THE SCOURGING OF IRAQ

The Scourging of Iraq

Sanctions, Law and Natural Justice

Geoff Simons

Second Edition

Published in Great Britain by
MACMILLAN PRESS LTD
Houndmills, Basingstoke, Hampshire RG21 6XS and London
Companies and representatives throughout the world

A catalogue record for this book is available from the British Library.

ISBN 0–333–74629–5 hardcover
ISBN 0–333–72681–2 paperback

Published in the United States of America by
ST. MARTIN'S PRESS, INC.,
Scholarly and Reference Division,
175 Fifth Avenue, New York, N.Y. 10010

ISBN 0–312–16182–4 clothbound (first edition only)
ISBN 0–312–21519–3 paperback (second edition only)

Library of Congress Cataloging-in-Publication Data
Library of Congress has cataloged the hardcover first edition as follows
Simons, G. L. (Geoffrey, Leslie), 1939–
The scourging of Iraq : sanctions, law and natural justice /
Geoff Simons.
p.   cm.
Includes bibliographical references and index.
ISBN 0–312–16182–4
1. Sanctions (International law)   2. Economic sanctions—Iraq.
3. Economic sanctions—Moral and ethical aspects.   4. Persian Gulf
War, 1991—Iraq.   5. United Nations—Iraq.   6. United Nations.
Security Council—Resolutions.   I. Title.
JX1246.S47   1996
341.5'82'09567—dc20   96–33706
                                                                          CIP

This book is printed on paper suitable for recycling and made from fully managed and
sustained forest sources.

10   9   8   7   6   5   4   3   2   1
07   06   05   04   03   02   01   00   99   98

Printed and bound in Great Britain by
Antony Rowe Ltd, Chippenham, Wiltshire

Dedication

**To the one million Iraqi children killed
by US biological warfare through the 1990s
and to the hundreds of thousands more that
will join them in the months and years ahead**

Contents

List of Tables

List of Figures

ix

The Chronology of Genocide

... nothing that we had seen or read had quite prepared us for the particular form of devastation which has now befallen the country [Iraq]. The recent conflict has wrought near-apocalyptic results ... the flow of food through the private sector has been reduced to a trickle. ... Many food prices are already beyond the purchasing reach of most Iraqi families. ... The mission recommends that ... sanctions in respect of food supplies should be immediately removed.

Report of mission (10–17 March 1991) led by
Martti Ahtisaari, UN Under-Secretary-General
for Administration and Management

... it is a country whose economy has been devastated ... above all by the continued sanctions ... which have virtually paralyzed the whole economy and generated persistent deprivation, chronic hunger, endemic undernutrition, massive unemployment and widespread human suffering ... a vast majority of the Iraqi population is living under most deplorable conditions and is simply engaged in a struggle for survival ... a grave humanitarian tragedy is unfolding ... the nutritional status of the population continues to deteriorate at an alarming rate ... large number of Iraqis now have food intakes lower than those of the populations in the disaster stricken African countries.

UN Food and Agriculture Organisation,
World Food Programme, Special Alert No. 237, July 1993

Alarming food shortages are causing irreparable damage to an entire generation of Iraqi children. ... 'After 24 years in the field, mostly in Africa starting with Biafra, I didn't think anything could shock me,' said Dieter Hannusch, WFP's Chief Emergency Support Officer, 'but this was comparable to the worst scenarios I have ever seen.' .... 'There actually are more than 4 million people, a fifth of Iraq's population, at severe nutritional risk,' said Mona Hamman, WFP's Regional Manager. 'That number includes

x

2.4 million children under five, about 600,000 pregnant/nursing women and destitute women heads of households as well as hundreds of thousands of elderly without anyone to help them . . . 70 per cent of the population has little or no access to food . . . Nearly everyone seems to be emaciated. We are at the point of no return in Iraq . . . The social fabric of the nation is disintegrating. People have exhausted their ability to cope.'

UN World Food Programme, *News Update,*
26 September 1995

. . . findings illustrate a strong association between economic sanctions and increase in child mortality and malnutrition rates . . . The moral, financial and political standing of an international community intent on maintaining sanctions is challenged by the estimate that since August 1990, 567 000 children in Iraq have died as a consequence.

Sarah Zaidi and Mary C. Smith Fawzi,
The Lancet (London), 2 December 1995

The Red Cross has strongly criticised the 'dire effects' of sanctions on civilians. . . . There is chronic hunger . . . with 20,000 new cases of child malnutrition every month.

Victoria Brittain, *The Independent,* 4 December 1995

. . . health conditions . . . are deteriorating at an alarming rate under the sanctions regime . . . the vast majority of Iraqis continue to survive on a semi-starvation diet . . . The damaging effects of poor nutrition are being compounded by epidemics . . . and by a precipitous decline in health care . . . The most visible impact of these problems is seen in the dramatic rise of mortality rates among infants and children.

UN World Health Organisation, 25 March 1996

Our policy is to keep Iraq in its box.

Western diplomat, *The Guardian,* 18 October 1995

Preface to the Second Edition

The US-contrived economic siege of Iraq has now lasted well over seven years, as I write . . . with, according to all the estimates, millions of casualties – perhaps 2,000,000 dead through starvation and disease, more than half of them children, and many millions more emaciated, traumatised, sick, dying. . . .

There are thousands of independent witnesses – aid workers, UN staff, journalists. One, Kathryn Casa (Clark, 1996), tells of 'a young mother standing over her child who lay listlessly on a dirty sheet, too weak to do much more than whimper, his abdomen swollen to the size of a large melon . . .'. This was a four-month-old baby boy . . . 'flies crawling in and out of his eyes and mouth . . . this little Iraqi . . . starving to death.' This baby is one of millions, dead or dying. . . .

The United States is the conscious architect of this years-long genocide. Knowingly, with a cruel and cynical resolve, US officials work hard to withhold relief from a starving and diseased people. And the grotesque facts are not even disputed by Washington. *Madeleine Albright, now Secretary of State, was prepared to assert in public that the killing of 500,000 Iraqi children was justified.*

Procrastination or veto in the Sanctions Committee, harassment of aid workers, threat (of up to $1 million fines and 12 years in jail) to American citizens taking medicines and toys to dying infants – these are some of the tools sanctioned by an American government committed to the slow extermination of a people. The old and the sick, emaciated pregnant women, the kwashiorkor children, grossly under-weight babies with no chance of survival, the desperately weak and vulnerable – these, by the million, are those most directly targeted for extinction by Washington. At the same time, Clinton, Albright *inter alia* smile their public-relations smiles and talk of compassion and human rights.

This edition provides more evidence of the 'new Holocaust', indicates the role of US propaganda, and profiles the cynical farce of 'food-for-oil' Resolution 986. It is shown how US policy, a slow and knowing extermination of a national people, falls unambiguously within the terms of the UN Genocide Convention; how US malevolence is not confined to Iraq; and how superpower arrogance can render a government deaf and blind to all the demands of decency, justice and international law.

GEOFF SIMONS
December 1997

xiii

Preface to the First Edition

The researching and writing of this book have been an education. I have learnt not only about one of the twentieth century's many unpublicised genocides, the subjecting of an entire people to a total years-long siege, but also about the psychology of comfortable, unthreatened human beings. Try to impress upon people – politicians, government officials, publishers, journalists, relatives, friends – what they are doing, or what they are allowing to be done in their name, and what happens?

Tell them about the innocent thousands, hundreds of thousands, forced to drink sewage; about the silent shrivelled women holding their dying babies; about the thousands of children trapped in unrelieved trauma; about the stick infants, the ballooning 'sugar bellies'; about the children now going blind for want of insulin; about the millions today being denied adequate food and medicine – and what is the response? Incomprehension, blocking out, a refusal to believe or feel – what psychologists have called *psychic numbing*. And *guilt transference*: if people are suffering, it cannot be *our* fault, *my* fault . . . There must be someone else to blame. Let us rely on the propaganda to tell us who it is.

While I was writing this book, a number of distressing and tragic child murders were copiously reported in Britain. Wrecked families struggled to adjust to a desolate new reality. No-one doubted that whoever had perpetrated such crimes must be monsters. So how are we to regard Western leaders and others who, stubbornly and knowingly, support policies that cause the deaths not of isolated children (or even 16), but of very many: 100,000 in 1994, 100,000 in 1995, perhaps half a million so far, with all the genocidal policies still in place. Are we and they, as the international human-rights worker Elias Davidsson asks, 'accomplices to mass murder'?

I propose a provocative and unfashionable theory: that any Iraqi child matters as much as any American or British child. And the corollary: that we are so ethically derelict that it needs to be said.

It is not necessary to visit Iraq. It is enough to acknowledge the copious testimonies and reports, some of which are quoted and cited here. I still feel the heavy shadow of Chapter 3, and something of what these inadequate words signal of human suffering. And I still

xiv

feel the impotent shame to which my government, and all the other psychically numbed and guilt-transferring accomplices to genocide, have condemned me. It is enough.

GEOFF SIMONS

Acknowledgements

Many people, either knowingly or unknowingly, have provided invaluable help during the researching and writing of the present book. Particular thanks are due to: Tony Benn, MP, for providing his characteristic support and for offering the pre-publication comment; Felicity Arbuthnot, journalist and Middle East expert, for her remarkable generosity in allowing me access to her entire Iraq archive; Alexandra McLeod, Librarian at the United Nations Information Centre, London, for highlighting reports, letters, resolutions and other essential material.

I am grateful also to individuals who took trouble to locate relevant papers and reports and for making them available: John O. Field, School of Nutrition, Tufts University, Massachusetts, US; Sarah Graham-Browne, the Gulf Information Project, London; Greg Steddy, Kluwer Law International, London; and the staff of the London-based charity Medical Aid for Iraq (MAI), whose detailed and regular reports have provided a valuable insight into the suffering of a people under siege.

Thanks should also be expressed to all those (politicians, journalists, human-rights campaigners and others) who through their independence and commitment have worked to change genocidal policies perpetrated in the name of Western virtue. They include: Tony Benn, MP, Tam Dalyell, MP, George Galloway, MP, Felicity Arbuthnot, Miriam Ryle, Eric Hoskins, Ramsey Clark, Henry Gonzalez, Elias Davidsson, Hugh Stevens, Jan van Heurck, Riad Al-Taher, Sabah Al-Mukhtar and many others.

Colette Simons provided valuable research assistance. Christine Simons helped with research and in many other ways.

GEOFF SIMONS

Introduction

The main purpose of this book is to highlight the continuing and un-justifiable punishment of the Iraqi people through economic sanctions. It rests on the simple principle, enshrined in the Protocol 1 Addition (1977) to the Geneva Convention (1949), that the starvation of civilians as a method of warfare is illegal and ethically indefensible. The book does *not* represent apology or exculpation for Saddam Hussein (I have charted his bloody rise to power in *Iraq: From Sumer to Saddam*, 1994). It is important to remember that many of the politicians, business leaders, pundits and journalists who today are keenest to maintain economic sanctions on Iraq are precisely the people who in the 1980s did all they could to build up and sustain the tyrannical Iraqi regime. What is argued here is that it is unjustifiable in both law (Protocol 1; UN General Assembly Resolution 96(I); the UN Genocide Convention; etc.) and natural justice to target helpless men, women and children as a method of overthrowing a national leader.

The reality is that the Western powers are pursuing a strategic policy, linked to the control of Gulf oil, that has nothing to do with support for human rights or condemnation of military aggression (Western leaders have long tolerated abuses of human rights and military invasions when they were judged to serve Western economic and strategic interests). What this means is that the United States has consistently manipulated the United Nations to serve its foreign policy objectives; and where this option has not been possible it has acted unilaterally in defiance of UN majority opinion. As Madeleine Albright, the US ambassador to the United Nations, has admitted: 'we will behave with others multi-laterally when we can and unilaterally when we must'. At the same time the United States remains in constant violation of its UN obligations – in deciding which national derelictions to ignore, which UN resolutions to support, and when, if ever, to pay its financial dues. Washington's financial debt to the UN, the largest of any Member State, has mounted over the years: in September 1995 it stood at $1.6 billion.

Chapter 1 profiles something of the impact of the Gulf War on Iraq, the suffering of the people and the devastation of the land. In this brief conflict alone there was enough to justify copious charges against the United States of war crimes; of serious violations of the Geneva

xvii

Conventions, the Hague Conventions, and other international agreements signalling what is and what is not permissible in war (these
charges have been amply justified by former US Attorney-General Ramsey
Clark, Congressman Henry Gonzalez and many others). But the war
was only one phase in the onslaught that the Iraqi people would be
forced to endure. Even before the war the harshness of the economic
blockade was bringing immense suffering to Iraq's civilian population
and forcing the Iraqi economy to its knees. After the war, what were
set to be years-long sanctions remained in place, compounding the chaos
and devastation already wrought by months of economic embargo and
weeks of unprecedented military destruction.

It soon became plain to the international community what the sanctions were achieving. The celebrated human-rights worker Elias Davidsson
was later to ask: '*Are we accomplices to mass murder?*'; pointing out
that 'many more civilians have died as a result of these quiet sanctions than from the massive bombings against Iraqi cities and villages
in the Gulf War'. In the same spirit Ramsey Clark emphasised that the
economic blockade was a weapon of mass destruction, 'a crime against
humanity, in the Nüremburg sense . . .'. He stressed, as was now abundantly clear: 'The blockade is a weapon for the destruction of the masses,
and it attacks those segments of the society that are the most vulnerable. Inherently, it attacks infants and children, the chronically ill, the
elderly and emergency medical cases.'

In the US Congress and the British Parliament, voices were raised
to protest at the genocidal impact of economic sanctions on the Iraqi
people. Congressman Henry Gonzalez began impeachment proceedings
against the President; and in the British House of Commons Members
of Parliament who had visited Iraq reported on the horrors that they
had witnessed. Thus the Labour MP George Galloway spoke of conditions that 'would have moved a person with stone for a heart. . . . We
visited hospitals where there was no medicine and no spare parts for
the medical equipment . . . women were having caesarian sections without
anaesthetic . . . garbage lay uncollected in the streets. . . . The great
waterways of the Tigris and Euphrates . . . are teeming with waterborne diseases. . . . The Minister knows about the tremendous increase
in marasmus, kwashiorkor and malnutrition of all kinds, as well as in
polio and cholera. . . . Iraq is a developed country which is being de-
developed by the United Nations. . . . The peace that we are keeping is
starving the ordinary people of Iraq' (*Hansard,* 13 December 1993).
In the same vein the Labour MP Tam Dalyell declared: United Nations sanctions are causing the deaths of more than 2000 people a

week in Iraq through lack of medicine, medical services, food and diet supplements, bad water, and a lack of equipment and parts needed for health care, good water, agriculture and food processing. . . . UNICEF estimates that between 80,000 and 100,000 children under five will die in 1993 if sanctions remain' (*Hansard*, 23 February 1993).

Chapter 2 charts the chronology of sanctions, with particular emphasis on the disarmament question – the main US pretext for denying the Iraqi people food and medicine. Attention is also given to 'the 706/712/986 ploy', the cynical US tool designed to transfer the guilt for the genocide from the strategic planners in Washington to the Iraqi regime itself.

In Chapter 3 some indication is given of what the Iraqi people are being compelled to endure: the shortage of food and medicine; the spread of disease in human beings, animals and plants; the inevitable rise in morbidity and mortality rates for all sections of the population. In assessing the plight of an entire nation, Eric Rouleau, a former French ambassador to Turkey and Tunisia, declares:

ABANDON HOPE, IRAQ . . . *Iraq has been irrevocably damned . . .* Iraqis understood the legitimacy of a military action to drive the army from Kuwait, but they have had difficulty comprehending the Allied rationale for using air power to systematically destroy or cripple Iraqi infrastructure and industry: electric power stations (92 per cent of installed capacity destroyed), refineries (80 per cent of production capacity), petrochemical complexes, telecommunications centers (including 135 telephone networks), bridges (more than 100), roads, highways, railroads, hundreds of locomotives and boxcars full of goods, radio and television broadcasting stations, cement plants, and factories producing aluminium, textiles, electric cables, and medical supplies.

The Arab Monetary Fund estimated the losses to be around $190 billion.

In the same paper ('America's Unyielding Policy Toward Iraq', *Foreign Affairs*, January/February 1995), Eric Rouleau comments also on the 'straitjacket' of the 'multifaceted embargo': the total collapse of food production in Iraq, rocketing price inflation on basic foodstuffs, and the *inexplicably proscribed articles on the 'red list'* stipulated by the UN Sanctions Committee (electric light bulbs, socks, wristwatches, ovens, sewing machines and needles, nails, textiles, grain mills, refrigerators, etc. – see also Table 3.1). Rouleau notes also that the sanctions are threatening the lives of millions of people: 'According to UNICEF, the calorie deficit among Iraqis is now putting at risk some 3.5 million persons, including 1.58 million children under the age of 15 and 230,000 pregnant or nursing women. Many children . . . will be born mentally handicapped; the infant mortality rate, which has doubled in three years, will continue to rise.'

By 1995 there was growing recognition that economic sanctions were having a devastating and cumulative effect on the Iraqi civilian population; and, moreover, that Washington's efforts to transfer the guilt to the Iraqi government (via the '706/712/986 ploy') were unreasonable. Thus the British Liberal-Democrat MP Sir David Steel commented: The UN argues that resolutions permit the Iraqi sale of limited oil to import food and medical supplies. That is true, but *the conditions on distribution internally by external agencies are not ones that any sovereign nation could reasonably be expected to accept*' (my italics) (*Glasgow Herald*, 11 November 1994). In the same spirit the eminent British politician Lord Healey, speaking at a symposium on sanctions in February 1995, highlighted the double standards that applied to the implementation of UN resolutions.

The mounting evidence of the genocidal character of sanctions on Iraq was now stimulating an international response. The International Commission of Inquiry on Economic Sanctions was highlighting the massive 'human cost' of the embargo, not least the high death rate among children ('sanctions are a violent weapon of mass destruction which targets most directly the weakest in society'). A report on war crimes and sanctions (by the campaigner Jan van Heurck) emphasised that some 11,000 US service personnel had refused to serve in the Gulf; and that several thousand, having made public statements, were tried and imprisoned. Here it is suggested that by 1992 around 300,000 Iraqis had been killed by bombing and sanctions. In July 1994 a petition (from a composer, a physicist, a priest, a playwright, a theatre director and others) was presented to the Icelandic government urging an end to the 'collective punishment' being inflicted against the civilian populations of Iraq, Libya and Serbia through sanctions ('The punitive actions by the Security Council can be regarded as acts of war. As Iceland is formally a party to these immoral measures, we are all guilty of causing innocent civilians irreparable harm').

In August 1994 an international seminar on 'US-imposed sanctions and blockades on Third World countries' was held in London (in association with The International Commission of Inquiry – see above). The seminar acknowledged the harm being done by sanctions, recognising also that they had been imposed to further Washington's global strategy. Thus Jaime Ballesteros, a former Spanish Member of Parliament, argued that sanctions should evoke the same revulsion as does the idea of using nuclear weapons. Taj Mohammad Khan Langah, a lawyer and Chairman of the Pakistan Saraiki Party, declared that sanctions violated international law and the UN Charter. Laura O'Sullivan, of the Irish in Britain Representation Group, said that a main purpose of sanctions was 'to destroy the independence of Third World countries' by causing hardship to civilian populations. And the Iraqi representative, Khalaf al-Sabaawe, declared that sanctions had been imposed on Iraq because that country did not obey the West. In this context it is easy to see UN sanctions as a convenient tool of American foreign policy.

Chapter 4 considers the use of sanctions, particularly in modern times and particularly as exploited by the United States. Consideration is given also to the treatment of genocide in UN resolutions and in the Genocide Convention, with attention to how such international agreements are directly relevant to what the Western powers are perpetrating in Iraq. Who are the guilty? Governments? Civil servants? The wider publics? How are we to respond to charges that we are implicated in genocide? By blocking out the information and by stifling our natural humanitarian instincts? Or, with the ready aid of the multi-billion-dollar propaganda machines, by transferring the guilt? In Britain the Archbishop of Canterbury points the way. A letter (13 May 1994) written on his behalf by a Secretary for Public Affairs points out the Archbishop is 'greatly saddened' by the suffering of the people of Iraq, and that in fact he prays for them. Of course he is in no position 'to assess personally . . . the complex international diplomatic arguments'; and he is certainly not in a position 'to comment on how the exemption of medical supplies' is working. The profound ethical question of the perpetration of genocide is no concern of the Archbishop of Canterbury. Instead, one should contact the Foreign and Commonwealth Office, 'the appropriate and authoritative body . . .'.

The matter of oil is mentioned briefly at the end of Chapter 4, for this is one of the principal elements in the protracted Gulf crisis. Let Iraqi oil back onto the markets and perhaps Saudi revenues will collapse, making it hard to pay US arms suppliers for their $billions-worth of shipments. Better by far to stoke up the tensions, if only to provide opportunities to test-fly a new generation of cruise missiles (the cruise-missile raid on Bosnia in September 1995 tested the satellite navigational systems that had replaced the earlier computer-mapping systems: Bosnia might not suffice for further laboratory tests).

Control the oil, signal US hegemony to difficult nations, sell more arms, test more weapons and communication systems, wreak destruction from time to time and then send in the US contractors, spend the munitions and stimulate the arms industries. What do genocides matter when all this exciting entrepreneurial activity is in the wind?

1 The Legacy of War

The United States might obliterate Iraq.

General Norman Schwarzkopf, 1 November 1990

We are closer to war with a Third World country. However, we are making plans as if it will be the Third World War.

General Merle MacBec, 3 November 1990

We will return you to the pre-industrial age.

Secretary of State James Baker, 9 January 1991

There was no water, no food, no milk – no people. . . . And this hell was still pouring from the skies. . . . Radi whispered through his dry lips, 'Grandma', and died in my lap. I looked at the sky and saw nothing. No flashes of bombs and bullets, no rubble. . . . Praise be to Allah, I have gone blind . . .'[1]

PREAMBLE

The 1991 Gulf War, fought between the US-contrived Coalition forces and the armies of Saddam Hussein, followed the Iraqi invasion of Kuwait on 2 August 1990. It followed also the period during which Kuwait was part of the Ottoman *vilayet* of Basra and the 1922 Uqair Conference at which Sir Percy Cox, High Commissioner under the (British-controlled) Indian Army for Mesopotamia, wishing to cut through 'impossible arguments and ridiculous claims', resolved with a cavalier flourish of his hand what would constitute the frontiers of Kuwait, Iraq and Saudi Arabia. And it followed the 1930 judgement of the British High Commissioner in Baghdad *'that Britain should encourage the gradual absorption of Kuwait into Iraq'*, with representatives of the British government contending *'that Kuwait was a small and expendable state which could be sacrificed without too much concern if the power struggles of the period demanded it'*.[2]

1

In the event the power struggles of the time required that Kuwait –
later depicted as an oil well with a seat in the United Nations – be
maintained as a Western proxy. The demands of erstwhile British colonialism and US economic imperialism had evolved a mutually congenial accommodation whereby a feudal outpost, buttressed by other
regional feudalisms, could be induced to protect the Western hegemony
over Gulf oil in the interests of freedom and democracy. How unsurprising
that, in the context of the West's insatiable appetite for cheap energy,
the cataclysm of 1990 should so dramatically spur the Western powers
to protect the pliant feudalisms.

There is now abundant evidence for the period late-1990/early-1991
that the Washington strategists wanted a war with Iraq. At first (early
1990) there were many signs that the United States would be indifferent to conflict between Iraq and Kuwait. Saddam was taking American
advice to pursue aggressive oil pricing policies, commissioning a study
from the Washington Centre for Strategic and International Studies
and no doubt hearing the advice of Henry Schuler, the Centre's energy security programme director, that Arab oil exporters should maximise their oil revenues instead of 'leaving money on the table'. In
April 1990 Senator Robert Dole, doubtless well aware of Saddam's
human-rights record, travelled with four other US senators to propitiate Saddam in Baghdad; and US Assistant Secretary of State John Kelly,
testifying before a House Foreign Affairs subcommittee, emphasised
the administration's continued financial support for Iraq. When, on
1 May, Secretary of State James Baker was asked before a Senate
appropriations subcommittee whether the United States should respond
to Iraq's willingness to use chemical and biological weapons and to
threaten Israel with missiles he replied that such a judgement would
be 'a little bit premature', emphasising that 'in all probability our
allies will be very quick to move in there and pick up our market
share'.[3]

In the same spirit US State Department spokeswoman Margaret
Tutwiler, in response to news that two Iraqi armoured divisions had
taken up positions on the Kuwaiti border, commented that the United
States did 'not have any defence treaties with Kuwait, and there are
no special defence or security commitments to Kuwait'.[4] The next day,
25 July 1990, the US ambassador April Glaspie delivered to Saddam
Hussein in Baghdad the most publicised 'green-light' signal of them
all: '. . . *our opinion is that you should have the opportunity to rebuild
your country . . . we have no opinion on Arab–Arab conflicts like your
border disagreement with Kuwait*'. On 31 July, with mounting evi-

dence of Iraqi intentions, US Assistant Secretary of State John Kelly, when asked what would happen if Iraq invaded Kuwait, emphasised that 'we would be extremely concerned' but again stressed that there was no treaty commitment that would obligate the United States to engage its own military forces. Saddam Hussein, doubtless estimating the likely US response to his planned invasion (and doubtless remembering US support for his earlier aggression against Iran), was being given an unambiguous, albeit coded, message from Washington: 'Go Ahead!'[5]

When, in the event, the Iraqi invasion of Kuwait occurred the United States moved speedily on many fronts: economic, military, political and propaganda. Saudi Arabia, much against its early judgement, was pressured by Washington into accepting a massive influx of Western troops;* comprehensive economic sanctions against Iraq were introduced under UN auspices (see Chapter 2); the United States began its systematic suborning – by dint of threat and bribery – of Security Council members and other useful states; and Saddam Hussein was routinely dubbed a 'new Hitler', the usual epithet that is thrown at any national leader reckless enough to challenge Western imperial arrogance. In the US, Britain and elsewhere Saddam was ridiculed, denounced and abused – where rational criticism, amply justified, was submerged in a torrent of counter-productive rhetoric. The unrestrained, often racist, demonisation of Saddam inevitably – and perhaps intentionally – rendered him impervious to pleas or arguments, made it easy for the Western powers to ignore their own contribution to the problem (by, for example, building up Saddam, ignoring his atrocities for so long, and aiding his aggression against Iran), and made it easy also to ignore Iraq's stated grievances and conciliatory gestures. The United States, having comprehensively manipulated the Security Council, thereafter excluded the UN Secretary-General from virtually all the proceedings, made no effort to negotiate on a serious basis, and thus – in violation of Article 2(3) and (4) of the UN Charter – made war inevitable.

Washington had signalled no serious opposition to Iraq's developing plans for an invasion of Kuwait. Indeed, just prior to the invasion

---

* As with other wars where the perceived US interest was at stake Washington lied persistently and comprehensively to gain the required international support. For example, the US claimed to have satellite pictures showing a massive Iraqi military build-up on the Saudi/Iraqi border. When sample photographs were later obtained from Soyuz Karta by an enterprising journalist, no such evidence was discernible (Maggie O'Kane, *The Guardian Weekend*, London, 16 December 1995).

the US was continuing to aid Iraq in various ways. But once Saddam's tanks rolled convincingly into Kuwait, causing the feudal Al-Sabahs to flee in panic, Washington was committed to war. It was plain, more so with hindsight, that a war would well serve the US strategists: new families of untried weapons and communication systems could be tested in a real-world environment; the fortunes of an unpopular Bush administration could be improved; a further shake could be given to the collapsing Soviet empire; the vast US military expenditures could be justified; and the US global military hegemony could be unambiguously demonstrated. Moreover, with a successful round of begging-bowl diplomacy, the enterprise need not entail the dissipation of much American treasure: the United States was happy to play the mercenary in the US-framed New World Order.

It was important for domestic reasons that the war involve few American casualties: a United States still afflicted by the enervating Vietnam syndrome would not tolerate a protracted inflow of body-bags. The answer was simple. Overwhelming force would be used against the enemy. The hapless Iraqis, already trapped in a remorseless tyranny, would be slaughtered in their hundreds of thousands with the total casualties, of one sort or another, set to be numbered in millions. Above all, US strategic objectives would be achieved while at the same time American virtue would be demonstrated and American sensitivities protected.

THE WAR

Without Saddam Hussein's invasion of Kuwait there would have been no 1991 Gulf War, though the mounting tensions in the region would still have made conflict likely at some time and in some circumstances. It is probable also that without US posturing and intransigence (and no doubt the hidden agenda set on war) – exemplified not least by the arbitrary setting of deadlines that reportedly distressed UN Secretary-General Javier Perez de Cuellar[6] – the war that began in January 1991 could have been avoided. When the war started, it was soon obvious that American missiles and American aircraft would be the principal agents of destruction. Between 16 January and 27 February some 88,000 tons of bombs were dropped on Iraq, an explosive tonnage judged equivalent to seven Hiroshima-size atomic bombs. Thus *for the period of the war Iraq was subjected to the equivalent of one atomic bomb a week, a scale of destruction that has no parallels in the history of* *warfare.** Moreover, whereas the horrendous destructive potential of an atomic bomb is focused on a single site the missiles and bombs ranged over the whole of Iraq.

The Coalition forces – principally the United States – used a wide variety of armaments in the Gulf War, some traditional (though improved) and some relatively untried. Extensive use was made of depleted uranium projectiles (see also 'The Environment', below), used because of their capacity to destroy armour and other defences. One estimate suggests that American tanks fired between 5000 and 6000 depleted uranium projectiles, while tens of thousands of these weapons were fired by aircraft. Many Iraqi soldiers 'were killed either directly by depleted uranium projectiles or as a result of their exposure to them'; and it is suggested that these weapons caused the deaths of around 50,000 Iraqi children 'during the first eight months of 1991 as a result of various diseases including cancer, kidney failure and internal diseases not known before ...'[7] It is arguable that depleted uranium projectiles fall within the category of prohibited weapons of mass destruction according to UN General Assembly Resolution 33/84(b), passed on 13 December 1978.

Use was also made of napalm, in part to incinerate entrenched Iraqi soldiers (*Washington Post*, 23 February 1991). A patent for napalm – today a weapon that attracts particular odium – was applied for in the United States on 1 November 1943; and thereafter napalm devices were used against the Germans and Japanese in the Second World War, and later against the Koreans and Vietnamese. The effects of napalm, today much 'improved', are well known. The substance is spread over wide areas in clumps of burning jelly at temperatures exceeding 800 degrees C, and in its 'improved' versions is almost impossible to extinguish and cannot be easily removed from human flesh. The well documented results include deep burning, local thrombosis, necrosis, pulmonary damage, heatstroke, oxygen starvation, carbon monoxide poisoning and infection – with all manner of scarring and disability in survivors.[8] It is likely that the Americans, as in earlier wars, also used white phosphorus incendiary devices which cause burning chemicals to remain active in human flesh for hours or even days.

Many observers commented that the 1991 Gulf conflict was not a

---

* Vietnam, well instructed in the benefits of American virtue, received a much larger tonnage of bombs but over a period of years rather than weeks. Thus between 1965 and 1968 around 700,000 tons of bombs were dropped on this small peasant nation. The US Congress concluded that 1,350,000 Vietnamese civilians had been slaughtered in the war, a manifestly conservative estimate.

'war' in the conventional sense: throughout its most decisive phase –
from the beginning of the air strikes on 16 January to the onset of the
Coalition ground offensive on 24 February – allied aircraft (mostly
American) ranged over the whole of Iraq, bombing at will (by the end
of February well over 100,000 air sorties had been flown). By contrast
the Iraqi forces had little opportunity to strike counter-blows: the Scud
attacks on Israel and Saudi Arabia produced relatively few casualties
and relatively little damage. It was widely acknowledged that the Coalition bombing missions over Iraq were a 'turkey shoot. . . . It's almost like you flipped on the light in the kitchen at night and the
cockroaches start scurrying, and we're killing them.'[9] The Iraqi Red
Crescent, quoted by former US Attorney-General Ramsey Clark, estimated before the end of the war that the bombing had caused between
6000 and 7000 civilian deaths. Clark himself described the state of
Basra – extensively carpet-bombed by B-52 deliveries – as 'a human
and civilian tragedy . . . staggering in its expanse'. Little attention was
given in the Western media to the 'carpets' of total destruction laid
out in village, town and desert; to the human impact of the Rockeye
cluster bombs, each containing 247 'anti-personnel' grenades that individually explode into 2000 high-velocity razor-sharp fragments that
effectively 'shred' people and that are ill-equipped to distinguish between soldier and civilian (the Iraqis claim that cluster bombs were
used against 'civil vehicles, taxis, coaches and lorries'[10]); or to the
vast destruction wrought by fuel-air explosives (FAEs), dropped to create
massive fireballs over Iraqi positions (causing, according to weaponry
expert Michael Klare, 'nuclear-like levels of destruction without arousing
popular revulsion').[11]

The American forces in the field rejoiced in the mounting evidence
of their unprecedented capacity to destroy the enemy. Film was taken,
most of it kept out of the public domain, to record the vast slaughter
of human beings. Thus, one high-tech video, taken at night and used
in a briefing by the US XVIII Airborne Corps, showed helpless Iraqi
conscripts shot to pieces in the dark, some blown apart by cannon
shells. The Iraqis, reported John Balzar of *The Los Angeles Times*,
were 'like ghostly sheep, flushed from a pen . . . bewildered and terri-
fied, jarred from sleep and fleeing their bunkers under a hellstorm of
fire. One by one they were cut down by attackers they couldn't see or
understand. Some were literally blown to bits by bursts of 30mm exploding cannon. One man dropped, writhed on the ground and struggled to his feet. Another burst tore him apart.' Said Ron Balak, one of
the US pilots: 'When I got back I sat there on the wing, and I was

laughing. . . . I was probably laughing at myself . . . sneaking up there and blowing this up and blowing that up. A guy came up to me and we were slapping each other on the back . . . and then he said, "By God, I thought we had shot into a damn farm. It looked liked somebody had opened the sheep pen." ' And Chief Warrant Officer Brian Walker was looking forward to more action of the same sort: 'there is nothing that can take them out like an Apache [attack helicopter]. It will be a duck hunt.'[12]

The comprehensive array of hi-tech armaments accomplished a massive slaughter of a largely helpless enemy, with much of the killing occurring after the time when constructive diplomacy would have brought an end to the conflict and a secure liberation of Kuwait. Use had been made of depleted uranium shells, napalm, cluster bombs, fuel-air (nuclear-scale) explosives, and conventional free-fall bombs dropped in vast tonnage by B-52s. The US Navy alone dropped more than 4400 cluster bombs, with many thousands more delivered by the US Air Force. In addition, British Jaguar strike aircraft dropped thousands of BL755 cluster devices, designed to 'mince' human beings in the field. The US and British armies used also the MLRS tracked missile launcher, each vehicle able to project twelve missiles more than twenty miles. MLRS missiles, each releasing 8000 anti-personnel fragmentation grenades, spread out over a target area of 60 acres. During the final phases of the war the US Army launched 10,000 MLRS missiles, while the British forces launched a further 2500. It is not hard to imagine the cumulative effect of these and other weapons on the hapless Iraqi conscripts trapped in the desert. Unofficial Saudi sources were suggesting at the end of the war that the Iraqi casualties numbered around 100,000, with a leaked report from the US Defence Intelligence Agency estimating around 400,000 Iraqi casualties.[13]

The US authorities took great care to disguise the scale of the slaughter.[14] Film shot by the US Army was not made available to journalists or other independent observers; journalists and others were routinely excluded from most of the killing fields, even at the end of hostilities when all the Coalition military objectives had been accomplished. Two massive Iraqi retreats from Kuwait, difficult to conceal because of their scale, received some attention in the Western media – but even here the scale of the slaughter was largely hidden from Western publics (vast columns of pulverised and incinerated vehicles were shown in television broadcasts but with the thousands of Iraqi corpses mysteriously absent).

This phase of the slaughter began when US aircraft spotted columns of desperate men, carrying loot from a ransacked Kuwait, in queues of military and civilian vehicles headed back home. Now the Iraqis were complying with UN demands that they leave Kuwait but this manifest withdrawal would not save them. With American aircraft queueing for the kill, the carnage was total: the fleeing Iraqis, and their Kuwaiti captives, were remorselessly attacked with 'flesh-shredding' cluster bombs, napalm and depleted uranium shells – a hellish slaughter protracted over hours. By the morning of 28 February a stretch of the Jahra–Basra road at Mitla Ridge 'had been turned into a giant scrapyard, with some 2000 military and civilian vehicles destroyed, some charred, some exploded, some reduced to heaps of tangled metal, with dead bodies and their severed limbs scattered all over, some corpses petrified in their vehicles, and others incinerated, with their faces reduced to grinning teeth'.[15] A *Newsweek* correspondent, a pool reporter attached to the 2nd US Armoured Division, described the 'vast traffic jam of more than a mile of vehicles, perhaps 2000 or more. . . . As we drove slowly through the wreckage, our armoured personnel carrier's tracks splashed through great pools of bloody water. We passed dead soldiers lying, as if resting, without a mark on them. We found others cut up so badly, a pair of legs in its trousers would be 50 yards from the top half of the body . . .'.[16] Other reporters noted that the carnage extended many more miles to the north. The journalist Greg LaMotte, having brought the first videotape from the site, commented that what had ensued – aerial strikes on a traffic jam – 'was in essence what you could only describe as a massacre'.[17] The tape, he warned, was 'somewhat graphic. . . . This was the most horrific thing I have ever seen in my life: bodies everywhere, body parts everywhere.'[18]

The Mitla carnage was not the only such event in the closing hours of the Gulf War. A similar merciless slaughter occurred on the Jahra–Umm Qasr highway, a coastal road running through the desert: here too a column of fleeing vehicles was spotted – and pulverised and incinerated into oblivion from the air. Witnesses noted the similar chaos of destroyed vehicles, scattered loot, and charred and bloated corpses. Dogs 'snarled around the corpse of one soldier. They had eaten most of his flesh . . . the dogs had eaten the legs from the inside out, and the epidermis lay in collapsed and hairy folds, like leg-shaped blankets, with feet attached . . .'.[19] One man who had tried to flee in a Kawasaki front-end loader finished up with half of his body hanging upside down, the 'left side and bottom blown away to tatters, with the charred leg fully 15 feet away'; others were flash-burned 'skinny and black wrecks', one with his exposed intestines and other organs 'still coiled in their proper places, but cooked to ebony'.[20]

The American journalist Bob Dogrin wrote of 'scores of soldiers' lying 'in and around the vehicles, mangled and bloated in the drifting desert sands'; and his companion Major Bob Nugent, an army intelligence officer, commenting that even in Vietnam 'I didn't see anything like this', wondered whether the great number of Iraqi casualties with so few allied deaths meant that divine intervention had played a part ('some sort of good against evil thing').[21] A nice doctrine: the Christian loving god had contrived a bloody massacre. British and American soldiers, witnessing the carnage, offered individual responses. 'Crispy critters', said one, surveying a group of incinerated corpses; 'Just wasn't them boys' day, was it?', said another.[22] Tony Clifton of *Newsweek* went up 'to see what we'd done . . . there were bodies all over the place . . . I was up to my ankles in blood . . . there were very white-faced men going round saying, "Jesus. Did we really do this?" '[23]

Even such testimony did little to expose the scale of the slaughter. Journalists and others had been barred from most of the desert killing fields – where, it is known, the US Army dug mass graves to accommodate the Iraqi dead. Pentagon officials were quoted as saying that 'heaps of Iraqi corpses are being buried in mass graves across the desert';[24] and there were reports that the allied forces were 'using bull-dozers to bury thousands of enemy dead in trenches as the allies advanced'.[25] But such scenes – which must have resembled the disposal of corpses in the Nazi extermination camps – were never publicised. Reasons of taste, decency and ideology meant that the publics had to be permanently shielded from the horrors perpetrated by governments in their name.

Many Iraqi soldiers were killed by the simple expedient of burying them alive: in one report, American earthmovers and ploughs mounted on tanks were used to attack more than 70 miles of trenches. Colonel Anthony Moreno commented that for all he knew, 'we could have killed thousands'. One US commander, Colonel Lon Maggart, estimated that his force alone had buried about 650 Iraqi soldiers. 'What you saw was a bunch of buried trenches with peoples' arms and things sticking out of them,' observed Moreno.[26] Such methods conspired with the many other modes of killing to produce hundreds of thousands of Iraqi fatalities, most of them – at least in the early stages of the war – among demoralised conscripts drawn from the Kurdish and Shia groups traditionally persecuted by Saddam Hussein. Now there can be little doubt that civilians too were targeted. Basra in particular was carpet-bombed by B-52s – to the point that, according to Ramsey Clark, hospitals, night clubs, coffee shops, clinics, law offices and whole residential areas were destroyed.

On 4 February 1991 – as a typical bombing strike in a civilian area – a bridge in Nasiriyeh was destroyed, killing 47 civilians and wounding more than a hundred; when the bridge exploded, many people were tossed into the Euphrates and carried downstream. And on 13 February, in a much publicised atrocity of the war, more than four hundred civilians – men, women and children – were incinerated by the US bombing of the Amiriya shelter of Baghdad. At about 4.30 a.m. a Stealth bomber attacked the shelter with a laser-guided missile, blasting a hole through the roof and ceiling, and exploding in the shelter's hospital on a lower level. A few minutes later, a second missile was delivered precisely through the hole made by the first. The explosion of the second missile blasted shut the 6-ton, half-metre-thick steel doors, and incinerated several hundred people on the upper level, many of whom actually evaporated in the few-thousand degree heat generated by the explosion. Several hundred people on the lower level were boiled to death by the water from the vast boilers destroyed in the blast.

It is not known for certain how many civilians were killed that night in the Amiriya shelter: the written record of the people who had sought refuge from the nightly bombing had itself been stored in the supposed safety of the building, and now was no more. What *is* known is that before 13 February more than 1500 people signed in to the shelter every night. After the massacre, eleven injured people, thrown out of the shelter by the blast, were found; and over a deeply harrowing period of several hours the mutilated black remains of 403 people were retrieved from the building. Thus it is estimated that several hundred people were burnt and evaporated into nothingness, with no means of determining their identities or even their precise numbers. Later witnesses – including Tam Dalyell, a British Labour Member of Parliament – described the carbonated imprints of women and children on the walls of the shelter. The imprints of tiny feet and hands are charred into the walls and ceilings; and on the walls at the lower level the tide mark of the water from the burst tanks is marked by a 5-foot-high scum of human flesh.

We need to recall Article 52 (Protocol 1) of the 1977 Addition to the 1949 Geneva Convention:

1. *Civilian objects shall not be the object of attack or of reprisals . . .*

2. *Attacks shall be limited strictly to military objectives . . .*

3. *In case of doubt whether an object which is normally dedicated
to civilian purposes . . . is being used to make an effective contribution to military action, it shall be presumed not to be so used.*

The Protocol, clearly relevant to the Amiriya massacre, applies equally
to many of the sites targeted in the Gulf War. Once the war was over,
the broadcaster Andy Rooney opined to nineteen million American
viewers of the televised '60 Minutes': *'There are some good things
about war sometimes. Everyone accomplishes more in times of war.
Our hearts beat faster. Our senses are sharper. . . . This war in the
Gulf has been, by all odds, the best war in modern history, not only
for America, but for the whole world, including Iraq, probably.'*[27] In
fact Iraq experienced a pace and scale of destruction not known since
Hiroshima. We need to remember what the Gulf War meant for the
Iraqi targets – the people and the land.

THE TARGETS

The Geneva Convention, as noted, prohibits military attacks on civilians and civilian property. Most governments pay pragmatic lip service to such demands, though their behaviour in war is an entirely
different matter. It is useful to note that the US forces in Iraq, in addition to attacking obvious military assets, carried out a prodigious
onslaught on many civilian targets.

The scale of the onslaught escalated throughout the period of the
bombing. It is significant that in the initial phase of the crisis the US
military planners had identified 57 sites in Iraq as strategic targets but
during the war some 700 targets were specified. Here it is specifically
acknowledged by US sources that the identified targets went far beyond the requirements of military necessity, a principal goal being to
maximise the economic and psychological devastation of the Iraqi nation.[28] A further consideration is that many targets were destroyed in
the cynical calculation that this would amplify Iraq's dependence on
foreign assistance, primarily from the United States, in the post-war
world: 'Some targets, especially late in the war, were bombed primarily *to create post-war leverage over Iraq, not to influence the course
of the conflict itself*. Planners now say their intent was to destroy or
damage valuable facilities that Baghdad could not repair without foreign assistance' (my italics).[29] In the event, one study subsequently

estimated that it would cost around $200 billion to replace the Iraqi assets destroyed during the war.[30]

There can be no doubt that a principal aim of the US military planners was to destroy Iraq's civilian infrastructure and so to reduce the country to a pre-industrial condition. Secretary of State James Baker announced this policy in his meeting with Iraq's deputy premier Tariq Aziz on 9 January 1991: 'Iraq will be turned into a backward and weak state.' In the subsequent escalation of the conflict a wide range of civilian assets – only a proportion of which were directly relevant to Iraq's illegal occupation of Kuwait – were targeted and destroyed. These included:

- electric power stations, relay and transmission systems;
- water treatment facilities, reservoirs, water distribution systems;
- telephone exchanges, relay stations;
- radio exchanges, transmission systems;
- food processing plant, food warehouses, food distribution facilities, infant milk formula factories, beverage factories;
- irrigation sites;
- animal vaccination facilities;
- buses and bus depots, trains and railways;
- bridges, roads and highway overpasses;
- oil wells, oil pumping systems, pipelines, oil refineries, oil storage facilities, petrol stations, fuel delivery vehicles;
- sewage treatment plant, sewage disposal systems;
- textile factories;
- automobile assembly plant;
- universities and colleges;
- hospitals and clinics;
- places of worship;
- archaeological sites.

One estimate suggests that perhaps as many as 20,000 homes, apartments and other dwellings were destroyed, with thousands of commercial centres – including shops, retail stores, banks, offices, hotels, restaurants and other public buildings – targeted and destroyed.[31] A main purpose of the sustained US campaign – extending to the destruction of schools, mosques, churches, private vans, tractors, taxi cabs, research institutes, water purification facilities, etc. – was 'to terrorize the entire country, kill people, destroy property, prevent movement, demoralize the people and force the overthrow of the government'.[32]

The massive destruction of the civilian infrastructure inevitably produced substantial numbers of fatalities – particularly among the very young, the old and the sick. Before the end of the war, before the prolonged sanctions had swelled the volume of casualties, the Red Crescent Society of Jordan estimated 113,000 Iraqi civilian dead, 60 per cent of which were children.

The US-orchestrated bombing campaign, with ambitions far beyond the enabling UN resolutions (see Chapter 2), was designed to destroy Iraq's morale and social cohesion. The wanton destruction of mosques, schools, invalid homes, institutes for the disabled, civilian shelters and agricultural plant had nothing to do with the eviction of the Iraqi forces from Kuwait, everything to do with destroying the social fabric of a relatively sophisticated nation. One report notes that the bombing destroyed 350 commercial stores and markets, 120 farms, 58 banks, 157 centres for water and electricity services, 646 elementary and secondary schools, 16 universities and colleges, 28 hospitals, 45 health centres and many other economic and social facilities, including laboratories, dispensaries, pharmacies, grain silos, military hospitals (for example, in Basra, Kut, Amara and Baghdad) and ancient archaeological sites.[33] The conduct of the US-led forces in Iraq violated many provisions of international law and morality, including the UN Charter, the Hague and Geneva Conventions, the Nuremberg Charter, and the laws of armed conflict (see Chapter 4).

The accumulated evidence suggests that the main aim of the US military planners was to destroy Iraq as a viable social system. From the outset a principal target was Iraq's oil resource, the substantial national asset that had supported all economic and social development. In March 1991 US satellite photographs were released that showed the destruction of key centres of the Iraqi oil industry. Images for the first week of the bombing campaign showed toxic plumes from the northern oil processing centres of Baiji and Kirkuk and from the Al Zubayr oilfield in the south. On 21 January 1991 US aircraft bombed five Iraqi supertankers in the Gulf, each capable of holding 100,000 tonnes of crude oil. Four days later the Mina Al Ahmadi oil terminal was destroyed. Before Saddam Hussein resorted to 'eco-terrorism', the allied bombing had produced 2-mile-wide oil slicks in the Gulf. However, it was 'politically expedient to condemn Saddam Hussein's ecological aggression and take the sting out of any accusations that the Allies were using similar tactics in their 100,000 sorties into Iraq'.[34] The Allies had targeted 'the root of the country's development'; this had been a war '*that simply went for everything that could nourish*

life; that caused identical damage to power plants, so that cannibali-
zation to provide limited power for hospitals, air conditioning, refrig-
eration was impossible; that took out irrigation pipes for farming, and
communications for reporting disease; in sum, it was a war which
destroyed people's environments and the potential for economic
activity . . .'[35]

The American decision to target the morale and social fabric of Iraq
was well illustrated by the attitude of Air Force chief General Michael
Dugan. Presented with a conventional list of Iraqi military targets (such
as air defence systems, missile sites, communication and command
centres, and armour formations), Dugan commented that while he accepted the list, 'that's not enough'. It was important also to target
'what is unique about Iraqi culture that they put very high value on';
it was important to know what it was 'that psychologically would make
an impact on the population and regime' in Iraq. Perhaps 'decapita-
tion' was the answer: to strike at Saddam's family, personal guard and
mistress – since he was a 'one man show'.[36] Another option, designed
to have a psychological impact on Iraqi culture, was to strike at mosques,
other religious centres and the renowned archaeological sites.

Throughout the war various archaeological sites (for example, the
Ur sites in Dhiqar province) were subject to air raids and plunder.
There is no doubt that some of the bombing damage to archaeological
sites was accidental – as Robert McCormick Adams, Mesopotamia expert
at Washington's Smithsonian Institute, said: 'You couldn't drop ordnance on much of Iraq without hitting an archaeological site!' At the
same time we can assume that US military planners welcome the impact on Iraqi morale of such damage. And plunder was no accident!

One archaeological expert, Andrew Petersen of the School of Orien-
tal and African Studies, London University, pointed out the likelihood
of archaeological damage being caused (4 February 1991) by the largest aerial bombardment in history. He reminded us that the Ur ziggurat
was being used as a platform for an anti-aircraft gun, that the bombed
gas plant at Salman Pak was adjacent to the ruins of Ctesiphon, which
includes the largest arch in the world, and that some major archaeological sites must have been destroyed.[37] Patrick Cockburn, writing six
months later, reported that the Ctesiphon arch, the oldest free-standing
brick arch in the world, was then in danger of collapsing because of
allied bombing. At the start of the war Muwayyad Sa'eed, director-
general of Iraq's Department of Antiquities, closed the main museums
in Baghdad and moved the archaeological treasures to many other sites
to escape the anticipated bombing. In the event the air attacks caused

widespread damage – for example, bringing down some of the bricks from the Ctesiphon arch – but most of the losses were caused by looting. During the Kurdish and Shia rebellions in March 1991 eight provincial museums were looted and destroyed; 8500 artefacts went missing; and an invaluable manuscript collection of 2000 items went missing from Kirkuk. Further losses were incurred when the Iraqi Army retook Kerbala, Najaf and Kufah from Shia rebels.[38] It is reported also that American troops stole priceless artefacts from many of the archaeological sites.

One report suggests that thefts took place from many of the remote sites, some of which (such as Uruk, Nippur, Tell Um-Alaqarib and Tell Chokka) are of inestimable worth. The archaeologist Dr Muayad Damirji, editor-in-chief of the Iraqi journal *Akkad*, reported that US troops had removed important parts of archaeological sites to house their trucks, tanks and other armoured vehicles. He claims also that the troops made their own bayonet excavations to obtain ancient artefacts.[39] The Ur ziggurat, hit by allied air attacks, now had 400 holes in the brick façades. According to Damirji, some 4000 antiquities had been looted from Iraqi museums as a result of the war. In 1993 reports appeared in the Western press indicating that Iraqi artefacts were being acquired by private collections in the United States.[40] Iraq protested and a few items were returned.[41]

The US onslaught on Iraq was massive and indiscriminate, extending far beyond the obvious military targets to every element of the social infrastructure and the nation's cultural heritage. Targets in all the main towns and cities were comprehensively bombed – some repeatedly, as if the military planners were running out of targets (even isolated villages and remote Bedouin camps were bombed and strafed). We need to note the impact – on both the people and the land – of this unremitting onslaught.

THE PEOPLE

Of the many estimates – Iraqi, American, British, Red Crescent, etc. – of Iraqi fatalities due to the Gulf War, none number the dead at less than thousands (compared with the 137 Americans killed). Even the most risible US attempts to minimise the volume of Iraqi casualties suggest tens of thousands of dead and wounded, with most estimates much higher. Paul Flynn, a British Member of Parliament, reflects a widespread view when he comments (*The Guardian*, 21 June 1991)

that the most recent estimate is that 100,000 to 200,000 Iraqis were
killed and 300,000 to 700,000 injured. British estimates, quoted soon
after the end of the war, suggest around 100,000 Iraqi soldiers killed;
with a French military expert estimating about 150,000 Iraqi fatalities.[42] American sensitivity about the scale of the slaughter was well
demonstrated by the case of Beth Osborne Daponte, a demographer in
the US Census Bureau. When in good faith she published her own
estimates of 158,000 Iraqis (half of them women and children) killed
in the war and its immediate aftermath, efforts were made to fire her.
Her boss, Barbara Torrey, rushed to accuse Daponte of using 'false
information' and of showing 'untrustworthiness and unreliability'. When
lawyers from the American Civil Liberties Union (ACLU) threatened
legal action, Daponte was reinstated. The official attitude remained
unambiguous: the horrors of the Iraqi killing fields had to be kept out
of the public domain. Said Daponte: 'They wanted to suppress the
figures because I had broken them down to show how many women
and children had died. . . . I find it extremely disturbing that the US
Census Bureau tried to suppress and delay the release of information
that is embarrassing to the current administration. Government employees should not be fired for speaking the truth . . . in this case the
figures were clearly politically embarrassing.'[43] Few independent observers doubted the one-sided nature of the conflict, with the inevitable massive scale of slaughter that this entailed. Thus Robert J. Lifton,
Professor of Psychiatry and Psychology at the City University of New
York, highlighted a widespread view when he quoted a taxi-driver:
'This ain't no war. It's just us dropping bombs and killing people.'[44]

Whatever the precise casualty figures there can be no doubt that the
ordinary Iraqi people – helpless in a political tyranny – had suffered
an appalling catastrophe. With the likelihood of hundreds of thousands
of dead and wounded, the bereaved and traumatised necessarily numbered hundreds of thousands more. And with the massive destruction
of Iraq's economic and social infrastructure – the removal of the necessary means to life – the civilian casualties were set to swell into the
millions (in a population of around 18 million). The obscene currency
of war (incineration, dismemberment, asphyxiation, burying alive, shred-
ding, blinding and the rest) had produced its predictable holocaust,
exploiting the obvious killing mechanisms and others that may not
have been widely suspected. For example, radioactive dust from the
depleted uranium shells had been released in copious quantities (see
'*The Environment*', below), and was known to cause kidney failure,
cancers and other diseases. When US aircraft bombed the oil refineries

there were necessarily many civilian casualties, among plant workers and people living in the vicinity. Thus when the Basra oil refinery was bombed at the start of the war many civilians were killed when their nearby homes were demolished, while others died in the clouds of suffocating smoke that poured from the massive fires. (At this site alone, more than 1.5 square miles became deeply contaminated, affecting not only the local flora and fauna but also the scarce sources of groundwater.) To these methods of killing and destruction were added the comprehensive efforts to block Iraqi access to the very necessities of life.

An immediate response of the Bush administration to the Iraqi invasion of Kuwait was to impose an embargo on Iraqi access to not only goods that might have industrial or military significance but also goods that are essential to civilian survival. The speedily enforced embargo (see Chapters 2 and 3) covered such items as medicines, water purifiers, hospital equipment, infant milk formula and food. A US naval blockade of Iraq was introduced, without congressional authority, as in effect an act of war to deny the Iraqi population the means to life. Iraqi funds were frozen and Iraqi oil sales prohibited – so reinforcing the blockade by denying Iraq the means to purchase as usual essential food and other supplies. Steps were taken also to discourage international agencies from supplying necessary aid and from investigating the mounting health crisis in Iraq. The plight of Iraqi minorities, deemed useful to American strategic aims, was given publicity while the desperate plight of the bulk of the Iraqi people was ignored. As early as 7 February 1991 the Red Crescent Society of Iraq estimated that the blockade and the bombing, by causing infant milk formula and infant medication shortages, had already caused 3000 infant deaths.

It is now clear that Iraq suffered its first civilian casualties (quite apart from the horrendous toll through the period of the Iran–Iraq War, when Iraq was supported by Kuwait, Saudi Arabia, Britain, the United States and others) in 1990, before the onset of military hostilities in February 1991. Already the scene had been set for the human catastrophe that would continue to roll in the months and years ahead. At the end of the war, with the military onslaught having compounded the early effects of the blockade, the Iraqi people faced a survival crisis of apocalyptic proportions. The water and sanitation systems had collapsed; food was already in short supply; and hospital supplies (drugs, disinfectants, equipment, etc.), already massively depleted, were not being replenished (see Chapter 3). In early March 1991 the Tigris river, a source of drinking water for thousands of civilians, was receiving gushing streams of raw sewage. All the sewage treatment facilities had been massively eroded and faced further deterioration. There were predictions – in the event fulfilled – of outbreaks of cholera, typhoid, hepatitis and polio (before the war all virtually eradicated from Iraq). Dr Mohammed Ani, director of immunisation and primary care for the Iraqi Ministry of Health, commented: 'We are being killed indirectly.'[45]

In October 1991 a report undertaken by a Harvard team of lawyers and public health specialists revealed that deaths among children under 5 in Iraq had nearly quintupled since the Gulf War, that close to one million children were malnourished, and that as many as 100,000 were currently starving to death. The children, according to the team, resembled Hiroshima survivors, with a listless air and drained of emotion. One of the team members, Dr Magne Raundalen, director of the Research for Children Programme at the Centre for Crisis Psychology at Bergen University, Norway, commented that the children were 'like living dead', that they had 'eradicated all their feelings and have no joy in their lives'.

The 87-strong team of international professionals from a wide variety of disciplines carried out investigations in Iraq's thirty largest cities and in rural areas across the country. Team members visited 46 hospitals and clinics, industrial plants, and 28 water and sewage facilities; and in addition made around 9000 random household surveys. Dr Eric Hoskyns, who presented the team's findings in London, noted that the report was 'the most comprehensive study ever done of the impact of conflict' and had provided 'a definitive assessment of the impact of the Gulf crisis on children'. The report indicated that Iraq's electricity, water and sewage services were close to total collapse and that their massive deterioration had caused a public health catastrophe throughout the country. Children with treatable leukaemia and diabetes were dying because of the shortage of anti-cancer drugs and insulin; and such preventable diseases as polio and measles were now resurgent. It was estimated that overall the mortality rate in children under 5 had risen by 380 per cent, with as many as a third of all survivors grossly malnourished.

The children of Iraq – according to a group of child psychologists with a decade of experience of the wars of Uganda, Sudan and Mozambique – were 'the most traumatised children of war ever described'. Said Dr Raundalen, expert in child trauma:

We must not keep this a secret, what has happened to these children. The international community must fulfil the promise made in the UNICEF summit just a year ago that children have the right to be looked after and brought back from despair and trauma.

Three-quarters of the children interviewed by the team members showed signs of despair; four out of five expressed fear of losing their families; and two-thirds could neither sleep nor concentrate properly, and doubted that they would survive to adulthood – 'exceedingly high figures', even for a conflict zone. The psychologists concluded that a majority of Iraq's children would suffer from severe psychological problems throughout their lives; and demanded a 'substantial national and international response' to help the vast traumatised child population. The report noted that the children were fighting to understand what they had seen ('planes bombing, houses collapsing, soldiers fighting, blood, mutilated and crushed bodies'), were fighting to forget what they had heard ('people screaming, desperate voices, planes, explosions, crying people'), were haunted 'by the smell of gunfire, fires and burned flesh', were struggling with the memories of what they had touched ('remains of planes, blood, carrying dead bodies and wounded relatives'), and every night the children went to bed 'with the memories of the terrible, shaking ground, and the prospect of the whole family being buried in the ruins of the house'. Of this hapless generation of Iraqi children the report commented:

> *The trauma, the loss, the grief, the lack of prospects, the feeling of threat here and now, that it will all start again, the impact of the sanctions, make us ask if these children are not the most suffering child population on earth.*[46]

Raundalen himself made two visits to Iraq to survey the plight of the children. On his second visit he retraced 90 per cent of the 230 children he had interviewed on his first visit (August 1991, Basra and Amiriya). On his first visit he had encountered 'a highly traumatised child population' and, contrary to his expectations, the second visit, some months later, revealed no reduction in the amount of distress in the children: 'It seems that time has stopped for the traumatised children, they are trapped within their own trauma, surrounded by reminders of what has happened . . . the children's minds appear a landscape of mental craters and destruction. The children have given insight into the disastrous psychic injury it represents to see family and friends killed, homes destroyed. There is no safe place. They expect the worst to happen again.' The Raundalen study revealed that 80 per cent of the children had lost friends in the bombing, that some had rescued friends or relatives from collapsed buildings, only to see them die later. One child, Luay, found the body of a mother and then her baby; the 13-year-old carefully put the dead baby on its mother's breast and put her dead arms around it. Luay tells also of a disembodied head handed round for identification; he recognised it as that of a school friend.

The impact of the war and of the draconian economic sanctions on Iraqi civilians in general and on Iraqi children in particular was well known to Washington and the rest of the international community in 1991. Eight detailed reports had been compiled by academics from various countries, and there was broad agreement on the dire situation that Iraq faced: an impoverished and increasingly diseased population was suffering a progressive decline into social decay, malnutrition and starvation. In fact the US-driven UN Security Council was alarmed enough to lift the *de jure* blockade of food, but the *de facto* embargo remained in place: Iraq, nominally with prodigious saleable assets, would still be denied the means to purchase the necessities of life. The situation, apocalyptic by the end of 1991, was set to deteriorate further. Few observers imagined that the punitive sanctions, already responsible for such widespread suffering, were set to remain in place for years to come.

THE ENVIRONMENT

The Gulf War, reinforced by comprehensive economic sanctions (many of which violated international law), transformed much of Iraq into a polluted and radioactive environment. At the end of the war, the Iraqi and Kuwaiti deserts – and many urban sites – were littered with wrecked armaments, unexploded mines and other munitions, chemical pollutants and radioactive debris. There was evidence that the United States had drawn up contingency plans for the use of nuclear and chemical weapons against Iraq. Thus Major Johan Persson, a liaison officer at a Swedish army field hospital, testified in Stockholm that he had seen official guidelines concerning the allied use of nuclear and chemical weapons. Said Persson: 'There was such an order. I saw it. I had it in my hand. It was the real thing.'[47] US Secretary of State James Baker declared to Tariq Aziz on 9 January 1991, days before the start of the US-led bombing campaign, that if Iraq were to use chemical weapons the US 'reply will be unrestrained'. From this, Aziz understood – according to the authoritative commentator Mohamed Heikal – 'that Baker was hinting at the use of nuclear weapons'.[48] Paul Rogers, a defence analyst at Bradford University's school of peace studies, commented that both the US Marines and Navy were equipped with tactical nuclear weapons.

The use of nuclear weapons is widely condemned, not only because of the massive destructive power of such devices but also because the hazards of radioactive contamination are visited on succeeding generations. Thus UN General Assembly Resolution 32/84 (12 December 1977) condemns *weapons of mass destruction*, defined as 'atomic explosive weapons, radioactive material weapons, lethal chemical and biological weapons and any weapons developed in the future which might have characteristics comparable in destructive effect to those of the atomic bomb or other weapons mentioned above'. Thus the American use of the BLU-82 fuel-air explosive (FAE), a 15,000-pound device capable of producing 'nuclear-scale' explosions to incinerate everything within hundreds of yards, stands condemned in international law. Similarly, depleted-uranium ordnance, as a 'radioactive material weapon', is condemned by GA Resolution 32/84. In fact, as noted, such ordnance was widely used by the US and British forces in the war.

The allied forces left at least 40 tons of depleted uranium on the Gulf War battlefields, according to a secret report produced by the United Kingdom Atomic Energy Authority (AEA).[49] The report suggests that there was enough depleted uranium (DU) in Kuwait and southern Iraq to cause '500,000 potential deaths'. Commenting that this indicates 'a significant problem', the report states: 'The DU will be spread around . . . in varying sizes and quantities from dust particles to full size penetrators and shot. It would be unwise for people to stay close to large quantities of DU for long periods and this would obviously be of concern to the local population if they collect this heavy metal and keep it. There will be specific areas in which many rounds will have been fired where localised contamination of vehicles and the soil may exceed permissible limits and these could be hazardous to both clean-up teams and the local population.' Though worry was expressed that 'a political problem' might be created by the environmental lobby ('It is in both the Kuwait and the UK interest that this is not left to rear its head in the years to come'), nothing was being done. It was acknowledged that 'if DU gets in the food chain or water this will create potential health problems' but, according to a senior AEA official, talks about possible remedies 'have not gone as quickly as we would have hoped'.[50] Soldiers, mine-clearing experts and reconstruction workers in Kuwait were told nothing of the hazards caused by the extent of the radioactive contamination.[51]

In the period after the Gulf War, Iraqi and international medical personnel noted a rapid increase in the number of childhood cancers, particularly leukaemia. At the same time UN and humanitarian aid workers were reporting that Iraqi children were playing with empty ammunition shells, tanks that had been destroyed by DU ordnance, and radioactive bullets that still litter wide areas of Iraq. It seemed reasonable to conclude that links existed (and continue to exist) between the radioactive debris – 'radioactive bullets . . . now being used by many children in Iraq as toys'[52] – and the growing incidence of cancer. (It is significant that the testing of DU penetrators in New Mexico has been linked to ground water poisoning; and that for similar reasons there has been fierce local opposition to the locating of test ranges in Minnesota and South Dakota.[53]) In fact the hazards of DU ordnance are widely recognised. The US Food and Drug Administration (FDA) has estimated that tank crews firing DU shells receive the equivalent of one chest X-ray every 20 to 30 hours. When, in late 1992, the director of the Albert Schweitzer Institute arrived in Berlin carrying a DU penetrator found in Iraq he was immediately arrested and charged with 'releasing ionising radiation'. The radioactive penetrator was quickly consigned to a lead-lined box. An aid worker in Basra testified that he had witnessed a child playing with hand puppets made out of DU penetrator shells. Another child, known to have played with DU shells, later developed leukaemia.

The UK Atomic Energy Authority had warned the Ministry of Defence that children would be badly affected by radiation if DU ordnance were used in the Gulf. Thus a memorandum sent to the ministry noted that when DU shells strike tanks and other targets they throw up 'toxic and carcinogenic' dust: 'Children playing in, or even looking in, burned-out vehicles could be affected.'[54] It was subsequently reported that Iraq's soil and water table had been contaminated, with such contamination set to last as long as the earth. Documents released under the US Freedom of Information Act stated that the American, British and Saudi armies fired about 4000 depleted-uranium-tipped tank rounds, and that US Air Force A-10 aircraft fired around 940,000 30mm bullets. The A-10s used DU ordnance against tanks, other armoured vehicles, trucks and roads. Here it is suggested that as much as 300 metric tons of radioactive uranium litter wide areas of Kuwait and Iraq; and that the ionising radiation (both alpha and gamma) is known to be carcinogenic.[55] The US Army has admitted that some soldiers were unknowingly exposed to DU radiation during the Gulf War – a circumstance thought by many observers to have contributed to the so-called Desert Storm syndrome that continues to afflict tens of thousands of Coalition personnel.

A research paper published in June 1994 by the Amsterdam-based Stichting LAKA documentation centre noted that DU ordnance had 'passed the battlefield tests in Iraq'; and pointed out that supplying depleted uranium to the US forces was the cheapest way to dispose of nuclear waste. Again emphasis is given to the mounting evidence of the growing incidence of radiation-linked diseases in the Iraqi population: *'The new types of lingering morbidity introduced by the most toxic war in history will include an estimated 800 tons of DU dust and fragments that will continue blowing across the devastated Arabian peninsula ecosystem for enough decades into the future to make this process well known in the annals of medicine.'*[56] In January 1992 the US Census Bureau estimated that life expectancy for the surviving Iraqi population had declined by 20 years for men and 11 years for women. Radioactive pollution had contributed to this situation. Nuclear bombs had not been used but Iraqi nuclear plant had been bombed, releasing radiation into the atmosphere, and the use of depleted-uranium ordnance had ensured that massive volumes of radioactive substances would remain a permanent feature of the Iraqi environment.

Radioactive uranium was not the only pollutant inflicted on the Iraqi people. There are also scientific reports, from Iraqi sources, to suggest that toxic chemicals were used by the Coalition forces. Thus a detailed report produced by the non-governmental Iraqi Society for Environmental Protection and Improvement (ISEPI) claimed that the US-led forces had resorted to chemical warfare in the Gulf.[57] It is stated that examined samples of vegetation, water, soil, blood and urine revealed the presence of highly poisonous myotoxins that were not indigenous to the region. Such trichothecene toxins are known to produce vomiting, diarrhoea, tachycardia, haemorrhaging, edema, skin lesions, nervous disorders, nausea, coma and death in human beings. In areas not exposed to bombing there was no evidence of such toxins. One Iraqi witness described a stinking yellow smoke that appeared after a rocket bombardment.[58] The victims of the alleged chemical attacks reportedly suffered from chest and stomach pains, vomiting with blood, nausea, vision impairment, rash blisters and other symptoms. Victims whose blood samples contained T-2 and HT-2 toxins suffered from vomiting, fever, headaches, backaches, swollen eyes and chest pains.

Massive volumes of pollutants were released when industrial plants, electrical power stations and oil facilities were bombed during the war. Some 20 main power plants, more than one hundred secondary power stations and scores of other industrial establishments were bombed between 17 January and 28 February 1991, with many of the sites bombed repeatedly. For example, the Daura refinery (Baghdad) and the North Oil refinery (Baiji) were both bombed twice, the South Oil Company and oil refineries in Basra were bombed several times, and

TABLE 1.1   Some bombed establishments and power plants with associated
environmental damage

Name of Establishment or Power Plant (P.P.)	Location	Date of Bombardment	Environmental Damage
1 Mulla Abdulla (P.P.)	Ta'mim, 45 km South Kirkuk	25/1	Burning of 3 million litres of crude oil
2 Taza (P.P.)	Salah al-Din	17/1	Burning of 5 million litres of gas oil
3 Mosul/Al-Yarmook (P.P.)	Ninevah	17/1	Burning of $\frac{1}{2}$ million litres of gas oil
4 Hartha (P.P.)	Basra	17/1	Spillage of 17 million litres of crude oil into the river
		17/2	Spillage of 60,000 litres of kerosene into the river
		13/2	Spillage of 76,000 litres of transformer oil (PcBs) into the river.
		22/2	Spillage of 50,000 litres of engine oil into the river
		24/2	Spillage of 150 tons of HCL
		28/2	Spillage of 164 tons of NaOH
5 Najaf (P.P.)	Najaf	27/1	Spillage of 3 million litres of engine oil into the soil
6 Taji (P.P.)	Baghdad/Taji	17/1	Burning of 1 million litres of gas oil
7 Glass/Ceramic (Est.)	Anbar/Ramadi	21/1	Spillage of 427,000 litres of liquid gas into the river
8 Iraqi Cement (Est.)	Anbar/Qaim and Karbala	2/2	Burning of 36 million litres of heavy oil

Name of Establishment or Power Plant (P.P.)	Location	Date of Bombard-ment	Environmental Damage
9 Phosphate (Est.)	Anbar		
Phosphoric acid refining factory		26/1	Spillage of 5000 tons of acid
H_2SO_4 factory		22/2	Spillage of 5616 tons of acid
Fluorine salt factory		16/2	Burning of 180 tons of fluorocylicic
Shelter		16/2	Burning of 53,600 tons of liquid sulphur to SO_2 gas covering an area of 20 km in diameter
Sulphur storage area		22/2	Burning of 18,000 tons of solid sulphur
10 State Enterprise for Fertilisers	Salah al-Din/Baiji	17/1	Spillage of 200 tons of Ammonia into the river
11 State Enterprise for Rubber Industry	Qadisiah/ Diwaniyah	13/2	Burning of 36,729 car and bicycle tyres and 6000 car tubes
12 Ministry of Trade's Gas Plant	Missan	22/2	Burning of 23,000 car and bicycle tyres
13 State Enterprise for Drugs and Medicine	Salah al-Din/Samana	17/1	Burning of 2.6 million litres of gas oil
14 State Enterprise for Sugar Industry	Missan	22/2	Spillage of 1 million litres of gas oil into the soil

the North Oil Company (Kirkuk) suffered 13 air raids. Tables 1.1[59] and 1.2 indicate the scale of the environmental damage caused by bombing raids on particular industrial establishments and power plants.

Substantial air and ground pollution was caused by the bombing of oil wells and other oil facilities. Thus at Basra alone the bombing caused the burning of 1.44 million barrels of oil, 12.6 million barrels of oil products, and 1.13 million cubic metres of natural gas. At Al-Anbar 240,000 barrels of oil were burned, as well as 72,000 tons of

TABLE 1.2   Chemical releases from bombed installations

Bombed Installation	Quantities	Substances
State Sugar Refinery	95,191 kg*	Pesticides
State Organisation for Geological and Mining Surveys	7874 kg	Mercuric nitrate, potassium nitrate, mercuric chloride, arsenic oxide, potassium cyanide, ammonium thiocyanide and potassium thiocyanide
	2 litres	Concentrated solutions of sulphuric acid and nitric acid
Iraqi State Cement Factory	4.5 kg	Ammonium thiocyanide and potassium thiocyanide, potassium nitrate
State Organisation for Fertiliser Production	700,000 kg	Ammonia
State Organisation for Phosphates	5,606,000 kg	Concentrated solution of sulphuric acid
	5,000,000 kg	Concentrated solution of phosphoric acid
	180,000 kg	Fluosilicic acid
	53,600,000 kg	Liquid sulphur dioxide
State Organisation for Electricity (Production and Transport)	1,350 kg	Alum
	150,000 kg/200 litres	Hydrochloric acid
	1,360 litres	Anti-rust solution
	75 kg	Polyelectrolyte
	164,000 kg	Caustic soda
State Organisation for Pharmaceutical Products and Medical Supplies	200,000 kg	Polythene and polypropylene
	100,000 kg	Wrapping and packaging products
Al Numan Factory	328,371 kg	Plastics (granules and residue)
	7,476 kg	Pigments
	400 kg	Fibreglass
	67,500 metres	Low-density polyethylene pipes
	9,960 kg	Resin
	350 kg	Solid and liquid wax
	19,925 kg	Black graphite
	600 kg	Dyes
	500 units	Used tyres

* 1 ton = 907.18 kg

Source: Note verbale (1 June 1993) from the Permanent Mission of Iraq to the United Nations Office at Geneva, addressed to the Secretary-General of the World Conference on Human Rights held in Vienna, 14–25 June 1993.

sulphur to generate sulphur oxides. At Al-Tamin some 30 million cubic metres of H_2S gas were burned, while 2.8 million barrels of oil
products were burned at the Baiji refinery at Salah Aldin. At these and
many other sites high concentrations of air and ground pollutants were
monitored. One estimate suggested that 1613 hectares of agricultural
land had been destroyed, with high densities of hydrocarbons detected
over large areas spreading hundreds of miles from the bombing-in-
duced fires. The high levels of air pollution – involving complex mix-
tures of sulphur products, hydrocarbons, nitrogen products, free radicals,
aromatic compounds, etc. – have been associated with unfamiliar plant
and animal diseases (causing, for example, the destruction of thousands
of eucalyptus trees and around 120,000 palm trees), in addition to the
catastrophic deterioration in the health of the Iraqi civilian population.

High levels of environmental pollution were caused by the war and
the punitive sanctions, now well into their sixth year (Chapters 2 and
3). The economic blockade means that Iraq has been denied the opportunity to begin social and industrial reconstruction by importing
the necessary goods and equipment. Today (early 1996) the US-induced plight of millions of ordinary Iraqi civilians continues to deteriorate.
Some observers have likened Iraq to a vast and forgotten concentration camp, denied the means to life and with no end in sight.

THE DESOLATION

The Iran–Iraq War (1980–88) had left Iraq massively in debt (to such
sponsors as Kuwait and Saudi Arabia); but the profligate dissipation
of lives and treasure had accomplished nothing, except to prepare the
way for another Gulf war. In Iraq all the baleful features of the regime
remained in place – disinformation, torture and the persecution of dissident and minority groups. At the same time, despite the harsh rig-
ours of the war, many social gains had been protected. By 1990 infant
mortality had fallen to 35 per 1000 births; life expectancy was 68
years; the population of 18.8 million (26.6 per cent under the age of
5) had a literacy rate of 90 per cent; immunisation cover had reached
95 per cent of the population; and a comprehensive health service –
with 135 modern and well-equipped hospitals (more than 37,000 beds)
and 850 community health centres – remained in place. Saddam's tyranny represented many of the familiar aspects of totalitarian repression,
but the less publicised benefits of Ba'athist socialism were also part of
the picture. With the reckless and ill-judged invasion of Kuwait in

1990, all these benefits were to be swept away. The ensuing conflict – what William Arkin, director of military research in the US, was to call 'the most destructive war in modern history' – was set to reduce Iraq to little more than an extermination camp.

The military devastation of the social infrastructure, with the subsequent denial of all the means to remedial reconstruction, inevitably resulted in a mounting toll of civilian casualties – in one estimate, 200,000 fatalities by the end of 1991. With three-quarters of the Iraqi population living in cities by the late 1980s, the bulk of the social provisions – hospitals, clean water, sewage treatment, communications, manufacture, agriculture, etc. – depended on electrical power. But the attack on the infrastructure (with power stations one of the principal target categories) resulted in comprehensive erosion of all these provisions. In many areas water treatment was no longer a practical option, raw sewage flooded into rivers that supplied drinking water, and hospital and other health provisions had virtually collapsed. In the immediate aftermath of the war much of the Iraqi population was driven to pre-industrial subsistence methods of survival, with all the inevitable social consequences that this situation implied: hospitals struggling to cope, with only a trickle of medicines and other supplies; surgical operations, including caesarians, performed without anaesthetics; no spare parts to repair resuscitation and laboratory equipment; hospital wards full of dying children; a growing incidence of nutritional and other diseases; and an ever diminishing government food ration (see Chapter 3). At the same time the collapse of the social infrastructure, coupled with the impossible economic pressures on ordinary families, was leading to a substantial increase in the levels of illegal abortions, social violence, theft, suicides and family collapse.

In 1991 the scale of the catastrophe afflicting the Iraqi people was clear. In Baghdad alone the massively degraded water and sanitation services were causing a public health crisis of vast proportions. Since mid-January most civilians had been deprived of running water and electricity. The Tigris, supplying virtually all the drinking water for many of the capital's inhabitants, was being fouled by torrents of untreated sewage. The postal, telephone and telex facilities had been destroyed, making it impossible to communicate information about sanitation and health needs. Mohammad Furat, manager of the Rustumiya sewage treatment plant, which, like most other such facilities, had come under allied bombing attacks, estimated that 65 million cubic yards of raw sewage was flowing into the Tigris every month. The health problems were compounded by the destruction of pumping stations and the bombing of the plants that manufactured water purification chemicals.

The international community knew well what had transpired. In March 1991 Martti Ahtisaari, the UN Under-Secretary-General for Administration and Management, led an investigation team to Iraq to report on the situation. His subsequent report to the UN Secretary-General included the comments:

> I and the members of my mission were fully conversant with media reports regarding the situation in Iraq and, of course, with the recent WHO/UNICEF report on water, sanitary and health conditions in the Greater Baghdad area. It should, however, be said at once that nothing we had seen or read had quite prepared us for the particular form of devastation which has now befallen the country. The recent conflict has wrought near-apocalyptic results upon the economic infrastructure of what had been, until January 1991, a rather highly urbanized and mechanized society. Now, most means of modern life support have been destroyed or rendered tenuous. Iraq has, for some time to come, been relegated to a pre-industrial age, but with all the disabilities of post-industrial dependency on an intensive use of energy and technology.[60]

The report emphasised the *'inexorable reality that, as a result of war, virtually all previously viable sources of fuel and power (apart from a limited number of mobile generators) and modern means of communication are now, essentially, defunct'*. The post-war civil unrest, encouraged by the United States, had conspired with the infrastructure collapse to make it impossible for the Iraqi authorities *'even to measure the dimensions of the calamity, much less to respond to its consequences ...'*. There was *'much less than the minimum fuel required'* for transportation, irrigation and the pumping of water and sewage. Most employees were *'unable to come to work ... approximately 90 per cent industrial workers have been reduced to inactivity and will be deprived of income as of the end of March'*. Iraq had formerly imported 70 per cent of its food needs, but now imports were blocked and food prices were already rising *'beyond the purchasing reach of most Iraqi families.'* In particular, the energy vacuum was perceived as *'an omnipresent obstacle to the success of even a short-term, massive effort to maintain life-sustaining conditions ...'*[61]

The impact of the UN-mandated economic sanctions was already plain in March 1991:

The mission noted that Iraq has been heavily dependent on food imports, which have amounted to at least 70 per cent of consumption needs. Seed was also imported. Sanctions decided upon by the Security Council had already adversely affected the country's ability to feed its people.[62]

All food stocks were at critically low levels or had already been exhausted; powdered milk was only available for sick children on medical prescription; and livestock farming had been 'seriously affected by sanctions because many feed products were imported'. The authorities were no longer able to support livestock farmers in combatting disease because the sole laboratory producing veterinary vaccines* had been destroyed in the bombing. The grain harvest was compromised because of the destruction of the drainage/irrigation system, the lack of pesticides and fertilisers (formerly imported), and the lack of fuel and spare parts for the harvesting machines. '*Widespread starvation conditions*' were '*a real possibility.*'[63]

Many Iraqi families were unable to draw their government-set rations because the distribution centres were depleted and it was difficult, in the absence of adequate transport services, to travel to other centres. With hyperinflation (prices of many basic necessities having increased by 1000 per cent or more), many employees unable to draw salaries, and most of the banking system having closed down, most Iraqi families were unable to supplement their food rations by purchases on the open market. At the same time, with the collapse of the sewage and sanitation systems ('Pools of sewage lie in the streets and villages'), it was predicted that health hazards would 'build in the weeks to come . . . a catastrophe could be faced at any time if conditions do not change'. The report, dated 20 March 1991, is now (early 1996) five years old. It concluded with words that signalled the importance of urgent humanitarian action in a matter of weeks rather than months: 'Time is short.'

Already the scale of the US destruction of Iraq was being exposed. Thus in a damning article in *The New York Times* Zbigniew Brzezinski, the former national security advisor to President Carter, emphasised that the damage-toll in Iraq 'raises the moral question of the proportionality of the response' to Saddam's invasion of Kuwait. In the same vein the respected British journalist Peter Jenkins, responding to the

---

* This important laboratory facility, destroyed by UN bombing in the effort to remove Iraqi troops from Kuwait, was established as part of a UN Food and Agriculture Organisation (FAO) regional project.

Brzezinski comments and other material, declared that the peace 'has turned into a nightmare, the continuation of the war by other means'.[64] Another observer, Joost Hiltermann, the Middle East organiser for Physicians for Human Rights (PHR), commented that the allied bombing had taken 'the brain out of the country's ability to survive'; with the PHR president Jack Geiger, after a tour of the Basra area, describing the US policy as 'Bomb now, die later!' The PHR findings confirmed other reports: malnutrition, a deteriorating health situation, dangerous drinking water, and a collapsed economy. The Harvard medical team was reporting that over the coming year 170,000 children would die because of the Gulf War and its aftermath.

In August 1991 official Iraqi sources reported that so far more than 11,000 people had died of starvation and that more than 14,000 children had died because of the lack of drugs since the start of the US-led economic embargo. Now Western aid donors were warning that only a relaxation of international sanctions would prevent malnutrition and disease on an unprecedented scale. UN officials were reporting an upsurge in such nutritional diseases as marasmus and kwashiorkor, with such infectious diseases as typhoid, hepatitis, meningitis and gastroenteritis surging out of control. In July a UN mission led by Prince Sadruddin Aga Khan, focusing on the humanitarian needs in Iraq, confirmed that economic sanctions were having a substantial adverse effect on the civilian population. Raw sewage continued to flow in city streets and into rivers used for washing and drinking. The unavailability of spare parts meant that medical and laboratory facilities, industrial and agricultural plant, and water sewage systems could not be maintained. The Sadruddin mission urged that immediate steps be taken to alleviate the desperate and worsening plight of the Iraqi people. On 14 November the Iraqi agriculture minister, Abdul Wahab al-Sabagh, declared that thousands more children and old people would die soon unless UN sanctions were lifted: ' . . . only 15 per cent of our people can afford to buy food on the free market. The rest must accept hunger. That is the reality of the embargo.' Where the national Iraqi grain requirement was 200,000 tonnes a month the country had been allowed to import only 100,000 tonnes in the eight-month period since the end of the war: 'Today we have a great lack of food and medicines. We lack spare parts for agricultural machinery. We lack fertilisers and pesticides as well as spares to get our power stations and oil refineries working again . . . we need pumps to bring the water to the fields and these require electricity which we do not have.'

The situation was well understood by the international community but the United States blocked all serious proposals for humanitarian action to address the suffering of the Iraqi people. On 20 November 1991 the director of Oxfam, Frank Judd, emphasised the need for urgent action to help the millions of Iraqis facing a winter without medicines, adequate food or housing. A doctor in a Baghdad hospital reported the vicious circle in which people became weaker and weaker through malnutrition, and then became increasingly susceptible to disease, which then weakened them even more. By now children with matchstick limbs and distended bellies, 'like drought victims from Ethiopia', were dying in their hundreds in Iraqi hospitals and could be seen on the streets of Baghdad and the other cities. In Basra Louise Cainkar, director of the Chicago-based Database Project on Palestinian Human Rights, having carried out detailed fieldwork in Iraq, encountered 'the same scene I was to see over and over again . . . Iraqi women holding thin, bloated and malnourished children . . .'.[65] On 20 May 1991 President Bush declared that there would be no end to the trade embargo 'as long as Saddam Hussein is in power'; and in the same spirit, Robert Gates, nominated by Bush to head the CIA, stated that the Iraqi people – by any reckoning, helpless in their predicament – would be made to 'pay the price' while Saddam remained in power.[66]

The Iraqi nation had been thrown back a century: 'no electricity, no running water, reliance on contaminated water, food and fuel shortages, transportation problems, for many no work, no income and thus no food, unreliable or total lack of access to medical care and medicine, massive inflation, and a real severing of human relations . . . most Iraqis appeared to be in silent shock . . .'[67] But all this was not enough for the Washington strategists. There were too few Iraqi wounded, diseased, traumatised, dead. The US-imposed humiliation and suffering of a helpless national people would continue. The genocidal economic sanctions would not only continue but would be intensified in the years to come. And other world crises would come to the fore. The international community would be happy to forget the dying of the Iraqi people.

2 The Chronology of Sanctions

> *... No, not war but something more tremendous than war. Apply this economic, peaceful, silent deadly remedy and there will be no need for force. The boycott is what is substituted for war.*[1]

> President Woodrow Wilson

> *The great advantage of economic sanctions is that on the one hand they can be very potent, while on the other hand they do not involve that resort to force which is repugnant to our objective of peace.*[2]

> John Foster Dulles

PREAMBLE

Economic sanctions – as a 'silent, deadly remedy', a 'very potent' measure – represent the prosecution of war by *nominally* non-violent means. In public-relations terms, sanctions are more respectable than biological warfare, more ethically acceptable than bombing, unlikely to generate a heavy toll of fatalities. Instead, we are encouraged to believe, economic sanctions are relatively civilised, an undeniable method of coercion, when adequately enforced, but one that is unlikely to cause the vast suffering associated with a military onslaught.

In fact to deny a nation the means to purify water or to treat sewage – and so to encourage the spread of disease – is a form of biological warfare. To deny a nation access to antiseptics, antibiotics and other essential medical supplies – thus to render disease untreatable – is a form of biological warfare. To litter a land with radioactive substances, and to deny the people the necessary remedial means, is again a form of biological warfare – striking not only at the living but also at the unborn generations. To deny people adequate electricity for hospitals and factories, to deny people – including pregnant women, babies, infants, the sick, the old – sufficient food and clean water is, if not

33

semantically a violent onslaught, undeniably a gross violation of humanity. No keen advocate of economic sanctions can doubt that untreatable diseases, malnutrition and starvation produce their own characteristic toll of suffering, disability and death.

It is now abundantly clear that economic sanctions, rigorously applied and sustained over time, strike hardest at the most vulnerable. Before we indicate what this means in human terms (see Chapter 3), it is useful to profile the chronology of events that followed the Iraqi invasion of Kuwait in 1990.

THE CHRONOLOGY OF SANCTIONS

The invasion of Kuwait on 2 August 1990 stimulated an immediate international response. The UN Security Council passed Resolution 660 (14 votes to none, with Yemen abstaining), condemning the invasion, demanding an immediate Iraqi withdrawal, and calling upon Iraq and Kuwait to begin immediate 'intensive negotiations' (Appendix 1). At the same time, before any sanctions resolution had been authorised by the Security Council, the United States took immediate economic measures. On 2 August President George Bush signed two executive orders to freeze all Iraqi and Kuwaiti governmental assets (these latter now under nominal Iraqi control).*

The freeze order, the third in recent years, followed a series of such orders that began with the First World War when the US Congress passed the Trading with the Enemy Act. This legislation authorised the president to respond to various situations; in particular, where an enemy government had acted illicitly to take control of property in time of war or national emergency. The powers authorised by the Act have been used by successive presidents to block assets and to regulate financial transactions involving such countries as China, Cuba, Vietnam and many others. The International Emergency Economic Powers Act (IEEPA, 1977), enacted in response to the increasing globalisation of the financial markets, added to the president's powers by authorising action against 'any unusual and extraordinary threat, which has its

---

* The economic measures taken against Iraq had many consequences, not least denying Iraq complete control over its nominal assets. This meant that Iraq was no longer able to pay its contributions to the United Nations, which in turn allowed the US to insist that Iraq be denied its voting rights, under the provisions of Article 19 of the Charter. That the conditions that had led to non-payment were now 'beyond the control of the Member' (Article 19) was ignored. Iraq was virtually expelled from the General Assembly. This, when the US owed the UN $1.6 bn.

source in whole or substantial part outside the United States, to the national security, foreign policy, or economy of the United States . . .'. It was under the terms of IEEPA, an effective substitute for the Trading with the Enemy Act, that President Bush acted to freeze Iraqi and Kuwaiti assets. The US banks and other financial institutions – with experience of earlier IEEPA freeze orders affecting Iran, Libya and Panama – moved promptly to take the necessary actions. It was comforting to Washington that countries that had formerly objected to the extraterritorial application of US measures against Iran and Libya now had no compunction about introducing measures against Iraq. There was no problem about whether US sanctions could be legitimately applied to the many overseas branches of US banks. Perhaps, opined one financial expert, 'a norm of customary international law has been created that recognises the validity of extraterritoriality in such circumstances'.[3] It was also highly significant that what was to become a virtually worldwide regime of economic sanctions – perhaps the most draconian economic measures ever faced by a country – was to be enforced by an unchallenged military blockade.

On 6 August 1990 the UN Security Council passed Resolution 661 (13 votes to none, with Cuba and Yemen abstaining), the first of the sanctions resolutions (Appendix 1). Now the full scope of the world action against Iraq was made plain. All states were called upon to prevent the import into their territories 'of all commodities and products originating in Iraq or Kuwait'; the transfer of all funds to Iraq or Kuwait for trading purposes was prohibited; the supply of all goods – except 'supplies intended strictly for medical purposes, and, in humanitarian circumstances, foodstuffs' – to Iraq and Kuwait was prohibited; and a Sanctions Committee was established to help supervise the sanctions regime. On 9 August President Bush issued further executive orders to strengthen US sanctions in response to UN Resolution 661. It is significant that these orders were relevant not only to Iraqi and Kuwaiti interests in the United States but also to the overseas branches of US companies. President Bush, with a stroke of the pen, was in a position to affect the patterns of world trade.

At this time there was no suggestion – at least in the public domain – that it would be necessary to launch an international military invasion of Iraq to liberate Kuwait. The initial declaration of the 12 member states of the European Economic Community (EEC), issued on 4 August 1990, reflected a widespread view in urging a peaceful solution to the crisis: '*The European Economic Community and its Member states reiterate their firm conviction that any dispute between*

countries should be resolved pacifically . . .' (Appendix 2). The subsequent EEC Regulation No. 2340/90, issued on 8 August and making
reference to UN Security Council Resolutions 660 and 661, reaffirmed
the 661 embargo conditions and listed in an annex the medical products that (along with 'foodstuffs intended for humanitarian purposes')
should be excluded from the embargo (Appendix 2).* Though, at this
stage, there were no reports indicating plans for a military solution to
the crisis it was clear that the United States was keen to inject an
element of force into the situation.

On 13 August 1990 Secretary of State James Baker declared that
the US was ready to impose an 'interdiction' of Iraqi oil exports as a
means of enforcing the UN sanctions regime. He refrained from using
the word 'blockade' – which is widely perceived internationally as an
act of war – but expressed the hope that other Western navies would
help to 'interdict' Iraqi oil exports. Already there was some dissent in
the Security Council. The Soviet Union considered that a separate Council
resolution would be required to authorise what amounted to a military
blockade on the high seas. Even Britain, normally supine in the face
of US pressure, inclined to the view that Iraqi traffic should be monitored for some time before any resort to force. Some 40 large US
naval vessels, three British and four French were reportedly in and
around the Gulf and the Red Sea, with ships from Canada and Australia on their way to the area. Moreover, solely as a means of deterring further aggression, 100,000 American troops would be in Saudi
Arabia within a month. Defense Secretary Dick Cheney emphasised
that the United States had no aggressive plans.

Many states had by now enacted domestic legislation to give effect
to the mandatory sanctions specified in Resolution 661. On 3 August
1990, anticipating the UN response, the Canadian Superintendent of
Financial Institutions issued a Direction to all banks (under subsection
313.1 of the Bank Act, authorising government control over selected
bank practices). This measure, deemed controversial, instructed the banks

---

* The exemption of medical products and foodstuffs 'intended for humanitarian purposes', as specified in Resolution 661 and other documents, was in fact a matter of
political packaging rather than humanitarian intent. It meant that the aid agencies
would be allowed to operate in Iraq but ensured that, through the freezing of Iraqi
assets and the prohibition of oil purchases, Iraq would not have the revenue to buy
medical products and foodstuffs in adequate quantities. Moreover, the condition '*for
humanitarian purposes*' imposed a disguised embargo. Washington had an interest in
denying that the sanctions were having genocidal consequences, so would 'humanitarian' need ever be recognised? At best there would be protracted delays in food
delivery; at worst, in the absence of any practical action, the matter would be *endlessly* debated.

not to act 'on instructions from or on behalf of, or purporting to be from or on behalf of, a Kuwaiti government agency', unless the instructions were approved in writing by the Superintendent. Once UN Resolution 661 was passed, the Direction was rescinded in favour of the United Nations Iraq Regulations, issued pursuant to Canada's United Nations Act. The validity of regulations issued under this unique legislation rests specifically on a Security Council resolution. The issuing of regulations in the present context had immediate consequences for trade and financial transactions between Canada on the one hand and Iraq and Kuwait on the other.

In France, Decree No. 90-681 (2 August 1990) stipulated: 'Foreign exchange transactions, transfer of funds and settlement of any kind between France and other countries made on behalf of individuals or companies resident in Kuwait and in Iraq, or of Kuwaiti or Iraqi nationality, are subject to the prior authorisation of the Minister of Economy.' Thus French–Iraqi/Kuwaiti financial transactions now depended upon government permission. A further decree (4 August 1990), citing earlier enactments, strengthened further the embargo on trade and financial transactions with Iraq and Kuwait. On 6 August the German Federal Government froze all Kuwaiti accounts and deposits held in Germany, as a means of blocking Iraqi appropriation of Kuwaiti funds. Export guarantees were suspended and fresh powers taken to control 'the trading of arms and nuclear weapon products on the territory of the Federal Republic of Germany'. Over the next few days other legislative measures were taken to protect the trade embargo of Iraq/Kuwait. Similar actions were taken in Italy, Switzerland, Japan and elsewhere. Few observers doubted that the reckless and illegal Iraqi invasion of Kuwait had generated an unprecedented international response.

At the same time there were some signs that the trade embargo was not total. For example, the Jordanian authorities appeared to be doing little to block the flow of trucks crossing into Iraq at their usual rate. There were reports of oil tanker trucks moving in a steady flow, carrying Iraqi crude oil to the refineries at Zerqa. Some tankers, it was noted, bore Kuwaiti licence plates; more lorries, with Jordanian, Iraqi and Egyptian haulage plates, plied their way into Iraq. King Hussein of Jordan commented that the government fully understood its obligations under the UN Charter: 'How this resolution physically will be implemented is under study . . .'.[4] Fahed Fanek, a leading Jordanian economist, noted that a total trade ban with Iraq would be a disaster for Jordan, accustomed to Iraqi oil and to exporting a quarter of its total commodity exports to Iraq: 'Such a step will break the back of the Jordanian economy. The imposition of sanctions by Jordan against Iraq might not cause major damage to the Iraqi economy, or to its military effort, but it will devastate the Jordanian economy and cause a loss in excess of half a billion dollars a year. It will also raise unemployment by a further 12.4 per cent over the current rate of 16 per cent and this is before adding the tens of thousands that are working in Kuwait and who may return to join the army of unemployed.'[5] In such circumstances, considering also the popular support for Saddam Hussein in Jordan, it is easy to understand the Jordanian tilt in favour of Iraq through the period of the Gulf crisis. It is equally easy to see why today (early 1996) Washington is working so hard to drive a political wedge between Iraq and Jordan in the interest of further isolating and punishing the Iraqi people.

By the middle of August 1990, a mere fortnight after the invasion of Kuwait, the economic embargo on Iraq was already beginning to bite. Already, by sea and by land, Iraq was becoming isolated from the outside world. The export of the bulk of Iraqi oil, the principal revenue earner, had been stopped. On 13 August an Iraqi tanker was turned away from the Red Sea terminus of Iraq's trans-Saudi pipeline; another tanker, turned away from French ports and docked at Rotterdam, was prevented from selling its cargo. Already Iraq had been deprived of hard currency revenues of around $15 billion in 1990. Moreover, the impact on food imports was already being felt. Accustomed to importing 70 per cent of its food needs, Iraq – with frozen assets and blocked oil revenues – was now no longer able to do so. Food stocks would soon be exhausted. In this increasingly dire situation, UN officials seemed uncertain how to react. Should the threat of starvation be pressed to its dreadful conclusion, or would such a policy – in violation of the Geneva Convention but much favoured by Washington strategists – merely generate sympathy for Saddam? Already the United States, Canada and Australia, suppliers of most of Iraq's wheat, rice, poultry and soyabean, had stopped shipments. The White House, well aware of Iraq's deteriorating food situation, commented on 13 August: 'It appears far too early to consider any foodstuffs as being in the humanitarian need category.' It was this sort of comment that exposed the emptiness of the food exemption in Resolution 661. Already there were ample signs that the United States would always be reluctant to recognise *humanitarian need*, however much the plight of the Iraqi people might worsen in the terrible months and years ahead.

In 1990 about one-third of the Iraqi workforce was engaged in agriculture, though their efforts were being steadily eroded by the impact of sanctions that made it impossible to import fertilisers, insecticides and spare parts for machinery. It was easy to predict that the rice and barley crops, grown along the lower Euphrates and Tigris, would drastically diminish, as would the harvesting of dates around Basra. Efforts to improve irrigation – in some cases following earlier advice from Western specialists but none the less routinely denounced in anti-Iraq propaganda – were relatively unsuccessful. The slightly saline water from the Tigris and Euphrates did not help: insufficient drainage, made inevitable through war and sanctions, was rendering the land increasingly infertile by depositing a thin layer of salt. Again, even a few weeks after the ending of the Gulf War, it was clear that Washington intended to build on the early effects of sanctions and use starvation as a political tool against the Iraqi people.

The Bush administration remained keen to portray the enforcement of the embargo as a police operation, not only serving the requirements of Resolution 661, but fulfilling also the provisions of Article 51 of the UN Charter allowing 'the inherent right of individual or collective self-defence if an armed attack occurs against a Member of the United Nations'. President Bush – asked if US enforcement would cover food and other essentials – replied: 'Just watch. Everything. Everything.'[6] If anyone doubted that starvation was to be used as a tactical weapon, here was further evidence. The Bush administration expressed the belief that the embargo would hold, while continuing diplomatic pressure to block the loopholes, such as Jordan's substantial trade with Iraq.

At the same time the United States continued to push for the maintenance of an 'interdiction' regime. Only rarely, it was argued, was a US vessel required to attack. A suspect merchant vessel was first warned by radio, and then by officers on a warship alongside the vessel. If the warnings were not heeded then a shot would be fired across the merchantman's bows. Only if this was ignored would guns or missiles be fired at the vessel. In fact in mid-August 1990 there were significant divisions in the UN Security Council about both the wisdom and the legality of the interdiction policy. France and the Soviet Union expressed 'very strong opposition' to US enforcement of the blockade, while Canada and Malaysia pointed out that in the absence of an enabling UN resolution they had declined Kuwait's invitation that they help to enforce the embargo. Already anxieties were being expressed that Washington intended to tackle the Gulf crisis without consulting other Security Council members; and that military enforcement of the embargo – a *de facto* blockade, an acknowledged act of war – required the approval of the US Congress. UN Secretary-General Perez de Cuellar, though by now increasingly marginalised by Washington, took pains to emphasise that only the United Nations, 'through its Security Council resolutions, can really decide about a blockade'. But such an observation had little impact on the course of events. The United States was pushing its own agenda and – by dint of characteristic threat and bribery – was securing enough international support for its policies. For example, Saudi Arabia, bullied into receiving the colossal influx of US troops, perceived it had little option but to support the US war effort. On 13 August the 155,000-tonne Iraqi tanker *Alqadisiyah*, waiting off the Saudi port of Yanbu, was informed that it would not be allowed to load crude oil. In similar (at first hesitant) support for the US posture, London ordered its naval vessels into the Gulf to participate in the interdiction activities. The UK Foreign Office Minister of State William Waldegrave declared that Britain was taking steps to ensure that the 'economic stranglehold does its work'. And on the same day the White House issued a further confirmation that food was included in the ban. The 'humanitarian' exemption included in Resolution 661 counted for nothing.

The Bush administration was continuing to pressure Jordan to close the only serious loophole in the trade embargo. On 15 August King Hussein arrived in the United States, with most commentators predicting that he would be given a frosty reception. Turkey, at one time a doubtful player, was now supporting the US policy of blocking food shipments to Iraq. By mid-August the transport of food across the Turkey–Iraq border had been brought to an almost complete halt. On one day a single truck laden with food crossed the border, in comparison with the usual 5000. A few days later none were crossing. It was now being reported that dozens of foreign trucks, even those carrying medicine, were being refused permission to cross the border. The reasons for this rigorous implementation of the sanctions regime – in violation of the exemption provisions in Resolution 661 – were not hard to fathom. US Secretary of State James Baker had recently visited Ankara and the usual American largesse was evident in the interest of securing strategic objectives. There would be cash for arms, World Bank loans, and American support for Turkey in such problem areas as Cyprus, Armenian charges of genocide, and Turkey's application to join the European Community (EC). A World Bank credit of $1.4 billion, held up because Turkey had not met World Bank financial criteria, was to be released. Some 40 F-4 fighter-bombers, held up for six years because of Greek objections, would now be made available to Turkey, and there was also an offer of an Eximbank loan for Turkish military investment. Turkey, like most states keeping an eye on the mercenary main chance, had been bought off. Jordan was a more difficult case, mainly because of the traditional links between that country and Iraq.

Threats from the Bush administration that it might be necessary to impose a naval blockade on Aqaba, to prevent the shipment of goods overland to Iraq, had already reduced the flow of traffic. The US was not satisfied: a complete trade embargo was deemed essential to the success of sanctions. On 15 August some nine ships were unloading goods in the port, with others waiting instructions. Some shipping companies were already reluctant to use Aqaba in case their vessels became trapped in the event of a US naval blockade. Already President Bush had promised to compensate Jordan for any financial losses through the embargo, but the question of popular Jordanian support for Iraq remained a stumbling block. The European Community (EC) was reportedly willing to assist in the compensation of Jordan for any loss of trade, which Jordanian officials were estimating would amount to around $500 million. In this context it should be remembered that the right of Jordan to claim compensation was protected under Article 50 of the UN Charter: '*If preventive or enforcement measures against any state are taken by the Security Council, any other state . . . which finds itself confronted with special economic problems . . . shall have the right to consult the Security Council with regard to a solution of those problems.*' As with many Charter provisions, the acknowledgement of this right does not guarantee that a solution will be found. The members of the Security Council, obliged to consult, are not obliged to act. In the event President Bush declared himself 'very encouraged' by his talks with King Hussein. The King's statement that Jordan would observe UN sanctions was 'widely welcomed' and the 'differences that possibly existed with Jordan have been narrowed'. A difference remained over precisely what goods were covered by the embargo. Where Bush wanted to block the shipment of everything except medicines, King Hussein suggested that the transport of food should be allowed.

It was now being reported that, even in the absence of UN authorisation, US warships had been ordered by President Bush to fire on recalcitrant merchant vessels sailing to and from Iraq in the Gulf. In fact the Pentagon had established three 'primary interception zones': to cover the Gulf south of Kuwait, the north-eastern waters of the Red Sea, including the Gulf of Aqaba, and the Gulf of Oman outside the Straits of Hormuz. Where illicit cargo was detected, the US captains had orders to take the ship into custody, with 'minimum force' – disabling shots fired at the ship's rudder or engine – to be used against vessels that refused to stop. An Iraqi spokesman declared that the US posture amounted to 'flagrant piracy' – a predictable response but one that had a measure of support from an important source. On 16 August 1990 UN Secretary-General Javier Perez de Cuellar commented that the United States was going too far and that the economic sanctions should be given time to work. The Pentagon responded by urging other Western navies to assist in the interdiction of Iraqi shipping.

In fact it seemed clear that sanctions were already having a serious impact on the Iraqi economy. The US Agriculture Department estimated that Iraq had no substantial food stockpiles, except in wheat, and even here the stocks would be exhausted in a matter of weeks. There were no meat stocks, and shipments from key suppliers such as Australia and South America had stopped. It was predicted that corn for chickens would be exhausted in less than a month. There were already serious shortages of cooking oils, vegetables and other foodstuffs. With the lack of spare parts and raw materials, industry and agriculture were grinding to a halt. Hospitals, schools, sewage treatment, transport – all were severely affected by the harsh sanctions regime, months before the US-led war brought unprecedented levels of destruction to the Iraqi nation. Iraq had a national debt, following the Iran–Iraq War, of $100 billion, and now no means of raising revenue from sales of the massive oil resource.

The United States – by dint of blandishment, threat and bribery – was succeeding in tightening the sanctions regime, but the Iraqis managed to chalk up a few minor victories. Captain Sami Ahmed Abdullah's oil tanker *Khanaqin*, ordered to halt by the US Navy as she sailed through the Gulf of Oman, refused to obey the orders and forced the crew of the US frigate *Reid* to abandon battle stations. In another incident the US frigate *Bradley* fired warning shots across the bows of Captain Tahir Juma Mohamed's tanker *Baba Gurgur* off Bahrain, but the vessel did not even slow down. In addition a merchant ship carrying goods to Aqaba refused to stop when challenged, though US ships did manage to turn round an innocent ferry sailing to collect stranded Sudanese refugees in Jordan. But the successes of the Iraqi oil tankers and the merchant ship *Zein al-Qaws* were exceptional: US and British ships were succeeding in blocking the passage of numerous vessels, many of them carrying food, bound for Iraq. Moreover, as US Defense Secretary Dick Cheney emphasised, the American 'interdiction-interception operations' were only just beginning. The crisis was only three weeks old and sanctions were set to remain in place for years.

At this time there were evident constraints on the declared US policy of using 'minimum force' to block the passage of Iraqi shipping. The Iraqi oil tankers breaking the blockade had not been attacked, despite earlier American threats. Now Washington was putting serious pressure on the Security Council to pass an enabling resolution. On 21 August the US bowed to opposition from other Council members opposed to the use of force, though it was felt that the necessary enabling resolution would not be long delayed. British premier Margaret Thatcher, predictably enough, was eager to support American efforts to secure UN authorisation for the use of force. In a press conference statement (21 August 1990) she emphasised that the use of force was already authorised under Article 51 of the UN Charter ('. . . the inherent right of individual or collective self-defence if an armed attack occurs . . .') but declared: 'We would like to have the extra authority, I think, of the whole world through the United Nations resolution to take the requisite action to enforce the embargo.' The embargo, she emphasised, 'must be effective . . . it must therefore be enforced and we must have the means to enforce it'.

Some Security Council members, primarily China and the Soviet Union, still remained reluctant to agree the introduction of a force element into the framework of UN authorisation. China and the Soviet Union indicated that they would not accept such a resolution unless Washington conceded close UN supervision of any military action. This condition was in fact in full accord with the demands of Articles 46 and 47 of the UN Charter, which stipulated joint control by the permanent Security Council members of military action under UN auspices. Soviet representatives emphasised that the Council should not authorise the use of force until there was clear evidence that the sanctions regime was being violated. *The position, to be sustained over the coming months and years, was plain. The United States was always characteristically pushing for the use of military force to fix this or that problem. Other members of the Security Council, more reticent, usually only succeeded in delaying, rather than permanently blocking, the resort to force option.* This pattern was clearly discernible in the attitude to the enforcement of the sanctions regime, the securing of UN authorisation for the US-led Gulf War, and the various military strikes against Iraq thereafter. Under Washington's unremitting pressure, key US military requirements found their way into authorising UN resolutions. When Washington could not secure enabling resolutions – as, for example, with the imposition of the southern 'no-fly' zone after the war – it was well prepared to take military action in their absence.

For four days the permanent members of the Security Council negotiated behind closed doors, with US militancy reportedly threatening
the established Big-Power consensus on the UN resolutions already
passed. The Soviet Union and China had both voted to support Washington on the previous four resolutions but now were anxious that the
United States was asking for *carte blanche* to use force. Soviet efforts
to implement the Charter requirement (Articles 46 and 47) for a Military Staff Committee, to ensure that the United States did not have a
military monopoly, were predictably opposed by Washington. China
was concerned that the US was taking *de facto* control of the UN
operation, as had happened during the Korean War.

On 25 August 1990 the five permanent members of the Security
Council agreed on a framework for the use of force to support the
embargo. The Soviet Union had supposedly secured the condition that
force would not be used until a clear violation of sanctions had been
established. At the same time the Soviet Union remained hesitant and
the vote on the resolution was delayed. There was anxiety also that
China, though not active in the Middle East, might abstain, so ruptur-
ing the permanent-member unanimity. In the event Resolution 665 (25
August 1990) was passed by 13 votes to none (with only Cuba and
Yemen abstaining). Washington had succeeded in securing the first
'force resolution' of the Gulf crisis. A key section of 665 declares that
the Security Council

> Calls upon those Member States co-operating with the government
> of Kuwait which are deploying maritime forces to the area to use
> *such measures commensurate to the specific circumstances as may
> be necessary* under the authority of the Security Council to halt all
> inward and outward maritime shipping in order to inspect and verify
> their cargoes and destinations and to ensure strict implementation of
> the provisions related to such shipping laid down in resolution 661
> (1990). (my italics)

The wording was highly significant. 'Such measures . . . as may be
necessary' made it plain that force was not prohibited. In the main,
US and British naval captains would be the judges as to what measures would be necessary to interdict Iraqi shipping: the UN, having
provided a *de jure* authorisation for the use of *any* measures deemed
necessary, no longer had a role in the matter. The UN 'flag of convenience' to sanctify military action had been raised. Now there was a
precedent for UN authorisation for a full US-led war against Iraq. The

eventual wording of Resolution 678 (29 November 1990) included the key phrase '... authorises Member States ... to use all necessary means ...'. Again the wording appeared moderate and reasonable: who could object to the implementation of 'necessary' measures? The problem was that the Pentagon now had a UN blank cheque authorising the United States to wage war – when it wanted and how it chose – without further reference to the Security Council or the Secretary-General. As in Korea the United Nations, having served its enabling purpose, was marginalised.

Having secured Resolution 665 it seemed increasingly clear that matters were moving Washington's way. Jordan was moving to close its border with Iraq, at the same time emphasising that steps should be taken to avert war. Reports suggested that sanctions – particularly the block on food imports – were having a growing impact on the Iraqi people. In response to the stopping of a shipment of baby milk to Iraq, Iraqi television asked how the United Nations could present itself as a humanitarian organisation *'when it conspires to starve Iraq's children?'* The UN Sanctions Committee, indifferent to such matters, seemed prepared to address the Jordanian economic plight. Said one Western diplomat: 'The international community had no option but to promise that it would fill the begging bowl when it was finally extended.' The cynical metaphor showed little understanding of the problems that Jordan faced due to loss of export earnings, freight fees, and the remittances (amounting to $800 million a year) from Jordanian workers in Iraq and Kuwait.

By the end of August 1990 there were US intelligence reports that Baghdad was instructing Iraqi captains to allow their ships to be stopped and searched when challenged by US patrols. This suggested that Saddam Hussein was increasingly concerned to avoid an outbreak of hostilities that might spill over into Iraqi territory. Secretary-General Perez de Cuellar, having appeared hesitant in the face of mounting American pressure, now seemed interested in working for a diplomatic solution to the crisis. In anticipation of a meeting with Iraqi foreign minister Tariq Aziz in Amman, Perez de Cuellar pledged that he would discuss 'all aspects of the problem' with the Iraqis. Washington, prepared to acknowledge that the Secretary-General had 'an appropriate role to play', emphasised that the United States would tolerate no compromise on the basic issues – signalling yet again that this was a matter for US rather than Security Council discretion.

There was now mounting evidence of food shortages in Iraq and Kuwait, leading to fears that foreigners from Third World countries trapped in Kuwait might be dying of starvation. Particular concern was being expressed about the plight of 172,000 Indians and 60,000 Filipinos, said by their respective governments to need international relief on an 'extremely urgent' basis. The United States and its allies expressed their fears that any food shipped into the area might *fall into the wrong hands*; that is, starving Iraqis may have something to eat. Yemen and Cuba, as temporary members of the Security Council, had repeatedly argued that the United Nations should not conspire to starve the people of Iraq and Kuwait to achieve the goal of expelling the Iraqi forces from Kuwait. Some independent observers had already pointed out that the use of starvation to achieve political objectives is a violation of the Geneva Convention (see Chapter 4 and Appendix 9).

By now there was general agreement that economic sanctions were having a serious effect on the Iraqi people, though there was debate as to how long it would take sanctions 'to work'. On 1 September the Iraqi authorities introduced rationing – which at least gave the lie to the common Western assertion that Saddam was content to watch his people starve. Efforts were made to make basic supplies such as flour, rice, sugar, tea and cooking oil available at controlled prices. Food and other supplies were being supplemented by provisions looted from Kuwait, though it was clear that such a stratagem could be effective only for a short time. The markets of Baghdad and other Iraqi cities continued to display a wide variety of foodstuffs, but with rocketing prices on most items these were beyond the reach of most families (for example, with an Iraqi labourer typically earning around 150 dinars a month, when work was available, a small packet of tea was selling for 10 dinars in Baghdad). In September 1990 stores were still reportedly full of peppers, onions, pomegranates, cucumbers, okra, beans and (imported) oranges and bananas – but prices in the private sector shops and markets sometimes doubled overnight.[7]

The embargo was being maintained on an effective basis, though it was inevitably porous to a small degree. Iran reported that it had arrested 29 people for trying to smuggle food to Iraq, while a new economic analysis published in Washington suggested that the Iraqi economy would be able to withstand the impact of sanctions on food supplies by low-level smuggling, boosting Iraqi agricultural production, and selling such assets as gold stocks. The report, from the Washington Institute for Near East Policy, stated that an element of smuggling was inevitable across the Iranian, Syrian and Turkish borders – though the volume of the smuggled goods would be limited by Iraq's capacity to pay. It was estimated that the Iraqi government would be able to mobilise around $2 billion: from such sources as stolen liquid assets from

Kuwaiti banks, friendly governments such as Libya, and crooked banks. This suggested that Iraq would be able to withstand the worst effects of sanctions for perhaps a year, until the end of 1991. At the same time there was no doubt that the standard of living of the ordinary Iraqi family would continue to plummet. The rationing introduced on 1 September meant that, at least in theory, each citizen would be guaranteed 1270 calories a day, supplemented by domestic produce of around 490 a day. Thus the diet was now only 57 per cent of pre-crisis levels, with a diet of less than 2000 calories meaning that Iraq, formerly a relatively well developed country, had been reduced to one of the poorest on earth. The report concluded with the '*basic point . . . that sanctions cannot be counted on to produce a sure result*'.

There was now a growing consensus that the economic embargo – at least in the short term – would be unlikely to secure the eviction of Iraqi forces from Kuwait. And there would be no *long*-term attempt to test the efficacy of the sanctions regime. Washington, well prepared to wait for years, decades even, for UN resolutions to influence the aggressive postures of such countries as Israel and Indonesia, was impatient with the impact of sanctions on Iraq that had been in place for less than six months. And America's supine allies were well prepared to echo US impatience. The British Foreign Secretary, Douglas Hurd, declared to Members of Parliament on 15 January 1991 that, because UN sanctions showed no signs of ever having a 'decisive effect' upon Saddam Hussein's capacity to wage war, Britain was resigned to the necessity of having to fight for the liberation of Kuwait. The key Security Council enabling vote had secured Resolution 678 (29 November 1990) by 12 votes to 2 (Cuba and Yemen) with China abstaining. Washington had threatened, cajoled and bribed Council members into authorising the United States to go to war (Cuba and Yemen, though doing no more than exercising their sovereign rights under the UN Charter, would soon be punished for their negative votes). Now it seemed that nothing could prevent a vast US-led military onslaught on Iraq once the specified deadline (15 January 1991) had been reached. There were still those who urged that sanctions be given longer to work. Thus Neil Kinnock, leader of the opposition Labour Party in Britain, argued that sanctions were working by impoverishing the Iraqi economy: 'Part of the reason for arguing for the longest-possible use of sanctions, and it is in no sense a concession to Saddam Hussein or appeasement, is to try to ensure the killing rate is as low as possible. . . . A war in the Gulf may ultimately have to be fought.' In the United States the CIA director, William Webster, had already testified before

Congress that sanctions had cut down Iraqi exports by 97 per cent and imports by 90 per cent, with various prominent former government and military officials agreeing that sanctions had devastated the Iraqi economy. Even General Colin Powell, a key player in the crisis, reckoned that the embargo was having its intended effect: 'He felt that containment or strangulation was working. An extraordinary political–diplomatic coalition had been assembled, leaving Iraq without substantial allies – condemned, scorned and isolated as perhaps no country had been in modern history. Intelligence showed that economic sanctions were cutting off up to 95 per cent of Saddam's imports and nearly all his exports. Saddam was practically sealed off in Iraq and Kuwait. The impact could not be measured in weeks, Powell felt. It might take months. There would come a point . . . when the sanctions would trigger some kind of a response.'[8] But such arguments did nothing to block the war agenda.

The war* succeeded – as everyone predicted – in expelling Iraqi forces from Kuwait, and so the main requirement set out in Security Council Resolution 661 had been achieved. Now, it seemed, there was no longer a requirement for economic sanctions. Perhaps they had failed, though not given long to achieve all their objectives, but now Kuwait had been liberated.

In fact the winning of the war gave Washington the chance to impose a fresh sanctions resolution. The goalposts would be changed – at the time of the ceasefire and repeatedly thereafter – with the express intent of maintaining sanctions on Iraq for the indefinite future. No attempt was made to articulate the new objectives in a consistent fashion: they varied from week to week, from month to month. Of the few constants in the post-war situation one of the most evident – for anyone who cared to notice – was the pitiful suffering of the Iraqi people.

Even at the start of the war there were signals – without UN authorisation – that the economic embargo would be maintained once the crisis had been resolved. On 17 January 1991 Thomas Pickering, the US ambassador to the United Nations, gave no indication in his address to the Security Council of how Iraq would be treated after the

---

* The course of the 1991 Gulf War is considered in detail elsewhere and need not be rehearsed here. Some key events of the war are highlighted in Chapter 1 of the present book. See also, for example, Geoff Simons, *Iraq: from Sumer to Saddam* (Macmillan, London, 1994), pp. 327–46; Dilip Hiro, *Desert Shield to Desert Storm* (Paladin, London, 1992); and Rick Atkinson, *Crusade: the Untold Story of the Gulf War* (HarperCollins, London, 1994).

war, but senior diplomatic sources were in no doubt that 'ironclad sanctions would remain in force against Iraq so that it could not easily rebuild itself militarily . . .'.[9] There were signs also that Washington's immediate aims went far beyond the objectives set in the dozen Security Council resolutions passed by the start of military action. The main aim of ejecting the Iraqi forces from Kuwait, as specified in Resolution 678 (referring to 660), was to be supplemented by various objectives that were authorised by no Security Council votes: such as the overthrow of Saddam, putting him on trial for war crimes, the destruction of Iraq's chemical and nuclear warfare potential, and the destruction of Iraq's conventional military capacity.[10] Here the point is not whether such aims were desirable, but whether they derived from UN authorisation or US fiat. Authorisation for Member States 'to restore international peace and security in the area' (Resolution 678(2)) could scarcely be cited to provide *carte blanche* for any US military initiative – if only because the earlier supposed 'peace and security' was evidently consistent with a heavily-armed Iraq well buttressed at the time by most of the permanent members of the Security Council.

In the immediate post-war situation there were some doubts among the Coalition allies on how to proceed. One point of dissension was how much Iraq should be expected to pay in war reparations. Another was the extent to which sanctions should be relaxed to enable Iraq to make such payments. A British Foreign Office source emphasised that if Iraq were to be allowed to sell oil such permission would not be granted on a 'wholly altruistic' basis: the sooner Iraqi oil began to flow again the sooner reparations could be paid. There were differences also on the question of frozen overseas Iraqi assets, with Britain and France disinclined to support seizure to facilitate payment of war damages and settlement of pre-war commercial debts. It was felt that US proposals to share out the frozen Iraqi assets would 'set dangerous precedents' and might lead to a flight of capital from the London markets. Any seizure of Iraqi assets would be likely to make Arab and other investors nervous about their financial deposits in London and Paris. Moreover, who would decide how any sequestered Iraqi assets would be distributed? Many Third World countries had suffered massive financial losses because of the Gulf War. It was unlikely that such countries would have first claim on any sequestered funds.

The Western allies were now moving to protect the punitive sanctions regime. On 3 April 1991 the Security Council – following the usual backstairs diplomacy – passed Resolution 687 (see Appendix 3) by 12 votes to 1 (Cuba) with 2 abstentions (Ecuador and Yemen).

This resolution, a veritable compendium of demands and conditions, addressed the border question, the deployment of a UN observer unit, the question of Iraqi weapons, the payment of compensation, and other matters. It also stipulated (F 20–29) the conditions that would continue to govern the sanctions regime. The 'sale or supply to Iraq of commodities or products' would still be banned, though foodstuffs 'notified to the [sanctions] Committee' would be exempted – a meaningless concession because Iraq was still to be denied access to any revenues. The 'prohibitions against financial transactions' would be maintained.

The resolution also stated that the Council would review Iraq's compliance with the specified terms and conditions 'every sixty days', a phrase that in itself suggested that sanctions would be maintained for a protracted period. Only if Iraq was seen to comply with all the terms of Resolution 687 (which included in its preamble thirteen earlier resolutions) would the prohibitions on Iraqi trade and financial transactions 'have no further force or effect'. All 'States and international organisations' were called upon to continue supporting the sanctions regime, with a further insistence that the situation would be reviewed on a regular basis 'and in any case 120 days following passage of this resolution, taking into account Iraq's compliance . . .'. The resolution concluded with the declaration of a formal ceasefire – subject to Iraq's acceptance of the stipulated provisions – between Iraq and Kuwait and the other 'Member States co-operating with Kuwait in accordance with resolution 678 (1990)'.

It was clear that Washington had succeeded in establishing the sanctions regime on a permanent basis. Where the sanctions specified in Resolution 661 related solely to the main requirement specified in 660, namely the withdrawal of Iraqi forces from Kuwait, now the imposition of sanctions was linked to a complex set of conditions where Iraqi compliance could be endlessly discussed, disputed and questioned. And the US strategy for the indefinite prolongation of sanctions even went beyond the ambiguities and complexities of Resolution 687. Fresh resolutions would be passed (for example, Resolution 688 (5 April 1991) condemning Iraqi persecution of minority groups within Iraq) and deemed to fall within the compass of 687, even though 687 itself listed in preamble the specific resolutions to which it was relevant. Furthermore, activities that had nothing to do with any United Nations resolution – such as Saddam's alleged refurbishment of his palaces – would be seriously cited by Washington as a reason why sanctions could not be lifted.

The United States had built a sanctions framework – complex, often ambiguous, sometimes risible – to ensure the continued punishment of the Iraqi people and that Iraq remain an impoverished nation. There would be no respite. Iraqi civilian casualties – soon to be numbered in millions – would continue to mount long after the end of the war.

In May 1991 the White House spokesman Marlin Fitzwater reiterated the familiar US position to the effect that 'all possible sanctions will be maintained until he [Saddam Hussein] is gone'. Again it was of no consequence to Washington that this policy had no authorisation in UN resolutions or in statements issued by the Secretary-General. Nor was it of concern that the economic sanctions were manifestly devastating the Iraqi people but doing nothing to undermine the Ba'athist regime. The worsening health of the Iraqi civilian population became increasingly obvious through the summer of 1991, though London and Washington – as key players on the Security Council – lost no opportunity to insist that the sanctions regime be maintained. Steps were taken also for the Security Council to secure access to any available Iraqi oil revenues. Thus Resolution 692 (20 May 1991) established a war damage fund into which Iraqi contributions would be paid 'with respect to all Iraqi petroleum and petroleum products exported from Iraq after 3 April 1991 as well as petroleum and petroleum products exported earlier but not delivered or paid' following the prohibitions set out in Resolution 661. The new resolution (passed by 14 votes to 0 with Cuba abstaining) emphasised yet again that full sanctions would be maintained in the absence of Iraqi compliance with the demands of the Security Council. It was unnecessary to repeat the point. Nothing would satisfy Washington except the disappearance of Saddam Hussein from the political scene. President Bush, Marlin Fitzwater and others had constantly reiterated the simple point: *sanctions would remain until there was a change of government in Iraq.* In May Robert Gates, President Bush's choice as the new CIA head, added his voice to the chorus: 'Any easing of sanctions will be considered only when there is a new government.' In this context the precise meaning of any particular UN resolution was an irrelevance.

Now reports were appearing on American television and in the press about Iraqi civilians dying of hunger and disease. The Harvard team had reported that 170,000 children under five would die in 1991 because of the war and the trade embargo. One member of the team, Rob Moodie, stated that the official Iraqi ration was a half that required to maintain normal health. Another member, Megan Passey, told of many people in the areas of Baghdad and Basra surviving on nothing more than bread and tea; and she described a health centre in Basra, massively afflicted by typhoid, where two doctors were struggling to care for 80,000 people.

On 15 July Britain declared that it would not support any lifting of the trade sanctions if Iraq failed to release Ian Richter, a British businessman jailed in 1986 on bribery charges. This had nothing to do with any UN resolution, and it was plain that even Richter's release would do nothing to change the British posture. Prince Sadruddin Aga Khan, the UN executive delegate for humanitarian aid to Iraq, was warning that without an easing of sanctions the Iraqi people faced a calamity. In a report to Secretary-General Perez de Cuellar he predicted that disease would spread and that there would be 'massive starvation'. The desperately urgent Iraqi need for food, medicine and supplies to restore health services, clean water, sanitation systems, power and communications facilities was put at $6.85 billion for a 12-month period, even if Iraq were allowed to import the necessary supplies. The UN appeal for humanitarian aid in the Gulf had raised no more than $216 million. The situation was absurd. While UN and other aid agencies were struggling with totally inadequate resources to meet the humanitarian needs of the Iraqi people, another UN body, the Security Council, was insisting that Iraq be denied the opportunity to sell its own oil in order to buy food, medicines and other supplies. As one UN aid worker was to observe: 'We first break their legs and then offer them a crutch.' On 29 July Maurice Gourdault, a spokesman for the French government, urged the Security Council to ease the trade embargo. The scene was set for the first phase of the 706/712/986 ploy (see below), a political device whereby Washington could make hypocritical nods to humanitarian concern while at the same time maintaining punitive sanctions that were by now having genocidal consequences.

On 20 November 1991 the Iraqi government issued a $1 billion list of urgently needed medical supplies that could not be purchased because of the block on oil sales. In London the director of Oxfam, Lord Judd, was urging that 'far greater priority' be given to the immediate humanitarian needs of the Iraqi people: '*Millions of innocent people are suffering and that is intolerable. They are the last in the nutcracker. They have not been able to influence events, but my God they are being squeezed.*' Iraq indicated that it had placed orders for drugs, medical equipment and other items through letters of credit, though there was no realistic expectation that deliveries would be made. Another list showed the urgent requirement for $2 billion-worth of food imports, though attempts to open credit lines with the Midland Bank,

Chase Manhattan and Société Générale had been blocked. Lord Judd commented further: 'While the aid agencies are working flat out, we feel like people trying to put a finger in the dike – of sewage. There is no way the infrastructural problems can be solved by the agencies alone.' Washington was of course working hard to ensure that any attempt to solve the infrastructural problems would be frustrated.

The US posture was further exposed by the decision to redraw the Iraq–Kuwait border in Kuwait's favour. It was now clear that Baghdad was about to lose strategic territory to Kuwait and be further squeezed out of the Gulf. This meant that Iraqi oil wells in the Rumeila field were being given to Kuwait, as was the territory of the Iraqi naval base at the port of Umm Qasr. The UN commission charged with the task of demarcating the disputed border – one of the sources of tension that led to the Iraqi invasion of Kuwait – was now expected to rule in favour of Kuwait's claims. In April 1992 the commission – ironically enough, chaired by a representative from Indonesia (condemned for invading East Timor in UN resolutions that Washington carefully ignores) – confirmed its recommendation that the Iraq–Kuwait border should be shifted northwards, giving Kuwait more territory in various sensitive areas and quashing Iraqi claims for the Warba and Bubiyan islands, another traditional source of tension in the region. One independent expert commented that the UN commission, by giving Kuwait 'the benefit of the doubt in the historical interpretation of the rival to the border issue', had simply stoked up the fires for further political tensions in the future.

A further pressure was exerted on Iraq by the US-led move in the Security Council to secure a resolution authorising the seizure of overseas Iraqi assets to fund a variety of UN programmes. Iraq continued to plead that it was not in breach of the ceasefire resolution, though now it was widely recognised that this was a secondary matter: sanctions would remain as long as Saddam Hussein was in power, and even thereafter the existence of sanctions might be welcomed by the West as providing leverage on a new regime. The maintenance of sanctions, coupled with the seizure of assets, continued to advertise the economic stranglehold on the Iraqi nation. None the less Iraq was attempting a measure of reconstruction in immensely adverse circumstances. In the United States a classified intelligence report, a so-called National Intelligence Estimate, suggested that Iraq was rebuilding parts of the shattered infrastructure by importing goods through Jordan in violation of UN sanctions. The report also confirmed that the condition of the Iraqi civilian population continued to worsen. At the same time a

Bush administration spokesman confirmed that sanctions were not eroding Saddam's capacity to survive: 'He is clearly stronger than he was a year ago. As long as he's able to get his hands on enough stuff to buy off his cronies, the Republican Guard, his chances of staying in power are pretty good ... it doesn't look as if he's going to fall any time soon.'

In early September 1992 a UN inspector, Maurizio Zifferero, deputy director of the International Atomic Energy Agency, declared that Iraq was now in compliance with the requirement (specified in Resolution 697) that it demonstrate its ending of any nuclear weapons programme. David Kay, who led earlier inspection missions, rushed to brand the judgement as 'naive and imprudent', while Britain chipped in to denounce the 'grotesque' jail sentences on two Britons, Michael Wainwright and Paul Ride, for illegally entering Iraq. Again the pattern was plain. Any suggestion that Iraqi compliance might contribute to a relaxation of the draconian sanctions regime must immediately be rubbished. However Iraq *seemed* to be complying with UN demands Saddam could not be trusted. There would never be a way out of this impasse: the very absence of evidence that the Iraqi government was seeking to frustrate the US-imposed conditions would itself be taken as evidence of Saddam's devious machinations. And spurious grounds, outside the spirit and letter of all the relevant UN resolutions, could also be cited to justify continuing with the sanctions regime. But precisely which Security Council resolution authorised a punitive economic embargo on the entire civilian population of Iraq because the authoritarian Ba'athist government unjustly imprisoned two Britons? When in due course Saddam released the various imprisoned foreigners, long before the expiry of the sentences, it earned him no favours. The sanctions, denying millions of ordinary people the necessities of life, were set to continue from one year to the next.

On 22 October 1992 Iraq and the United Nations signed a humanitarian accord to prepare the way for an injection of humanitarian aid into the country. It was estimated that $200 million-worth of food, medicine and other emergency assistance would be supplied, with a half of this allocated to the north (where the West was interested in cultivating a degree of Kurdish separatism). The accord allowed up to 300 UN guards to be sent to the north and an unspecified number of relief workers to be sent to other parts of the country. It was obvious that, with Iraq needing billions of dollars worth of food, medical supplies and reconstruction investment, the amount of aid entering the country – much of it targeted to achieve political rather than humanitarian objectives – was pitifully inadequate. In November the Security

Council yet again blocked any easing of economic sanctions, noting that Iraq had failed to recognise the newly-demarcated Iraq–Kuwaiti border, to provide information on long-range missiles, and to permit verification of industrial plants that might have military applications. The Iraqi foreign minister Tariq Aziz commented: 'No matter what Iraq does in fulfilment of obligations imposed upon it, the unjust sentence passed by the Council to starve the people of Iraq will remain in place because this is the will of certain influential governments.' Few observers doubted that the United States and so Britain would continue to support sanctions while Saddam Hussein remained in power – a Western posture that had no authorisation in any UN resolution. In December the United States handed over $50 million of frozen Iraqi assets to help fund UN operations in Iraq.

The Western propaganda offensive continued unabated. Thus Douglas Hogg, the Minister of State at the British Foreign Office, declared in February 1993 that there was 'nothing to prevent the Iraqi government using its own resources to pay for humanitarian supplies' – apart from the minor matter, unremarked by Hogg, that Iraqi financial assets were either blocked or seized and that Iraqi oil sales were prohibited. In the same vein Ronald Newman, head of the Northern Gulf Bureau in the US State Department, asserted that it was necessary to point out 'that the measures taken by the world community are not aimed at the Iraqi people. Iraq may import (and indeed does) foodstuffs, medicines and essential civilian consumer goods' – though Newman neglected to mention the pitifully small volume of such imports or the fact that the people of Iraq were sliding helplessly into famine conditions. The food supply was now 50 per cent, and medical supplies less than 10 per cent, of pre-war levels. And throughout the period there was the persistent Catch-22 interpretation of all actions by the Iraqi government. Even if the Iraqis met the demands imposed upon them, they could not be trusted. Thus a Western diplomat commented in March 1994 that even when the Iraqi government complied with UN resolutions it was '*not because they have seen the error of their ways . . . but because they are in such desperate straits*'. With this sort of Western attitude – insisting that nothing the Iraqis did could ever be taken at face value – there would always be a reason for maintaining the sanctions that were bringing such suffering to an entire national people.

There were some signs that the sanctions blockade was leaking. In February 1993 Iran reopened a border post between the Iraqi town of Khanaqin and the Iranian town of Qasr Sharin, north-east of Baghdad. In March the Turkish government sent a chargé d'affaires to reopen the Turkish embassy in Baghdad, while it emerged that the Egyptians were sending a senior diplomat to Baghdad, ostensibly to look after the interests of their nationals. Both Turkey and Egypt continued to urge the maintenance of sanctions on Iraq but some observers suspected that the diplomatic moves might herald minor trade concessions to Baghdad. There were still Iraqi–Jordanian trade links in operation with King Hussein unwilling to block Iraq's tenuous access to food and medicine in limited quantities. Washington, perennially sensitive to any accommodation made by any regional powers with the Iraqi regime, continued to exert diplomatic and economic pressures. The US goal was plain and frequently rehearsed: it was essential to contrive the collapse of the Iraqi regime – by means of the on-going covert CIA destabilisation activity or via the protracted route of economic strangulation. In March the White House press secretary Dee Dee Myers declared: 'It is inconceivable that Saddam Hussein could remain in power if he complied with all UN resolutions.' Now, to Washington's growing alarm, there were fresh reports that Iraq was selling quantities of oil, fertilisers and cement to Iran and Turkey.[11] The United States responded in predictable fashion. A protest to Tehran through diplomatic channels was issued, while US sources reiterated the familiar refrain: there would be no relaxation of sanctions until Iraq complied 'with all UN resolutions' – and of course it would be Washington or its proxies that would continue to monitor the degree of compliance.

The sanctions regime was routinely renewed on 29 March, with the Clinton administration now proclaiming its intention to 'depersonalise' the issue of Iraq. The ending of sanctions would not be dependent on the fall of Saddam Hussein, but on Iraqi compliance with UN demands. None the less the United States did not accept that Saddam could comply with all UN resolutions and still remain in office. It was soon plain that the 'depersonalisation' comment was no more than a spasm, intended no doubt to lay emphasis on the primacy of UN resolutions in justifying the endless imposition of economic strangulation on the Iraqi people. In any event the world focus was now beginning to shift away from Iraq. The deteriorating situation in the former Yugoslavia was increasingly the focus of international attention – a development that aided Washington's attempts to maintain the diplomatic and economic isolation of Iraq. Where, in the immediate aftermath of the Gulf War, journalists and others had been prepared to publicise the suffering of Iraqi civilians, the Iraq question was now slipping out of the world consciousness. Saddam, in widespread consensual perception, remained a sore on the body politic, but the desperate predicament of the diseased and starving Iraqi civilian population now had an ever diminishing profile in the eyes of the international community.

In June 1993 the UN Department of Humanitarian Affairs (DHA) Special Unit for Iraq called a conference of aid donors to discuss the mounting funding crisis. It was still the case that a nominally wealthy Iraq (debts apart) was being denied the opportunity to purchase the foodstuffs and medicines that the aid agencies could not afford to supply. A year-long aid 'Co-operation Programme' (1 April 1993 to 31 March 1994), run under UN auspices, had called for an aid budget of $489 million; but at the donor conference (1–2 June 1993) this amount, already insufficient to meet basic needs on a widespread basis, was reduced to $220.38 million by indicating priorities for basic survival needs. It was soon apparent that even the reduced aid target would not be achieved: donor pledges amounted to no more than $50 million.[12] Relatively small aid funds were being made available through the DHA's revolving fund, from Turkey and from the Pak-Arab Council, channelling aid to Iraq through the World Health Organisation (WHO).[13]

It is important to note that *a proportion of donated funds were being designated for non-humanitarian purposes*; that is, donor funds were being used for various purposes that had little to do with the relief of suffering. Thus, as of 15 April 1993, less than half of $101.5 million-worth of donations had been spent on the humanitarian programme, with expenditure targeted on five main areas:

- the commission for compensation – $21 million;
- the commission for weapons of mass destruction – $33 million;
- UN costs for return of Kuwaiti property – $4 million;
- half the cost of the UN boundary demarcation commission – $2 million;
- humanitarian programme – $41.5 million.[14]

Against these levels of expenditure it was estimated that Iraq had about $4 billion of assets, to which it was denied access, in 30 countries. According to the US Treasury Department there were $1.1 billion of Iraqi assets in the United States, which would not be released for humanitarian purposes. By contrast, the United Kingdom had released $120 million, Switzerland $120 million, Canada $3 million and Italy $4 million.[15] In this connection it has been emphasised that not all these released assets were oil-related – an important consideration in view of the asset seizure authorisation granted by Security Council

Resolution 778. The central point was that Iraq was still being denied the chance to use the bulk of its own resources to supply its own people with the basic necessities of life.

On 1 September Tariq Aziz, now Iraqi deputy prime minister, met with UN Secretary-General Boutros Boutros-Ghali to discuss the sanctions issue; but the 'frank and constructive' meeting yielded no practical results. A further meeting, on 21 November, was equally fruitless: a week later the Security Council again confirmed that sanctions would remain in place. The Iraqis had now fulfilled many of the conditions of Resolution 687, and had substantially agreed the terms of Resolution 715, designed to ensure long-term monitoring of Iraq's weapons production. Washington, to counter any good will that Iraq might have created by its obvious degree of compliance with 687 and 715, yet again expressed its concerns about the persecution of the Shias in southern Iraq. This concern was registered under the terms of Resolution 688 ('Condemns the repression of the Iraqi civilian population in many part of Iraq. . . . Demands that Iraq . . . immediately end this repression . . .'), which – for at least three separate reasons – could not be licitly invoked to justify the prolongation of sanctions:

- Resolution 688 (5 April 1991) was not passed as a *mandatory* resolution (that is, one passed under Chapter VII of the UN Charter);

- It was passed *after* Resolution 687 (3 April 1991), which stipulates the post-war sanctions regime and lists in preamble the Security Council resolutions – necessarily excluding 688 and all later resolutions – that 687 is intended to cover;

- Article 2(7) of the UN Charter stipulates that the United Nations is not authorised 'to intervene in matters which are essentially within the domestic jurisdiction of any state . . .'. It is acknowledged that 'enforcement measures under Chapter VII' may be necessary, but the clear implication is that these are only justified when, for example, there is an act of aggression. Thus 'enforcement measures', which may have domestic consequences, may be justified – but not to achieve a domestic objective.

None of this means that the sentiments enshrined in Resolution 688 are not to be supported (who cannot applaud a condemnation of repression?), though such sentiments are *politically* mediated: one man's repression is another man's restoration of civil order. The important point, such considerations apart, is that *there is no way in which Reso-*

lution 688 can be reasonably used to protect the sanctions regime.

By the end of 1993, as the privations of the Iraqi people became increasingly obvious, there were many calls for an easing of the economic embargo. On 12 December the former British premier Sir Edward Heath called for Britain to resume diplomatic links with Iraq, acknowledging that the Iraqi people were in desperate need of humanitarian assistance: 'We are not thinking about medicine for the regime. We are thinking about medicine for the nearly 20 million people who are in Iraq. . . . The shortages are acute. I have a whole list of them in front of me.' Even then the veteran Tory politician did not support an end to sanctions ('Not until the UN resolutions have been complied with'). None the less Heath was prepared to concede that the continued imposition of sanctions was counter-productive, putting the Iraqi people on Saddam's side 'because they resent very strongly the way they are being treated'. Now Washington was hardening its position, insisting that the Iraqi regime recognise Kuwait as a sovereign country. Only then, declared President Clinton, would it be possible to consider any relaxation of the economic embargo. Of course when Saddam eventually moved to recognise Kuwait the United States immediately found other reasons why sanctions could not be relaxed at that time.

Madeleine Albright, the US ambassador to the United Nations, was now spelling out (primarily in an interview to *The New York Times*) Washington's policy on the Iraqi oil sales ban. There was, she declared, a 'two-stage approach': Iraq would first have to abandon its nuclear, chemical and biological weapons programmes (as demanded in Resolution 687). Rolf Ekeus, head of the special disarmament commission, would have to certify that the programmes had been abandoned, after which the commission would be required to monitor the situation: 'I've said we want a proven track record of six to 12 months' monitoring.' The second stage required that Baghdad prove 'its readiness to rejoin society', a vague stipulation that had nothing to do with any of the UN resolutions authorising the economic embargo. Here was further evidence, if any were needed, that the so-called UN sanctions had become an instrument of US foreign policy, a means of leverage to protect American interests in the Middle East. There would have to be, declared Albright, 'an overall package here – which clearly gave Washington the facility to include any conditions they chose on a week-to-week, month-to-month basis. Again Washington was allowing Baghdad no clear route to a relaxation of the punitive trade embargo. Now President Clinton, despite earlier indications, was showing that he had adopted the old Bush hard line. At first Clinton had announced that he was not 'obsessed' with Saddam. Now it seemed that nothing but the fall of Saddam would be allowed to relieve the desperate plight of the Iraqi people.

In early 1994 Turkey, to the surprise of many observers, began calling for an end to the sanctions regime, a development that compelled British Foreign Secretary Douglas Hurd to insist in Ankara that Britain and the United States were still committed to the embargo. One reason for the new Turkish posture was plain: any erosion of Iraqi sovereignty in the north could only serve to strengthen the Kurdish 'safe haven' and so pave the way for an independent Kurdistan that would bolster the dissident Kurds in Turkey. Said Douglas Hurd, speaking on Turkish television: 'We do not believe that an independent Kurdistan is possible.' But now the pressures for a relaxation of the sanctions regime were growing also among other key members of the former anti-Iraq coalition. A senior Russian diplomat was signalling dissatisfaction with the Western position, indicating that the Russian Federation would welcome developments that would give Baghdad the chance to repay its long-standing debts to Moscow. Rolf Ekeus had insisted that, following Iraq's observance of Resolution 715, there would have to be monitoring to ensure six-months of compliance before any relaxation of sanctions could be considered. When, Russian diplomats were wondering, would the six-month period be allowed to begin? One Russian official was even quoted as saying that Moscow should now be standing up for its national interests 'and that those interests lie in reverting to Soviet alliances [that is, with Iraq] because that's where the money is'. Perhaps economic self-interest among Security Council members would succeed in denting the sanctions regime where widespread declarations of concern for the Iraqi people had so clearly failed.

The United States, in response to the growing international opposition to the embargo, was redoubling its efforts to keep sanctions in place. On 29 April the US Secretary of State Warren Christopher urged other countries not to be taken in by 'illusory' gestures of good will that might emanate from Baghdad: 'The stakes are too high to give Mr [sic] Hussein the benefit of the doubt, or to let our policy be dictated by commercial interests or simple fatigue.'[16] Now there were signs that France was joining Russia in urging a relaxation of sanctions as a means of securing commercial advantage. There remained in Iraq, declared Christopher, an 'instinct for repression' – as if Washington had never cultivated Saddam through the 1980s or rejoiced in accommodations with countless other repressive regimes. Saddam should be allowed no leeway, even though, as Christopher was forced to admit,

'Iraq is beginning to comply with the UN's requirements on weapons of mass destruction.' So, whether Iraq complied or not, the Catch-22 meant that it would derive no benefits in either case. Even if Saddam met UN demands he would still be harbouring dark thoughts. Christopher had no doubt that for Iraq to comply – but with deep resentment – was a 'cynical tactic' that the international community could not allow to succeed. Britain too, as a supine extension of the US State Department, was happy to juggle the Catch-22. Saddam would not be allowed to get away with cynical compliance. Nothing in fact would be allowed to count as acceptable Iraqi behaviour. Even if Saddam appeared to be meeting the spectrum of UN conditions we could always assume a hidden agenda. Sanctions would remain.

The embargo was upheld in May and June 1994 with no hint of any relaxation in the future. It now seemed that the Iraqis were complying with UN requirements. Rolf Ekeus of the monitoring commission (UNSCOM) had reported that most of the information demanded had been obtained, and the weapons monitoring systems were being set up (see 'Weapons Monitoring', below). There were still divisions in the Security Council about how to evaluate the degree of Iraqi compliance. In particular, how long should the monitoring systems be in place before an easing of the sanctions regime could be considered? As usual it was principally Washington and London that were resisting a 'premature' debate on any alteration to the terms of the embargo. Even if UNSCOM were satisfied on the degree of compliance regarding weapons programmes it would be an easy matter to find other reasons why sanctions should not be lifted. There was general agreement that Saddam had lain low for more than a year, and there was even talk of a 'charm offensive'. But he was gaining nothing. The sanctions remained in place and the plight of the Iraqi people was worsening. Would the stalemate drive Saddam into some new military adventure? Washington, few observers doubted, would have welcomed the excuse for a fresh military onslaught on Iraq.

In August reports appeared that Russia had reached agreement with Iraq, subject to a relaxation of sanctions, on the reconstruction of the Iraqi oilfields. The Interfax news agency, quoting anonymous sources in the Russian foreign trade ministry, said that the planned project would involve more than $2 billion-worth of work on three of Iraq's largest oilfields, and that some work might begin before sanctions were lifted. The Russian deputy foreign minister, Boris Kolokov, said on 3 August that Baghdad would have to recognise Kuwaiti sovereignty and the newly demarcated border, but emphasised also that Iraq was now complying on the disarmament question. There were signs also that Moscow was prepared to support the controversial Turkish plan for the flushing of the disused pipeline as a prelude to a resumption of oil sales. On 28 August King Hussein of Jordan and President Suleyman Demirel of Turkey called for an easing of the sanctions on Iraq. The joint press conference was held in the Jordanian capital of Amman while at the same time a party of 70 businessmen and 15 journalists from Turkey was being welcomed in Baghdad. Washington, we may assume, remained unimpressed by any of these developments.

On the eve of yet another review of sanctions there were signs of a minor shift in the UN position. Again the sustained imposition of the trade and arms embargo was 'rolled over' automatically under US pressure, despite the persistent disagreements in the Security Council. But the previous day (13 September 1994) Rolf Ekeus had pronounced his intention to announce the start of a trial period for weapons monitoring after which a recommendation for the lifting of sanctions could be made. Washington and London were growing increasingly concerned that it might no longer be easy to argue for an *ad infinitum* prolongation of the sanctions regime. One British official complained: 'The difficulty with cut-off points is that all the Iraqis have to do is to sit back and be good boys. The Iraqi horse has started to run a little but there are still a lot of hurdles left for it to go over.' How much more congenial it would have been to London and Washington diplomats for the Iraqis to have continued behaving consistently as bad boys! Nor were the anti-Iraq Western strategists much heartened by reports that business interests in both France and Italy had signed lucrative new oil contracts with Baghdad. The commercial pressures for a relaxation of the embargo were mounting. Turkey, Jordan, Russia, France, Italy, even some low-profile business stirrings in Britain and the United States – all were combining to increase the pressure on the hard-line US policy makers. Russia, for example, was now admitting that it had signed a post-sanctions trade accord with Baghdad to cover industrial and oil projects, and many other business groups in various countries were moving into position in what was now perceived to be a shifting international attitude to the embargo.

In one account, 'intense pressure' was building up in the United Nations for the sanctions to be lifted.[17] A meeting between Tariq Aziz and the French foreign minister, Alain Juppé, was one of a number of manoeuvres aimed at securing a part of future Iraqi markets. The need in Iraq for a relaxation of sanctions was becoming ever more pressing. In September 1994 the rations of basic foodstuffs were halved, inevitably plunging thousands more families into malnutrition, disease and premature death. The United States and Britain, characteristically unmoved by this development, refused to meet Tariq Aziz in New York and instead began to consider new UN resolutions to punish Iraq yet more.[18] Rolf Ekeus, while doubting that he had all the necessary weapons information but still sceptical about the more extreme charges against Iraq, reckoned that there was now movement towards 'a decisive situation' where the Security Council would be forced to look at procedures for the lifting of sanctions. Washington and London were still unwilling to accept a limited-term weapons monitoring period; to them, monitoring must be open-ended, possibly stretching over years. Ekeus himself urged a more constructive approach: ' . . . we do want Iraq to see the light at the end of the tunnel, to know that there is a process and that there is progress towards that light. Without progress Iraq can conclude it is not worth co-operating.' Baghdad now seemed increasingly committed to a compliant posture – even to the point that a move towards recognition of Kuwait was being anticipated. It was possible for observers to note – writing in October 1994 – that 'most UN diplomats now privately admit the embargo will be history within a year'.[19] It seems that such commentary under-estimated the persistence of the Washington and London hawks.

By the end of 1994 Iraq was suffering rampant and rising unemployment; inflation was running at around 24,000 per cent a year; the gap between rich and poor was vast and increasing; and the great majority of the civilian population was destitute. Saddam had been wooing former friends with promises of lucrative contracts if they supported the campaign against the embargo. Already, it was widely noted, such countries as Russia, China and France had shown a willingness to respond to such overtures. Iraq had even floated rumours that it was prepared to join the Middle East peace conference with Israel – if Israel would use its pull in Washington to accelerate the ending of the embargo. At the same Saddam was managing to rebuild his military forces by acquiring spare parts from Eastern Europe, by secretly negotiating with French intermediaries to rebuild his Mirage aircraft, and by relying on smuggled goods able to penetrate the embargo. One arms expert has noted that many of the front companies set up in the 1980s to supply Saddam's weapons programmes with Western technology continued to service Iraq's military needs from France, Monaco, Switzerland, Germany, Britain and the United States.[20]

The evolving situation was now breeding a fresh confidence in the highest echelons of the Iraqi regime. While attempting to cultivate international support by on the one hand demonstrating compliance with UN demands and on the other promising mega-contracts to sympathetic states, Saddam was also hinting that if there were to be no end to the embargo then Iraq would have to reconsider its policy of co-operation. Thus on 3 October 1994 the Iraqi information minister, Hamed Youssef Hammadi, declared to the national news agency in Baghdad that if the embargo continues. 'we will have no choice but to find another way to deal with the Security Council and its American plans'. The following day, the Iraqi authorities announced that they would not co-operate with a visiting UN envoy on arms control if no assurance were given that sanctions would be eased. The government daily newspapers *Al-Jumhuriya* supported this new Iraqi posture by commenting that Rolf Ekeus was no longer trustworthy. In the same vein a statement (6 October), from the Iraqi Revolutionary Command Council and broadcast on Radio Baghdad, was conveyed to the President of the Security Council to indicate the 'clear and unequivocal threat' now emanating from Baghdad. The statement, contained in a letter (S/1994/1137) from the Kuwaiti permanent representative, asserts that the United States, assisted by the Chairman of the Special Commission, Rolf Ekeus, is determined to harm Iraq. *The US 'and its collaborators in the region, in particular the rulers of Kuwait, are determined to prolong the embargo as long as they can in order to kill the largest number possible of Iraqis through the policy of starvation and deprivation'; the Iraqi leadership had no alternative but to 'reconsider a new stand which will restore justice and relieve the Iraqi people from the distress imposed upon it . . . we shall wait until 10 October 1994, and after that, every party will assume the responsibility of its own position'.*

The statement – if accurate, as alleged by the Kuwaiti permanent representative – signalled an important Iraqi departure from the general posture on broad compliance and conciliation. The Security Council, then under the presidency of the UK's Sir David Hannay, issued a document (S/PRST/1994/58) noting 'with grave concern' the Iraqi statement and underlining 'the complete unacceptability of the implication therein that Iraq may withdraw cooperation' from the UN Special Commission. The Council document also made reference to reports that 'substantial numbers of Iraqi troops' were being deployed towards the border with Kuwait. Again, if true, this represented an important development showing that Saddam had not abandoned his aggressive intentions. In fact it would be naive to take the reports of hostile Iraqi troop movements at face value.

The United States was now on the propaganda defensive, forced to concede the growing threat to its policy of inflicting starvation on the Iraqi people through sanctions. It was time to launch a fresh propaganda initiative. Thus, as a new ploy to justify the continued imposition of the embargo, the US and its allies announced that Iraq was again threatening Kuwait. Washington acted decisively to counter this new 'threat', moving extra troops and warplanes to the region; and with President Clinton, unconsciously signalling the difference between Washington and the rest of the world, declaring: 'We will not allow Saddam Hussein to defy the will of the US and the international community,' the US Defense Secretary declared that US forces might launch a pre-emptive military attack on Iraq. In such circumstances, Washington was keen to emphasise, there could be no thought of relaxing sanctions.

Few commentators were prepared to question the fresh tide of US-orchestrated propaganda or to consider the suborning of the Security Council in support of Washington's new anti-Iraq campaign. The journalist Robert Fisk, one of the few truly independent observers, noted that reporters on the Kuwait–Iraq border had not managed to detect any signs of aggressive Iraqi intent. One Kuwaiti tank was spotted near the border, and on the other side 'there were even slimmer pickings'.[21] UN officials, seemingly reluctant to support US propaganda, disclosed that their reconnaissance aircraft, which provide a 20km view across the border, 'had not observed a single tank or personnel carrier'. Even Israel, surprisingly out of step with its principal backer, suggested that the 'crisis' had been manufactured by the United States. Yitzhak Rabin and senior Israeli army officers 'stated frankly that Saddam Hussein had neither the air cover nor the manpower to invade Kuwait, that the Republican Guard divisions were not deployed in an aggressive posture, that there was, in short, no impending catastrophe'.[22]

However, the US propaganda campaign had achieved its objectives. The conventional wisdom, shaped by misinformation, was that Saddam had yet again threatened the peace. The Security Council had issued its condemnatory statement; and soon, to buttress the US posture, there would be a further Security Council resolution denouncing the 'hostile and provocative' movements of the Iraqi forces. Thus Resolution 949 (15 October 1994), unanimously adopted, condemned the 'recent military deployments by Iraq in the direction of the border with Kuwait' and demanded a withdrawal of the forces and no repetition of the threat. Yet again the United States had cultivated an atmosphere in which it would be easy to insist that the embargo remain in place. But now the situation was being complicated by a further factor: Iraqi moves for the recognition of Kuwaiti sovereignty.

On 14 October 1994 the Iraqi government, through the mechanism of a joint Iraqi–Russian statement, agreed to recognise Kuwait as a sovereign state, 'as decreed by Security Council resolution 833. . .'. Now yet another US pretext for maintaining sanctions had been removed. But moves for a vote on Resolution 949 were now in hand as a means of aborting the important Iraqi concession. Even Iraq's declared willingness to recognise Kuwait – long proclaimed by Washington as a principal objective of the embargo – could be dismissed, with the predictable connivance of the British government. Douglas Hurd was quick to brand the Iraqi concession as 'inadequate', noting that there would still be an Iraqi 'threat when American and British soldiers have gone home . . . his [Saddam's] mailed fist will still be over Kuwait and her neighbours'. So the Catch-22 was alive and well. How unhelpful it was for Saddam Hussein to agree to UN resolutions! Sanctions would remain.

The passing of Resolution 949 – even deriving, as it did, from 'black propaganda' – allowed Washington not only to undermine the diplomatic significance of the Iraqi recognition of Kuwait but also to threaten fresh air attacks against Iraq. The Iraqi–Russian statement affirming Iraq's readiness to abide by the demands of Resolution 833 was issued, as noted, on 14 October. Two days after Iraq, via this statement, had agreed to recognise Kuwait, Washington was threatening Iraq with fresh air attacks. There was, declared Secretary of State Warren Christopher, 'no occasion for doing Saddam Hussein any favours at the present time'. There was of course a further reason why the international community should maintain its vigilance against Saddam. Madeleine Albright righteously informed the Security Council that he was building 'pleasure palaces'; and distributed photographs around the Council to prove it. Sergei Lavovr, the Russian UN envoy, was quick to point out the absurdity of this new American argument: 'I don't recall that building palaces was prohibited by Security Council resolutions.' And voices were being raised to suggest that if Washington *were* contemplating further military action against Iraq perhaps it might first raise the matter with the United Nations. Thus the French foreign minister Alain Juppé commented that 'I think it belongs . . . to the Security Council to decide what must be done.' But Madeleine Albright had already shown her contempt for such suggestions. Speaking on a television talk show she had blandly announced that the area of Iraq south of the 32nd parallel was 'vital to US interests' and that the United States was prepared to go it alone: 'We will behave multilaterally when we can and unilaterally when we must.' Whether or not Resolution 949 authorised fresh air attacks against Iraq was irrelevant: Washington would launch bombing raids, with or without the approval of the 'international community', whenever it felt like it.

In early November the Iraqi National Assembly passed a formal resolution to confirm the earlier decision to recognise Kuwait. The move, predictably enough, did nothing to encourage a lifting of sanctions. White House spokeswoman Dee Dee Myers emphasised that there were 'a number of other elements in UN resolutions that Iraq must adhere to' before any lifting of sanctions could be discussed; and the familiar Foreign Office echo sounded in London: ' . . . this is only one of the things we have been looking to Saddam to do'. Again it seemed plain that '*sanctions will never be lifted* because the US and Britain do not trust Saddam not to pose a threat' (my italics).[23] Sanctions could not be lifted, '*whatever the degree of Iraqi compliance with UN resolutions*, as long as President Saddam remains in power' (my italics).[24] Washington in particular appeared 'determined to maintain sanctions and avoid discussion of the underlying issues'.[25]

Now there were deepening divisions among the Western allies and in the Security Council on the question of the embargo. On 6 January 1995 Tariq Aziz held talks with Alain Juppé in Paris to explore conditions for lifting the sanctions, while at the same time Russia was lobbying for a relaxation of the embargo within a matter of months. British and American officials moved to play down the significance of such developments, while rebuking France for its independent initiative. A US State Department spokeswoman, Christine Sholley declared that the French decision to open an interests section in Baghdad was not a 'timely action'; such a decision was, she said, neither 'helpful or constructive'. In London the Foreign Office acted swiftly to provide the usual echo: this was 'not the moment to relax pressure on Iraq . . .'.[26] As the time approached for another Security Council review of sanctions, Washington was making it plain that it opposed any acknowledgement of Iraqi compliance with UN resolutions. UN officials were now insisting that only if Iraq would 'see some light at the end of the tunnel' would full compliance be achieved. But again the sanctions regime was upheld. The pressures exerted by France and Russia in the Security Council, the mounting commercial pressures, the full knowledge in the international community of the desperate suffering of the Iraqi people – none of this was allowed by the US/UK faction in the Security Council to dilute the rigour of the embargo or to suggest the likelihood of a relaxation in the future.

At the end of January 1995 further evidence emerged that Russia was prepared to support an ending of sanctions. Sa'di Mahdi Salih, the speaker of the Iraqi National Assembly, held a series of meetings in Moscow to discuss the embargo, after which the Russian premier Viktor Chernomyrdin announced that Russia was prepared to encourage the gradual lifting of sanctions. The Iraqis agreed that they would co-operate in settling such outstanding matters as the missing Kuwaiti servicemen and confiscated Kuwaiti property, with a view to linking this to an ending of the embargo. The State Duma Chairman Ivan Rybkin declared Russia's friendship towards Iraq, while Valeryan Viktorov, the deputy chairman of the Federation Council, stated that the Iraqi regime was a matter for the Iraqi people.

These developments received little attention in the Western media. Instead reports appeared that Iraqi agents were allegedly using the deadly poison thallium to eliminate opponents of Saddam who had thought themselves safe. Thus major Safa al-Battat, a member of the Iraqi National Congress (INC), had been poisoned in northern Iraq – possibly in an attempt to kill the INC head, Ahmed al-Chalabi – and was now being treated in Britain.[27] Opposition Iraqi sources claimed that other INC members had been killed in this way. Said a Foreign Office spokesman in London: 'This is yet another graphic example of the brutality of Saddam Hussein's regime and clear violation of the Charter which requires Iraq to cease acts of terrorism.' It was obvious that, with pressure growing for an end to sanctions, publicity for Iraqi acts of terror would make it easier for Washington and London to uphold the embargo. The British spokesman, affirming the posture that had won the applause of INC vice-president Latif Rashid, declared: '*We must continue pressure to apply all the Security Council resolutions and believe there should be no question of relaxing sanctions until that time.*'[28] Again it was acknowledged that sanctions had brought 'terrible suffering' to the Iraqi people.

Now there were fresh signs of mounting commercial pressures for an end to the embargo. The reports of the Iraqi discussions in Moscow at the end of January made reference to various commercial considerations, in addition to the specific matters that related directly to the lifting of sanctions: 'The sides discussed the possibility of future fulfilment of major Russian–Iraqi oil and gas projects, construction and the Iraqi use of Russian high technologies.'[29] And the growing commercial interest of such countries as France, Italy, China, Egypt, Jordan and others in establishing links with Iraq was increasingly obvious. There were even signs that American business groups were active in

Baghdad, and the British government was coming under growing pressure from businessmen who felt that the posture of Britain would put them at a disadvantage once sanctions were lifted. At the beginning of February representatives of.70 British companies visited the headquarters of the Middle East Association in London to express their concern that British exporters were losing market opportunities because Whitehall was being too strict about the terms of trade with Iraq under the conditions of the embargo.[30]

It was repeatedly suggested that the government's interpretation of the embargo meant that British firms were increasingly losing out to competitors. Thus Frank Coates of the Middlesbrough-based pharmaceutical supplier Anglo-Mid-Eastern Enterprises commented: 'We are manacled. Iraq was a strong market for British goods and, because of the way the government here interprets sanctions, we're losing out to companies from France, Italy and the Far East.' The meeting, organised by the Iraqi British Interests (IBI) group, exposed the harsh interpretation of the embargo being sustained by the Department of Trade and Industry. Anyone wishing even to discuss trade with Iraq needs a licence, a rigorous provision that is unique to the British view of sanctions. The 'licences to communicate' may be granted relatively easily but no activity outside the humanitarian area is tolerated, even with a view to positioning business interests favourably pending an end to sanctions.[31]

The British government has argued that the frustrations of British business interests are exaggerated, emphasising that sanctions will only be lifted gradually, that there will still be import controls imposed on Iraq, and that a substantial proportion of any eventual oil revenues will be paid into a UN-administered escrow account to fund UN operations, war damages and Iraq's massive foreign debt. It was conceded that Iraq's wrecked infrastructure would offer many business opportunities, but suggested also that Saudi Arabia and the United Arab Emirates remained attractive markets that would scarcely welcome any expansion of British business interest in Baghdad. Humanitarian considerations were being given minimal attention: the suffering of the Iraqi people was rarely weighed in the balance. Frank Coates, having recently returned from Iraq, said that the Iraqis were suffering terribly, with raw sewage in the streets, no drugs and a rising infant mortality rate. Such matters remained of minimal concern in the context of *realpolitik*, strategic calculation and contemplation of business advantage.

On 23 February 1995 the British foreign secretary Douglas Hurd, speaking in London, reassured his Kuwaiti counterpart, Sheikh Sabah al-Ahmad al-Sabah, that Britain and the United States remained committed to a rigorous defence of the sanctions regime. It was important, declared Hurd, not to 'reward' the 'untrustworthy' Saddam Hussein. Russia and France were continuing to press for a relaxation of sanctions, while Kuwait was lobbying hard for the economic stranglehold on Iraq to be kept in place indefinitely. Officials were now speculating that no change could be expected at the March review of sanctions but that there might be some movement in mid-April when Rolf Ekeus was due to report on Iraq's compliance with the weapons monitoring demands. It was now generally acknowledged that Ekeus had made 'very considerable progress' in some of the areas covered by the principal sanctions resolution (687). Again the mounting business pressures were evident, the British government freshly embarrassed by the visit to Baghdad of a trade delegation that was now calling for an end to sanctions. Iraqi opposition groups continued to assert that any relaxation of sanctions would simply play into Saddam's hands. Said Clive Furness, a spokesman for the Campaign Against Repression and for Democratic Rights in Iraq (CARDRI): '... various commercial interests ... see sanctions being lifted and the prospects of new markets being opened up ... the whole sanctions issue is simply a Trojan horse by which to rehabilitate Saddam'. On 24 February Madeleine Albright reasserted US opposition to any relaxation of the sanctions regime. Speaking in London, she insisted that there would be no let-up while Iraq failed to honour its obligations, and a British Foreign Office spokesman duly declared, of Saddam: 'This is a leopard that has not changed its spots. Pressure has got us to where we are now and it needs to be maintained.' Albright had no doubt that France and Russia were 'wrong' to be seeking any lifting of sanctions, and she reiterated her goal of pre-empting 'any attempt at premature lifting'. In Baghdad there was growing confidence that Washington was increasingly isolated in the United Nations. Thus the official newspaper *al-Iraq* announced: 'America is cornered in the Security Council' – the world would not forsake its economic interest for 'Washington's whimsical interpretation of UN resolutions'.

In March, as predicted, the United States succeeded in keeping the sanctions regime in place. No-one doubted that, unless confronted by overwhelming international opposition, Washington would seek to maintain the embargo until a pliant proxy could be installed in Baghdad. Western reports highlighting instability in the Iraqi capital were denounced by Baghdad's official media as 'a feverish campaign ... for the unjustified blockade imposed on Iraq'. Now, despite all the predictions of late 1994, it seemed increasingly unlikely that 1995 would see an end to the sanctions regime.

Fresh controversy erupted when two Americans, William Barloon and David Daliberti, were jailed in Baghdad after 'straying across' the Iraq–Kuwait border into Iraqi territory. The US rightwingers Patrick Buchanan and Senator Richard Lugar immediately suggested that air strikes be launched against Baghdad, a proposal that President Clinton criticised as 'irresponsible'. As always, a White House spokesman was on hand to declare that no option had been ruled out and none ruled in. Media commentators rushed to opine that the imprisonment of the two men could only harden US resolve to keep sanctions. When, as a gesture of conciliation, the Iraqi authorities subsequently released the men there were no media pundits or others prepared to suggest that this initiative would hasten the ending of the embargo. At the same time reports were appearing that the American CIA had asked Congress for a further $12 million for 1996 to continue covert operations against Iraq. The reports did not say which UN resolutions authorised these fresh plans for US state terrorism against a sovereign member of the United Nations. In May the Security Council, under characteristic US prompting, again confirmed that sanctions would be retained. This time Washington relied on the April report of Rolf Ekeus that he had been unable to obtain satisfactory Iraqi explanations of what had happened to 17 tons of material that could be used to manufacture biological weapons. Little attention was given to the fact that this material had been accumulated in the late 1980s with the aid of Saddam's Western sponsors.

Now, with it being made abundantly clear that even *total* compliance with UN demands would never induce Washington to agree an end to the embargo, Baghdad was again examining its relations with the United Nations. There were again signs that Saddam was contemplating a break with UNSCOM, if only because Iraq could never rely on its capacity to resist US pressure. In June he chaired a joint meeting of the Ba'ath party's 'pan-Arab' and 'regional' (Iraqi) leaderships, from which emerged an important announcement: the 'Iraqi people, their legislative institutions and leadership' would determine their attitude to the United Nations in the light of the new report that Ekeus was due to deliver to the Security Council on 19 June. The Iraqi government, it was asserted, would only address the question of biological weapons if formal UN recognition of progress in other weapons fields was given. In short, what was the point of further concessions if earlier ones had not been acknowledged? Where was the light at the end of the tunnel? It was inevitable that this fresh attempt to put pressure on the United Nations would fail. Washington would never sanction any conciliatory move, and Ekeus predictably rejected the Iraqi proposals. The UN Food and Agriculture Organisation (FAO) was again warning of famine conditions in Iraq, and so this was obviously a time for the West to sit back and watch the Iraqi nation move into terminal collapse. The London-based *al-Quds* Arabic newspaper, while opposing Saddam Hussein, noted that the Iraqi regime was now faced with famine and insurrection. Reports of a mutiny on the outskirts of Baghdad served to strengthen Western resolve to keep the sanctions in place. If the Iraqi state was falling apart the end of Saddam could not be long delayed.[32] At the same time there were signs of serious divisions in the main opposition faction, the Iraqi National Congress (INC). Opponents of Saddam were no longer able to assume that a united political organisation would be in a position to exploit the growing disarray in the Iraqi regime.[33]

In early July Turkish forces again invaded northern Iraq in a further attempt to crush Kurdish separatists in the Kurdistan Workers' Party (PKK). This event did not play well – from Washington's perspective – in the Western media. Invasions across frontiers were what the containment of Iraq was supposed to be about. Why should one invasion attract punitive sanctions lasting years, while another invasion should be not only tolerated but facilitated (by the provision of NATO weapons in abundance)? The double standards were plain. At a time when Saddam seemed to be facing unprecedented disaffection at the highest levels of his regime, INC in-fighting and Turkish aggression in violation of international law were doing little to assist the prolonged anti-Iraq campaign. Saddam responded to the new situation by freeing the two imprisoned Americans, which predictably failed to impress Washington (Christopher: 'Perhaps he is trying to court some international opinion. The two men were unjustifiably detained'); and by hinting yet again that if there were not some movement on the sanctions question then Iraq would be forced to reconsider its relations with the United Nations. Thus on the 27th anniversary of the 'glorious July revolution' Saddam declared: 'Iraq can no longer comply with Security Council resolutions or co-operate with UNSCOM without linking these steps to the lifting of the embargo.' Some observers noted that the warning was given no deadline and that it had been less forceful than anticipated. Perhaps the emphasis was still on conciliation. The official Iraqi news agency INA reported that a general political amnesty had been granted by the government to all those convicted inside or outside the country.

Sceptics were quick to denounce the gesture as meaningless.

In early August 1995, in a dramatic blow to the tightly-knit Iraqi leadership, two sons-in-law of Saddam Hussein – Lieutenant-General Hussein Kamel Hassan and Lieutenant-Colonel Saddam Kamel Hassan (later killed in Iraq) – fled to Jordan seeking political exile. Accompanied by their wives, their cousin Major Izzedine Mohammed Hassan and others, they declared their intention to rally the opposition to Saddam. Said Hussein Kamel, himself stained with the blood of repression in Iraq: 'We will seriously and continuously work towards changing the existing system. . .', at the same time calling on 'all officers in the Iraqi army, in the Republican Guards, in the special Republican Guard units, and all government officials to be prepared for the coming change, which will turn Iraq into something modern'.[34]

The United States moved quickly to exploit the situation. Fresh forces were despatched to the region, heralding joint US–Kuwaiti and US–Jordanian military exercises. Washington pledged to defend Jordan from any Iraqi military threats – of which there was no evidence whatever; and US intelligence officers rushed to Amman to interrogate the defectors. King Hussein was now under growing pressure to co-operate with Washington in tightening the screws still further on the Iraqi regime. Robert Pelletrau, the US Assistant Secretary of State for Near Eastern Affairs, and Mark Parris, a national security official, arrived in Amman to try to persuade King Hussein to sever all Jordan's remaining links with Iraq. Hussein, prepared to welcome the defections as heralding 'a new era and a new life for the Iraqi people', was *not* prepared to agree further economic strangulation of his neigbour. Jordan would not close the border because this would cut off food and medicine: '*This is a matter that we do not contemplate because we are with the people of Iraq as much as we can until the long night of their suffering ends.*' Washington had no such interest. On 25 August 1995 Madeleine Albright announced that, because new revelations about Iraqi arms had shown that Saddam Hussein was not to be trusted, an early ending of sanctions was less rather than more likely. The United States would continue to do whatever it could to prolong the long night of suffering of the Iraqi people.

THE DISARMAMENT ISSUE

The United States and Britain have given many reasons why it is essential to maintain sanctions on Iraq. Principal among these is the insistence that never again should Iraq be allowed to become a military threat to its neighbours in the region. In particular, any programmes dedicated to the development and production of nuclear, chemical and biological 'weapons of mass destruction' had to be dismantled; and any existing weapons in these categories had to be destroyed.* If, as Rolf Ekeus has suggested many times, there is found to be a substantial degree of Iraqi co-operation in these areas then other reasons are given for maintaining the embargo: Saddam is persecuting the Iraqi minorities, is again moving troops towards Kuwait, is sponsoring terrorism, is refurbishing his palaces, is not to be trusted, etc. The disarmament issue remains central but, if and when the UN inspectors eventually declare themselves satisfied with the degree of Iraqi compliance in this area, Washington will move quickly to justify the embargo on other grounds. Today no independent observer believes that Iraq is a military threat to anyone. The arms issue is one of a number of pretexts for maintaining an embargo designed above all to secure the collapse of the Iraqi government. For this key US objective there is no authorisation in any UN resolutions and no justification in international law.

It is useful also to note the much rehearsed fact that it was the United States, Britain, France, the Soviet Union and other states that helped Saddam Hussein to build up his military capacity. Through the 1980s Washington and London showed no concern for persecuted Iraqi minorities or about Iraq's protracted aggression against Iran. On the contrary, the US, Britain and others actively aided Saddam's schemes by providing weapons, technology, financial credits, intelligence, and, in some cases, direct military support. In the nuclear field alone, Iraq was supplied with reactors and other equipment, nuclear materials, expertise and training. The US and British governments permitted staff from Saddam's Al-Qaaqaa nuclear weapons factory to receive specialist training in the West. Three Iraqi physicists were allowed to attend a conference on 'The Physics of Detonation', sponsored by US nuclear weapons laboratories in 1989 and held in Portland, Oregon. Other Iraqi scientists came to Britain the same year to train at Hadland Photonics (Bovington, Hertfordshire), a company that specialises in the flash X-ray photography used in the analysis of nuclear and other explosions.

---

* It is useful, when considering chemical and biological weapons development, to remember US and British interest in these areas: for example, the vast (840,911 acre) CW and BW research site at Dugway, Utah, in the United States; how the US protected Japanese war criminals in exchange for their CW/BW expertise (see Sheldon H. Harris, *Factories of Death*, London: Routledge, 1994); and a new UK Ministry of Defence complex for carrying out CW experiments on human beings (*Independent on Sunday*, London, 27 August 1995).

Such events show the ease with which Saddam Hussein could gain access to the high technology of weapons development and production. By early 1990, with substantial Western assistance, Iraq had moved a long way towards acquiring nuclear weapons; and what was true in the nuclear field was true also in other areas of weapons technology. The West had helped Saddam acquire weapons of mass destruction[35] (just as the United States, in violation of the 1970 Non-Proliferation Treaty (NPT), had protected Israel's development of nuclear weapons[36]). Today the West, keen to denounce all Saddam's perfidies, shrugs off any responsibility for shaping the events that led to the Iraqi invasion of Kuwait. Does no guilt attach to the man who hands a loaded gun to a known psychopath?

The West, having helped Saddam Hussein to build up a substantial part of his military capability, then resolved to destroy it. In the Gulf War the Coalition forces undertook a massive campaign to obliterate any industrial plant, research facility, transport system, power plant, etc. that might have supported, however indirectly, Saddam's ability to develop and manufacture a weapons capability. One of the early principal targets was Iraq's nuclear power technology: for example, the Tuwaitha reactor that began generating electrical power in 1968. There was no evidence that this reactor, regularly inspected by International Atomic Energy Agency (IAEA) personnel, had any connection with weapons development; and yet the Tuwaitha scientific centres including the reactor were, according to Iraqi testimony, 'bombarded severely and almost daily' during the Gulf War.[37]

In his televised speech after the beginning of the bombing campaign President Bush declared that a high priority was to crush Iraq's nuclear capability, though little distinction was drawn between peaceful power generation (protected by the Non-Proliferation Treaty) and the development of nuclear weapons. On 31 January 1991 the British Defence Secretary Tom King confirmed that the first achievement of the air campaign had been 'the destruction of all nuclear reactor capacity' in Iraq. These statements immediately raised questions about the amount of radioactive contamination that the bombing attacks had caused, and whether the targeting of peaceful nuclear reactors constituted a violation of international law. The Israeli bombing of Iraq's Osiraq nuclear reactor in 1981 resulted in the passing of Security Council Resolution 487, condemning the Israeli action as a violation of the UN Charter; and at a more recent IAEA conference a resolution stressed the need 'to prohibit armed attacks on nuclear installations from which such [radioactive] releases could occur' and affirmed 'the urgency of concluding an international agreement in this regard'. At the NPT review conference, held in Geneva 1990, a collective statement declared that 'this conference recognises that an armed attack on a safeguarded nuclear facility, operational or under construction . . . would create a situation in which the Security Council would have to act immediately in accordance with the provisions of the United Nations Charter'.[38] Despite this statement of the NPT conference, at which the United States was a leading participant, the US then voted in the UN General Assembly (December 1990) – the only country to do so – against a resolution prohibiting bombing attacks on nuclear reactors. A few weeks later, American aircraft – against the spirit and letter of NPT conference and General Assembly resolutions – began the sustained bombing of Iraqi nuclear plants. These events revealed what was to become a defining feature of the Gulf War and the imposition of the sanctions regime: any US-inspired policy would be justified by Washington, however disproportionate such policies might be, however lacking UN authorisation, and however unrelated to specific overt policy objectives.

At the end of the war the United States drew up the terms for a formal ceasefire, at the same time pushing the UN Security Council to accept the US formula. Already there were differences among the Council's permanent members, some declaring that Washington was going 'too far' in trying to add a number of strategic objectives far beyond that of liberating Kuwait. On 1 March 1991 the draft US resolution imposing a host of demands on Iraq was issued to all fifteen members of the Security Council. President Bush was now declaring that it was difficult to imagine normal relations with Iraq while Saddam Hussein remained in power, though Washington balked at the idea that Saddam's removal should be a condition in the ceasefire resolution. None the less it was still taking some time to finalise the wording. Said Bush: 'There is quite a lot to get in.'

The draft resolution, still being considered at the end of March, was calling for the destruction of Iraq's remaining chemical and biological weapons, for the dismantling of its ballistic missiles, and for the destruction of all facilities for their development. Many other conditions were also included, with some commentators now prepared to question the wisdom of maintaining Iraq as a permanently weak state in the Middle East. It was noted that many other states of the region had ballistic missiles (Saudi Arabia had the powerful CSS-2 missiles), chemical weapons (Syria had fitted chemical warheads to its Soviet-built SS-21 *tochka* missiles), Egypt was designing its own long-range ballistic missiles, and nothing was being done to discourage Israel from developing its own nuclear weapons. Would it be acceptable, as a permanent arrangement, to deny a sovereign number of the United Nations adequate means of defence when surrounded by increasingly militarised potentially hostile neighbours?

On 3 April 1991 the Security Council passed Resolution 687 (see Appendix 3) by 12 votes to 1 (Cuba) with 2 abstentions (Ecuador and Yemen). A principal part of 687, one that was to attract much attention in the months and years to follow, is the part (Section C(7)–(14)) dealing with the destruction of Iraq's military capability. This section required Iraq to reaffirm its obligations under the Geneva Protocol banning the wartime use of asphyxiating, poisonous and other gases, and the Convention prohibiting the development, production and stockpiling of biological and toxic weapons. Iraq was asked to agree the destruction of its chemical and biological weapons, its ballistic missiles with a range greater than 150 kilometres, and all the associated repair and production facilities. A special commission was to be established to verify that the demands were being met. At the same time Iraq was asked to reaffirm its commitment to the Non-Proliferation (of Nuclear Weapons) Treaty, and to agree that it would not acquire or develop nuclear weapons or any related materials and systems. The IAEA Director-General, working with the Special Commission, would inspect Iraq's nuclear capabilities with a view to confirming IAEA safeguards. The various actions specified in Section C of Resolution 687 were to be regarded as '*steps towards the goal of establishing in the Middle East a zone free from weapons of mass destruction and all missiles for their delivery and the objective of a global ban on chemical weapons*' (Section C(14)). The steps were of course ones that affected only Iraq. All the other states in the region – with the exception of Libya (like Iraq, branded a 'pariah state' by Washington) – would be allowed to develop, manufacture and purchase a wide range of military equipment, technology and expertise.

In early June 1991 Saddam Hussein indicated by letter to UN Secretary-General Perez de Cuellar that Iraq would hand over a list of nuclear materials sought by the UN inspection teams and allow the inspection teams unimpeded access to the relevant sites. Already, however, there were signs that the Iraqi authorities would be reluctant to comply fully with UN demands.[39] When, on 24 June, UN inspectors tried to enter the Abu Gharaib military base north of Baghdad in the search for nuclear material the Iraqis refused to admit them. Said US representative Alexander Watson: 'If we can't get this one right the problems for the future will be really bad.' In Washington the State

Department spokeswoman Margaret Tutwiler commented on the 'ample evidence from multiple sources' that Iraq had been carrying out a covert programme for the development of nuclear weapons. When, after a delay, the UN team gained access to Abu Gharaib there were no nuclear materials or equipment to be found. Either there had been none earlier or the Iraqis had purposefully delayed the UN inspectors in order to remove the suspect items. Previous inspections, following a significant degree of Iraqi compliance, had allowed the IAEA personnel visiting the Tuwaitha and Tarmiya sites to seal about 87 pounds of uranium (27 pounds of 93 per cent highly enriched uranium and 60 pounds of 80 per cent enriched uranium, both openly declared by Iraq).

On 26 June the United States urged Iraq to release without further delay 'any and all nuclear equipment' in its possession. To support its charges of Iraqi non-compliance eight US intelligence experts gave an audio-visual presentation of US spy-satellite photographs to diplomats, having asked all officials below the rank of ambassador to leave the closed-door session, showing what they said were Iraqi efforts to hide nuclear weapons equipment. Computer-enhanced images of three alleged nuclear installations were shown to identify equipment for enriched uranium which Iraq had not declared. There were also US claims that the clothing of American hostages contained traces of radioactive graphite, indicating that they had been held at undisclosed nuclear sites. Now the UN inspectors were lodging a protest that they had not been allowed to visit certain sites, and Washington was threatening 'further steps as may be required' – taken to mean fresh military action – to enforce Iraqi compliance with Resolution 687. On 28 June Iraqi soldiers reportedly fired live rounds to prevent UN inspectors from following and videotaping a convoy of 60 army trucks carrying undeclared military equipment. Commented President Bush: 'We can't let this brutal bully [Saddam] go back on this solemn agreement and threaten people that are there under UN jurisdiction, and that's exactly what he appears to have done. This man has no shame.' Asked what action Washington intended, Bush replied: 'Stay tuned.'

Fresh warnings were issued to Baghdad. On 29 June Rolf Ekeus, the head of the special disarmament commission, Hans Blix, the IAEA head, and Yasushi Akashi, the UN disarmament chief, delivered a stern message in Baghdad that Iraq was obliged to release all its nuclear weapons equipment. It was emphasised that until there was full Iraqi compliance the crippling economic sanctions would not be relaxed. President Bush was continuing to emphasise his belief that the UN authority for a fresh American military attack on Iraq already existed:

Washington would decide, even in the absence of further enabling UN resolutions, when new bombing raids would be launched to force Iraqi compliance. The US Deputy Secretary of State Lawrence Eagleburger, speaking on the Cable News Network, commented: 'I cannot believe the Iraqis will be so stupid as to think they can get away with this for very long'; and in the same spirit *The Washington Post* (30 June 1991) declared: 'Continued evasion of the conditions of the ceasefire, and resistance to them, would justify further resort to military force by the allies.' Already it was widely known that the sanctions were inflicting massive suffering on the Iraqi people.

This fraught situation, characterised by Iraqi recalcitrance and US threats, was set to continue. Bush, intent on subjecting the Iraqi people to the harshest deprivations, emphasised that his quarrel was not with them but with their leader – who should 'step aside' as a means of bringing 'relief to the people of Iraq'. It was clear, declared Bush, that Saddam Hussein was 'lying and cheating' about his nuclear programme, and so a fresh allied military intervention could not be ruled out. Britain and France were expressing concern at the degree of Iraqi non-compliance, but other countries meeting at the G7 London summit – notably Japan and Germany – seemed unwilling to support fresh ultimatums that might render a new military campaign inevitable. Some observers surmised also that China, not a G7 member, might be less than enthusiastic about ringing declarations emanating from a powerful international body from which it was excluded.

The games and tensions ran into July and beyond. President Hosni Mubarak sent a letter to Saddam Hussein warning him of the dangers of ignoring the US-imposed ceasefire terms, whereupon Saddam invited the Arab League to send representatives to inspect Iraqi nuclear installations. On 15 July 1991 the Iraqi premier Saadoun Hammadi commented that there was a 'probability' of Iraq again being bombed when a new UN deadline (25 July) for full Iraqi weapons disclosure expired; and that the purpose of sanctions was to 'starve the Iraqi people so they revolt and change their leader, Saddam Hussein'. Hammadi claimed also that the UN inspectors were largely satisfied with the degree of Iraqi disclosure. Already Iraq had acknowledged that it had developed a three-track nuclear programme and produced about a pound of enriched uranium using a primitive low-tech method. Such disclosures had 'made a nonsense' of IAEA efforts to prevent the spread of nuclear weapons.[40] At the same time the United States was infuriated at Iraqi attempts to disguise not only the extent of such nuclear developments but also the size of the Scud missile stockpiles and the quantity of chemical weapons that survived the war. Senior UN sources were now declaring that 'there is no doubt' that the US and its allies would resume bombing if Iraq had not provided the necessary information by 25 July. [41]

Already the UN inspectors had found evidence of two industrial-scale factories, at Tarmiya and al-Sharqat, that could have produced enough weapons-grade uranium for two nuclear bombs a year. Massive air handling and filtration systems, built and maintained by Western companies, had been used 'to prevent isotopic signatures from escaping from the plant' and revealing to IAEA inspectors the principal purpose of the production facilities. The factories had been destroyed in the war or subsequently demolished by the Iraqis, but with much of the equipment first taken by the Iraqis to undisclosed locations. Now the UN inspectors had no doubt that Iraq 'had been pursuing an undeclared uranium enrichment programme', and that the pre-war IAEA inspections had manifestly failed to detect the nuclear development programmes then in progress. When the deadline (25 July) was reached, Baghdad had still not provided the required information, but Washington was now backing off from the idea of immediate bombing raids – possibly because of insufficient international support for such action. Now it was clear that the stranglehold of trade sanctions would be maintained for an indefinite period. Reports were appearing that starving Iraqis were eating weeds and grass, and that there was a real threat of widespread famine in the country. Abdallah al-Ashtal, Yemen's UN ambassador, commented that the Iraqi people were being 'victimised' and that 'the Security Council will eventually be blamed for the catastrophe'. Washington and London continued to insist that the mounting suffering of the Iraqi civilian population was entirely the fault of Saddam Hussein.

In early August 1991 Iraq admitted for the first time that it had conducted germ warfare experiments but claimed that these had ceased soon after the start of the Gulf crisis. Said an Iraqi foreign ministry spokesman: 'The Iraqi side has informed the inspection team that there is a laboratory for biological research for military purposes within a general research establishment. Iraq dropped this biological research completely in autumn 1990 because of the possibility of an attack [by the US and its allies].' Still Washington was railing at what it considered to be the totally inadequate degree of Iraqi disclosure of its weapons programmes. On 9 September, with President Bush declaring himself 'plenty fed up', a White House official announced that US F-117A Stealth bombers and F-17 jets would be despatched to Saudi Arabia 'in the next day or so' and that the Saudis would also be given Patriot missiles as a 'safeguard' against possible Iraqi attack.

The degree of Iraqi compliance with the UN weapons inspectors remained patchy. Baghdad granted permission for UN helicopter flights over parts of Iraq, but demanded that Iraqi officials be on board and that no aerial photography be carried out, whereupon a UN spokesman declared that no such conditions could be tolerated. President Bush again threatened military action. On 23 September Iraqi soldiers ejected a UN team from a building in which documents had been found that confirmed Iraq's nuclear intentions. Washington immediately issued a 48-hour ultimatum for Iraqi compliance and declared that US aircraft would be sent in to accompany the UN helicopters. A former US ambassador to Iraq, Marshall Wiley, reflecting the mounting frustration in Washington, commented: 'I don't think we can ever be sure we have removed all hi-tech weapons capability from Iraq unless we occupy the country and put in maybe a million men and keep them there for a period of years. That is a cost I don't think we are prepared to pay.'

On 25 September the Pentagon announced that 100 targets had been selected for possible punitive raids against Iraq, and General Colin Powell, chairman of the joint chiefs of staff, declared to Congress that 'patience is wearing thin'. Some 44 UN inspectors were now beleaguered in a Baghdad car park and the Iraqis were showing no signs of relenting. Baghdad issued a statement charging that the team leader, David Kay, was working for US intelligence and that 'he was the main source of the difficulties that we have encountered'. President Bush was reportedly viewing the impasse as a 'very serious matter'. On 27 September, under the terms of a face-saving formula, the Iraqi authorities granted the UN inspectors permission to carry out an inventory of crucial documents giving details of Iraq's secret nuclear programme and details of procurement agreements with Western companies. David Kay reported to Cable Network News that he was 'happy to say that as of seven minutes ago the siege is officially over'. However, Kay and Robert Gallucci, the deputy head of the special commission, then earned a rebuke from UN Secretary-General Perez de Cuellar. Key sections of the 25,000 documents seized in Baghdad were transmitted to the State Department in Washington without going through UN channels. It was known also that an American U-2 spy plane and spy satellites were collecting surveillance data on Iraq. Suddenly there seemed to be substance in the Iraqi charges that American UN inspectors were working as spies for the US State Department. David Kay's role was reportedly causing growing concern among UN officials.[42]

The Security Council was now moving to ensure that Iraq never again developed weapons of mass destruction. On 11 October 1991 the Council passed the highly intrusive mandatory Resolution 715* establishing a monitoring scheme of indefinite duration and authorising UN inspectors to roam at will anywhere in Iraq, by land or air, to remove or photograph any item or document, to take any sample, to interview any personnel, and to install any surveillance equipment. The resolution also authorised UN inspectors to intercept vehicles, ships and aircraft, and to check any imports and exports. Few observers doubted that the new resolution – according to a senior Western diplomat 'as strong as it can be – reduced Iraq, in theory a *de jure* sovereign member of the United Nations, to virtual trusteeship status. Even so-called 'dual-use' machinery, essential for a wide range of industrial purposes, and chemicals that have no military uses, were to be prohibited. In short, Iraq was to be prevented from possessing any industrial base: it was to be indefinitely consigned to a pre-industrial, impoverished status. The crippling sanctions, that had already reduced the Iraqi people to unprecedented levels of suffering, were to be intensified.

The draconian scope of the new conditions were supposedly justified by Iraq's failure to comply with UN inspection demands; in particular, by its unwillingness to reveal the extent of its weapons stocks and weapons development. But there were now reports that Iraq's nuclear weapons capability had been greatly exaggerated,[43] and that in any case there was now a substantial degree of Iraqi compliance with UN demands. Over a period of six months the UN inspectors had exposed most of Iraq's weapons plans. At the al-Muthanna chemical weapons complex (according to an inspector, 'the most dangerous place in the world'), rocket projectiles, mostly empty, were being destroyed; most of the nuclear secrets had been exposed; and records had been compiled of Iraq's 46,000 missiles, bombs and other munitions that contained, or were ready to contain, nerve and mustard gas. Two 'superguns' had been destroyed, and the scale of the Scud missile stockpiles, not wholly accounted for, determined. By any reckoning, much of the work authorised in ceasefire Resolution 687 had already been completed.

The pattern was repeated in subsequent years: Iraqi evasions within the context of broad compliance and frequent US threats of military

* Reinforcing Resolution 707 (15 August 1991) (see Appendix 4 for both 707 and 715).

intervention. Washington charged constantly that Iraq was failing to co-operate in revealing its Scud missile stockpiles, the volume of chemical and biological weapons still to be destroyed, and the extent of the nuclear programme. The charges, predictably rebutted by Baghdad, led to further threat of air strikes and other military initiatives:

'Iraq told it faces military action for defying UN'[44]

'US raises the stakes in new game of chicken with Iraq'[45]

'US plans renewed air raids on Iraq'[46]

'Iraq warned of possible armed strike'[47]

Now Iraq was continuing to question the motives of the US-dominated Security Council. What was the purpose of the unremitting pressures and threats? Was it to secure peace in the region or to destroy the Iraqi nation? The Iraqi deputy prime minister Tariq Aziz, speaking for Baghdad newspapers, commented: *'They* [the Council] *make no mention what measures have been carried out concerning the scrapping of weapons of mass destruction. They only concentrate on claims that Iraq has not complied. In New York we will ask the Security Council: Is your aim to destroy Iraqi industry or implement Resolution 687? If your aim is to carry out 687, you have our approval. But if your objective is to annihilate Iraqi industry and deny Iraq the chance of becoming a prosperous industrial country, that would be a different matter.'* Aziz added that Iraq had implemented the UN measures so that the United States 'and its biased allies in the UN establishment' would not be able 'to fabricate excuses to maintain the embargo'. Such comments were of course entirely fruitless. While Saddam Hussein remained in power Washington would work to maintain the sanctions regime, whatever the degree of Iraqi compliance with 687 or any other Security Council resolution.

On 12 March 1992 Tariq Aziz made a lengthy statement to the Security Council, answering US charges of Iraqi non-compliance point by point. He insisted that military equipment that could be converted to civilian use should not be destroyed, and demanded that respect be shown for Iraqi sovereignty. At the end of the meeting Aziz was publicly thanked for the 'goodwill' he had expressed, while at the same time reports were appearing of six B-52 strategic bombers of the US 42nd bomber wing arriving at the RAF Fairford base, possibly in anticipation of further air attacks on Iraq.

The United States continued to work hard to fuel anxieties about Iraq's military potential. Perhaps the UN measures had only delayed rather than destroyed Iraq's nuclear programme. Rumours persisted that the Iraqis had managed to build an underground plutonium plant and secret production centres where cascades of imported centrifuges were making large quantities of uranium-235. In the absence of firm evidence the rumours were sufficient. Everyone knew that Saddam Hussein could not be trusted – so clearly the sanctions would have to remain in place.[48] Still the UN and IAEA inspectors were continuing to identify nuclear-related components and to destroy key elements in the Iraqi nuclear programme. Thus by the end of April 1992 the al-Atheer nuclear weapons establishment had been largely destroyed and the explosives-testing bunker filled with concrete: one thousand reluctant Iraqi workers were enlisted to aid in the destruction process. There were still various deliberate Iraqi impediments to the efforts of UN inspectors ('Iraq ignores UN deadline', 'Standoff between UN team and Iraqis', etc.). As always, part of the problem was that the UN inspectors, far from being objective officials of the international community, were too easily portrayed as little more than agents of US strategic interest. Saddam himself denounced the United Nations as *'an advertising agency'* for Washington: 'What is needed is a jihad to purge the Arab nation of these treacherous leaders who have become a shameful burden on our region!' In such a perception the leaders of Kuwait and Saudi Arabia were, like the despised UN inspectors, shameful agents of a hostile foreign power.

Fresh problems erupted when UN personnel were denied access to the Iraqi Ministry of Agriculture – where, it was suspected, weapons documents might be concealed. Fadhil Mahmoud Khareer, an Iraqi trade union leader, expressed the prevailing mood in Baghdad: 'Tell the whole world, Iraqi workers have lost patience. They can no longer stand the humiliation. . . . We are under great pressure from our workers. If we could control them in the past, we won't be able to contain them in the future.' Again, before the stand-off was resolved, the predictable threats were issued from Washington:

'UN may resort to force over Iraqi weapons'[49]

And again observers were noting the evident subservience of UN operations to American control. The Special Commission, established under the terms of Resolution 687, though based at UN headquarters in New York, was directed from Washington and 'had close links with US

army intelligence, the CIA and the National Security Agency'. Moreover, US army officers had 'played a prominent role' in the commission's many missions to locate and destroy Iraq's weapons of mass
destruction.[50]

Now the US–Iraq tensions were being fuelled by the exigencies of
the American election campaign. Where the Gulf War had boosted
Bush's popularity, people were now noticing that Saddam was still in
power while the Bush administration was looking increasingly rocky.
Perhaps fresh air attacks on Iraq might again boost George Bush's
attempt to secure a second term in the White House. So yet again the
prospect of war loomed large:

'Iraq war could start in days'[51]

'Allies threaten air strikes on Iraq'[52]

'Gulf war threatens as Bush in crisis talks'[53]

'Iraq defiant as America warns of war'[54]

The crisis, like the many before it, passed. The Iraqis agreed to allow
UN inspectors access to the Baghdad Ministry of Agriculture, provided that a new United Nations team be appointed to carry out the
necessary work. Rolf Ekeus announced that the 'immediate problem is
now settled' and indicated that he would leave for Baghdad immediately to supervise the operations. A disappointed George Bush, now
cheated of the chance to launch electorally attractive bombing raids,
commented peevishly: 'The international community cannot tolerate
continued Iraqi defiance of the UN and the rule of law. There is too
much at stake for the UN and the world.' The Iraqis declared themselves satisfied with the composition of the new inspection team: no
longer dominated by American personnel, it now contained staff from
Sweden, Switzerland, Germany and Russia. Ekeus commented that
'certain sensibilities' had been taken into account in picking the new
team but without 'compromising the quality of the inspections'. The
American eagerness for a fresh military onslaught had been thwarted.
Moreover, Ekeus had observed, of the destruction of Iraqi weaponry:
'*What has been destroyed is through the peaceful means of inspection.
It is that way to destroy weapons, and not through bombing and at-
tacks.*' The American Republicans may have wished for a more stal-
wart ally in election year.[55]

In August it seemed that Baghdad and Washington were yet again
lurching towards a military confrontation. An Iraqi announcement,

reversing a 12-day-old agreement that UN inspectors should be allowed access to the Ministry of Agriculture, now declared that access to all its ministries would be denied to UN personnel. Marlin Fitzwater, a White House spokesman, immediately declared that while there would be no comment on military operations, 'all options are open to us'. President Bush declared that Iraqi 'defiance' would bring a fast, aggressive response. Then, in characteristic fashion, the Iraqi authorities again modified the earlier prohibition and allowed certain UN inspections. But by mid-August the Bush administration was again contemplating a military response to Iraqi non-compliance: ' . . . if Mr Bush wants to try to provoke a confrontation, there are ample opportunities to do so through UN inspections'.[56] Again the familiar headlines appeared:

'President poised to bomb Iraq'[57]

'Bush plans air strikes on Baghdad'[58]

Now there were UN officials prepared to say that Iraq's nuclear threat 'remains at zero'. Thus Maurizio Zifferero, the leader of the latest team in Baghdad to monitor Iraqi compliance, emphasised that Iraq was no longer developing nuclear weapons (so repudiating the view of one of his predecessors, David Kay): 'There is no longer any nuclear activity in Iraq. They have no facilities where [they can] carry out this activity.' This reflected the now widespread view of UN inspectors that the Iraqi nuclear programme had been halted by a combination of the war and subsequent inspections. Zifferero stressed that he was not taking the Iraqi word at face value but was confident that UN personnel had carried out the necessary investigations for themselves. Iraq had been stripped of its ability to develop nuclear weapons using electromagnetic isotope separation, and inspectors, having travelled to many parts of the country, had uncovered no evidence of Iraqi attempts to conceal the centrifuges that might be used to produce weapons-grade uranium. On 7 September Zifferero commented that Iraq still had to give full details of foreign suppliers but at the same time praised Iraqi co-operation with his team, noting that Baghdad had agreed to accept various UN-controlled monitoring methods.

On 16 October 1992 a 50-strong UN team arrived in Baghdad on what team leader Nikita Smidovich called a 'very important mission' that would include searches for Scud missiles. A principal task was to determine whether Iraq was still holding ballistic missiles that should be destroyed according to Resolution 687 (said Smidovich: 'We will visit both declared and undeclared sites'). Now the emphasis had shifted.

The nuclear question had abated, though set to open up again in the future. Now other reasons had to be found for maintaining sanctions.

Fresh tensions developed early in 1993 when a plane chartered by UN inspectors was denied permission to land in Baghdad, and some 200 Iraqi personnel crossed into Kuwait to seize armaments, including surface-to-surface missiles. Major-General Dibuama, the chief of the United Nations Iraqi–Kuwaiti Observer Mission (UNIKOM), immediately requested a meeting at the Iraqi foreign ministry to protest at the incursions into Kuwait. In fact the Security Council had granted Iraq until 15 January to remove Iraqi property from land now controversially donated to Kuwait by the 5-man commission appointed by the UN to demarcate the new border. The Iraqis, it appeared, had been careless in notifying the appropriate authorities about their intentions to remove items from the territory in question. None the less the incident generated predictable warnings from Washington that more US military strikes would follow. On 13 January some 114 aircraft had again bombed Iraqi targets, with both US and British aircraft involved. Bush described the operation as a Baghdad 'big success' but reports suggested that many of the intended targets had not been hit. A Pentagon spokesman, Pete Williams, conceded that not all the targets had been hit, 'but that was never our measure of success'.

It soon transpired that the block on the UN-chartered plane had caused a delay rather than a fresh crisis. Observers were even prepared to note what they dubbed Saddam's 'peace offensive' – possibly designed to discourage further allied bombing raids over Iraq. Bush had indulged his final spasm. For months he had wanted to launch further military strikes against the Iraqi people, and now, with his presidential term ebbing away, he had managed to kill a few dozen more Iraqis in addition to those who had succumbed to the crippling pressures of the embargo. But if Saddam was calculating that a change of president would do anything to alter the character of the US–Iraq relationship he would soon learn that everything would continue as before. There would be no respite for the Iraqi people while Saddam Hussein remained in power.

On 21 January 1993 UN inspectors arrived in Baghdad to continue with the destruction of chemical weapons, and to search yet again for nuclear and missile equipment. Officials reported a new tone of conciliation in Baghdad as Saddam Hussein tried to capitalise on the change of American president. But now US personnel were doing all they could to undermine the new spirit of accord that was developing between UN inspectors and Iraqi officials. Thus Gary Milhollin, an anti-nuclear proliferation campaigner, declared that the Iraqis were 'outfoxing' the inspectors at every turn, 'harassing them and making it more and more likely that Saddam Hussein will wriggle out from under the current embargo with large parts of his A-bomb effort intact'. One UN source branded the charge a 'grotesquery . . . biased, unfair, and misinterpreting the facts'. By March the UN inspectors were claiming that their job was almost done: many colleagues of Zifferero now shared his view that the Iraqi nuclear programme was 'at zero'. It now seemed clear that – by early 1993 (three years ago at the time of writing) – a substantial proportion of the UN inspectors were satisfied that Iraq no longer posed a military threat to its regional neighbours: the 'aggressive hunt' was 'quietly giving way to a lower key programme of long-term monitoring'.[59] Even in this changed atmosphere the United States deemed it well worth while to continue punishing the Iraqi people by blocking their access to food, medicines and the other basic necessities of life.

In February surprise visits to Iraqi sites had revealed nothing; the destruction of 70 tons of declared nerve gas stocks was nearing completion; and stockpiles of irradiated uranium were being prepared for despatch from the country. In May the IAEA announced that a contract for disposing of the radioactive waste from Iraq's atomic weapons programme would be given to Chelyabinsk-65, the Russian nuclear city. Since no UN inspectors had examined safety there, it was a questionable decision. Said one IAEA official: 'Our hands are tied. UN rules say that we have to accept the lowest bid and the Russians' is the lowest. None of our people have ever been to the site but we have heard about the conditions. If it is so bad, 35–40kg more waste won't make much difference.' The aim was for irradiated highly-enriched uranium from the French-built Tammuz-2 and Russian-built IRT-5000 research reactors at Tuwaila to be separated into eight 5kg consignments, each of which would then be entombed in 20-tonne blocks of lead and stainless steel for transport in Russian military aircraft. There was no prospect of the British or French handling the irradiated material since their legislation says that reprocessed fuel has to be returned to the country of origin: there was no question of returning anything to Iraq.

By now the rumour of a hidden Iraqi nuclear reactor had been dispelled by persistent UN investigations. Thus Bob Kelly, a senior IAEA official, commented: 'Having looked at this for two years, I think it is time to put it on the backburner. We have analysed a huge body of data and I think it is a good time to put the story to bed. . . . I have tramped around Iraq looking at things we felt were suspicious.' The IAEA would be ready to reopen the reactor file 'if anything new comes up'. Now, however, fresh tensions were growing because of Iraqi reluctance to agree long-term monitoring of selected sites. In mid-June 1993 UN inspectors were prevented from installing cameras to monitor two missile testing sites; and in July the US was again warning of the likelihood of a fresh confrontation. On 4 July Secretary of State Warren Christopher commented that it was 'a bad sign' that the inspectors were having to leave Baghdad before accomplishing their monitoring tasks. Washington could be heading for a new confrontation, opined Christopher: 'Our next step would be discussed with our allies.' There seemed little doubt that if the Iraqis were to persist in denying the inspectors permission to install the cameras at the Yam al-Azim and al-Rafah sites, 65km south and south-west of Baghdad, the tensions would again mount, leading to the possibility of US air strikes.

On 27 June President Clinton authorised the firing of 23 Tomahawk cruise missiles at Baghdad, in retaliation for Iraq's alleged involvement in an attempt to assassinate George Bush on a visit to Kuwait in April. US spokesmen conceded that some of the missiles had hit residential areas and that there had been civilian casualties. The Iraqis subsequently reported that children had been killed and also Leila al-Attar, an Iraqi painter revered throughout the Arab world. Madeleine Albright attempted to justify the fresh attack on Baghdad, but even *The New York Times* felt compelled to comment that to swallow the US case 'as it stands requires a leap of faith and a complete suspension of political cynicism'.[60] On 1 July, partly in response to Iraqi reluctance to accept long-term intrusive monitoring, the United States, Britain and France were reportedly finalising new plans – without UN authorisation – for a fresh 'full-blown air attack' on Iraq.[61] The UN inspectors had been forced to abandon, at least for the moment, their monitoring plans, but they had placed seals on the sites to prevent their use (Ekeus: 'We will place seals on machines . . .'). Again, as far as Washington was concerned, Saddam Hussein was yet again playing his familiar game of 'cheat and retreat' with the West.

Now there were signs that the US posture was beginning to alarm Washington's Western allies. While both Britain and France publicly supported the military option in the event of Iraqi non-compliance, there had been anger that Washington had launched missiles without adequate consultation. In London a Ministry of Defence source noted: 'The notice was so short that it was not possible to give the prime minister proper advice about the possible collateral damage. We did not even know that the missiles would be flying over Baghdad.' Again President Clinton was warning that the use of force against Iraq 'is entirely possible', with US officials declaring that if Iraq failed to comply fully with UN demands a military strike was certain. Mohammed Said, Iraq's foreign minister, wrote to the Security Council in an attempt to forestall yet another punitive raid: 'Iraq calls on the Security Council to shoulder its responsibilities . . . so as to prevent the launching of yet another military aggression . . .'.

On 19 July the Iraqi authorities, reversing their earlier policy, agreed to let UN inspectors monitor Iraq's weapons programme. Rolf Ekeus rejoiced that the two sides had come out of the 'vicious cycle' of threats and counter-threats, and noted in a position paper that Iraq was ready to agree 'on-going monitoring and verification as contained in Resolution 715' (see Appendix 4). Now Iraq was again insisting that its full compliance meant that the trade sanctions should be immediately lifted. To such appeals Ekeus was responding by saying he could recommend no easing of sanctions until Baghdad was prepared to give a full and detailed disclosure of its weapons capabilities and suppliers. Nothing had changed. There would always be reasons why the West could not possibly agree the ending of the embargo at any particular time, and why the possibility of fresh military action against Iraq should always be on the agenda. Even after this new sign of Iraqi compliance the UK Foreign Secretary, Douglas Hurd, chose to declare: 'We will not hesitate to use force if necessary . . .'. Of course the West had 'no quarrel with the Iraqi people . . . . They have suffered enough.' Hurd *et al.* would continue to ensure that the suffering of the Iraqi people deepened yet further. No-one denied that there had been a significant degree of Iraqi compliance with UN demands, yet the thirteen 're-views' of the sanctions (to mid-July 1993) had not eased them in the slightest. The US policy

fails to distinguish between Saddam Hussein's regime and the Iraqi people, who are the major victims of both the sanctions and any Western military action, and which is akin to 'burning down a house with all its occupants because of the wrongdoing of one of them.'

Compounding the tragedy is the fact that virtually the entire community of nations has been forced to rubber-stamp US policy, with most countries not daring to risk the retribution which objecting to American behaviour might earn them.[62]

In early August 1993 the UN inspection team left Baghdad after installing the long-term monitoring cameras at the two designated sites; Bill Eckert, the team leader, praised the Iraqis for their co-operation. A month later, a new and more intrusive monitoring phase began, involving the use of helicopters flying at roof-top height and equipped with French nuclear radiation-sensitive devices. A principal aim was to provide a 'radiation profile' of Iraq to serve as a base for comprehensive long-term monitoring. At the same time UN plans were revealed for a substantial increase in the monitoring staff and equipment both in the air and on the ground, yet another pressure on the Iraqis to comply with the expanding US-contrived inspection regime. Saddam Hussein had complained that the new scale of surveillance smacked of a CIA plot to chart his movements as a means to his subsequent assassination. Ekeus commented that he was anxious to be on site when the new planes arrived 'so that if there is a conflict, I can confront it head on'; and he confirmed that the lifting of sanctions was not on the agenda: 'We're starting a comprehensive and intensive programme of overflights across the entire country, with new planes, new helicopters and new sensors being brought in. . . . Saddam has said that there must be no air capability and no new sensors without a lifting of the oil embargo. But of course *there isn't going to be any lifting of the oil embargo now*' (my italics). Still, Ekeus claimed, the Iraqis had not named all the suppliers 'on the chemical weapons front and the missile front. . . . We know he [Saddam] is hiding some things'.

The familiar charade was being played again. After months of obstruction the Iraqis finally produced a comprehensive list of foreign suppliers who had helped with the chemical and nuclear weapons programmes. Rolf Ekeus, after eight days of talks in Baghdad, managed to secure the required list: 'We have, as a matter of fact, last night received the answers of the Iraqi cabinet which has approved the release of data which we have requested.' Still there would be no recommendation for a lifting of the embargo – until 'long-term' (1-year?, 5-year?, 50-year?) monitoring of Iraqi arms development had been accomplished. Again the Iraqis had suspected that the list would find its way into CIA hands: the information was provided only after the IAEA had 'signed a letter promising to use the information about the suppliers for technical ends and to keep it secret'. But this concession had done little to advance the Iraqi cause. The blight of sanctions would continue to plague the Iraqi people.

By 1994 Iraq had divulged substantial amounts of information in response to UN enquiries, had formally agreed to long-term monitoring of its weapons potential, and had granted UN inspectors unprecedented access to buildings and locations throughout the country. Still Rolf Ekeus and other UN officials, quite apart from the predictably hard-line Washington strategists, remained dissatisfied with the extent of Iraqi compliance. On 6 February 1994 Ekeus again declared that Iraq had not given him enough information on its chemical weapons, where-upon an Iraqi newspaper denounced him as 'evil' and 'wretched'. Still he persisted with his efforts. UN inspectors were again visiting various sites in the country to develop the facilities for long-term monitoring of Iraqi weapons programmes. In April the UN Secretary-General reported on the extent of the 'on-going monitoring and verification of Iraq's compliance' with the relevant parts of Resolution 687.[63] Here it was acknowledged that the 'major development' in the period under review was Iraq's acceptance of Resolution 715 (see Appendix 4), designed to extend the scope of the inspection regime. The failure of Baghdad to provide requested data was also noted, as was the 'good Iraqi co-operation' with the inspectors in their ballistic-missile protocol-building efforts.

Other matters covered in the report included: an incident in which Iraqis threw stones at a helicopter as it was evacuating two injured UN soldiers ('the Iraqi government has firmly denied any involvement in the attack'), the activities of UNSCOM 66 following Iraq's accept-ance of Resolution 715 (development of monitoring and verification facilities), the activities of UNSCOM 69 and UNSCOM 71, the inves-tigation of documentation released by the Iraqi authorities, and spe-cific investigations in particular areas (biological, nuclear, etc.). Finally, the scale of the aerial inspection regime was summarised: high-alti-tude U-2 reconnaissance aircraft were now flying once or twice a week (having so far flown a total of 201 missions), and UN helicopters had flown 273 missions to cover some 395 suspected sites. No mention was made of satellite surveillance.

The picture was now one of broad Iraqi compliance, but with many suspicions in the international community that Saddam was striving to escape the worst consequences of the embargo and to rebuild his weapons-procurement programme. In October 1993 Hans Blix, the IAEA direc-tor-general, had reported that 'in all essential aspects, the nuclear-weapons program is mapped and has been neutralized through the war or there-after'. Rolf Ekeus, for his part, now believed that Iraq's chemical pro-grammes had been dismantled, and that the UN inspectors had accounted for all 890 Scud-B missiles provided to Iraq by the Soviet Union through the 1970s and 1980s. Doubts remained that the biological weapons programme had been fully exposed and destroyed.[64] It was now being acknowledged that 'Saddam's aim is plainly to fulfill the letter of UN law by coming clean about Iraq's unconventional-weapons programs in order to get the sanctions lifted'; but at the same time 'monitors like Ekeus suspect he has no intention of obeying the spirit of the ban'.[65]

In October 1994 a further report was issued by the UN Secretary-General to note the progress to date in implementing the relevant parts of Resolution 687.[66] Again, in a detailed 20-page document, significant progress in many weapons-control sectors was described. Now 'the situation is much improved . . .', but there were still 'gaps and discrepancies', with great difficulties experienced in obtaining 'the necessary data, particularly in the biological area'. However, the report noted that such difficulties could be ascribed in large part to the fact that the Commission was roaming ever more widely, visiting new sites and so coming into contact 'with Iraqi personnel who have not previously had to deal with the Commission. . . . The Commission has received assurances that the missing information will be provided.'* In conclusion the report emphasised that the system for ongoing monitoring and verification, 'a highly complex and sizeable undertaking', had been established. This, of course, was far from the end of the story: 'Enough operating experience will have to be gained' to show that the system is able to provide the Security Council (i.e. the United States) with the assurance that it needs. Finally, the imaginative packaging of the report, in which – not for the first time – a tantalising reference to the ending of the embargo is made: '*After the lifting of sanctions, the system, if it is to be effective and endure, will have to be a dynamic one, refined and augmented in the light of experience, of technological developments and of the growth of Iraq's economy.*' What *lifting of sanctions*? What *growth of Iraq's economy*? Eighteen months later (early 1996), the United States strives not only to maintain sanctions but (for example, by new pressures on Jordan) to tighten them yet further.

By 1995 the questions were still being asked. Had the UN inspectors uncovered all the information they needed? Was the monitoring system adequate to its intended purposes? Was the confusion about

---

* As I carefully read this report, and its predecessors and successors, I increasingly felt trapped in a Kafkaesque world. Endless protracted queries, repetitions, seemingly petty details endlessly rehearsed with no way out. UN inspectors satisfied on this or that point, but then a quick shift to other areas. No real light at the end of the tunnel. Never the slightest hint that the health and very lives of an entire population were being ransomed through the bizarre cynicism of a handful of comfortable Washington strategists.

the existence of biological-weapons materials, dating back to the late 1980s, a sufficient reason for prolonging the misery of the Iraqi people? Was Washington still insisting on Saddam's removal before the punitive sanctions could be lifted? Would the embargo, now well into its sixth year, survive another year? Another ten years? By 1995 the UN inspectors were claiming that they had destroyed Iraq's entire capacity to produce weapons of mass destruction. Morever, they were claiming also that the Iraqis had co-operated fully with all their demands. Said Jaako Ylitalo, the chief UNSCOM field officer in Baghdad in October 1994: *'They [the Iraqis] have done an excellent job. Our commission is convinced it's all over. It is watertight. We have faith in the work we have done.'* A report presented in New York on 13 October confirmed these broad conclusions. Now Washington was under growing pressure to explain its main objectives. Was it really interested in the implementation of UN resolutions (primarily the crucial Resolution 687), or was the United Nations little more than an increasingly transparent cloak for a covert strategic agenda?

A further report (December 1994) from the UN Secretary-General to the Security Council raised the familiar doubts, criticisms and uncertainties, but at the same time acknowledged that 'much progress' had been made: 'All items verified as being proscribed have now been destroyed. The ongoing monitoring and verification system is provisionally operational. The major elements for chemical and missile monitoring are in place.'[67] So was this the end? In fact it was a new beginning: 'Interim monitoring in the biological area is *about to commence*' (my italics). If the nuclear and chemical questions had been settled, biological matters could now present further pretexts for an indefinite prolongation of the embargo. The Iraqi defector General Wafiq al-Samarra'i, a former head of Iraqi military intelligence, declared to *The Sunday Times* in London that Saddam had retained an arsenal of biological bombs – by burying them, as well as 80 Scud missiles, around the Salah al-Din region of Iraq. Ann Clwyd, British Labour Member of Parliament and CARDRI supporter, noted that the new information 'could jeopardise Saddam's chances of rehabilitating his reputation' – as if this were ever an option. Rolf Ekeus now moved to confirm that Iraq was still hiding details of its past biological arms programme, so crushing the faint hopes for a lifting of the embargo.

By March 1995 the biological issue had been inflated into a new Iraqi 'threat'. In the 1980s, according to the new revelations, up to 3.3 tons of bacteria – more than could have been needed for medical purposes – had been cultivated; but when UN inspectors asked for the growth media and documentation the Iraqis claimed that everything had been destroyed in the post-war uprisings. A senior UN official commented that the Iraqi 'stories were the most fanciful so far'. It was conceded that Iraq had complied fully in the nuclear and chemical areas. Now 'Baghdad's huge secret biological weapons effort' was 'the main obstacle to lifting economic sanctions'.[68] Madeleine Albright was now touring the Middle East to garner enough support so that an increasingly defensive United States would not have to use its Security Council veto for the retention of sanctions. Said White House spokesman Mike McCurry: 'Any modification of the sanctions regime that ameliorates the pressure that Saddam Hussein must feel is not at this time warranted.' Albright, with characteristic creative US diplomacy (i.e. threat and blackmail), secured her majority and sanctions were yet again retained. The British premier John Major had no doubt what he was expected to say: *'We are determined to ensure that the whole of Iraq's biological capability is detected and destroyed before there can be any question of adjustment to the sanctions regime.... We shall continue with good reason to approach sanctions rigorously in the interests of Iraq's peoples ...'**

In April an anticipated joint French/Russian resolution for the suspension of the oil embargo did not materialise because of the freshly-fuelled concerns about Iraq's biological weapons potential. By allegedly failing to meet all UNSCOM's demands – this time regarding stockpiles of biological material – Iraq had, in the words of one Western diplomat, 'shot itself in the foot'. He commented: 'Their game all along has been one of deception, but they're not very good at it and they keep getting caught.' Rolf Ekeus remained convinced that, biological weapons apart, the bulk of UNSCOM's work had been done: 'Our conclusion, and what we will present to the Security Council, is that we feel confident that, with the exception of the biological area, Iraq will not be able to develop any weapons of mass destruction or long-range missiles without being detected by the international controls.' Iraq had admitted that it had last imported 32 tonnes of complex biological 'growth media' – ideal for producing biological weapons – as late as 1991. About half of this material remained unaccounted for – a revelation that Washington greeted with glee. Yet another pretext had been contrived to continue the operation of the sanctions regime. In the event sanctions were retained in May 1995 and in the various 'reviews' for the rest of the year.

* See Chapter 3.

Iraq was finally driven to admit – just as it had done in other areas – that it had developed an extensive biological weapons programme, contradicting past statements to UN weapons inspectors. Ekeus now declared that Iraq began its research on biological weapons, including anthrax, in 1985, and by 1990 had stored large quantities in concentrated form. The Iraqis were now claiming that all the agents had been destroyed in October 1990, just three months before the start of the Gulf War; and was now promising to provide a full and final report on its biological weapons research by the end of the month (July 1995). Washington and London, predictably enough, remained unimpressed, and highlighted Iraq's failure to destroy some missile-manufacturing equipment as further evidence that Saddam Hussein could not be trusted and that the sanctions would have to remain. On 20 July, in further significant concessions, Iraq agreed to destroy the equipment in question, and also submitted a draft report to UN inspectors giving details of its past biological weapons programme.

In August the Iraqi defector Lieutenant-General Hussein Kamel, one of Saddam's sons-in-law, allegedly stated that Iraq's plans to test an atomic bomb had been forestalled only by the Gulf War. Here, Washington decided, were fresh reasons to keep sanctions. Iraq had only admitted the extent of its biological weapons programme for fear of what revelations the defectors might offer to the West. Clearly, in such a context, Saddam could not be trusted. All the efforts of Rolf Ekeus and the other UN personnel were counting for nothing. At this time Ekeus himself was declaring that the Iraqi government had taken 'a new turn' in its degree of compliance: 'At last we have come to a situation where Iraq voluntarily and actively provides the Commission with information.' Still he conceded that more information was needed; in particular, regarding the biological development of botulism and anthrax agents. Fresh information on the nuclear programme would have to be taken back to Vienna for analysis by IAEA experts. Doubtless it would all take time, and doubtless the sanctions regime would be preserved intact throughout the entire period of the new investigations. Ekeus, even while maintaining his demands for more data, was still looking to the end of the embargo: *'The Iraqi leadership declared to me that its policy from now on is 100 per cent implementation of the ceasefire arrangements. So with that the Security Council, all members without exception, should have no choice about lifting the embargo.'*[69] Aware of Iraq's mounting despair in the belief that sanctions would never end, Ekeus urged Baghdad not to 'slam the door when we are so close to the end'. But, in August 1995, after five years of the most punishing sanctions, was the end in sight?

Now the Clinton administration was convinced that the collapse of the Iraqi regime was imminent: the defections, it was surmised, showed that soon Saddam would be consigned to history. Until then, many stratagems could be used to justify the indefinite prolongation of sanctions. On 18 August the US purported to have detected new hostile military moves in Iraq: perhaps Kuwait would again come under attack. No realistic observers believed it but in public-relations terms it was useful to stress that any relaxation of sanctions would be unwise. A few days later Rolf Ekeus reported that the Iraqis had now provided comprehensive information on germ warfare and missile programmes, but the surfeit of fresh data inevitably meant further delay: all the new information would have to be assessed, and there was no way that any useful conclusions could be reached before the sanctions regime was considered by the UN in September. None the less Ekeus commented: 'At last we have come to a situation where Iraq voluntarily and actively provides the commission with information.' But it remained clear that such co-operation would bring the Iraqis no rewards: the US priority remained the indefinite maintenance of the sanctions regime. In September, as expected, Madeleine Albright announced that the sanctions would continue. The availability of new weapons information had demonstrated that Saddam was not to be trusted. If no information were made available it showed that the Iraqis were concealing something; if comprehensive data was provided it proved that the Iraqis had lied in the past. In either case it was essential that Iraq 'be kept in its box'.

In late September 1995 the Pentagon was again asserting that Iraqi troops were menacing Kuwait. Said one official: 'We simply do not know if he is testing us, planning an attack on Kuwait or planning to murder more of his own people. Any action by him is madness; but then he's mad, so who knows?' Few journalists had any interest in questioning the familiar Pentagon assertions: with Saddam comprehensively demonised, anything could be said by Western pundits. On 11 October Ekeus reported to the Security Council that the Iraqi regime had concealed vast amounts of data on its chemical, biological and nuclear programmes. Madeleine Albright professed to find the observations 'chilling', while a British official noted that the Iraqis had 'made a nonsense' of earlier UN efforts to investigate their weapons plans.

By now the ploys were familiar: Washington remained committed to the indefinite prolongation of the sanctions regime. Anything could

be said: the Iraqis had lied; Saddam was not to be trusted (who could
know when he might not strike again?); what fearsome devices might
he not have hidden away (on one occasion a massively corroded gadget
was fished out of the Tigris to demonstrate Iraqi perfidy – 'Believe
me,' said a Washington spokesman, 'it contains very sophisticated technology'). There would always be ample reasons – many of them clearly
spurious and absurd – to justify the continued imposition of sanctions.
Serious journalists could observe that Iraqi weapons were no longer a
threat to the regime (thus Jonathan Rugman, *The Guardian*, 14 October 1995: 'It is generally agreed that Iraq has already destroyed all of
its weapons of mass destruction, either under UN supervision or in
anticipation of allied bombing raids . . .'). But sanctions were set to
run on through 1996. Washington remained committed to the genocide
of the Iraqi people.

THE 706/712/986 PLOY

From the time of the first post-war UN report (Ahtisaari, March 1991:
' . . . nothing . . . had quite prepared us for the particular form of devastation which has now befallen the country'), the scale of the suffering being endured by the Iraqi people was well known to politicians,
UN officials and others. It was partly in response to the Ahtisaari findings that paragraph F(20) was included in Resolution 687:

> . . . the prohibitions against the sale or supply to Iraq of commodi-
> ties or products, other than medicine and health supplies, and prohi-
> bitions against financial transactions related thereto, contained in
> resolution 661 (1990) shall not apply to foodstuffs . . . or . . . to materials
> and supplies for essential civilian needs . . .

The inclusion of this supposedly humanitarian provision was largely
an exercise in cynical *realpolitik* – as were a number of related US
initiatives in the months and years that followed. It was essential to
Washington that it deflect widespread charges that, by denying Iraq
food and medicine, it was perpetrating a deliberate genocide on the
Iraqi people. President Bush had portrayed the anti-Iraq campaign as a
highly virtuous venture: the crusade could not now be tarnished by
evidence of American crimes against humanity. Yet paragraph F(20)
had minimal practical consequences. It nominally allowed Iraq access
to food and medicine, *but only after individual requests, most of them*

desperately urgent, had been subjected to protracted bureaucratic scrutiny, and only to the extent that inadequately funded charities or Iraq itself could purchase the necessary supplies. But now Iraqi assets throughout the world were frozen, Iraqi access to the international financial markets was blocked, and there was a complete ban on the sale of Iraqi oil, the country's principal national resource. These restrictions, supported by US military power, meant that there was no way that Iraq could purchase the supplies that were essential to meet the basic needs of the Iraqi people.

In May 1991 the UN Sanctions Committee nominally authorised the unfreezing of about $1 billion in Iraqi assets held in US, Swiss, British and Japanese banks to enable Baghdad to purchase essential supplies. This move was followed by a further decision on 12 June that 31 countries be allowed to release $3.75 billion for the same purposes. However, the committee stipulated also that any release of funds should be *at the discretion of the particular governments*, which meant in reality that few if any of the funds were made available to the Iraqi government for the specified humanitarian purposes. Already there were many claimants – some, not all, acting in good faith and with good cause – with an eye on Iraqi assets. It was by no means certain that, even with a genuine unfreezing of Iraqi assets, the Iraqi people would see an early end to malnutrition, disease and starvation.

Now the Sanctions Committee had access to further information about the deteriorating condition of the ordinary civilian population of Iraq. On 22 July 1991 the results of a 'field-based' mission to Iraq were presented to the committee in New York. A 'food sector team' had conducted market surveys in 16 out of the 18 governorates, covering most provincial capitals and accounting for 95 per cent of the national food crop production. A 'water and sanitation team' visited the governorates of Kut, Amarah, Basra, Erbil and Dohuk to conduct extensive investigations; and inspected water treatment plants, and had discussions with ministry officials in Baghdad. A 'health team' carried out detailed investigations covering paediatric wards and health centres in 5 governorates in the south and 6 in the north. An 'energy sector team' visited 15 power generating plants and many transmission substations from Basra in the south to Mosul in the north. Extensive discussions were held between team members and Iraqi officials at all levels, including the Deputy Prime Minister, Tariq Aziz.

The mission produced a detailed report which was submitted by the UN Secretary-General to the Sanctions Committee. At the July presentation the following 'basic facts' were emphasised:

There is a clear and undeniable humanitarian need in Iraq;

It is absurd and indefensible for the United Nations to pay for these needs when numerous other urgent crises and disasters, from Bangladesh to the Horn of Africa, cry out for our attention;

Iraq has considerable oil reserves and should pay to meet these needs itself;

If this committee were to decide that Iraq should be allowed to use funds from oil sales or facilitate the use of blocked accounts to meet "essential civilian needs", a suitable control mechanism and monitoring system should be identified and put in place.

The mission findings and the thrust of the presentation were unambiguous ('Given the solid and thorough work done by our teams, I do not believe we are crying wolf'): the teams had confirmed the 'near-apocalyptic' conditions that Ahtisaari had described a short time before. It could not be denied that Iraq was on the brink of famine. What was to be done?

Washington faced a dilemma. Not to act would be rightly seen as callous in the extreme; yet the US strategists had no inclination to mitigate the harshness of the sanctions regime to any degree. The task facing Washington was to keep the embargo intact while at the same time providing a propaganda weapon that could be used to demonstrate its humanitarian concern. The mechanism whereby this was accomplished was Security Council Resolution 706 (15 August 1991) and two supplementary Council resolutions passed at strategic moments in the public-relations agenda. In unguarded moments US spokesmen revealed the true purpose behind 706 and its successors. Thus a Bush administration official told *The New York Times* that Resolution 706 was 'a good way to maintain the bulk of sanctions and not be on the wrong side of a potentially emotional issue' – the *potentially emotional issue* being the US-induced starvation of the Iraqi people.

Resolution 706, passed by 13 votes to 1 (Cuba) with one abstention (Yemen), has been consistently represented in the Western media as allowing Iraq to sell 'up to $1.6 billion-worth of oil to buy food and medicines'. Iraq's failure to take up this offer has demonstrated yet again, according to the mass ranks of concerned Western pundits and politicians, Saddam Hussein's willingness 'to watch his people starve'. The fact that it is only Iraq's rationing system that has prevented mass starvation under the pressure of sanctions is ignored. It is useful to consider the terms of Resolution 706 and its successors (see Appendix 5), and what their adoption would mean for the Iraqi nation.

The main provision of 706 is that sales of Iraqi oil, subject to approval by the Sanctions Committee, will produce revenues (not to exceed $1.6 billion) that will be paid into a UN-administered escrow account, with the revenues then to be used for various purposes – *not only to meet Iraqi humanitarian needs*. The following points should be emphasised:

1. The realised revenues, in addition to funding Iraqi humanitarian needs, would be used also 'to cover the cost to the United Nations of its activities under the present resolution . . .'; to make 'appropriate payments to the United Nations Compensation Fund . . .'; to cover 'the full costs of carrying out the tasks authorized by Section C of resolution 687 . . .'; to cover 'the full costs incurred by the United Nations in facilitating the return of all Kuwaiti property seized by Iraq . . .'; and to cover 'half the costs of the Iraq–Kuwait Boundary Demarcation Commission'. This means that only a proportion – perhaps a *small* proportion – of the stipulated $1.6 billion would be available for Iraqi humanitarian purposes.

2. The entire scheme – oil sales, administration of the escrow account, food distribution, etc. – would be administered by non-Iraqis; that is, by the Sanctions Committee, the Secretary General, other UN officials, and other personnel acting under UN auspices. This means that Iraq would suffer a massive loss of sovereignty, an important violation of Article 2(1) of the UN Charter. It would mean that Iraq was well on the way to trusteeship status, where the management of the national economy and the provision of key social services were no longer under the control of the Iraqi government. That Washington *intended* to reduce Iraq to trusteeship status is further demonstrated by the intrusive provisions of Resolution 715 (11 October 1991) (see Appendix 4).

3. No country could be reasonably expected to surrender its principal national resource to an international body dominated by a power overtly and covertly committed to the overthrow of that country's government.

4. Even if Iraq were to accept loss of sovereignty in exchange for the relatively small realised revenues over which it would have

no control, there could be no confidence that the Sanctions Committee would be primarily motivated by humanitarian considerations in its allocation of the realised sums. This is the committee that has denied Iraq access to disinfectants, sanitary towels, glue for school textbooks, and shroud materials for the dead (see Chapter 3). No independent observer can imagine that the committee would have a fresh interest in the good of the Iraqi people. Washington, with its committee veto, would continue to control the committee in the light of the principal US objective – the collapse of the Iraqi regime.

In this context it was inevitable that Iraq would reject Resolution 706 – an outcome that Washington clearly calculated. Baghdad would scarcely be likely to sacrifice its national sovereignty, hand over its oil resource to a US-dominated committee, fund its declared enemies, and grant hostile states the means to further destabilise the regime. The July 1991 investigatory mission, led by Prince Sadruddin Aga Khan, the UN Secretary-General's executive delegate, had confirmed that Iraq was 'on the brink of calamity' and had estimated that to provide food and medicines, and to restore some basic services including sanitation, would need expenditure of about $6.8 billion over a 12-month period. In couching the designated aid (Resolution 706(1)) at an uncertain proportion of $1.6 billion the US strategists had further ensured that the resolution would have little appeal to the Iraqi government. But the propaganda purpose, the sole objective of the exercise, had been accomplished. A pliant and unreflective press could be relied upon to advertise the reasonable magnanimity of Resolution 706, with the essential corollary that Saddam's indifference to the suffering of his people was again demonstrated. There was no dent in the sanctions regime and the new propaganda tool could exploited repeatedly.

In early September 1991 the UN Secretary-General issued a report 'pursuant to Paragraph 5' of Resolution 706.[70] This document, running to 37 pages (including annexes), sets out the detailed provisions for the implementation of 706 on the apparent assumption that its authorisation by the Security Council means that it can now have practical effect. Apart from the insufficiency of the stipulated sum (UN Secretary-General Perez de Cuellar had himself indicated an estimated shortfall of $800 million), the central question was how 706 could be implemented without Iraqi co-operation. One suggestion was that Iraqi oil from the disputed Kurdish region of Kirkuk might soon start flowing along the pipeline to the Turkish city of Yurmurtalik, a clear signal that the West intended to access Iraqi oil reserves with or without the approval of Baghdad. In September 1991 a new Security Council resolution was passed, seemingly to bolster 706. Now Resolution 712 (19 September 1991), passed by 13 to 1 (Cuba) with one abstention (Yemen), reaffirmed the terms of Resolution 706 and called upon states 'to cooperate fully' in its implementation. There was no reason to suppose that 712 (see Appendix 5) would succeed in attracting Iraqi support where 706 had failed. On 24 November Prince Sadruddin reported that there had been no breakthrough in his talks over Baghdad's bitter refusal to accept Resolution 706 (and by implication 712): 'The government of Iraq may be held responsible for failing to take advantage of the window of opportunity – *narrow and constraining though it may be* – afforded by the arrangements for oil exports and imports of essential needs.' Iraq continued to complain that 706 would undermine national sovereignty, turning the country into a virtual UN protectorate.

The desultory discussions continued into 1993 and beyond, with Iraq seemingly wavering on occasions in the light of the mounting privations of the Iraqi people. Arguments that Iraq be allowed to administer the sales of its own oil were consistently opposed by Washington, though Baghdad continued to rail against what it perceived as 'humiliating political preconditions'. Talks in July 1993, between the Iraqi deputy foreign minister Riyadh al-Qaysi and UN legal personnel, yet again ended in failure, while at the same time pressure continued to mount for an end to the embargo. In June 1994, under growing international pressure, Washington reluctantly agreed to allow a partial reopening of the Iraqi oil pipeline through Turkey, a significant psychological boost to Baghdad but one with no revenue benefits to the Iraqi regime.

In early 1995, with mounting evidence of the destitution and suffering of the Iraqi people, the West decided it was necessary to relaunch the 706/712 propaganda exercise. This was accomplished by the passing of Resolution 986 (see Appendix 5) in the Security Council on 14 April. According to the preliminary hype, this resolution was designed to increase the money involved, to change the distribution monitoring mechanisms, and to change the proportions that would be allocated to specific purposes. Now $1 billion-worth of oil could be sold under United Nations control every 90 days, though still with the familiar constraints on Iraqi sovereignty. Now a number of states – Russia, France, China, Indonesia and others – were prepared to argue that it was time to consider the lifting of sanctions altogether; with Russia and France declaring that there was no point in adopting a resolution merely as a 'public relations tool enabling the US and Britain to continue blaming Iraq for hardships caused by sanctions . . .'.[71] In the event, Iraq predictably rejected Resolution 986, declaring that only a total lifting of the oil ban would be acceptable. An Iraqi television broadcast, announcing the decision of the Iraqi cabinet chaired by Saddam Hussein, depicted 'this unfair resolution' as a 'dangerous violation of Iraq's sovereignty and national unity, for which the Iraqi people have paid rivers of blood'. Iraq, it was claimed, had now met all the UN conditions for a total lifting of the oil ban. In early 1996, with the plight of the Iraqi people growing ever more desperate, the regime indicated its willingness to discuss with the UN yet again how oil might be sold to relieve the widespread suffering.

Resolution 986, like 706 and 712 before it, appeared to be no more than a cynical political ploy, a fresh public-relations diversion from on-going US efforts to tighten the embargo yet further. Any estimate of the significance of the 706/712/986 stratagem can only be made in the context of overall US policy on Iraq. Any pretensions to humanitarian concern must be set against the known and protracted effects of the sanctions regime on the Iraqi people. We need to remember what it means to use economic sanctions against ordinary helpless people, against babies, pregnant women, the sick and the old. We need to remember what it means to target the powerless . . .

3 Targeting the Powerless

As a lawyer . . . I see the blockade clearly as a crime against humanity, in the Nüremburg sense, as a weapon of mass destruction . . . a weapon for the destruction of the masses . . . it attacks those segments of the society that are the most vulnerable . . . infants and children, the chronically ill, the elderly and emergency medical cases.

Ramsey Clark, former US Attorney-General

Perhaps the general western public will agree with the apparent official view that emaciated Iraqi children are either legitimate pawns in a just struggle or a future threat to be extinguished.

Sabah Jawad and Kamil Mahdi[1]

PREAMBLE

The scale of the Western onslaught on Iraq in the Gulf War, totally disproportionate in view of the declared objective of expelling Iraqi forces from Kuwait, resulted in the virtual destruction of a society. The early post-war reports from journalists, aid agencies, UN officials and others conveyed a consensual picture of a civilian population facing unprecedented catastrophe. The Ahtisaari report (20 March 1991)[2] set the scene for what was to follow: a spate of unambiguous portrayals of collapsed communities, of traumatised and confused people struggling desperately to survive in a shattered environment. For example, an early report from the Save the Children Fund (compiled by a team that formed part of a delegation, hosted by the Iraqi Red Crescent, that included members of Oxfam, Care, the Jordanian Red Crescent and the Libyan Red Crescent) noted that the Iraqi health, water and sanitation services had collapsed 'as a result primarily of the bombing of infrastructure and communications facilities . . . and the shortages of fuel and parts under the continued application of international sanctions'.[3]

The 'severe and increasing problem of food supply', caused by Iraq's 'inability to import food – which it did previously for 70 per cent of national requirements', was highlighted; as was the fact that the problems facing the civilian population could only worsen if the prevailing conditions were allowed to continue.[4] The report further noted that the sophisticated infrastructure of Baghdad, which had formerly provided services for one-quarter of the Iraqi population, had been 'systematically crippled and destroyed' and that equal devastation 'was also witnessed in towns along the road leading from Jordan to Baghdad (reports confirmed 'that the destruction is similar in other parts of the country').[5] The various essential services (electricity, water, sewage treatment, telecommunications, etc.), already eroded by sanctions before the war, were now in a state of almost total disarray (for example, electricity generation, essential to other services, was now 4 per cent of pre-war levels). The missile attacks had caused 'identical damages' to virtually all the power stations, so preventing the cannibalising of equipment and blocking attempts at reconstruction. Under sanctions, the country was 'sliding downhill fast. . . . All industry has come to a standstill, people are without work and there is no real economic activity. . . . *This is a new kind of war which understands and takes advantage of the vulnerability of technological advances. . . . The situation is deteriorating rapidly and it will get worse in the months ahead . . .*' (my italics).[6]

American medical workers who had visited Iraq were reporting in April 1991 that the country's problems were insurmountable while the sanctions remained in force. Joost Hiltermann, the Middle East organiser for Physicians for Human Rights (PHR), observed that the allied bombs had taken 'the brain out of the country's ability to survive'. In the same spirit the PHR president Jack Geiger, having witnessed the devastation around Basra, described the effect as: 'Bomb now, die later . . . you just cause the system to collapse.' The group's report painted what was by now becoming a familiar picture: malnutrition, diarrhoea and dehydration among children, sick people being given contaminated drinking water, water purification plants destroyed by the bombing, and a crippled economy.[7] On 10 May 1991 British Prime Minister John Major, in a speech to the Scottish Conservative Party Conference, declared that Britain would veto any UN attempt to weaken sanctions against Iraq 'for so long as Saddam Hussein remains in power'. This was said at a time when the United Nations Children's Fund (UNICEF) and the World Health Organisation (WHO) were warning of a potentially disastrous situation facing Iraq if the present circumstances were allowed to persist. There was growing evidence of a cholera epidemic, and UN workers were reporting cases of the formerly-eradicated diseases of marasmus and kwashiorkor, indicating severe malnutrition.[8]

The war, devastating but of relatively short duration (see Chapter 1), was over but there was no end to the systematic onslaught on the Iraqi people. Before the war Iraq was a relatively prosperous nation with a sophisticated health and welfare system, good transport and communications facilities, and ample food and water. Now this formerly modern nation was being forced into progressive decline. Bernt Bernander, the UN Co-ordinator and Special Representative for Relief Operations in Iraq, declared: 'Sewer systems have failed; water purification plants don't function. People are seeing an incidence of malnutrition where previously there was none.'[9] The vast bulk of the population were suffering, 'but the poorest people are being hurt the most'. The block on food imports and the rocketing prices of domestically-produced foodstuffs were forcing most people to scale back on their diets. This, added to the unavoidability of drinking contaminated water, was making young children, the sick and the elderly 'highly vulnerable to severe malnutrition, marasmus, gastrointestinal illnesses and other diseases'. Medicines in what were formerly well-equipped hospitals were 'rapidly dwindling', and even the requirement of feeding babies was rapidly becoming 'a luxury that poor people simply cannot afford'.[10]

The situation in Iraq continued to deteriorate through 1991 and thereafter, with the comprehensive block on imports hampering all efforts at industrial and social reconstruction. In early 1993 UN-linked aid agencies were reporting that the 'socio-economic situation in Iraq . . . is expected to deteriorate further . . . because of United Nations sanctions, there are shortages of all imported goods, including food'. The escalating prices in local markets were subjecting ordinary Iraqis to 'severe hardship . . .'.[11] In February the United Nations Children's Fund (UNICEF) commissioned Dr Eric Hoskins, a Harvard expert on public health, to compile a 'situation analysis' for Iraq. The resulting 32-page 'preliminary draft' identifies 'the impact of war and sanctions on Iraqi women and children', stating that 'nearly three years of economic sanctions have created circumstances in Iraq where the majority of the civilian population are now living in poverty . . . the greatest threat to the health and well-being of the Iraqi people remains the difficult economic conditions created by . . . internationally mandated sanctions and by the infrastructural damage wrought in the 1991 military conflict'. The 'executive summary' concludes:

Sanctions, unless applied in a manner which safeguards the civilian population, may threaten the more vulnerable members of society –

especially children and women. Indeed, it may be that one funda-
mental contradiction remains: that politically motivated sanctions
(which are by definition imposed to create hardship) cannot be im-
plemented in a manner which spares the vulnerable.[12]

This conclusion, added to the disturbing finding of the report, proved
far too embarrassing to the West: a UNICEF official declared that the
report's conclusions were 'not entirely based on fact', and the report
was shelved. The official suggested that the problems were caused in
part by Iraq running down its own social services. Dr Hoskins continued to defend the 'good document' that he had produced. In fact his
findings were completely confirmed by the 'Special Alert' report jointly
published in July 1993 by the UN Food and Agriculture Organisation
(FAO) and the World Food Programme (WFP).[13]

An FAO/WFP Crop and Food Supply Assessment Mission visited
Iraq from 14 to 28 June 1993 to assess the current food situation throughout the country. Mission members travelled through Iraq, visiting 17
of the 18 governorates, interviewing farmers, traders and others, and
carrying out independent investigations to determine food availability
and market prices. The Mission reported good co-operation from the
Baghdad-based UN agencies and the Iraqi government agencies concerned with food and agriculture. The subsequent report emphasises at
the outset that Iraq would not normally be a 'food insecure' country:
'Rather it is a country whose economy has been devastated by the
recent war and subsequent civil strife, but *above all by the continued*
sanctions since August 1990, which have virtually paralyzed the whole
economy and generated persistent deprivation, chronic hunger, endemic
undernutrition, massive unemployment and widespread human suffer-
ing' (my italics). This meant that 'a vast majority of the Iraqi population is living under the most deplorable conditions and is simply engaged
in a struggle for survival; but with increasing numbers losing out in
the struggle every day a grave humanitarian tragedy is unfolding'.[14]

The report confirms 'a substantial deterioration' in the food supply
situation 'in all parts of the country'; and notes 'the commonly recognized pre-famine indicators' (exorbitant prices, collapse of private incomes, soaring unemployment, massively reduced food consumption,
drastic depletion of personal assets, high morbidity levels, escalating
crime, rapidly increasing numbers of destitute people, etc.). Only the
public rationing system had so far prevented 'massive starvation' throughout the country, though the average calorific intake was now about
half the pre-war level and the rations were deficient in essential micro-

nutrients and protein: 'the nutritional status of the population continues to deteriorate at an alarming rate . . . large numbers of Iraqis now have food intakes lower than those of the populations in the disaster stricken African countries'.[15] These facts and related data collected by the health expert Dr Salman Rawaf, collaborating with various international medical organisations, led him to depict the entire Iraqi population as '18.8 million in a refugee camp'; and led others, responding in the same spirit, to characterise Iraq as 'a concentration camp with a population of 18 million, one third of which are children – of whom at least a hundred thousand are already dead, not from war but from hunger'. The London-based charity Medical Aid for Iraq (MAI) noted that whereas from 1980 to 1990, even under the pressures of the Iran–Iraq War, the infant death rate had halved, under sanctions child mortality had quadrupled, there were no vaccines, and diseases of all types were seeing a massive increase.

All this was known to Western leaders who continued to represent the sanctions regime as a necessary and virtuous enterprise. It was now widely acknowledged that despite the Iraqi rationing system the food shortages were 'becoming acute,'[16] with no prospect of an early end to the embargo. Even if Iraq were seen to be complying over the weapons issue, other matters would remain: in early 1994 the London-based Economist Intelligence Unit (EIU), as one authoritative source, did not anticipate that sanctions would be lifted to allow any Iraqi trade in oil before the end of 1995, and 'it may be even longer than that . . .'.[17] Now it was widely perceived that Washington and London intended to maintain sanctions on an indefinite basis, not as a matter of legality or human rights but as a matter of long-term oil strategy and regional hegemony. It is useful to note the Iraqi environment to which sanctions were being applied, and to profile the working of the sanctions system, before considering in more detail the significance of economic sanctions for Iraqi communities.

THE RAVAGED ENVIRONMENT

The condition of the environment of Iraq (see also 'The Environment', Chapter 1) – the state of the air and the land, the condition of the water and other natural resources – continued to define the overall context in which all efforts at reconstruction had to be attempted. The devastating impact of the war, in Kuwait as well as Iraq, was seen in part as massive environmental degradation – with many questions yet to be answered. What were the immediate and long-term consequences of bombing hundreds of textile factories, petrochemical plants and oil refineries throughout the land? Of bombing chemical, biological and nuclear facilities? Of the huge quantities of unexploded ordnance, shell fragments, spent depleted-uranium (DU) ordnance and wrecked military vehicles? Of the massive troop movements throughout the region? What were the consequences of all this for both the devastated urban environments and the fragile desert ecology?

Ross B. Mirkarimi, an environmental specialist working for the US-based Arms Control Research Center, has commented that the environmental consequences of the war did not remain limited to the combat zone, that 'unless proper analysis is conducted for preventing the war's long-term effects, tens of thousands of hapless civilians, as far as a thousand miles away, could become "collateral casualties"'. Moreover, it is 'quite likely that *yet unborn children of the region may be asked to pay the highest price, the integrity of their DNA*'[18] (my italics). Such considerations should be weighed in the balance not only when deciding to wage war but also when choosing the methods and means to be used in the planned conflict.

The need for further scientific environmental research should not be allowed to obscure the important work, highlighted by Mirkarimi and others, that has already been carried out. For example, bacteriological analysis conducted for the Harvard study team found that more than half the population tested in 15 of the Iraqi governorates were exposed to faecal contamination in their drinking water, so providing a direct route for pathogens and the likelihood of waterborne disease epidemics. Research by Iraqi scientists and others revealed a complex mix of airborne pollutants, which in itself has posed fresh problems for economic reconstruction. Should bomb-damaged factories, newly prone to injecting pollutants into the environment, be allowed to operate? Or should they be closed down, in the absence of spare parts for remedial repairs, so guaranteeing further industrial collapse? In 1992, a year after the end of the war, the 'stew of contaminants' continued to make breathing a hazardous undertaking in many areas. The incidence of respiratory disease had risen sharply, with children and the elderly particularly at risk. And in all the areas where it was dangerous to breathe the air it was hazardous also to drink the water.

The investigation (September 1991) highlighted by Mirkarimi found that most of Iraq's entire population had been directly exposed to waterborne diseases in their potable water supply. Tests for coliform or faecal contamination yielded 156 positive, with 52 either negative or unconfirmed; about half the areas tested, weighted for population density, showed evidence of gross contamination. The researchers found solid waste accumulating in the streets, raw sewage overflows around homes and in the streets, raw sewage flowing into rivers in which children played and washed, drinking water being drawn from contaminated rivers, and drinking water being drawn from watermains contaminated from adjacent sewage pipes. About two-thirds of all people surveyed in 7 of 9 governorates had lost their access to tap water, primarily because the lack of spare parts had prevented the repair of pumps, watermains and electrical supplies.[19]

The comprehensive bombing of oil wells, oil refineries, industrial plant and power stations had resulted in the release of substantial volumes of pollutants (see Table 1.1). In Basra vast quantities of oil and suffocating smoke were released; at Dibis, oil, petroleum, naphtha, emulsifier, tofloc 300 and sulphuric acid; north of Kirkuk, sulphur (2.5 tons burned for more than a month), carbon monoxide, sulphur and nitrogen oxides, hydrogen sulphide, etc.; at Baiji, carbon monoxide, sulphur and nitrogen oxides, hydrogen sulphide and lead oxide; at the Baghdad baby milk plant, large quantities of CFCs (from freon refrigeration cylinders) were released, as well as carbon monoxide, sulphur and nitrogen oxides, and other emissions.[20] To these persistent hazards, caused initially through widespread and repeated bombing but prolonged through the economic embargo, were added the dangers associated with depleted-uranium ordnance and the massive quantities of unexploded bombs and shells. One US military expert, quoted in *The Washington Post* (1 March 1991), commented: 'At least 600 bombs, rockets and artillery shells dropped or fired every day of the war will have failed to explode and thus constitute a continuing hazard somewhere in the former combat zone.' This suggests that around 30,000 pieces of unexploded ordnance continued to litter the battle zone in the period after the war.* Kuwait, with substantial international assistance, estimated that it would take two to three years to clear unexploded ordnance on its territory. In Iraq, with no international help and subject to the unending embargo, the problem is inevitably deep-seated and interminably prolonged – a continuing cause of maimings and fatalities, as indeed is unexploded ordnance in many former battle zones around the world.

---

* The UK Medical Educational Trust reported that 6 people were being killed every day (as of November 1991) by picking up or standing on unexploded ordnance: 1000 deaths so far (*Continuing Health Costs of the Gulf War*, London, October 1992).

The punitive sanctions have meant the Iraq has been denied the opportunity for post-war reconstruction that typically takes place in defeated nations. In consequence the degraded and polluted environment reported in 1991/92 saw only minimal improvement in later years. Thus a 1994 assessment mission to Iraq organised by the International Federation of Red Cross and Red Crescent Societies discovered that, though repairs had been made to the infrastructure, they were significantly limited because of lack of spare parts and replacement systems. After visiting hospitals and interviewing officials the mission summarised the sanitation problems:

- Safe drinking water remained a problem in many of the governorates, with the poorer areas of the cities still not connected to the supply systems;

- Raw sewage was still being fed into rivers and canals;

- Sanitation facilities in many hospitals had collapsed, causing serious health problems;

- In Basra more than 100,000 displaced people were living in deserted houses, unfinished buildings, etc., with no water or sanitation facilities; children were playing in large ponds of polluted water that covered the streets;

- In the 3 northern governorates the lack of electrical power was affecting the sanitation facilities and the supply of drinking water to the 3 major cities. Sulaimaniya was having frequent power cuts; Erbil was experiencing power cuts every day; and in Dihok there was no electricity at all, apart from a generator powering one hospital.[21]

Reports from Iraqi sources, while often trying to present an optimistic picture, were tending to confirm the findings of foreign researchers, aid agencies, and UN workers in the field. Thus a report from the Iraqi Ministry of Culture and Information noted that main feeder water pipes were suffering some 18,000 to 24,000 blockages and breaks, a three-fold increase on pre-embargo levels, with the performance of water treatment systems reduced by as much as 80 per cent due to the lack of spare parts; that the quality of drinking water had been seriously affected by the insufficient levels of chlorine; that most sewage pumping stations had ceased to operate; that raw sewage was being discharged into rivers at the rate of 5 cubic metres per second, so promoting waterborne diseases; that there had been a reduction in solid waste collection and disposal because of the lack of spare parts for trucks and other equipment, so promoting airborne diseases; that the number of specialised vehicles for road building had decreased from about 6000 to 655, with most of these out of operation; that most civil engineering projects had been abandoned; and that green areas had diminished, both because maintenance equipment was no longer available and because trees had been used for fuel following the bombing of gas stations, oil stations and electricity generating plant.[22]

A broadly consensual picture emerges from all the available sources: one of an entire nation being denied the means to reconstruct the basic services that are necessary for human life. The means whereby this violation of human rights is not only maintained but progressively intensified is the sanctions system, an effective international bureaucratic tool for inflicting a silent holocaust on a people. It is useful to profile some of the principal features of this system.

THE SANCTIONS SYSTEM

A rigorous international system has been devised to block the flow of goods to Iraq. This system, nominally resting on the terms of the appropriate UN Security Council resolutions, has evolved as a genocidal instrument administered jointly by the official bureaucracies in individual countries and the UN Iraq Sanctions Committee.

If anyone wishes to send goods to Iraq it is necessary first to apply to the appropriate government department for a licence. In Britain applications are made to the Sanctions Unit, a department that functions under the Export Control Organisation of the Department of Trade and Industry (DTI); other countries have their own analogous arrangements. The application, which may be complex, is then processed over a period of time: the DTI Sanctions Unit, comprising about a dozen staff, is also administering sanctions on Libya, Serbia and Angola – so it is inevitable that licence applications sometimes wait in a queue, the first source of delay. If the application is seen to be defective in some way – for example, omitting crucial information – it is returned to the sender with a request for more details. When the application eventually satisfies the Sanctions Unit it is sent to the UN Iraq Sanctions Committee in New York, which is continuously receiving may application from various countries.

The Sanctions Committee, a reflection of the UN Security Council, comprises representatives of the five permanent members (the United States, the Russian Federation, China, France and Britain) and the ten rotating members who are on the Security Council at any particular time. Copies of the licence applications are circulated to all 15 committee members for consideration. Any single member can block an application or delay it indefinitely by asking for further details; only if no objection or delay is registered by any member is the application then approved. This means that every individual committee member has a decisive veto and can place a 'hold' on any particular application, pending further information and consideration. This is a deliberate recipe for delay and procrastination.

The meetings of the Sanctions Committee are held in closed session and at no fixed times. This means that objections to particular applications, many of which have humanitarian relevance, do not reach the public domain. Decisions cannot be openly debated or questioned; in particular, Iraq is allowed no voice in any of these proceedings. An official handout on the operations of the Committee notes that 'with 15 states represented . . . there is plenty of scope for debate on the application of sanctions'; and that debate usually concerns 'whether a particular application is humanitarian or not' and what advice to give to applicants. The 'scope for debate' inevitably means that decisions are often held over to subsequent meetings, by which time new objections may have surfaced. In all accounts the quickest decisions that result in approval involve a few months, from receipt of the initial application to the eventual despatch of goods; the most protracted, eventually yielding approval, very much longer. Clearly the use of the veto can yield a relatively speedy decision, though inevitable bureaucratic delays in the various Sanctions Units and the Sanctions Committee may mean that it is many weeks before an applicant is notified of the outcome.

The Sanctions Committee deals only with governments, which are required to submit applications through their Missions to the United Nations. As well as the powers of veto, 'hold' or approval, the Committee may also choose to modify an application as a prelude to further discussion or approval. There is nothing in the rules of the Committee that require it to meet in the event of an urgent humanitarian request. Again this is a sure recipe for delay cynically contrived for political purposes – principally the strategic agenda of the United States shadowed by Britain. The absence of any Iraqi voice on the Committee well illustrates the *realpolitik* character of the sanctions regime: *natural justice cries out for the manifest right of Iraq to appeal in such a forum for the basic humanitarian needs of the Iraqi people.*

The closed nature of the Committee deliberations prevents *details* of the discussions being publicly available but, as a somewhat feeble gesture to transparency, the *results* of Committee deliberations are made available to any UN member state that requests them. Via this route we may learn more about specific vetoes and approvals but rarely much about the discursive preamble to particular decisions. It *is* known that various states, pursuing their own covert agendas, frequently advance excuses and spurious justifications to block applications that have clear humanitarian relevance. It is important to stress that what to many people seem to be the reasonable *de jure* provisions of UN resolutions are not necessarily in accord with the *de facto* operation of the US-dominated Sanctions Committee. The well documented suborning of the Security Council by the United States is precisely echoed in the US manipulation of the Committee.

In September 1990, at a time when the sole UN authorisation for the trade sanctions rested on the terms of Resolution 661, the United States and Britain objected to a proposal from Yemen that the UN Office of the Legal Counsel should give guidelines on the relevance of humanitarian considerations to the situation of the Iraqi civilian population. Here the aim was to provide the Sanctions Committee with a framework for judging humanitarian applications, primarily those relating to drugs and foodstuffs, on a speedy basis to relieve human suffering as quickly and effectively as possible. The reason for the US/British objection was obvious: Washington wanted to retain sole power to decide what was or was not a humanitarian matter, with a view to imposing maximum deprivation on the Iraqi people. This cynical ploy was further exposed when, on 7 September 1990, the US representative, supported by its Western allies, vetoed a request by Bulgaria for permission to ship baby food to Iraq on the grounds that the food might be consumed by adults.

What was to be an enduring pattern soon became plain. On 10 September 1990 the United States, again predictably supported by Britain and France, blocked an Indian request to send foodstuffs to its nationals in Iraq and Kuwait; further consultations were needed. Similar requests by Yugoslavia and Sri Lanka were blocked on the ground that humanitarian need had not yet been verified, while at the same time the US, Britain and France continued to block all attempts to discuss the *nature* of humanitarian need as a way of addressing the worsening plight of the Iraqi civilian population. Washington was now even going so far as to insist on an investigation of reports that non-governmental humanitarian organisations, various aid charities, were sending food-stuffs through Jordan to Iraq – as if such activity were to be condemned.

The category of 'dual-use' products, where nominally humanitarian goods might be used for other purposes, became yet another device whereby Washington could maximise the suffering of Iraqi civilians. Who knows? Perhaps those surgical scissors might be melted down to make bullets, those children's clothes converted into military uniforms! Thus in March 1992 the Sanctions Committee blocked a request from the Netherlands to ship NCR computer equipment to Iraq, which according to the supplier company could only be used in specific haematology and hepatitis studies. In June the US representative blocked a request from Denmark to supply children's hospitals in Iraq, on the ground that the heaters might be useful elsewhere than in the designated hospitals. In the same spirit Britain objected to a request from the United Nations Food and Agriculture Organisation (FAO) for permission to supply 300 tons of insecticides to Iraq, since such chemicals might be used for other purposes.

A Turkish request to supply the Iraqi pharmaceutical company at Samarra with rubber tube and PVC sheet was blocked to prevent any enhancement of Iraq's crippled economy. This again was illustrative of what was to emerge as the prevailing pattern of obstruction: nothing that might help Iraq to reconstruct its devastated economy or to rebuild its social provisions was to be allowed. At every stage the sanctions regime operates to reduce Iraq to an impoverished state. A director of a small British company specialising in exports of mainly medical and hospital supplies describes what is involved in trying to trade with Iraq:

1. Before any individual or company can talk to an Iraqi buyer (private or public), they must apply for a licence to negotiate. . . . Licences to negotiate could take three to four weeks to issue.

2. Only when the licence is issued can you start talking . . . without fear of breaking the law.

3. Once the buyer and seller agree . . . the seller must then apply for a supply licence, which can take up to 20 weeks to issue.

4. In the meantime the Iraqi dinar is suffering daily devaluation and inflation beyond control.

5. 20 weeks later the seller receives the supply licence by which time the buyer's situation has changed.

In nearly 24 weeks, inflation and the continuous devaluation . . . will force the buyer to cancel the order or, at best, reduce the quality or quantity of the goods in order to raise the hard currency needed to finance the purchase. But any change to the application means that the whole process must start again.[23]

This trader, specialising in medical equipment, has no doubt that humanitarian supplies are 'certainly not' exempted from the operations of the sanctions regime; and he quotes the chilling figure that in 1994 was well known to anyone who bothered to notice: ' . . . UNICEF's expectation that 100,000 Iraqi children would die in 1994 as a direct result of the sanctions has, shamefully, been exceeded'.

The strategy of Washington, invariably supported by London, in blocking or delaying the bulk of possible exports to Iraq is well facilitated by the composition and powers of the Sanctions Committee. The Committee's capacity for disputation, delay, reconsideration, redrafting of applications, etc. significantly contributes to the use of cynical delaying tactics. Some of the difficulties have been admitted by UN officials. Thus the Austrian UN ambassador Peter Hohenfellner, one-time chairman of the Sanctions Committee, commented in interview that the need for the agreement of every member 'makes the work much more difficult'; with the so-called 'no-objection' procedure, designed supposedly to increase the Committee's effeciency (by allowing some applications through quickly), the problem remained 'that you could not necessarily respond very efficiently to the needs of the population'.[24]

Even efforts by non-aligned countries to allow innocent items such as books, pencils, other school supplies, blankets, shirts, boots, etc. through without obstruction were blocked by Washington. Hohenfellner: 'One school [of thinking] was the rather restrictive one saying we are not inclined to take . . . a more flexible view to all these goods as long as Iraq is not inclined to comply fully with the resolutions. We want to maintain the pressure on Iraq.'[25] This meant that everything possible – school supplies, clothes, toiletries, etc. – had to be blocked as a means of demoralising the Iraqi civilian population and so contributing to the collapse of the regime (Table 3.1 lists some of the items that the Sanctions Committee has either permanently vetoed or subjected to prolonged delays). Hohenfellner conceded that it was questionable to use Iraq's 'tough line' to 'make women and children and the other vulnerable groups, like handicapped and old people, hostage' – 'So, I had a very difficult time.'[26] But the culture of the Committee

TABLE 3.1   Items for Iraq vetoed by the UN Sanctions Committee

baby food	water purification chemicals
rice	medical swabs
various other foodstuffs	medical gauze
agricultural pesticides	medical syringes
shirts	medical journals
other adult clothes	musteen cancer drug
boots	angiseed heart stabiliser
children's clothes	cobalt sources for X-ray machines
leather material for shoes	incubators
thread for children's clothes	X-ray film
shoe laces	X-ray equipment
shroud material	catheters for babies
school books	specific umbilical catheters
glue for textbooks	suction catheters for blockages
school handicraft equipment	nasal gastric tubes
ping-pong balls	NO cylinders for women in labour
badminton rackets	medication for epilepsy
notebooks	canulas for intravenous drips
paper	disposable surgical gloves
pencils	bandages
pencil sharpeners	oxygen tents
erasers	surgical instruments
children's bicycles	stethoscopes
blankets	ECG monitors
nail polish	dialysis equipment
lipsticks	drugs for angina
soap	PVC for a private hospital
sanitary towels	ambulances
deodorants	polyester and acrylic yarn
tissues	nylon cloth for filtering flour
toothpaste	wool felt for thermal insulation
tooth brushes	all electrical equipment
toilet paper	concrete additives
shampoo	specific granite shipments
cleaning agents	all other building materials
rubber tubes	steel plate
PVC sheets	textile plant equipment

remained unchanged. Why, Washington would argue, should ping-pong balls be allowed: 'we don't believe that this is an essential civilian need'.[27]

The dominance of the Washington hard line in the Sanctions Committee, predicably echoed by London, has resulted in a massive number of vindictive and seemingly pointless vetoes. Thus:

6 February 1992 A consignment of ping-pong balls from Vietnam vetoed by United States, Britain, France and Japan.

3 April 1993 A consignment of tennis balls, children's clothes, adult clothes, pencils, sharpeners, erasers and school notebooks from Pakistan vetoed by United States, Britain, France and Japan.

4 August 1992 A consignment of children's bicycles vetoed by United States and Britain.

17 September 1993 Shroud material vetoed by United States and Britain; later released from UK; then export licence revoked under new UK DTI regulations; whole process of applications had to begin again.

26 April 1992 Water purification chemicals vetoed by United States and Britain.

24 July 1993 Cotton for medical use (swabs, gauze, etc.) vetoed by Britain.

1 June 1992 Application from Spanish consortium to help rebuild medical syringe factory (bombed in war) vetoed by Britain and France.

14 August 1993 Application from Japan to supply communication links for hospital use (i.e. pagers, hospital–ambulance links) vetoed by United States and Britain.

12 December 1991 A consignment of paper for hospital doctors vetoed by United States.

29 October 1992 Boxes of nail polish and lipsticks vetoed by Britain.

In 1994 a woman in Baghdad sent a pair of hand-knitted leggings to her daughter who lives in Britain and who had just had a baby, the woman's first grandchild. The daughter was contacted by the UK Customs and Excise department and informed that before being allowed to receive the leggings she had to apply to the Sanctions Committee for an import licence and be granted permission.

The Committee has also rejected various requests for the supply of textiles to Iraq, including thread for weaving children's clothes, on the ground that these items are an input to industry. Iraq, it seems, is to be denied a textile industry in case it threatens the peace and security of the region. A request from the French CIS company in Paris to supply Iraq with 1200 kilograms of nylon cloth for filtering flour was vetoed by the United States. The only purpose of such cloth is to serve the grain-mill filters to rid the flour of adulterants, stones and other foreign matter as a preliminary to baking. In the same punitive and vindictive spirit the Sanctions Committee rejected a number of requests for supplying Iraq with glue to be used in the preparation of textbooks and notebooks, needed by pupils at all educational levels. The permission was denied on the ground that the glue, typically used also in school handicraft lessons and technical education, was an input to industry. In the same way the supply of 120 tons of rock wool felt was blocked as an unjustified input to industry, just as blank audio cassettes were not allowed for the same reason. The Committee is therefore overt in its determination to deny Iraq any chance of rebuilding its industrial base, a prerequisite with the lifting of the oil-sales embargo for the reconstruction of the national economy and essential social services.

Again a common pattern had emerged. In June 1993 the United States vetoed the export to Iraq of 200 tons of polyester and acrylic yarn used in textile production on the ground that this constituted an input to industry; and at the same time Britain blocked the export of 300 tons of polyvinyl chloride (PVC) material for a non-governmental hospital on the ground that it was destined for the private hospitals sector – an eccentric reason from a British Tory government, explicable only on the assumption that every opportunity had to be taken to punish yet further the hapless Iraqi people. Britain objected also to the import of 103 rolls of galvanised steel plate by the Al-Fajr Plant as a further intended input to industry. When the Committee representatives of Morocco and Djibouti emphasised that the material was intended for the food industry Washington maintained its veto on the spurious ground that the identity of the end-user could not be verified. In the same way Britain blocked the export of 45 crates of cable joints, intended for schools and hospitals, on the ground that it was impossible to be certain that the products would be used by the specified institutions. Britain also objected to the export of 25,935 tons of concrete additives for the Al-Mamoon building company involved in the construction of housing. The reason again was that such materials constituted an input to Iraqi industry. Similarly, the export of 15,000 steel bars to the Ekur Trading Agency in Baghdad for the construction of houses, many of which were destroyed by allied bombing, was blocked by Britain as an input to Iraqi industry. The United States vetoed the export of 66 containers of granite for hospitals and health care centres on the ground that such material was not a basic item.[28]

Thus Iraq is to be denied any scope for reconstructing its industries, any opportunity to rebuild bombed houses and hospitals, any chance to convey to its civilian population that there is light at the end of the tunnel. The saga of the shroud material graphically illustrates the West's callous indifference to the suffering of the Iraqi people. In April 1993 the UK-based trader Kais al-Kaisy, specialising in the export of medical supplies, began his struggle to export ordinary shroud cloth to Iraq (see also note 23). On 6 May the DTI Sanctions Unit issued a licence permitting Kais al-Kaisy to enter into negotiations for the export of shroud material to Iraq. Then the UN Sanctions Committee issued a letter indicating that shipment to Iraq would be permitted, with a further payment of $500 per 20-foot container being demanded for UN inspector purposes. Then, after further delay, a letter arrived from the DTI on 23 September declaring that 'all UK individual export and certain supply licences are revoked with effect from 28 September 1993. . . . You should note that it will not be possible to export goods from the UK on or after 28 September 1993 unless you have a new, valid export licence.' Reasons for the revocation were given: 'it has come to our attention that there may have been falsification or fraudulent use of UK licences for Iraq' and it was necessary to bring the export licences 'into line with changes' in UN letters of authorisation for Iraq. A new device to delay exports to Iraq was now being introduced: exports formerly approved now had to start the whole tortuous process again.

In vain Kais al-Kaisy protested about his planned export of shroud cloth: 'This material can be used for nothing but dressing the dead. It is recognised for what it is – it could not be used for curtains or clothes – it is shroud material. We do not bury people in smart clothes or shining shoes. We have no funeral homes. We wash them, tend them, buy six or seven metres of shroud cloth from textile shops and put them in the ground, wrapped in a shroud.'[29] On 29 November 1993 Mr al-Kaisy received the following letter from Peter Mayne of the DTI Sanctions Unit:

I refer to your application dated 17 June 1993 for a licence to export shroud cloth to Iraq under the Export of Goods (Control) (Iraq and Kuwait Sanctions) Order 1990.

The application has been considered in the light of the United Nations Resolutions 661 and 667 (sic).* I have to inform you that a licence under the Order has not been granted under the current climate.

* The reference should presumably be to UN Resolutions 661 and 687.

The US representative on the UN Sanctions Committee are (sic) currently blocking the export of cloth to Iraq.

The treatment afforded to Kais al-Kaisy's attempt to export shroud cloth to Iraq is no isolated aberration but part of a general pattern affecting countless humanitarian products. For example, a letter (25 April 1994) from Dr Stella Lowry, head of the International Department of the British Medical Association (BMA), emphasised that 'the only mail that is entering Iraq at present is personal correspondence'; and that commercial mail, 'which includes scientific journals, is not allowed through because of United Nations sanctions'. In consequence, people in Britain trying to take out subscriptions, on behalf of people in Iraq, to the British Medical Journal (BMJ) were being warned that 'it is very unlikely that the journals will reach their targets . . . some journals are in fact in storage pending the lifting of the UN sanctions. . . . I understand that there is no way round the current situation.'[30]

What was happening with shroud material and medical journals was happening equally with countless other harmless items that had humanitarian significance. The operations of the Sanctions Committee, coupled with the parallel activities of national financial institutions in blocking Iraqi transactions,[31] continued to ensure that Iraq remained in an impoverished and deteriorating condition. We need to remember what this means for the most vulnerable members of Iraqi society.

SUFFER THE CHILDREN

What the West has done and continues to do to the children of Iraq is one of the genocidal crimes of the century. Many of us were first alerted to what was being perpetrated when the Harvard study team reported in 1991 that 'at least 170,000 young children under five years of age will die in the coming year' as a result of the war and the economic embargo. The many witnesses are unanimous:

A German Doctor Tells How Iraq's Children Are Being Killed[32]

Children condemned to a lingering death[33]

Child victims of the sanctions syndrome[34]

Sanctions that should shame the UN
('Denying Iraqi babies medicines amounts to cold-blooded murder')[35]

The early testimonies painted a grim picture that was set to deteriorate yet further in the years to come. When Dr Margit Fakhoury, a
German paediatrician, visited hospitals in Iraq in March 1991 she reported the unprecedented incidence of 'malnourished babies and tod-
dlers . . . with kwashiorkor, severe deficiencies of vitamins, or dying
of a simple flu or diarrhoea'. After her second visit four months later
she reported a worsened situation. A typical case was a malnourished
woman with a 40-day-old baby and no breast milk. When she found
milk on the black market she could not afford it, and so her baby was
being fed on water, sometimes with sugar added – one of the growing
generation of bloated Iraqi 'sugar babies'. The water was contaminated and the malnourishment inevitably depressed any natural resistance to infection: 'In all hospitals, be they in Baghdad, north or south
Iraq, the doctors see increasing numbers of cases of cholera and typhoid fever.'[36]

Before the war Iraq was able to produce penicillin, ampicillin and
other basic antibiotics. The bombing destroyed the production plants
and the sanctions meant that the Iraqis were prevented from rebuilding
such facilities. One consequence was that doctors were being forced to
use the increasingly unavailable antibiotics in lower and lower doses
via intramuscular rather than intravenous techniques – often leading to
'ineffective treatment, long-term brain damage, or, after a short time, a
second, fulminating infection'.[37] In children this has caused mental and
physical disablement and early death.

The cases were well documented: 3-year-old Sabreen, suffering from
a broken fibula and severe infection after a fall (wound still discharg-
ing after 4 months; doctors said they could do nothing more); 8-year-
old Alah, wounded in a bombing raid that killed her mother (severe
infection that was expected to cause at least permanent disablement);
19-year-old Ijad, lost both legs in a bombing raid on a shelter, sent
home from hospital with continuing pus discharge because of lack of
available treatment; 16-year-old Maisoon, badly burned but sent home
from hospital because of lack of treatment facilities (later found in
severely malnourished state).[38] Today such a list could be extended to
thousands and tens of thousands. In August 1991 Iraq claimed that
more than 14,000 children had already died from lack of drugs since
the trade embargo began.

It was soon apparent that the youngest were being severely affected
by the sanctions regime in the aftermath of the war. From January to
August (1991) infant deaths (under 1 year of age) per 1000 live births
more than tripled (from 23 to 80). In the same period the under-5

mortality rate had almost quadrupled, and the situation was set to deteriorate. The monthly average death rate (under 5) for August to December (1991) was 712; for May 1992 the figure was 3341 infant deaths. For over-5s (same period) the monthly average number of deaths increased from 1833 to 6730. Reduced birth weight was one of the factors contributing to the higher infant mortality rates. Thus in 1990 a monthly average of 4.5 per cent of babies was under 2.5kg at birth; in May 1992 the percentage was 17.1. At the same time, as may have been expected, the nutritional status of surviving infants was seeing a massive deterioration. For the under-5s the incidence of kwashiorkor had risen from 485 cases in 1990 to 12,796 cases in 1991 to 5578 cases for the period January to May 1992. Thus in a period of just two years one of the principal nutrition-deficiency diseases saw a 27-fold increase. Over the same period marasmus saw a 20-fold increase for the under-5s, with other cases of malnutrition for this age group reaching a monthly average of 89,021 cases for early 1991 (an 11-fold increase on 1990). It is estimated that *in 1991 there were some 1,056,956 cases of malnutrition in Iraqi children under 5 years old, with the incidence increasing through 1992 (an 11.5-fold increase in the total of kwashiorkor, marasmus and other nutritional diseases on 1990).*[39]

To the catastrophic impact of war and sanctions on the physical health of Iraqi children was added the traumatic devastation of their psychological condition. Thus Dr Magne Raundalen, Dr Atle Dyregrov (both of the Centre for Crisis Psychology, Bergen, Norway) and others began collecting data on a generation of Iraqi children 'trapped in trauma' because of the block on medical and other supplies that would otherwise have encouraged a gradual return to psychological health (see also Chapter 1).[40] This substantial research has revealed a highly disturbed child population characterised by intrusive thoughts about the war and various pattens of 'avoidance' behaviour. Around two-thirds of the children surveyed by Raundalen were experiencing sleep problems, and about a half (44.9 per cent in Al-Amiriya, 55.7 per cent in Basra) were worried that they might not live to become adult. Moreover, there were suggestions that the psychological problems were worsening. For a whole generation of Iraqi children, 'the world is not a safe place anymore, anything can happen, and it can literally happen out of the blue' (Raundalen, 1991). A majority of the children felt 'more alone inside': they had lost all sense of security and optimism. They could not talk to their parents because they too were traumatised. The older generation lacked both the skills and the psychological resources to help their children emerge from disturbance and pain.

In August/September 1991 Raundalen and Dyregrov interviewed a total of 214 Iraqi children of school age and used various psychological assessment methods to determine the psychological impact of the Gulf War (Dyregrov and Raundalen, 1992). The testimonies had a grim uniformity:

> I look at the girl beside me at school and I imagine she's my dead friend sitting right next to me . . .

> I can't believe that my friends are dead . . . that the whole thing was real.

> In front of my parents I try to act as if I'm cheerful, but deep inside I'm very sad.

> I dream, and the dreams are always about corpses . . . when I pass by my dead friends' houses, I can't look . . .

> It's the sight of the corpses I remember. All the corpses.

> Why doesn't God come for me the way he came for them. I should be finished with this life . . .

> I dreamed that I saw a burnt man with black scars on his stomach and I saw an image of a woman all crumpled, all burned.

> I prefer not to talk because it causes pain.

And through all this pain there is the knowledge that the West is determined to maintain the vicious sanctions. A child called Zaineb said:

> I want to ask you a question, could you please tell me when the sanctions will be lifted. We lost so many things during the war, we lost the furniture of the house. . . . We have no food, we have no water, we have to ask for water because Basra water is not drinkable . . . we don't have medicine, and when we took the children to the hospital they said 'we don't have medicine, you can take them where you like, it's not up to us'. So when will all this be over. Just tell me when, because yesterday our last ration of flour was consumed when we baked some bread and all my brothers ate it up.

More than four years after this testimony there is no relief: the war continues, albeit by other means. Iraq remains under constant threat of further bombardment, and in consequence the entire Iraqi people – not only the children – are denied any route to a post-war psychological

security. For the traumatised children, 'time seemed to have stopped.
. . . There had been little or no work-through of the war-traumas. *They
seemed trapped within their trauma, surrounded by reminders of what
had happened, and unable to escape . . . their minds seem to be a landscape of mental craters and destruction. . . . There is no safe place,
and they expect the worst to happen again'* (my italics) (Dyregrov and
Raundalen, 1992).

Throughout this period Western leaders continued to declare that
there would be no relaxation in the sanctions regime: the Iraqi civilian
population was now entitled to no respite. In June 1992 Abdul Jabbar
Abdul Abbas, a senior Iraqi health official, reported that in the first
four months of 1992 almost 41,000 Iraqis, including a further 14,000
children, had died because of the economic sanctions. Now many of
the deaths were taking place in hospitals that no longer had access to
basic provisions (see 'The Health Weapon', below). And again first-
hand accounts were appearing of malnourished children with no access to adequate food: 'Children are being fed on water or sugar and
water.'[41] A further academic study, made independently by a team of
international researchers, confirmed the massively increased scale of
child mortality throughout Iraq.[42] Here one conclusion was that '46,900
excess deaths among children under five years of age' had occurred
during the first eight months of 1991. This meant a three-fold increase
in child mortality, as compared with the average rates during the previous six years. The researchers concluded:

> Our data demonstrate the link between the events that occurred in
> 1991 (war, civilian uprising, and economic embargo) and the subse-
> quent increase in mortality. The destruction of the supply of electric
> power . . . with the subsequent destruction of the electricity-depend-
> ent water and sewage systems, was probably responsible for the re-
> ported epidemics of gastrointestinal and other infections.

It is emphasised further that the severe epidemics were made worse
'by the reduced accessibility of health services and decreased ability
to treat severely ill children'; and that the increased malnutrition had
contributed 'to the increased risk of death among infants and children'. The pattern of mortality was now resembling 'that observed in
the less-developed countries, where diarrhea and respiratory infections
account for most deaths in infancy and childhood'.[43] The West had
claimed that the use of high-precision weapons had produced only limited
damage to the civilian population: '*The results of our study contradict*

this claim and confirm that the casualties of war extend far beyond those caused directly by warfare' (my italics).[44] In April 1993 a document submitted by the Iraqi UN ambassador Nizar Hamdoon to the UN Secretary-General included various items of information indicating the effects of sanctions on infants and children:

- An increase in the per-month deaths of children aged 5 years and over: 3800 in August 1992, as against 2289 in August 1991 and 712 in August 1990. Main cause – malnutrition coupled with severe shortage of vaccines and other medicaments;

- 61,442 deaths of children under five years of age from August 1990 to August 1992 as a result of economic sanctions;

- Total number of deaths among children age 5 years and over: 6362 per month in 1992, as against 4872 in 1991 and 1833 in 1990;

- Low birth weight in more than 17.5 per cent of all newborns, compared with 10.8 per cent in 1991 and 4.5 per cent in 1990.[45]

The surviving Iraqi children – typically malnourished, sick and facing premature death – inevitably suffered in other ways as well. Many were orphans, without adequate housing, and facing shattered educational provision. The detailed report produced by Dr Eric Hoskins for UNICEF, shelved as politically inconvenient, emphasised that thousands of schools had been destroyed or damaged by bombing and that now they were in bad need of repair and lacked desks, blackboards and text-books.[46] There had been a massive increase in drop-out rates, and where education was still being attempted it was necessarily deteriorating. Basic items such as chalk, pencils, erasers, notebooks, paper were either absent or in short supply; many of the surviving schools were without electrical supply, water or sanitation facilities. It was estimated that in some governorates as many as 30 per cent of the windows in school buildings had been shattered by the bombing. In less than three years the price of pencils, as with other basic school items, had increased more than 50-fold (a dozen pencils: cost less than 1 dinar pre-August 1990, more than 50 dinars now).[47] One estimate suggested that 205 kindergartens and 1767 primary schools throughout Iraq had been destroyed in the bombing.[48]

The blockage of paper imports through the sanctions regime meant that an ever reducing number of children's books was available from one year to the next. In 1989 the Children's Publishing House in Baghdad

TABLE 3.2 Impact of sanctions on the health of children under 5

Type of Case	1990		1991			1992			1993			1994		
	number	monthly rate	number	monthly rate	increase times 1990	number	monthly rate	increase times 1990	number	monthly rate	increase times 1990	Jan. March	monthly rate	increase times 1990
Kwashiorkor	485	41	12,796	1,066	26.3	13,744	1,145	27.9	15,128	1,261	30.8	5,392	1,797	43.8
Marasmus	5,193	433	96,186	8,015	18.5	111,477	9,289	21.4	139,346	11,612	26.8	48,856	16,285	37.6
Other types of malnutrition (such as protein, calorie and vitamin deficiencies)	96,809	8,063	947,974	78,998	9.8	1,123,319	93,610	11.6	1,235,657	102,971	12.8	340,241	113,414	14.1
GRAND TOTAL	102,487	8,537	1,056,956	88,079	10.3	1,248,540	104,044	12.1	1,390,131	115,844	13.6	394,489	131,496	15.4

published 200 books; in 1991 fewer than 50, and thereafter none at all. Teachers, now often malnourished themselves and facing rocketing inflation (so eroding their capacity to supplement their food rations), were growing accustomed to falling class sizes and children fainting from hunger. A UNICEF report put the drop-out rate at approaching one-fifth in July 1993, where pre-war it had been negligible; for this and many other obvious reasons literacy was declining.

It had by now long been abundantly clear that the sanctions regime was devastating an entire generation of Iraqi children. From the dramatically increased number of stillbirths and deformities at birth, through the obscenity of the 'sugar babies' and early deaths, to the demoralisation and trauma of surviving children the US-dominated Sanctions Committee was achieving its evident objectives. In April 1994 the Iraqi minister of health reported that approaching a quarter of all Iraqi babies now had low birth weights, that infant mortality had reached 126 per 1000, and that diseases (polio, cholera, scabies, typhoid, measles, pneumonia, viral jaundice, malaria, diphtheria, etc.), many of which had been formerly eradicated, were now all seeing dramatic increases among children throughout the country. A UNICEF statement (20 July 1993) confirmed that child mortality had 'greatly increased' and that many diseases ('plagues and maladies') were now increasing among children. A report published by the Iraqi Ministry of Culture and Information (June 1994) confirmed the dramatic increase in the incidence of kwashiorkor, marasmus and other nutritional diseases in children under 5 years of age (see Table 3.2).[49]

The deteriorating condition of Iraqi children was plain and widely known. The many witnesses were testifying to the dying babies in the hospitals, the diseased and malnourished infants on public view in the main towns (with the assumption that children in the less well served distant villages were in an even worse predicament), the orphans on the streets. Thus one testimony: '. . . this traumatised child population . . . bear the brunt of the UN sanctions against Iraq. Destitute and orphaned children begging on the streets are now a common sight . . . poverty is forcing increasing numbers out of school and into the labour market . . . rations provide less than two thirds of the daily energy requirement and lack protein and micro nutrients. This state of chronic nutritional deficiency leaves children more susceptible to disease, which must often go untreated because of medicine shortages.'[50] And this observer notes that in 1990 Britain ratified the UN Convention on the Rights of the Child, which proclaims that children, 'because of their vulnerability, need special care and protection'.

Witnesses continued to report the effects of sanctions on the physical health and mental condition of Iraqi children; and how needless Western acts continue to sow terror and confusion. Thus Dr Siegwart Gunther, the president of Yellow Cross International, Austria, reflects on the 'devastating' psychological effects that the war has had on children and how these are being deliberately prolonged: 'Many children exhibit permanent damage of speech. During thunder storms they start shivering all over the body and begin to stutter in fear . . . in Mosul the suicide cases of children are very high.' And Gunther comments on his personal experience in Mosul: 'I witnessed myself, on a Friday, the day of prayer and celebration for Moslems, 12 Allied Jets appearing over the town, one after the other, at very low altitudes. Window panes rattled, the children ran screaming to seek protection in the houses, a terrifying experience, also for me as an old soldier.'[51]

In early 1995 the permanent Iraqi mission to the United Nations office in Geneva presented an important document (see Appendix 6) to the Centre for Human Rights. This document,[52] 'The impact of the embargo on Iraqi children in the light of the Convention on the Rights of the Child', rested on the interesting idea, outside the cognisance of the UN Sanctions Committee, that the General Assembly proclamation (20 November 1959) of the Declaration of the Rights of the Child should properly be regarded as having direct relevance to the current plight of Iraqi children. Here are spelt out the main principles of the Convention and attention is drawn (in Part II) to the impact of the embargo on children. It really was a measure of the depths to which the West had sunk that a member state of the United Nations felt it necessary to emphasise that children should be seen as having a right to life, a right to health care, a right to education and the rest; and that, in the context of suffering inflicted on children by the sanctions regime, 'such suffering . . . is totally incompatible with the provisions of the Convention . . .'. Should it really be necessary to have to argue in an international forum that it is morally wrong to deny children medical care and to starve them to death?

The document concludes (Paragraphs 21 and 22) with the words:

The people of Iraq, and particularly their children, are faced with destruction by a weapon that is just as horrendous as any weapon of mass destruction, namely the economic embargo weapon to which one million persons, half of whom were children, have fallen victim during the last four years.

This destruction is a form of genocide of the people of Iraq: it is an international crime punishable under international law, regardless of whether it is committed in time of war or peace.

Article 2 of the Convention on the Prevention and Punishment of the Crime of Genocide defines acts of genocide as: killing members of the (ethnic or religious) group; causing serious bodily or mental harm to members of the group; or deliberately inflicting on the group conditions of life calculated to bring about its physical destruction in whole or in part.

These acts are undoubtedly being committed deliberately through the imposition and maintenance of the economic embargo which can no longer be justified now that the reasons that led to its imposition no longer apply.

It is plain to anyone who bothers to look that we do not have to rely on Iraqi prompting to learn about the genocide being committed by the West against the children of Iraq. The non-Iraqi, anti-Saddam witnesses are copious enough. It is sufficient here to cite one more. The French deputy Yves Bonnet has described what he saw in August 1995 in the Saddam Hussein Children's Hospital in Baghdad. A mother slowly unwraps her 3-month-old baby, 4lbs in weight, emaciated, and medically judged soon to die: 'I look at the mother, two large black eyes silently reproaching me; then I turn away, guilty, ashamed. One after another, and each time this silent exchange with an incredulous yet resigned woman.'[53] Yet again the UN Sanctions Committee has 'endorsed its implacable mission: the death of 100 innocent under-fives each day through respiratory infections, diarroea, gastroenteritis and malnutrition, and the death of 200 over-fives a day of heart problems, hypertension, diabetes, renal and liver disease, and leukaemia'.[54] And Bonnet's final acknowledgement of his culpability as a Western politician: ' . . . *I am filled with shame and anger at myself, at my cowardliness, my silence, my complicity with those who, despite their claims to the contrary, have killed hundreds of thousands of civilians, without incurring the wrath of the (War Crimes) tribunal of the Hague, implacably going about their dirty, evil work*' (my italics).[55]

SUFFER THE WOMEN

Women suffer, as do men, at the pain of their children. And women suffer also in unique ways. Only the desperately hungry *pregnant* woman can experience the anguish of knowing that her foetus is already malnourished, that her baby will stand a greater chance of being born disabled or dead, and that if it survives it is destined to suck in vain on shrivelled breasts. Iraqi women, having lost husbands, sons and brothers in war, have been forced to shoulder an immense burden. More than 10 per cent of Iraqi women are widows, and so often the sole wage–earners in their families. Economic sanctions have produced greater unemployment, making it difficult for women to earn the money not being provided by war-maimed or absent husbands. So a generation of malnourished women has been driven to scavenging, prostitution, begging and the black market. Women typically go hungry to provide for their children and elderly relatives.

By August 1991, long before the full impact of sanctions was being felt, many Iraqi families had exhausted their savings and were being forced to sell their most valued personal possessions, solely to obtain food. More than half of the women interviewed by the international study team had sold their jewellery, given to new brides as a dowry asset. Many families were trying to sell furniture, domestic appliances, carpets, clothes, and even the doors of their houses. Half of all families had incurred heavy debts, increasing the economic vulnerability of women and their families. Nearly two-thirds of women interviewed were suffering from such psychological problems as depression, anxiety, headache and insomnia. Other problems included severe malnutrition, increased susceptibility to disease, menstrual irregularity and breastfeeding difficulties. Sick and weakened women were now having to queue for water, to collect firewood, and to cope with the consequences of marital breakdown through increased domestic tensions. While many marriages were breaking down, it was now increasingly difficult for families to afford marriage costs (to fund the traditional celebrations and to provide the expected dowries). The erosion of the education sector, the increased incidence of crime, the collapse of the family – all exacerbated by sanctions – were now combining to produce unprecedented levels of social dislocation. This deteriorating situation has impacted drastically on the condition of Iraqi women, by now increasingly bereaved, sick, abandoned, divorced and poor. Comments in the report of the international study team reflect a grim optimism: '*Iraqi women have experienced this whole crisis not only as victims, but also as crucial actors who have sustained the family and the society. The basis of the Iraqi society, the home, has been held together by their ingenuity and strength – despite their own economic, social, emotional and psychological deprivation.*' Hunger, in conditions of deepening pauperisation, represented the most crucial deprivation.

Testimony collected for the International Study Team well conveys the desperation created by the war and prolonged by sanctions:

Every night we sleep hungry. Faddila

How long will the Sanctions continue? We are tired. We are innocent. Fatin

All my life I was never sick. Now I am always sick. Look at my face, it is so thin now. Um Mohammad

We feel weak, but it's not that we can't go on. Um Amari

The war is over but the worries and uncertainties remain. Fatimah

With the blink of my eye I lost half my family. I just want God to save those who remain. They are my future. Um Samiri.[56]

These women and many others told of the extremes of deprivation: children crying for food that cannot be provided; one piece of bread divided into eight pieces to feed the entire family; families drinking dirty river water; the suffering of the most vulnerable groups (children, women, old, handicapped, the mentally ill and the destitute); homes flooded with sewage; the collapse of pre-natal care; the lack of affordable insulin; malnourished women suffering significant hair loss; irregular menstruation and teeth falling out; the growing incidence of infertility; the desperate efforts, following the closure of a local clinic, to find medical help for a child already dead.

The real income from employment and pensions had seen an almost total collapse, accelerating the growth of asset sales and debt as desperate attempts to meet the basic food needs. Still the women, often providing the only family support, had great difficulty in feeding their children. Thus the 60-year-old Majida Hamid testified of 'suffering like never before'. Every day was getting worse: 'I have sold all my gold, including my wedding ring. This was not enough so we sold our furniture and kitchen utensils. Even our water tank had to be sold. This too was not enough.' Many Iraqi families have now disposed of all their assets and are destitute, with all the inevitable consequences for access to food, water and other necessities often only available on the black market. The 32-year-old Saeda Bani Dana, living in Mosul, testified: 'Every waking moment I worry about how I will feed my eight children. It is the hardest thing for a mother not to be able to feed her child.'[57]

A half (49 per cent) of the women interviewed said that there had been an increase in illness among their children and themselves, with reports of diarrhoea, typhoid, malnutrition and infant deaths. With the progressive collapse of the medical infrastructure (see 'The Health Weapon', below), women were increasingly forced to take on the burden of health caretakers. This in turn put mounting stress on women, already struggling to find food and water, and usually unable to feed their families properly. Many women have taken their sick children to health centres and hospitals, only to find that the sanctions have blocked the medical access to drugs and to the spare parts necessary to keep medical equipment working. The women have then stayed with their dying children in hospital wards denuded of effective medical care provisions, so putting further burdens on the rest of the women's families at home.

The 21-year-old Alia from Najaf testified: 'Most women suffered terribly from trauma of miscarriages during the war and the disturbances. Many could not find medical treatment at the time and have continuing problems with their health. Effective treatment seems unavailable for most women. A doctor friend of mine estimated that 7000 woman had miscarriages because of shock in Najaf alone.'[58] The 1991 Sadruddin Aga Khan report estimated that about a third of all pregnant and lactating women were under-nourished and in need of nutritional support.[59] Dr Abed al-Amir, head of the Babylon Paediatric and Maternity Hospital, has stated that the much increased incidence of miscarriages, premature labour and low-birth-weight babies has been caused by the mounting physical and psychological pressures on women, the lack of medicines and pre-natal care, and the difficulty in reaching hospitals because of transportation problems.[60]

Dr al-Amir commented also that the lack of contraception facilities, a further consequence of war and sanctions, was having various adverse consequences. Now contraceptives were only being made available to women for medical reasons and in rare cases to older women with large families. The researchers for the International Study Team encountered one woman, anaemic and weak, who had had two caesarian operations in one year because of lack of contraception. Aid workers were soon to report caesarian operations taking place without anaesthetics – yet another consequence of sanctions. A teenage girl was cited who had bleeding problems that could only be countered by the birth control pill, which at that time had become unavailable. Another consequence, reported by a women gynaecologist from Hilla, was an increase in the incidence of illegal abortions and a related increase in the number of maternal deaths. The widespread deprivation, making it difficult for families to support existing children, constituted an additional pressure on women to abort. A large number of women were now testifying that they or their daughters were now suffering from irregular menstruations, excessive bleeding and severe pains; with an increase in the incidence of hair loss, skin complaints, weight loss, insomnia and other problems.[61]

Many women were claiming that whereas the long Iran–Iraq War (1980–88) had had only minimal effect on domestic life the war waged by George Bush on Iraq – by deliberately targeting the entire national infrastructure – had drastically affected the lives of all Iraqi civilians. And when the impact of the war was compounded by the most punitive sanctions no Iraqi households could survive unscathed. Some 80 per cent of women interviewed said that they had extra domestic responsibilities because of the destruction of the infrastructure (water supply, electrical power generation, fuel supply, etc.).[62] Women testified that they often gave their share of the food to their children.

In summary, the vast bulk of Iraqi women were having to contend with a variety of problems: more difficult roles, a greatly reduced ability to feed their families, an increased chance of unemployment, general impoverishment, lack of medical care and of an hygienic environment, anxiety and psychological trauma, marital collapse and family breakdown, increased problems in pregnancy and childbirth, an increased likelihood of sickness and disability. The report for the International Study Team concludes, speaking of Iraqi women: *'Their central role both as victims and as actors makes it all the more important to listen to their unheard voices.'*[63]

The plight of Iraqi women, like that of Iraqi civilians as a whole, is well reported and widely known. Thus a UN document can observe in May 1993: 'It is evident that the first group to suffer most from food shortages are children, pregnant and lactating women.'[64] The problem is not that the crucial information on the condition of the Iraqi civilian population has not been obtained, but that – in the teeth of this unambiguous data – the West is implacably committed to a policy of genocide. In April 1994 an international forum, 'Human Rights and Women', organised by the General Federation of Iraqi Women, was held in Baghdad. There the French representative Andrée Michel, a founder of Women Citizens for Peace in August 1990, represented the general view in denouncing the 'barbaric blockade'. Never before had an economic blockade been 'so dire and cruel'; the blockade violated 'all the resolutions of international law, particularly the articles of the Geneva Convention' that forbid depriving a civilian population of the goods necessary to its survival. The UN Security Council had lost its credibility, choosing only to implement 'the law of the strongest, the law of the dollar, the law of oil and the arms trade'. Michel then denounced François Mitterrand for complicity in war crimes and crimes against humanity in participating in the Gulf War and the economic embargo.[65] The complicity extends far beyond France. The plight and example of Iraqi women demonstrate plainly enough the character of the silent holocaust being perpetrated by Washington and its allies.

THE FOOD WEAPON

Control over food confers ultimate power: prevent people from eating for a few weeks and they will not cause you much trouble thereafter. The United States today celebrates this simple truism in various ways; for example, by blocking food aid if a country does not act in accord with US strategic interests (as when a food shipment to Sudan was blocked during the Gulf crisis[66]) and by maintaining the tightest possible food blockade in perpetuity on such countries as Cuba and Iraq. Today the role of economic sanctions in this regard is very well understood, as it has been throughout the entire history of human conflict. Thus one writer, commenting on the use of economic sanctions by the League of Nations, notes the school of thought that favours the drastic application of sanctions to ensure that *'sufficient number of women and children'* are *'starved in the aggressive country'*.[67] This is the philosophy that Washington began to apply to Iraq in August 1990 and which still prevails today (early 1998).

Many observers and researchers have charted the growing incidence of malnutrition in Iraq as a result of sanctions. For example, Hoskins points out that in 1992 the government food ration was providing only two-thirds of daily energy needs and was deficient in protein and micronutrients (see Figure 3.1).[68] This has meant a significant increase in a wide range of nutritional deficiency diseases (rickets, goitre, anaemia, marasmus, kwashiorkor, etc.) and deaths through starvation, akin to those in the famine-stricken regions of the Third World. In these circumstances the health of the next generation has been drastically impaired: anaemia of pregnancy has become common, with an associated increase in the number of stillbirths, and in the first two years of sanctions the incidence of low-birth-weight babies increased four-fold.

Through the 1980s, despite the war with Iran, Iraq maintained a very low rate of malnutrition. Food was heavily subsidised by the state and in plentiful supply, while the health services were seeing signifi-

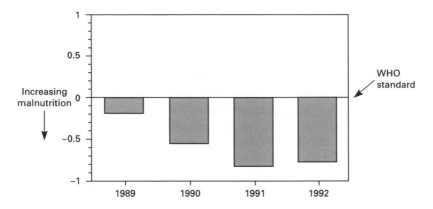

FIGURE 3.1   Increases in malnutrition among children in Baghdad

Source: UNICEF, Baghdad: Children 1–3 years, weight for age.

cant improvement. By 1988 the average per capita food intake was 3340 kilocalories (128 per cent of the WHO adult recommendation) but, with around 70 per cent of Iraq's food imported, the draconian economic sanctions soon achieved a massive decline in the amount of food available. The systematic bombing of Iraq's infrastructure had also helped to erode the civilian access to food: food processing plant was destroyed, refrigeration facilities had no electricity, and the normal mechanisms for food distribution (roads, bridges, transport) were totally disrupted. As early as February 1991 a WHO/UNICEF mission to Baghdad estimated that the daily per capita calorie intake had fallen (from the pre-sanctions level of 3340 kilocalories) to less than 1000 kilocalories (one third of the WHO recommendation). In June 1991 UNICEF reported an 'alarming and rising incidence of severe and moderate malnutrition among the population of children under age 5'; and in July the UN Food and Agriculture Organisation (FAO) warned that Iraq was 'approaching the threshold of extreme deprivation'. A subsequent UNICEF study monitored the changes in the nutritional status among Baghdad children over the 2-year period following sanctions. Again a significant increase in the incidence of both moderate and severe malnutrition was reported.[69]

By August 1991 official Iraqi sources were claiming that deaths from starvation had reached 11,000.[70] Now the gravity of the deepening food crisis was being acknowledged by UN officials, aid workers, journalists and other observers. Thus Michael Priestly, a senior UN official, declared at the end of August that unless sanctions were eased quickly Iraq could face malnutrition, disease and a food emergency unprecedented in modern times.[71] But such testimony had no effect on the rigour with which sanctions were being enforced. On 13 September 1990 the UN Security Council passed Resolution 666 by 13 votes to 2 (Cuba and Yemen), emphasising that foodstuffs could only be exported to Iraq in the case of 'urgent humanitarian need'. Far from any genuine attempt to relieve the suffering of the Iraqi people, Resolution 666 simply consolidated the bureaucratic delay and obstruction that were already determining how sanctions were being enforced on a day-to-day basis. The Secretary-General would obtain information, then produce reports which would be made available to the Sanctions Committee, whereupon the Committee would consider such reports, after which it would submit its conclusion to the Security Council, which would then consider what if anything should be done (Resolution 666, Paragraphs 3–5). Apart from the normal and inevitable bureaucratic delays in such a procedure it also allowed every opportunity for mischievous obstruction and procrastination. No-one observing how the US-dominated Sanctions Committee was operating could doubt that such obstruction would continue to occur. So much for *urgent humanitarian need*.

Any doubts about the humanitarian value of Resolution 666 were amply confirmed by later events. Despite the acknowledged urgency of the food need in Iraq, no information was gathered under the terms of 666 until 16 February 1991, no less than 5 months after the passing of the resolution. The WHO/UNICEF mission, already cited, duly reported its dire findings and some weeks later a reluctant Security Council declared a humanitarian emergency. Still no foodstuffs were to be allowed into Iraq unless provided by the United Nations or by 'appropriate humanitarian agencies' working with the UN. *Iraq would still not be allowed to purchase or distribute its own foodstuffs*. Again this was a formula for blocking the supply of food to the Iraqi civilian population. There was no way – even ignoring bureaucratic delay and malicious obstructionism – that the United Nations and the aid agencies, under the imposed restrictions, could hope to feed an entire population of more than 18 million people, particularly since a growing number also needed medical help that was being deliberately prevented (see 'The Health Weapon', below).

Moreover, the US-dominated Sanctions Committee was reluctant even to declare the recognised aid agencies as 'appropriate' (Resolution 666, Paragraph 6). If an aid agency, whatever its acknowledged international reputation, wished to ship food to Iraq it was first required to submit in advance a detailed application to the Sanctions Committee, detailing the exact foodstuffs and in what quantity they were to be shipped. The Committee would then deliberate on whether the aid agency was 'appropriate' and whether such foodstuffs should be allowed into Iraq. Washington's success in blocking the Iraqi population's access to food is well shown by the fact that, whereas Iraq's *daily* grain requirement was approximately 10,000 tons, this was about the amount that Iraq was allowed to import *from August 1990 to April 1991*. The United Nations itself declared that a minimum of $178 million was necessary to address the acknowledged humanitarian crisis in Iraq; in the event, less than a fifth of this amount was forthcoming. Washington's strategic policies were having their anticipated effect. No-one who knew how the Sanctions Committee was working was surprised to learn of mounting malnutrition throughout Iraq and starvation in various parts of the country. In June 1991 Dr Robert M. Russell and Dr John Osgood Field, two specialists from the Tufts University School of Nutrition, were sent under UNICEF auspices to assess the nutrition of children under 5 years of age in Iraq. Some 680 children in 14 rural and urban settings in the Basra and Amara governorates were examined for weight, height and mid-upper arm circumference as part of an assessment for clinical signs of anaemia, dehydration and vitamin A deficiency.[72]

The Tufts specialists, with support from local UNICEF staff, found evidence of 'both acute and chronic malnutrition' in large numbers of the children examined. Nutritional signs of impending famine were not evident, notwithstanding 'epidemic levels of infectious diseases, market prices for basic food items three to twenty times pre-war levels, and a reported crisis in mothers' ability to breastfeed'. It was concluded that child malnutrition was 'a serious problem' and that the embargo would be bound to make matters worse: 'Continuation of the trade embargo and of UN-mandated sanctions against Iraq for any significant length of time will place the health and very lives of hundreds of thousands of children at enormous risk ... the Security Council will have to decide how to balance the political objectives of the embargo and sanctions against the humanitarian fallout that is virtually certain to follow in their wake.'[73] At the same time there were signs of growing social dislocation as hungry Iraqi civilians became increasingly desperate. In November 1991 food riots erupted as people took to stealing and looting in order to stay alive.[74]

One of the main causes of hardship was the rocketing prices of many foodstuffs, an inevitable consequence of the shortages caused by sanctions (see Table 3.3). The massive price escalation that occurred in the first

TABLE 3.3   Food price increases in Iraq caused by one year of sanctions

Food Item	Price per unit (ID)		Percentage increase over 1 year
	Aug 90	Aug 91	
Wheat-flour	0.05	2.42	4,531
Milk (powdered)	0.75	27.33	3,661
Bread (per piece)	0.01	0.33	2,857
Baby milk (450g tin)	0.45	10.00	2,222
Sugar	0.20	4.42	2,208
Cooking oil	0.48	10.33	2,138
Rice	0.23	4.08	1,801
Tea	1.70	23.67	1,392
Tomato	0.27	1.25	469
Chickpeas	0.65	2.92	449
Potatos	0.45	1.92	426
Eggs (carton of 30)	3.83	12.50	350
Onions	0.37	1.25	341
Dates	0.52	1.75	339
Meat (lamb)	7.00	16.33	233
Meat (beef)	6.83	16.90	247
All items (high case)			2,004
All items (low case)			1,546
Cost (at current prices)*	66.00	6,010.00	1,546

* average 1990 food basket for a family of six ('low case' assumptions)

Notes:

(a) The commodity unit is 1kg unless stated otherwise. For each commodity, the stated price is an unweighted average of the prices reported in Mosul (northern Iraq), Baghdad (central Iraq) and Basra (southern Iraq).

(b) Food price indices are weighted averages of individual commodity prices; the weights are the corresponding shares of total food expenditure in 1990. Incomplete information on 1990 expenditure patterns was supplemented with more detailed information for 1971.

   The 'high case' and 'low case' correspond to different assumptions about the evolution of expenditure patterns between these two dates.

Source: Jean Dreze and Haris Gazar, 'Income and Economic Survey', in International Study Team, *Health and Welfare in Iraq After the Gulf Crisis: An In-Depth Assessment*, October 1991.

year of sanctions continued in subsequent years, with the result that by August 1995 the average salary in Baghdad of 4000 dinars a month was worth $2. This meant that ordinary Iraqi families had no opportunity to supplement the necessarily inadequate government rations by purchasing food on the open market. The only remaining alternatives were begging, prostitution, scavenging, theft, looting, malnutrition, starvation and death. As in all social sectors the crippling burden of sanctions came on the top of the devastation wrought by the war.

The food crisis, deliberately created by the virtually total block on foodstuff imports, was exacerbated by denying Iraq the opportunity to reconstruct its own devastated agricultural sector: sanctions applied not only to foodstuffs but also to seed, pesticides, agricultural machinery and plant, and the spare parts that would have allowed the repair of existing equipment. The bombing of the power stations had impacted dramatically on this industrial sector, as on all the others. Soil fertilisation in much of central and southern Iraq had depended on the highly-developed irrigation system, designed to regulate the flooding from the Tigris and Euphrates rivers and to limit the concentration of salt deposited in the soil by the saline waters. The collapse of the power system resulted in the long-term flooding of much agricultural land and increased salt concentrations in the soil. With spare parts for damaged pumps no longer available, large areas of agricultural land have been lost.[75]

At the same time Iraq's agricultural capability has been eroded in many other ways: for example, seeds and fertilisers, blocked by the embargo, are in increasingly short supply, and chemicals for agricultural pest control are no longer available. Thus in 1989/90 some 59,000 tons of pesticides were procured; in 1991/92 only 500. The Abu Ghareib potato seeds factory in Baghdad and the Al Qaim fertiliser plant were deliberately targeted by the allied bombers, with the embargo then blocking all imports of seeds and fertilisers. In 1989/90 some 269,000 tons of fertilisers and 6700 tons of seeds were procured to meet projected requirements; whereas in 1991/92, with increased projected requirements (300,000 and 7000 tons respectively), no fertilisers and no seeds were procured.[76] This meant that whole areas of Iraqi agriculture had died, with little hope of resurrection.

In the same way Iraq's animal wealth had seen significant decline (see Table 3.4).[77] In one estimate the country's total number of animals in December 1991 was 50–60 per cent of the pre-sanctions total. A number of factors had contributed to the decline: some of the animals had been killed in the war, others had succumbed to the increased

TABLE 3.4   Decline in Iraq's animals

Kind	(in 1,000s) 1986[1]	1989[2]	1991[3]
Sheep	8,981	9,038	4,160
Goats	1,476	1,882	752
Cattle	1,578	1,495	747
Buffalo	141	169	85

[1] Annual Abstract of Statistics, 1990, Central Statistics Organisation, Ministry of Planning, Republic of Iraq.
[2] Initially forecasted by UN Envoy Prince Aga Khan, 15 July 1991, verified by subsequent examination of data by team members in September.
[3] Forecasted by Study Team members, September 1991.

incidence of waterborne diseases, and the block on veterinary supplies had meant that many of the normal animal husbandry procedures were no longer possible. In addition the collapse of the crop sector, coupled with the embargo, meant that animal feed was now in short supply; and there was evidence that during the war and its aftermath many animals were smuggled into Iran and Turkey.

The International Scientific Symposium, held in Baghdad (10–12 December 1994), gave further evidence of the deteriorating condition of Iraqi agriculture. Thus Dr H. A. Ali noted that the rodent population had increased significantly, as had the extent of parasitic infestation of sheep, goats and cows. The yield of grain crops (wheat, barley, grain, corn and rice) had declined significantly in all categories between 1989 and 1994. For example, the wheat yield was 900kg/donum (1 hectare = 4 donums) in 1989, but only 165kg/donum in 1994; barley saw a similar decline, from 850kg/donum to 195kg/donum over the same period.[78] Thus food imports were blocked and domestic production was collapsing.

Dr Ibrahim J. al-Jboory drew attention to the impact of dust storms* on plant physiology: the dust particles close the stomata, rendering the plant weaker and less productive, and improving the conditions for mites. Some of the consequences were significant increases in the incidence of fall blight on citrus, dust mite on date palms, pomegranate false spider mite and tomato russet mite. The dramatic increase in air

* The military operations had seriously eroded the fragile top soil in many areas, making dust storms 5 times more frequent in May 1991 than in the same period in 1990.

pollution caused by the bombing of chemical factories resulted in 'date palm neck bending' (120,000 palm trees destroyed) and the loss of tens of thousands of eucalyptus trees. Increased pest infestation was noted for many trees and plants: date palms (chalaropsis, fusarium and thelaviopis fungi, heart wet rot, heart dry rot, lesser date moth, dubas bug), grains (rusts, sunn insect, soft scale insect, smuts, rotten neck), citrus (citrus leaf miner), and potato, egg plant and tomato (potato tuber moth).[79] The imposition of economic sanctions was a direct cause of these increased infestations. Sanctions operated not only against the importation of pesticides but also against pesticide dispensers (sprayers and dusters), and in any case aerial spraying was prohibited. This allowed the spread of agricultural pests to governorates where formerly they were absent. Thus in Baghdad, leaf miner (affecting citrus trees) appeared for the first time; in Basra, cover smut (wheat); in Babylon, spiklate drought disease (rice); in Diayla, neck bending (date palm); in Mousel, bacterial mould (barley), and so on.[80] The sanctions were known to be encouraging the spread of both human and agricultural disease.

The symposium considered many other topics, including the impact of sanctions on Iraq's animal resources. The embargo on the importation of feedstuffs, veterinary drugs and equipment meant a massive reduction, compared with pre-sanctions levels, in the amount of animal products available to the Iraqi population. Thus the per-capita consumption of milk (kg/year) rapidly fell from 15 to around 3.5; of egg (egg/year) from 85 to 25; of red meat (kg/year) from 13 to 2.8; of chicken (kg/year) from 12.5 to 1.5; of fish (kg/year) from 3.5 to 1.5; and of animal proteins in general from 18 gm/day to 5.[81] These figures, for 1993, decreased yet further in 1994, with still no end in sight. Here is an entire national people being deprived of the essentials to human survival.

It is now obvious that economic sanctions (introduced in August 1990) were having a dramatic impact before the start of the war in January 1991. As early as March 1991, after 7 months of sanctions and 7 weeks of devastating war, a large tin of milk powder was costing 45 dinars, with a typical government salary set at about 100 dinars a month. Prices were already beginning their massive and inexorable inflation: the price of tomatoes had already increased 6-fold, that of chicken 3-fold, that of eggs almost 4-fold. The reserve stocks of food required to serve the 18-million population were quickly exhausted, and there was no prospect of adequate domestic production at prices the majority could afford. In May 1991 Iraq said it was desperate for access to $1 billion of its assets to pay for the next food supply. Britain, in line with the United States and France, declared that it would veto any move to 'significantly ease' the sanctions on Iraq while Saddam Hussein remained in power. The Iraqi foreign minister, Mahdi Salih, said what was common knowledge, that Britain and the other Western states were trying to starve the Iraqi people as a way of putting pressure on the regime. Only the comprehensive system of rationing, albeit totally inadequate, introduced by the Iraqi government had so far prevented mass starvation.

The rationing system was established in September 1990, a few weeks after the imposition of the sanctions regime. Even at that time, when the government could rely on some food stocks, the allocation provided only 1300 calories per day per person, far below the necessary energy intake for an adult. People were already having to supplement the ration by purchases on the open market, an option that would become increasingly unrealistic with rocketing price inflation.

In November 1991 Max van der Stoel, the Special Rapporteur of the UN Commission on Human Rights, transmitted to the members of the General Assembly a report on the deteriorating food and health situation in Iraq.[82] The report acknowledged that the 'severe post-war conditions' were 'affecting large parts of the population through the destruction of various parts of the health-care infrastructure, food-producing and food-distributing systems'; and recorded the response of the Iraqi government to questions about the scope of its humanitarian provision.

It was claimed that the stocks of food and medicines in all Iraqi cities were intended for all citizens, without any discrimination (against charges that military personnel and government officials enjoyed an advantage). Foodstuffs were distributed to citizens, on the basis of ration cards, according to the size of their families. It was acknowledged that state-operated warehouses ('central markets') sold some consumer goods to civil servants ('on low incomes') and military personnel, but claimed that the same provision was available to other citizens via the consumer co-operative associations.

The main purpose of the rationing system was to ensure that every citizen received at least a certain secure food allocation (monthly per capita amount: '8kg of flour, 1kg of rice, 1.5kg of sugar, 50gm of tea, 1kg of legumes and 50gm of oil'), which, if purchased on the open market, would cost 20 to 30 times as much. At that time (November 1991) the monthly foodstuff allocation was being distributed by 48,823 agents of the State Enterprise for Trade in Foodstuffs, part of a nationwide system that had so far managed to stave off famine. Notwithstanding this degree of success, Iraq then drew attention to the impact of sanctions on the civilian population; in particular, to the spread of disease, the increase in the infant mortality rate, etc. (' ... thousands of children in Iraq would die unless they were rapidly provided with food and medicine ...'). In response, the Special Rapporteur, while broadly defending the UN posture, conceded that there 'can be no doubt that the capacity of Government of Iraq to ensure high standards of well-being in terms of access to food and health care has been impaired by events in the last year or so'.

The rationing system remained in place in subsequent years, though it became increasingly inadequate with time. In July 1993 a report* from the UN Food and Agriculture Organisation (FAO) noted that the public rationing arrangements had provided food to the population 'at highly subsidised prices which currently represent less than 1 per cent of the cost of market purchases'.[83] The rations were 'an exclusive and indispensable means of sustenance for a vast majority of the households', but though there had been some improvement in the rationing system from the very low levels after the war, it was now only able to provide 53 per cent of the average energy intake of the 1987/89 period. Massive famine had been prevented but the system had not been able to check 'the increasing malnutrition and morbidity rates, affecting a large section of the population'.[84] The rationing system, 'basically equitable ... and generally efficient', was coming under increasing strain: ' ... at current market prices the direct monthly cost of government subsidy on food rations amounts to 8.9 billion dinars ($108 million). Such a huge cost, a substantial part of which is composed of foreign exchange component, cannot be supported by the government for too long, without having the ability to earn foreign exchange. The inability of the country to resume international trade renders the public rationing system extremely vulnerable; a collapse of the system would spell a catastrophe for the majority of the Iraqi population.'[85]

There was now little prospect that the embargo would be lifted in the near future, even though, according to academic analysis, the 'most compelling manifestation of the embargo's effects was on food'.[86] The embargo had resulted in a halt to commercial food imports, causing food shortages 'and their intensification over time'. Moreover, with the growing scarcities of animal feed, the animal stocks, especially sheep and goats, 'had to be culled by more than one-half their previous

---

* This report came to form a substantial part of the FAO/WFP Special Alert No. 237, July 1993 (see note 88).

levels'. The litany of contributory factors is familiar: rising prices, acute shortages of spare parts for agricultural equipment, the exodus of foreign labour, the collapse of the transportation and electric-power infrastructure, a 'significant decline in breastfeeding . . . attributed primarily to psychological trauma', the unavailability of tinned milk and formula, the sale of household assets to buy food at rapidly escalating prices, and so on. The result was that 'Iraqi society suffered a health crisis superimposed on a worsening food crisis.' In 1993 the overall situation was 'still characterised by persisting food insecurity for most Iraqi citizens'.[87] Only the lifting of the embargo will allow Iraq to enjoy 'much of the food security it enjoyed' in the pre-sanctions period.

In January 1993 a tray of 30 eggs purchased in the open market in Iraq cost 72 dinars, compared with 1.5 dinars at the end of the Gulf War; lamb was costing 85 dinars a kilogram; and a tin of baby-milk formula 180 dinars. Most civil servants, the majority of Iraqis still employed, were earning between 250 and 500 dinars a month. The government rationing system continued to operate but by now was providing sufficient food for perhaps 10 days out of every month. The 'Special Alert', issued jointly by the Food and Agriculture Organisation (FAO) and the World Food Programme (WFP) in July 1993, suggested that the rationing system was providing perhaps one-half of the required per capita energy intake, and that the diet was deficient in essential micro-nutrients and protein. Furthermore, price inflation meant that much of the population was no longer able to supplement the ration by market purchases. In consequence, 'large numbers of Iraqis have now food intakes lower than those of the populations in the disaster-stricken African countries'.[88] Surveys were showing that an increasing number of children were dropping out of school 'to enter petty trading to supplement their family incomes'. Now beggars were becoming 'a common sight on Iraqi streets and most of them beg for food rather than cash'. A sharp rise in unorganised crime was being reported in many localities. The condition of the Iraqi people, after three years of punitive sanctions, was sinking into an ever deepening crisis:

The Mission found that for a large section of the population the coping mechanisms are fast running out. Recent surveys indicate a considerable deterioration of the nutritional status of the population, with the vulnerable groups worst affected. There has been a substantial increase in the number of people seeking destitute status who cannot be absorbed in the state support system for lack of government funds . . . the above indicators clearly demonstrate a widespread and acute food supply and access crisis which, if not averted urgently, will cause massive starvation in the country.[89]

The solution to the crisis was plain. The sanctions had caused 'persistent deprivation, severe hunger and malnutrition for a vast majority of the Iraqi population, particularly the vulnerable groups – children under five, expectant/nursing women, widows, orphans, the sick, the elderly and disabled'. To continue the sanctions in their present form would only serve to aggravate 'the already grave food supply situation'. The report declared: *'The lasting solution to the current food crisis would lie in the regeneration of the Iraqi economy which cannot be achieved without a resumption of international trade by the country. Such an action will not only relieve the grave human suffering in Iraq, but will also allow a release of scarce humanitarian assistance resources (currently being used in Iraq) for their most appropriate allocation to the benefit of large numbers of starving people elsewhere in the world.'*[90] This UN-linked joint initiative, at odds with the posture of the US-dominated Security Council, was emphasising an important fact: the embargo was not only pushing the bulk of the Iraqi population into destitution but also depriving countless suffering people elsewhere of essential aid.

A subsequent FAO report (December 1993)[91] confirmed the findings of the joint FAO/WFP Special Alert (July 1993). The Mission, following observations and interviews in several areas of Iraq, confirmed the presence of many acknowledged pre-famine indicators, 'such as very high food prices, collapse of private incomes, depletion of personal assets and rapidly increasing numbers of the destitute'; and noted that various coping strategies had been adopted, 'such as secondary employment, child labour, and the sale of household assets'.[92]

The earlier FAO/WFP Mission had optimistically forecast a significant recovery in domestic food production, but now it was noted that the familiar problems were combining to obstruct any real recovery: 'The lack of herbicides, pesticides, compound fertilisers, agricultural machinery and sprayer spare parts, and seeds still constitute a major obstacle . . . production of livestock is facing severe shortages of veterinary drugs and vaccines. As a result a number of animal diseases which pass to humans, such as brucellosis, have also increased and created problems in food safety.' And there was evidence that *the deliberately-contrived administrative delays in the UN clearance procedures were causing approved agricultural items to arrive too late to aid productivity.*

It was noted also that the sanctions were affecting not only productivity but the quality of food grains. The grains were of poor quality, 'indicating inadequacies in seeds, fertilizers, and crop protection, and contain high levels of foreign materials (e.g. wood, dirt, and stones)'. Moreover the low production levels were forcing producers to mix several lower-value grains (barley, millet, corn, etc.) to produce flour, which in turn was of very poor quality because of the deteriorating condition of the milling equipment. It was estimated that the 1993 production of eggs and poultry would barely reach 20 per cent of 1990 levels; and that livestock numbers would continue to decline because of the shortages of feed, veterinary drugs and vaccines.[93] The rationing system, though continuing to supply a totally inadequate diet to the majority of the Iraqi people, remained 'highly effective in reaching the population' (one computerised list of people entitled to receive rations, examined by the Mission in Baghdad, comprised more than 1 million names). After considering the composition of the government-supplied diet, the Mission concluded: 'The ration supplies a very important part of daily dietary needs ... It is, however, far from being nutritionally balanced both in relation of daily needs and also to what was available in 1988–90.' Food prices on the open market continued to escalate (see Table 3.5).[94]

One estimate suggested that in April 1994 the Iraqi government was spending about $750 million a year, a significant proportion of Iraq's meagre export earnings, on providing basic rations to prevent mass starvation. But this remained a deteriorating situation. In September 1994 the Iraqi government was forced to reduce the ration of cheap flour, rice and cooking oil by about a half. A few rations had been increased in January but now, the situation becoming increasingly desperate, some cut-backs were unavoidable. The government newspaper *Al–Jumhuriya* reported that President Saddam Hussein and his cabinet had decreed the cuts, forced on Iraq because of the embargo, to 'organise economic conditions because of the unjust sanctions and the short supply of cereals ...'. One aid group was now estimating that annual food imports to Iraq had reached about $1.2 billion, against an annual pre-war food import of $2 to 3 billion. When the domestic food output was taken into account this meant that Iraq continued to face a 40 per cent shortage of food supplies compared with pre-war levels.[95] Since 1990 salaries for those in work had increased 2–3-fold, against food prices that had risen 32–1000-fold in the same period with daily rises continuing. Thus from 1990 to 1994 meat had become 32 times more expensive, milk powder 375, vegetable oil 283, and

TABLE 3.5   Inflation of basic food prices (July 1990–November 1993)

Commodity (kg)	Food Prices July 1990[1]	Food Prices Nov. 1993[2]	Times increase
Wheat flour	0.060 dinars	24.300 dinars	405
Rice	0.240	16.500	69
Vegetable oil	0.600	63.000	105
Infant formula	1.600	532.000	332
Lentils	0.400	52.000	130
Potatoes	0.500	16.750	34
Sugar	0.600	57.000	95
Tea	2.000	153.000	77
Red meat	2.000	150.000	75

[1] 1990 prices as reported by the Ministry of Planning.
[2] 1993 prices as collected from markets in Baghdad and Basra by Mission members.

wheat flour 1000 times more expensive. In this context it was easy to see why, in the words of the aid group report, '*everybody is poor*'.[96]

The United Nations itself, charged through the Sanctions Committee with administering the crippling embargo, well knew what was happening. The UN-linked bodies active in the field had accumulated the information over a matter of years. Thus the UN-linked World Food Programme (WFP) was able to note in mid-1995 that *critical food shortages and international indifference were threatening the lives of more than 1 million of the most vulnerable people in Iraq*.[97] Because of a lack of donor pledges, the UN's own aid programme had slashed rations and cut by a half the number of Iraqis receiving assistance. The WFP predicted that by the end of May 1995 most food stocks would be exhausted. In the same vein the Food and Agriculture Organisation (FAO) of the United Nations reported in May/June 1995 that the amount of food imported to Iraq would be 'likely to be further reduced due to a worsening hard currency crisis . . . serious [food] shortages, a sharp drop in the value of the Dinar and a cut by up to 50 per cent in the Government subsidized food rations . . . has resulted in sharp increases in free-market prices which have further eroded the already low purchasing power of the majority of the population'.[98] An appeal launched by the UN Consolidated Inter-Agency Humanitarian Programme for 1995/96 emphasised that Iraq's food needs were enormous and that they could not be met 'solely through humanitarian assistance programmes'. A subsequent WFP report confirmed the deteriorating situation: '*The deterioration of the economic situation in the country and*

*lack of foreign exchange will result in a further reduction of food imports
in 1995. This, coupled with below-normal domestic production, will
result in a sharp decline in the country's per caput food supply.'* And
yet again the inadequacy of the humanitarian assistance programmes
was emphasised.[99]

This was the absurd situation that continued through 1995 and pre-
vailed in 1996. While various humanitarian arms of the United Nations (UNICEF, WHO, WFP, FAO, etc.) bewailed the appalling fact
that the entire Iraqi people were being denied access to adequate food,
medicine and other basic necessities of life, other arms of the United
Nations (the Security Council, the Sanctions Committee) were intent
on maintaining the genocidal sanctions regime that was causing all the
problems. Still Iraq was not to be allowed to use its own natural wealth
to buy food for its people. The silent holocaust would continue.

THE HEALTH WEAPON

One of the main pretexts for prolonging the sanctions regime rests on
assertions about Iraq's development of biological weapons. Iraq itself
has admitted research and development in this field, though there is no
evidence that such devices have ever been used. By contrast, Washington has used unremitting biological warfare against Iraq for more
than five years. Already we have considered how the US-dominated
Sanctions Committee is operating the embargo *to encourage the spread
of disease in Iraq – among human beings, animals and plants.* This is
an undeniable form of biological warfare, one moreover that is impacting on an entire nation. This is the 'health weapon'.

In late-1991 it was estimated that, following the imposition of sanctions and the destruction of medical facilities in the war, less than
one-thirtieth of Iraq's medicine requirements were being met. Iraq had
been accustomed to importing medicines ($500 million-worth a year)
and other medical supplies on a massive scale, a practice that was
almost totally blocked by the embargo. This meant that soon all medicines – including medicated milk for infants with diarrhoea, vaccines,
drugs (for diabetes, asthma, angina, tuberculosis, etc.), anaesthetics and
antibiotics – were in short and diminishing supply. In the same way
all other medical supplies (such as syringes, intravenous fluids, surgical supplies, new medical equipment and spare parts for X-ray machines, incubators, etc.) were rapidly becoming unavailable, either
deliberately blocked by the Sanctions Committee or mischievously delayed

by cumbersome and bureaucratic procedures (see Table 3.1). In addition the collapse of the infrastructure – power supplies, clean water, transportation, etc. – meant that many of the formerly sophisticated health provisions could no longer operate, substantially reducing the access to health care.

Despite the token exemption in Resolution 661 ('. . . not including supplies intended strictly for medical purposes . . .') and later associated provisions and assertions, it remained illegal for the government of Iraq to purchase and import any medicines and medical equipment. Many pharmaceutical companies, often intimidated by Washington, refused to supply their products to Iraq, even when a notional permission had been granted by the Sanctions Committee; and this often resulted in a block on the shipment of products for which Iraq had already paid. In one account more than fifty separate consignments of medicines and thousands of tons of infant formula and milk powder, purchased by the Iraqi government before August 1990, were held by governments that refused to authorise shipment.[100] The wording of the 661 exemption ('strictly for medical purposes') gave the Sanctions Committee licence to insist on detailed applications, protracted discussion, requests for further information, more deliberation – all a recipe for inordinate delays, even in cases where there was an obvious need for urgent medical aid.

In March/April 1991 health experts of the Gulf Peace Team carried out detailed assessments in 14 Iraqi towns, including Basra, Nasiriyah, Najaf, Kerbala, Kirkuk, Sulaimaniyah, Erbil, Mosul, Dohuk, al-Amadiyah and Baghdad. They found that the unavailability of clean water had led to gastroenteritis epidemics with thousands of deaths. More than 50 cases of cholera were diagnosed, though, with many laboratories bombed or otherwise inoperable, diagnosis was often impossible and the cholera incidence was judged to be possibly a hundred times the verified figure. Infants as young as 2 months old were being admitted to the Nasiriyah Paediatric Hospital suffering from severe malnutrition and dying of diarrhoeal diseases. In the absence of drugs and medicated milk such infants could not be treated. Many of the hospitals had been reduced to 'mere reservoirs of infection',[101] since there was a shortage of medicines, the laboratories were not working, there were no surgical supplies, and such basic services as food, clean water and electricity were no longer available. In Kirkuk Hospital a physician described how she had just performed an emergency caesarian section 'with flies swarming over the incision because operating room windows had been shattered during bomb blasts' and the sanctions regime would not allow their replacement.[102] It was now plain that thousands of innocent Iraqi civilians, denied access to food and medicine by the Sanctions Committee, were dying of disease and starvation.

The aid agencies were soon confirming the desperate plight of the Iraqi civilian population. On 12 March 1991 Ibrahim al-Nouri, the director of the Iraqi Red Crescent, told a representative of the French-based Médecins Sans Frontières that 'cases of cholera and typhoid' had been detected in many towns. With the water and sewage systems repeatedly attacked by allied bombers, the World Health Organisation (WHO) estimated that the Baghdad water supply was down to 5 per cent of its pre-war level, which meant that people were forced to take drinking water from heavily polluted rivers. The International Committee of the Red Cross in Amman was warning that there would be widespread epidemics unless appropriate measures were taken. At the same time the London-based Save the Children Fund (SCF) was reporting that 'health, water and sanitation services in Iraq' had collapsed 'as a result primarily of the bombing of infrastructure and communications facilities during the war, and the shortages of fuel and parts under the continued application of international sanctions'. The infrastructure in and around Baghdad, formerly providing medical and other services to one-quarter of the Iraqi population, had been 'systematically crippled and destroyed. . . . Reports confirm that the destruction is similar in other parts of the country. . . . The country is in a state of shock.'[103]

The SCF team reported that, because of the shortages of fuel and electricity, hospitals and clinics were working at around 20 per cent of normal capacity. The availability of stockpiled drugs was sufficient for current medical services in their much reduced condition. The collapse of the transport infrastructure (the destruction of roads, bridges, vehicles, etc. by the bombing) meant that fewer people could reach the hospitals that were still working: only a quarter of the 400 beds in the Saddam Children's Hospital in Baghdad were occupied, and surgeons and physicians were only turning up for work every third or fourth day. It was considered that conditions would be even worse in more remote hospitals. In the Saddam Children's Hospital there was no longer sufficient power to pump water to the tanks on the top floor, equipment could no longer be sterilised, and the operating theatre was out of use.

The Iraqi immunisation programme, formerly achieving around 95 per cent coverage and considered by WHO/UNICEF to be one of the best in the Middle East, had been totally disrupted by the bombing of the electric power infrastructure. Where no cases of polio had been reported in the previous 8 years, this disease, with others formerly eradicated, was again emerging as a public health threat. The nominal medical exemption specified in Resolution 661 was clearly meaningless. Many drugs required by the Iraqi Ministry of Health were produced only by specialist companies in the United States and Britain, and the governments in these countries were effectively blocking all exports to Iraq. In consequence, cardiac, cancer and other serious diseases were no longer receiving proper treatment. The value of medicines reaching Iraq had been reduced from $2 million-worth per day to $2 million-worth a month, 30 times less than before.[104] Before the war the Iraqi Ministry of Health was moving 1500 tons of medical supplies around the country every month using large trucks and trailers with 35-ton capacity; in the immediate post-war period about 90 per cent of the Ministry vehicle fleet had been immobilised.[105]

By May 1991 the main health problems in Iraq were gastroenteritis, dehydration and malnutrition – caused by the shortage of food ('near-famine conditions in certain areas'[106]), and the absence of clean water in most of the country. Some 20–40 new admissions per day for these diseases were being reported for the main children's hospitals in Baghdad, Basra and Kirkuk; two children were arriving dead every day at the Saddam Hussein Children's Hospital in Baghdad, with all the children's hospitals reporting infant mortality rates 2–3 times normal. In the immediate post-war period at least 100 children were dying every day from diseases that were treatable in normal conditions.[107] The bombing had severely eroded the food stocks and sanctions blocked any route to replenishment. Government food warehouses had been targeted by allied bombers, as had food production centres, seed and animal vaccination warehouses, and the only laboratory producing animal vaccines. This helped to produce widespread malnutrition, which in turn made people more susceptible to disease and encouraged the spread of epidemics. At the same time there was a significant increase in the incidence of the characteristic nutritional deficiency diseases, such as marasmus and kwashiorkor (see Table 3.2). Again the mounting evidence was available to UN officials in general and the UN Sanctions Committee in particular. Even if Western politicians and diplomats chose to ignore the information provided by the Iraqi government, it was cynical in the extreme to dismiss the mounting testimony from journalists, medical experts and the aid agencies. Before me as I write I have copies of photographs of children taken in Baghdad hospitals (supplied by the London-based Middle East Action Network). The captions say enough:

5 year-old Fatima Mohammed from Kerbala . . . suffering from severe diarrhoea and dehydration, followed by septicaemia and suspected cholera. . . . She died . . . a few minutes before this photo was taken.

1 month-old Shakar has marasmus and gastroenteritis. . . . He is unlikely to survive . . .

14 year-old Hayda Faraj will probably die from renal failure. There are no dialysis facilities in his hometown, Najaf, and finding transport to Baghdad was a nightmare.

$1\frac{1}{2}$ year-old Sadrin Abdulla has marasmus and kwashiorkor. He is the weight of a baby of 2 or 3 months.

4 month-old Ali Fadil from Najaf is so dehydrated by diarrhoea that he needs artificial tears to cry with. If he survives he'll be blind, as well as otherwise physically and mentally disabled.

5 year-old Habia Majad is severely malnourished. She should weigh at least 18kg, but weighs only 8.5.

5 year-old Sejwas Abdullah is on a respirator, brain-dead from diabetes, due to shortages of insulin.

1 year-old Riyam Majid . . . has been sick for 4 months from kwashiorkor, caused by lack of protein.

The Middle East Action Network (MEAN), formed in March 1991 by members of the Gulf Peace Team, was now reporting the mounting deaths from diarrhoea, malnutrition, marasmus, kwashiorkor, cholera and typhoid. Overstressed, malnourished mothers were producing little breastmilk, so exacerbating the effects of the bombing of the Abu Gharaib infant-milk factory which formerly supplied 80 per cent of the country's needs. Relatively minor illnesses were now often fatal, because of poor food, contaminated water, the lack of medical supplies, and the collapse of the telephone and transport systems. There were reports of babies dying in incubators after power failures, with others growing up with cerebral palsy due to insufficient oxygen. The al-Wiya Children's Hospital in Baghdad normally had a monthly average of 8 deaths by disease, but the total from mid-March to mid-April 1991 was 150. It was estimated that only about 10 per cent of seriously sick children were reaching the hospitals.[108]

The London-based charity Medical Aid for Iraq (MAI), carrying medical supplies to Iraq in September 1991, reported on the 'steady deterioration' in the hospitals. Machinery was breaking down and spare parts could not be obtained; 'nearly all medicines' were in short supply; the shortages of anaesthetics meant that only emergency operations could be performed; as always, 'in these situations the innocent continue to suffer and die'.[109] In Baghdad pharmacies a constant stream of people with prescriptions was arriving, only to be turned away. Some pharmacists were turning away 90 per cent of the people; elsewhere only 1–2 per cent of people were being served. One elderly man had tried 6 or 7 pharmacies; another, 30–40; elsewhere desperate parents were struggling to obtain an antibiotic cream to prevent their 4-year-old son from losing the skin graft on his head.

The MAI team witnessed depressingly similar conditions in all the hospitals they visited: medicine shortages and an increase in the incidence of disease, shortage of anaesthetics, power failure in the middle of emergency heart operation (Medical City, Baghdad); shortages of drugs and medicines, increase in malnutrition and typhoid, shortage of nurses, shortage of disinfectants, no polio or typhoid vaccines, lakes of sewage in the street (Basra General Hospital); marasmus and gastroenteritis, 20 cases of typhoid a week, increase in incidence of polio and meningitis, women unable to breastfeed through malnutrition and trauma, same needles used repeatedly for injections, equipment breaking down, increase in anaemia and the need for caesarian section (Nasiriyah Hospital); central heating/cooling systems inoperable, increase in leukaemia, typhoid increased 10 times, hepatitis 10 times, cholera 20 times, most malnourished children dying (Kerbala Children's Hospital).[110] Such findings served to confirm much of the information presented by the Harvard medical team which travelled throughout Iraq from 28 April to 6 May 1991 and was allowed unlimited access to medical facilities throughout the country, as well as to water purification plant, sewage treatment facilities and electrical power plant. The team commented that cholera, typhoid and gastroenteritis had reached epidemic proportions, and that 'the state of medical care is desperate and – unless conditions substantially change – will continue to deteriorate in every region and at nearly every provider level'.

The 28-page report from the Harvard team, released at a 22 May press conference in Washington, D. C., was largely ignored, as were the many other reports from the aid agencies, journalists, interested observers and the Iraqi health authorities. The findings of the Harvard team, led by Dr Megan Passey, were briefly reported in the Western media; and substantial extracts appeared in various specialist journals. The team concluded that Iraq was experiencing 'an emerging public health catastrophe', that infant and child mortality was set to double, and that 'at least 170,000 children under five' would die during the coming year as a result of the war and economic sanctions. Six crucial factors were identified:

- Mortality data, gathered in hospital visits, showed a 2- to 3-fold increase in infant and child deaths;

- Morbidity data showed the sudden onset of epidemics of gastro-enteritis, cholera and typhoid throughout the country in early 1991;

- These waterborne diseases, typically peaking during the hot summer months of June and July, had started months earlier and so would probably worsen;

- Severe malnutrition, previously uncommon, was now widespread in all regions of the country;

- The health system was operating at a fraction of its pre-war capacity, with many hospitals and community health centres closed and with acute shortages of medicines, staff and equipment;

- The basic infrastructure for water purification, sewage treatment and electrical power generation was operating at substantially reduced levels, with many facilities damaged beyond repair.

The findings of the prestigious Harvard medical team were now being confirmed, not only by journalists and the independent aid agencies, but also by various UN-linked bodies. Thus reports issued under the auspices of the World Food Programme (WFP) described the deteriorating health condition of the Iraqi population and, by implication, criticised the suffering being caused to ordinary civilians by the sanctions regime. In one account a child is rushed into the emergency entrance of the al-Wiya Children's Hospital in Baghdad. To the distraught grandmother the doctor says: 'He has chronic diarrhoea. He has no immunity; he will die any minute now. It has become a common problem now. We see this every day, among children from a few months to a few years ...'. The grim scenario is repeated elsewhere. In Erbil a mother sits on a bed, holding a severely malnourished baby. The doctor predicts that if the baby survives he will be mentally handicapped: 'What the baby needs is a therapeutic formula such as Isomil. But it's hard to find and too expensive.' Says Dr Adnam Al Asadi: 'On one hand we are trying to reconstruct and rebuild our hospitals and health centres but at the same time we are trying to cope with the problems of epidemics caused by returnees with viral hepatitis, typhoid and chronic diarrhoea. These are problems that we just weren't prepared for and we don't have the proper medicines.'[111]

Here it is pointed out that Iraq's health care system was the best in the region: 95 per cent of all Iraqi children immunised against polio, measles and diphtheria, even the poorest people given free medical care, paying minimal fees for drugs and consultations, and with the country proud of its physicians, many with degrees from the top medical schools in the United States and Britain. Now 'they must sit and watch their healing powers erode'. Said one doctor: 'We have lost patients because we didn't have any instruments. We can't monitor cardiac patients because the monitors don't work. Either we have run out of spare parts or laboratory kits. We have radiological equipment, but no X-ray paper. Because of the shortage of food and, prior to that, of fuel, it was difficult getting staff to the hospitals. The quality of our work has declined because staff are stressed and overtired ... many of us just don't want to practise medicine here anymore.'[112] By late 1991 the deteriorating health of the Iraqi population was widely known in the international community, as was the lifting of sanctions perceived to be the only realistic answer to the deepening crisis. Thus three medical experts working for the UNICEF Nutrition Programme in Baghdad highlighted the '*gradual descent of the children of Iraq into a state of malnutrition: severely malnourished children do not survive ...*'; and then concluded: 'There is a risk of acute food crisis unless economic sanctions are lifted soon.'[113]

At the same time a report to the United Nations was supplying further evidence of the medical catastrophe afflicting the Iraqi people.[114] The annual incidence of typhoid, paratyphoid, and amoebic and bacillic dysentery had increased 5- to 6-fold; viral hepatitis (types A and B) had increased more than 8-fold; the registered cholera cases now numbered 1217, of which dozens had already died; between August 1990 and August 1991 a total of 14,232 children under 5 died, whereas the corresponding 1989/90 number was 3188, indicating a 4-fold increase; over the same 1990/91 period 36,968 children over 5 died, a 3-fold increase over the equivalent 1989/90 period. It was found also that many specific diseases, in addition to those with obvious nutritional or hygiene roots, were seeing a large increase. Thus, as may be expected, there were more patients with psychological problems: 21,411 outpatients and inpatients for 1991; 24,857 for 1992; and 25,250 for 1993 (up to August). Cases of high blood pressure associated with mortality had risen from 609 cases in 1990 to 1707 cases for the first half of 1993; with cases of diabetes associated with mortality rising from 450 cases in 1990 to 1031 cases for the first half of 1993. One estimate suggested that about one million Iraqi children were malnourished in 1993, an incidence of nutritional deprivation that was inevitably associated with various diseases.

In July 1992 the Iraqi UN ambassador, Abd al-Amir al-Anbari, submitted to the UN Secretary-General a study prepared by the Iraqi Ministry of Foreign Affairs on the working of the Sanctions Committee.[115] The study highlighted a UN report which indicated that 40 per cent of water samples in Basra were polluted, a situation that also existed in the neighbouring governorates. It was emphasised that the drainage of untreated water had led to the pollution of agricultural land and overflowing drains in residential areas. This and other factors associated with the sanctions regime had caused further deterioration in the health of the Iraqi people: 'The situation which the Iraqi people is suffering . . . is extremely tragic . . . all the medical contributions of humanitarian organisations and bodies meet only a small portion of the actual needs of drugs and medical services.' The report included a table (see Table 3.6) showing the growing incidence of various diseases. In this connection it was emphasised that Iraq had relied upon sophisticated medical technology imported from around the world; and that now Iraq was prohibited by the sanctions regime from importing such equipment and the necessary spare parts for equipment already in Iraq. Iraq was no longer allowed to acquire X-ray plates, laboratory scanners, spare parts for incubators and intensive-care units, inks, paper and much else for which there was a clear medical need.

The report concluded: 'It appears . . . that the work of the Sanctions Committee and the way it performs the tasks entrusted to it under Security Council Resolution 661 (1990) are oriented towards the obstruction or rejection of any request by Iraq that enters into the area of civilian essential needs of a humanitarian nature, which has led to the increasing danger faced by vulnerable categories.'[116] Attention was drawn to the 'political motives' of the states controlling the Sanctions Committee; how the voting system in the Committee hinders the taking of decisions (and leads to procrastination on the pretext of seeking further information and clarifications); how the exclusion of Iraq from the Committee is a further means of obstructing approval for Iraqi humanitarian requests; how humanitarian requests are denied on the bogus ground that they might contribute to the Iraqi industrial structure; how the blocking of Iraqi funds prevents the purchase of products needed for humanitarian purposes; and how such practices contribute to an increase in the incidence of disease, particularly among children.

TABLE 3.6   Increase in disease incidence in Iraq (1989–91)

Disease	Number of cases		
	1989	*1990*	*1991*
Poliomyelitis	10	56	186
Angina	96	168	511
Whooping cough	368	489	1,537
Measles	5,715	7,524	11,358
German measles	514	693	2,848
Puerperal tetanus	42	393	936
Tetanus	32	87	933
Pneumonia	6,612	11,713	235,329
Mumps	9,639	15,962	22,718
Cholera	0	0	1,217
Typhoid	1,812	2,240	17,524
Giardiasis	73,412	113,222	501,391
Amoebic dysentery	19,615	32,957	58,311
Viral hepatitis	1,816	3,228	11,135
Meningitis	2,559	1,810	5,792
Domestic malaria	3,428	3,924	7,105
Baghdad rash	1,829	1,894	8,233
Black-water fever	491	576	3,713
Haemorrhagic fever	38	42	196
Malta fever	372	512	2,223
Ankylostomiasis	370	406	1,787
Scabies	0	198	1,892
Rabies	25	37	256

Still there seemed no prospect that the Sanctions Committee would address the basic humanitarian needs of Iraq in the way that the report suggested: as '*in reality a cohesive chain of humanitarian services, plus materials and equipment which extends from the sectors of electricity, agriculture, water, sanitation, medicines and health and medical requirements, food, clothes and other educational and living requirements . . .*'. The Committee was not ready to give prompt and positive consideration to basic humanitarian items, much less to agree the provision of a 'cohesive chain' or any other formula for the relief of the suffering now being endured by the Iraqi people.

On 18 February 1993 the former US Attorney-General Ramsey Clark, conducting his own tireless campaign against the genocide of the Iraqi people, wrote again to UN Secretary-General Boutros Boutros-Ghali to ask for an 'immediate end' to the sanctions. Clark had toured Iraq extensively and had no doubt what was being perpetrated by the US-dominated Sanctions Committee: 'The UN sanctions are causing the

TABLE 3.7   Increase in disease incidence in Iraq (1989–92)

Disease	Year	No. of cases	Year	No. of cases	Increase
Kwashiorkor	1990	485	1992	13,744	28 times
Marasmus	1990	5,193	1992	111,477	21 times
Cholera	1989–90	none	1991–2	2,100	
Measles and German measles	1989	6,229	1992	21,823	3+ times
Typhoid fever	1989	1,812	1992	19,276	10+ times
Pneumonia	1989	6,612	1992	17,377	2.5 times
Amoebic dysentery	1989	19,615	1992	61,939	3+ times
Viral hepatitis	1989	1,816	1992	13,776	7+ times
Brucellosis	1989	2,816	1992	14,546	5.9 times
Giardiasis	1989	73,416	1992	596,356	8.1 times
Whooping cough	1989	368	1992	1601	4.3 times
Poliomyelitis	1989	10	1992	120	12 times

deaths of more than 2000 people a week from the lack of medicine, medical services, food and diet supplements, bad water, and equipment and parts needed for health care. . . . There can be no doubt about the deaths . . . UNICEF estimates 80,000–100,000 deaths of children under 5 in 1993 if sanctions remain in place.' Again the United Nations was made aware of the increase in disease in Iraq as a result of sanctions (Table 3.7).

It was pointed out that the special report in the *New England Journal of Medicine* (24 September 1992), among others, had established the high death toll in Iraq. Every sector of Iraqi society was affected by the international blockade against the importation of food, medicines and other basic necessities of life. Again the most vulnerable were the worst affected. In 1990 4.5 per cent of births had low body weight; in 1992 the figure was 17.6 per cent, 4 times higher; and the figure was continuing to rise. People with physical disabilities, those with chronic serious illnesses and the elderly were dying at unprecedented rates, a significant component in the 3-fold increase in the death rate. Medical laboratory examinations had declined by 60 per cent (from 17,928,604 in 1989 to some 7,079,420 in 1992); over the same period major surgery had declined by almost two-thirds. Said Ramsey Clark: '*The sanctions are the actual, moral and legal equivalent of taking the lives and health of infants, the sick and the elderly hostage for the payment of money, or other acts of government. They violate humanitarian law because they are known to deprive a population of essential food and medical care.*' And he appealed to the UN Secretary-General to act at once: 'Hundreds of people are dying every day as a direct result of this continuing violation of humanitarian law . . .'.

In February 1993 the aid charity Medicine for Peace (MFP, New York) noted that it was 'quite clear that the functional embargo of medicines and biologicals (vaccines), hospital and laboratory equipment, and most critically, spare parts for medical equipment had resulted in a complete collapse of the health delivery system'.[117] Many hospitals and clinics had closed, and even the best hospitals in Baghdad has drastically reduced their number of beds and were unable to provide adequate medical care. The most acute needs identified were: *anaesthetics and surgical supplies*; *antibiotics, vaccines and other pharmaceuticals* ('only a few of the children with . . . cancer are now able to obtain treatment'); and *hospital and laboratory supplies* ('Iraqi hospitals are still without disposable intravenous and spinal needles, intravenous delivery packs, transfusion sets, sterile tubing, and all of the other supplies that allow a modern hospital to function properly'). It was noted that children with marasmus and kwashiorkor were still 'commonly seen' in emergency rooms and hospitals throughout Iraq. This report concluded with the familiar appeal: 'Iraq must be allowed to sell oil or borrow on assets in order to finance a major reconstruction of the entire hospital and public health system to prevent further unnecessary deaths.'[118]

The 1993 Hoskins report, shelved by politically sensitive UNICEF officials, also highlighted what it called the 'excess deaths' due to the Gulf crisis; in addition drawing attention to the Beth Osborne Daponte finding that Iraqi life expectancy at birth had been reduced from 68 years (pre-war) to 47 years by 1992.[119] She estimated that 30 times as many civilians had died after the war than during the military conflict itself, the largest contributor to the 111,000 excess deaths (60,000 of these children under 5) being the poor health conditions exacerbated by sanctions. Daponte, facing the sack for her politically embarrassing findings, was saved only by the American Civil Liberties Union (ACLU) threatening legal action (Daponte: 'I find it extremely disturbing that the US Census Bureau tried to suppress and delay the release of information . . .'). And Hoskins highlighted also the characteristic features of the deteriorating health situation in Iraq: outbreaks of cholera, typhoid, gastroenteritis, malaria, meningitis, brucellosis, measles, polio, hepatitis and other infectious diseases; the shortage of laboratory kits and reagents; poor hygiene and contaminated water; the unavoidable re-use of disposable needles and syringes; increases in the incidence of scabies and intestinal parasites; the increase in the incidence of malaria due to the lack of ground and aerial spraying; the increase in the number of abortions, miscarriages, premature labour and low-birth-weight babies; the lack of infant formula (baby milk), blocked by sanctions; the massively increased incidence of child malnutrition.

In early 1993 the charity Medical Aid for Iraq (MAI) found that the medical situation had worsened since MAI's last visit (May 1992). The children had 'been hit the hardest'. The need in the hospitals was now even greater, with the basic supplies (cotton wool, dressings, soap, etc.) 'in desperately short supply'; more hospitals had resorted to the re-use of cannulas, needles and syringes. Because of the absence of insulin, comatose diabetic children were arriving in hospital and then being left to die. The lack of intravenous fluids, anaesthetics and muscle relaxants was causing similar problems. The MAI workers also reported 'an ever increasing number of children with kwashiorkor due to protein deficiency ... the children's wards were full of malnourished children'. It was now obvious that 'aid is needed more than ever'.[120]

The individual hospitals visited by the MAI staff were suffering from the usual problems: severe shortages of staff and supplies, children dying for want of insulin, asthmatics dying for want of salbutamol, incubators out of order, lack of milk powder (Kerbala Children's Hospital); most children malnourished, increase in incidence of premature births, no protein food, no antiseptics, the hospital director Dr Saad al-Tibowi having given his own blood 3 times in the past week (Samawa Children's and Obstetrics Hospital); insulin in very short supply, no milk powder, malnourished children suffering from kwashiorkor, UNICEF's feeding programme in collapse (Nasiriyah Children's and Obstetrics Hospital); situation worsening, no insulin and few vaccines, severe lack of cannulas, syringes and intravenous fluids (Kut General Hospital Paediatric Unit); water and sewage problems, lice and worm infestation, constant re-use of cannulas, needles and syringes, cases of marasmus and kwashiorkor due to severe nutritional deficiency (Ibn al-Baldi Children's and Obstetrics Hospital, Baghdad); and so on.[121] In April the Iraqi UN ambassador, Nizar Hamdoon, submitted a letter (S/25653, 22 April 1993) to the UN Secretary-General, detailing the worsening health plight of Iraqi children and the elderly. Subsequent letters conveyed abundant information and the same message. Thus a letter (18 May 1993) addressed to the UN Assistant Secretary-General, Geneva, stressed how the economic embargo had led to 'an acute and widespread shortage of all medicines and medical supplies ... antibiotics, sedatives, endothermics, antiemetics, antidiarrhoeals and ointments are currently unavailable in the country'.[122] There were no

TABLE 3.8   Increases in under-5 and over-50 mortality as a result of sanctions

Under-5 mortality

| | Condition | | | | | |
| | *Diarrhoea* | | *Pneumonia* | | *Malnutrition* | |
Period	*Deaths*	*Rate of increase*	*Deaths*	*Rate of increase*	*Death*	*Rate of increase*
July 1989	142	–	98	–	138	–
July 1993	2001	1309%	901	819.3%	2102	1423%

Over-50 mortality

| | Condition | | | | | |
| *Period* | *Hypertension* | | *Diabetes* | | *Malignant neoplasm* | |
	Deaths	*Rate of increase*	*Deaths*	*Rate of increase*	*Deaths*	*Rate of increase*
July 1989	122	–	62	–	246	–
July 1993	272	123%	146	135.5%	699	184%

intravenous fluids, no hormones, no eye drops. Because of the shortages the number of laboratory tests had fallen by two-thirds (compared with the 1989 rate), as had the number of surgical operations.

Again emphasis was given to the impact of the sanctions regime on hygiene and food availability: 'The economic embargo has also produced a wide shortage of food and personal hygiene articles, which has in turn led to the outbreak of communicable diseases ... such as typhoid, infantile paralysis, tetanus, viral hepatitis, Giardia, German measles, kala-azar, undulent fever, haemorrhagic fever, croup, whooping cough, rickets, scabies, hydrocysts and rabies.'[123] Babies were underweight, children were malnourished, women were unable to breastfeed through malnutrition, and infant foods were unobtainable. A further letter (S/26353, 25 August 1993) charted the increase in under-5 and over-50 mortality as a result of sanctions (Table 3.8)

A further MAI report, following the delivery of medical supplies to hospitals in Baghdad and southern Iraq during September and October 1993, confirmed the continuing food-price inflation and the 'sharp deterioration of the health service within Baghdad over the past two years'.[124] Kwashiorkor and rickets were 'common'; milk rations for babies under 1 year old were half the normal requirement, tempting parents to dilute the ration, 'often using unsterilised water'; diarrhoea and gastroenteritis were 'rife'. Cannulas, syringes, catheters and surgical gloves were being re-used, but in the absence of soap, disinfectants and other cleaning solutions this was inevitably an unsafe practice. The lack of paper meant that prescriptions were being written on scraps of cardboard; dressings and nappies (diapers) were being improvised using tissues, plastic pants and plaster of paris; lactose-free milk (essential for children with gastroenteritis), vitamin drops for babies, drugs for asthma, insulin and other drugs were either completely lacking or in very short supply. There were many more cases of aplastic anaemia, often associated with chemical pollution, and cancers, especially leukaemia, among children. Aplastic anaemia can be treated only by a bone marrow transplant, which now could no longer be performed because of the embargo on the import of new medical equipment and spare parts for equipment needing repair. The cytotoxic drugs needed to combat leukaemia and other cancers were either unavailable or in very short supply.[125] The result was that children and adults with serious but treatable diseases were being left to die. And again the MAI workers reported the deteriorating conditions in Iraqi hospitals: shortages of cannulas, lactose-free milk (Isomil), asthma drugs, a 'vastly increased number of children with rickets', unsterile incubators ('port-hole doors missing, rags pushed into the holes to try and maintain the temperature within'), babies lying on soiled sheets, no vitamin D for rickets, 'unprecedented increase' in cases of amoebic dysentery and infectious hepatitis, cancer ward (Medical City Children's Hospital, Baghdad) full of dying children because of the lack of cytotoxic drugs, 'unprecedented upsurge' in the number of children with cancer, dirty wards with no soap or disinfectant, women giving birth on hard plastic tables, the last working blood gas machine in Iraq now broken and without spare parts unrepairable, sharp decline in conditions may force hospital (Ibn al-Baldi Children's Hospital, Baghdad) closure, doctors meeting to decide which children to leave to die, no spare parts for broken oxygen cylinders, no antiepileptic drugs, doctor performed emergency caesarian operation only to find that there was no catgut or silk left in the hospital (post-operative woman left open for several hours), child with hydrocephaly dying because of the lack of intracranial shunts that would have saved him, efforts to clean blood-stained single-use gloves without soap or disinfectants or sterilising solutions, sharp increase of mortality rate through septicaemia, meningitis 'very much on the increase . . .

with no medication available to treat the children', aplastic anaemia now 'relatively common', many more children with leukaemia, neonatal unit with 'rife septicaemia', many babies 'left to die', and so on.[126]

In February 1994 the British Red Cross reported that large numbers of Iraqis were now 'existing on food intakes which are lower than those of people living in disaster-stricken African countries'; and that 'pharmaceuticals, basic medicaments and spare parts for equipment are also in critically short supply at every level of the Iraqi health system'.[127] Scarce resources were tending to be focused on the towns, leaving the rural areas 'to suffer very badly'. Here it is acknowledged that pre-war Iraq could boast a 'very advanced health system' built up with oil revenues. Now Iraqi doctors accustomed to using high-technology equipment and the latest drugs were having to cope in a devastated health system denuded of equipment, drugs and most basic medical supplies. It is acknowledged also that the deterioration of the health facilities was coming at a time 'when there is an increased need due to the emergence of diseases caused by malnutrition and lack of clean drinking water'. The severe food shortage had resulted in widespread malnutrition, and 'there is a massive shortage of medical supplies to treat any illnesses which occur . . . water supplies are badly contaminated because water treatment plants have fallen into a state of disrepair due to a lack of spare parts, and raw sewage is now leaking into drinking water supplies'.[128] In the same spirit the Smit/Revel report for the International Federation of Red Cross and Red Crescent Societies noted that Iraq, which had formerly enjoyed a 'very well developed' health care system (with 'sophisticated health care facilities . . . nearly free of charge'), was now seeing massive deterioration in its health provisions.[129]

Most of the hospitals visited 'were in a rather poor condition with facilities worn out, broken down and overused', with sanitation remaining a major problem: 'Large ponds and stagnant water surrounding villages and suburban areas such as Kut, Basra and all cities in the south represent a major health hazard. Typhoid fever, cholera, hepatitis A and all kinds of gastro-intestinal diseases have been reported . . .'.[130] It is acknowledged that pre-war Iraq was free from malaria but that now it had reappeared in the northern governorates, which were reporting 'thousands of cases'. The shortage of insecticides and medicines left 'little hope for any improvement in the short term' and there were increased risks of further spreading of the disease; tuberculosis, kala-azar and other diseases, at one time almost totally eradicated, were now also reappearing.

Few observers doubted that the sanctions regime was now the main cause of the deteriorating health situation in Iraq. Drugs, equipment, spare parts, and all other medical supplies (even such basic items as soap, disinfectants and syringes) were either permanently blocked or delayed to the point that their usefulness was massively eroded. Western politicians and diplomats continued to assert that foodstuffs and medicines were exempted from the embargo – a claim that was belied by all the evidence. There was even a suggestion, quite apart from the cynical delays introduced into the discussions of the Sanctions Committee, that Washington and London were deliberately conspiring to tamper with the flow of medical supplies into Iraq. Thus Tim Llewellyn, the BBC Middle East correspondent, speaking on 16 February 1994 in Westminster at the monthly meeting of the Council for the Advancement of Arab–British Understanding (CAABU), declared: *'The claim by the Western governments that food and drugs flow freely into Iraq is not true. I have seen telexes and documents that showed clearly that the British and the American government interfered with the flow of crucial drugs into Iraq. That is unquestionable.'* And Llewellyn emphasised what Washington had made 'absolutely clear' – that the sanctions would 'not be lifted even if Iraq satisfies the United Nations Security Council on every single sanction report . . . the Americans are making it clear that the sanctions are not going to be lifted under any circumstances . . . the West's decision is . . . to keep squeezing the country. . . . I do not see any possibility that oil will flow in Iraq between now and the end of 1994, and probably after that.' After the same time the number of Iraqi dead – in effect killed by the Sanctions Committee – continued to mount. Where, according to the Iraqi health minister, the monthly average of individuals deceased in 1990 was 2545.4, the figure rose to 7161.8 in 1991, and to 11,193.5 in early 1994 – a rise solely attributable to the embargo on the essentials of life.

A further MAI team delivered medical supplies to hospitals in Baghdad and southern Iraq in April 1994.[131] Again the team was struck by further 'sharp deterioration of the health provision within Baghdad'. Even hospitals that were previously better supplied than those outside Baghdad were now in a much worsened state. The MAI workers reported: 'All medicines are lacking. . . . Cholera and typhoid are still a problem. A lack of spare parts obstructs repair of water processing plants. . . . Chlorine is in short supply, so that purification is not effective.' As before, essential medicines for children with chronic diseases (diabetes, epilepsy, asthma, etc.) were either unavailable or in very short supply, with intravenous drugs and fluids 'especially scarce'. Antibiotics, when available, typically ran out mid-course. Anaemic children, with no access to iron supplements, were being treated with blood transfusions, in the circumstances risking the transmission of hepatitis and AIDS. All the hospitals visited by the MAI workers lacked cleaning fluids, disinfectants, insecticides, bedsheets, theatre gowns and most other medical supplies. Staff shortages were continuing to rise because of transport problems and low pay. And there was the usual grim catalogue of medical decay and deterioration, with all the human suffering that this implied: 'Conditions have worsened considerably since MAI's last visit. All drugs and equipment are in short supply. . . . There are no disinfectants. . . . The neonatal unit was virtually empty, as there are no drugs available for sick babies' (Kerbala Children's Hospital); 'Conditions are deteriorating. . . . There are no antiepileptic drugs, antibiotics or insulin. . . . Milk powder is reserved for infants who have had diarrhoea for more than two weeks . . . flies are a serious problem' (Samawa Children's and Obstetric Hospital); 'The hospital serves 800,000 people. It receives only 5 per cent of the medicines required per month' (Diwaniya Children's and Obstetric Hospital); 'All medicines and equipment are needed. . . . The hospital has not been visited by any NGO [non-governmental organisation] supplying aid in the past year, and has received no medicines or equipment . . . in this time' (Kut General Hospital); and so on for all the hospitals visited (Feluja General Hospital, Bequba Women's and Children's Hospital, Ibn al-Baldi Children's and Obstetric Hospital, al-Wiyah Children's Hospital, the al Mansour (Medical City) Children's Hospital, etc.).

The general MAI conclusion was that the Iraqi health system, after nearly four years of crippling sanctions, was in a state of virtual collapse; and that the situation continued to worsen:

A general deterioration is widely reported over the last three months. Malnutrition and the increases in infection rates associated with it have resulted in a worsening situation and an increased shortage of medicines. Hospitals in Baghdad, where 25% of the population live, are experiencing particularly acute shortages.[132]

In this situation, largely hidden from Western publics, a British physician, Dr Harvey Marcovitch, could well ask – '*Saddam's atrocity – or ours?*'[133] Here a desperate letter from an Iraqi doctor is quoted. The points are familiar enough:

The sanctions imposed by the UN are taking their toll mainly on the children and women. . . . Working in paediatric departments in Iraq has become a daily nightmare. . . . Hospitals depend entirely on irregular and spasmodic donations brought in by charities, which are like a drop of water on parched earth . . . In the diabetic clinic we have to divide four small bottles of insulin between 20 or 30 children while trying to calm their parents' terror. . . . For children with leukaemia to begin treatment, parents are forced to send money to buy drugs from Jordan. . . . Parents sell their belongings and even their homes and even after bringing in the drugs the children are dying from uncontrolled infection.[134]

The letter was accompanied by photographs of starving children and ones suffering from vitamin deficiency diseases. Marcovitch circulated copies of the letter to British paediatricians – and received no response.

In June 1994 the Iraqi Ministry of Culture and Information published further information showing the growing incidence of disease through the Iraqi population (Table 3.9).[135] At the same time this report also indicated the reduction in the number of major surgical operations (from a monthly rate of 15,125 in 1989 to a rate of less than 5000 in early 1994), the fewer laboratory tests (from a monthly rate of 1,494,050 in 1989 to a rate of less than half a million in early 1994), and the reduction in the amount of food supplied (per person/per month) as a result of sanctions. In December 1994 a further MAI report again charted the unrelieved crisis in Iraqi health care: 'The situation has deteriorated sharply in the six months since MAI's last visit.'[136] This report notes that in October 1994 the government food rations, already wholly inadequate, were cut by a third: now a monthly ration was not sufficing for much more than one week: 'The further reduction will result in another increase in malnourished children and underfed pregnant or nursing women. . . . The major concern of most Iraqis is the question of how to feed their families.' The MAI team reported a decrease in the amount of food available in the shops, and a deterioration in the quality of what food was available. And yet again:

A severe deterioration is detectable in all the hospitals visited by MAI. The team had not expected to see such an extreme reduction of resources, given the desperate situation of the hospitals in April: further deterioration had been hard to imagine. Basic medicines are absent, routine surgery impossible, and more and more equipment is breaking down and put out of use because of the unavailability of

TABLE 3.9 Increase in incidence of some communicable diseases (1989–93)

Disease	1989 number	1990 number	1990 increase times 1989	1991 number	1991 increase times 1989	1992 number	1992 increase times 1989	1993 number	1993 increase times 1989
Poliomyelitis	10	56	5.6	186	18.6	120	12	75	7.5
Diphtheria	96	168	1.75	511	5.4	369	3.8	239	2.49
Whooping cough	368	489	1.3	1,537	4.1	1,601	4.3	767	2.08
Measles	5,715	7,024	1.3	11,358	1.9	20,160	3.5	16,399	2.87
German measles	514	693	1.3	2,848	5.5	1,663	3.2	928	1.8
Puerperal tetanus	42	393	9.3	936	22.2	233	5.58	171	4.1
Tetanus	32	87	2.7	933	29.1	98	3	64	2
Pneumonia	3,312	11,713	1.7	23,529	3.5	17,377	2.6	199,114	2.89
Mumps	9,839	15,963	1.6	22,718	2.3	23,883	2.4	46,916	4.87
Cholera	Nil	Nil	Nil	1,217	1,217	976	976	825	825
Typhoid	1,812	2,240	1.2	17,524	9.6	19,276	10.6	22,688	12.5
Giardiasis	73,416	113,222	1.5	501,391	6.8	596,356	8.1	602,011	8.2
Amoebic dysentery	19,615	32,957	1.6	58,311	2.9	61,939	3.1	62,864	3.2
Viral hepatitis	1,816	3,228	1.7	11,135	6.1	13,766	7.5	16,801	9.2
Meningitis	2,559	1,810	0.7	5,792	2.3	4,534	1.8	3,772	1.47
Local malaria	4,328	3,924	1.1	7,105	2	5,535	1.6	4,581	1.34
Oriental sore	1,829	1,894	1	8,233	4.5	8,779	4.8	7,378	4.03
Black-water fever	491	576	1.1	3,713	7.5	3,866	7.8	3,817	7.77
Haemorrhagic fever	38	42	1.1	196	5.1	65	1.7	48	1.53
Malta fever	2,464	2,816	1.1	13,106	5.3	14,546	5.9	14,989	6.1
Toxoplasmosis	372	512	1.3	2,223	5.9	2,754	7.3	3,145	8.54
Ankylostomiasis	370	406	1	1,787	4.8	1,991	5.3	2,108	5.69
Scabies	Nil	198	198	1,892	1,892	7,956	7,956	10,354	10,354
Rabies	25	37	1.4	256	10.2	84	3.3	49	1.96

*spare parts. . . . Children are referred to Baghdad because treat-
ment is unavailable at their local hospital. . . . But the Baghdad
hospitals cannot provide the treatment either.*[137]

The al-Wiyah Children's Hospital in Baghdad had run out of *all*
medicines, with the wards full of sick and dying children that could
not be treated. There had been an 'unprecedented deterioration' in the
period prior to MAI's visit. There was a reduced need for insulin: 'so
many diabetic children have died'. Now many children, unable to reach
hospitals where in any case there would be no treatment, were dying
untreated at home. At the Saddam Children's Teaching Hospital few
incubators were working, specialised surgery was no longer possible,
there was an increase in the number of children with leukaemia and
congenital heart disease with no available treatment, and babies and
children were dying at an ever faster rate. And yet again the inevitable
conclusion: 'The hospitals visited . . . reveal the extent of the rapid
deterioration of conditions in Iraqi society at large. . . . The result is a
deepening crisis which affects not only the present, but also the future,
hitting the vulnerable first.'

The International Scientific Symposium (Baghdad, 10–12 December
1994) helped to chart the impact of war and sanctions on the health of
the Iraqi people.[138] Here there is further information about the spread
of disease, increased child mortality rates, increased low birth weights,
increased incidence of child leukaemia, increased incidence of some
adult cancers, increased incidence of seminal fluid abnormalities, and
increased incidence of some congenital malformations (an increased
incidence of ambiguous genitalia, skeletal abnormalities, hydrocephaly,
etc.).[139] The information was available in abundance, if people cared
to notice.

In January 1995 Iraq submitted a note verbale, enclosing a study
entitled 'The impact of the blockade on Iraq', to the Centre for Human Rights at the United Nations Office in Geneva.[140] This substantial
38-page document (complete with some fancy title fonts and many
typographical errors) conveys much information about the impact of
the embargo on Iraq's health care system (see Appendix 7 for extract).
The facts were plain enough, long known to Western politicians and
diplomats but still rarely impinging on the consciousness of Western
publics. In March 1995 *The Sunday Times*, London, felt able to run an
item conveying the tribulations and anxieties of a typical Iraqi doctor.[141] The picture was familiar to anyone who had followed events:
shortage of food, rocketing prices, the progressive collapse of Iraq's

health care systems, and again the *nightmare* simile: 'Being in casualty is like living in a nightmare. The severe shortage of drugs means we can do very little to help. . . . Children die in front of me. The parents ask why and I cannot answer them. . . . Each night I pray for the embargo to be lifted.'

In April 1995 MAI workers again delivered medical supplies to hospitals in Baghdad and southern Iraq. A month later the usual report appeared.[142] It included the following comments: '*The situation has deteriorated yet further. . . . Morale is extremely low, and there is no expectation of improvement. . . . A severe deterioration in conditions continues to affect all the hospitals. . . . Malnutrition is even more widespread among children than it was six months ago . . .*'. A significant increase was noted in the incidence of underweight babies, rickets, marasmus, kwashiorkor, tuberculosis, hepatitis A, the number of children bitten by mosquitos, children dying at home, child blindness from lack of vitamin A, rheumatic fever, brucellosis, gastroenteritis and amoebic dysentery. The comprehensive biological warfare being waged by Washington against the helpless Iraqi people continued to wreak its predictable genocide.

EPILOGUE

The silent war being waged against Iraq has now continued for well over five years, as I write. Washington spares nothing of this nation. By denying trade *in toto*, everything and all life become a target: social infrastructure, human beings, livestock and plants; even the animals in Baghdad's famous zoo have been condemned to oblivion.[143] As the metaphors accumulate with the suffering, the whole of Iraq, once vigorous and thriving, has been reduced to *a vast refugee camp, a concentration camp, a nightmare.* In testimony before a UN Commission, Warren A. J. Hamerman of the International Progress Organisation likened Iraq to *a mediaeval city under siege*: 'cut off from outside assistance; its population, deprived of adequate food, water, medical care and the means to produce for its subsistence, is condemned to perish. It is only a matter of time.'[144] In the same vein Francis Boyle, Professor of International Law at the University of Illinois, issued a document of formal indictment against George Bush and the United States on behalf of 'the 4.5 million children of Iraq'. And the English journalist Edward Pearce signalled the biological warfare being waged by Washington against the Iraqi people: 'We *know* about cholera but we destroy power plants and electricity supply, we deny by embargo the means for immediate repair. That is different from deliberately seeding and spreading the cholera virus, only in the most etiolated fashion. It is different in the way that manslaughter is different from murder.... In the most lackadaisical and morally laidback way, we are killing people.'[145] And all this righteous protest – at the cholera and starvation brought 'to small brown children beyond the reach of our shrivelled imaginations' (Pearce) – was uttered in 1991, long years of suffering ago, when Washington's sanctions regime was already known to be taking its terrible toll.

The embargo was unambiguously contributing to progressive social collapse. Hospitals, health centres, clinics, laboratories, factories, farms, schools, homes – all were being reduced to pitiful inadequacy. Jihan, a psychologist and school counsellor, testified that malnourished children were fainting in class: 'Sometimes they are so hungry they steal from each other. Often we have to send students home because they are too sick from hunger to be able to sit up . . .'. And the social decay, leading inevitably to an increase 'in such crimes as murder, rape and armed robbery',[146] generated increased repression. By 1993 it was obvious that crime was eating into what had been a relatively law-abiding society. Violence, rape, prostitution, murder, robbery – all were on the increase. A thieves' market (*souk al-Harami*) flourished in a street in Baghdad, one sign among many of a society in decay. The authoritarian regime, predictably brutal, responded with brandings and amputations, obscene outrages that the West celebrated as signalling the character of the regime against which the 'robust' sanctions policy was properly deployed.[147] In reality the sanctions, in contributing so significantly to social collapse, had encouraged the increase in crime and the resulting intensified repression. Saddam's 'terror' was well known when he was a darling of the West, and Washington remains manifestly indifferent to amputations and beheadings in feudal Saudi Arabia. Western hypocrisy, with all its emotive diversions, could not disguise the genocide being perpetrated against the Iraqi people. It was all, as President George Bush had told us, a matter of '*right against wrong, a good-and-evil thing*'.

The US-contrived sanctions regime had killed perhaps one million Iraqi civilians by 1995, and today the embargo remains in place: there is to be no reprieve, no relief. On 17 February 1995 the Iraqi government newspaper *Al-Jumhuriya* commented: '*Remember the one million people killed by America. Remember the sufferings of the embargo which have entered every Iraqi house. Engrave in the memory of your children the name of the criminal [Washington] whose harm against Iraq has never been done by any other criminal in history.'* And we do not need to rely on Iraqi rhetoric for condemnation of the sanctions regime. The protests have been easy to discern, though not heeded by the Washington strategists, over the years; and they continue today. In May 1994 an international conference in Kuala Lumpur, Malaysia, issued a resolution condemning the economic sanctions on Iraq (see Appendix 8).[148] The Malaysian Declaration, appended to the resolution, includes the words:

> At present, even when Iraq has complied with all the relevant Security Council resolutions, and in particular resolution 687 (1991), the iniquitous economic sanctions imposed on Iraq in 1990 have still not been lifted. They are maintained, and indeed intensified even until this moment, despite the compliance and the mounting sufferings of the Iraqi people.

> We call upon the United States and its allies to withdraw all sanctions against the Iraqi people. A decent and humanitarian attitude towards the suffering of the people of Iraq would mandate the Clinton Administration to withdraw the United Nations sanctions immediately.

The Malaysian conference took place almost two years ago, and today the sanctions regime remains in place. On 16 March 1995, after the Iraqi deputy prime minister Tariq Aziz had met the Pope, the Vatican issued a statement declaring that sanctions must not be used to punish a people. The accumulating condemnation of the American posture had so far done nothing to bring relief to the helpless Iraqi population. Today Washington deems it essential that the genocide continue.

4 The Face of Genocide

We say to the rotten people – yes people not leadership – of Iraq that the Kuwaitis are much superior to you and much more honourable and pure than you can ever be. . . . We say to Iraq as a whole, its people, its regime – present and future – you are the lowest of the despicable and pray the Lord to vengefully chastise Iraq and O Lord leave not even a stone in Iraq standing upright.

Kuwaiti newspaper Al-Anbaa editorial, 19 January 1993

. . . we present our short list of "do's and don'ts" for the architects of a sanctions policy designed to change the policies of the target country . . . (3) Do pick on the weak and helpless . . . (5) Do impose the maximum cost on your target . . .

Hufbauer et al., 1990[1]

1. Starvation of civilians as a method of warfare is prohibited.
2. It is prohibited to attack, destroy, remove or render useless objects indispensable to the civilian population . . . foodstuffs, crops, livestock, drinking water installations and supplies and irrigation works, for the specific purpose of denying them for their sustenance value to the civilian population . . .

Geneva Protocol I, Article 54

Today the supporters of the embargo against Iraq rarely argue that the Iraqi people are not suffering. Only the perversely ignorant could doubt the miseries of that tortured nation. Rather the upholders of sanctions choose to argue that all the suffering of the Iraqi civilian population is caused by the brutal intransigence of Saddam Hussein. If he would only observe all the UN Security Council resolutions, if he would only 'step aside', if he would only . . . then the embargo could be lifted and the terrible suffering of the Iraqi people brought to an end. We can of course debate the extent to which the relevant resolutions (principally

661 and 687; 688 and others are not *mandatory* resolutions) have been observed (Rolf Ekeus, UN official in charge of dismantling Iraq's 'weapons of mass destruction', concedes that there has been substantial Iraqi co-operation), but such a debate – much favoured by cynical US strategists – represents a deliberate diversion from the central ethical and legal question: *to what extent, if at all, is it justifiable to subject a helpless civilian population to disease and starvation in the furtherance of a political objective?* Before considering this crucial question, before examining the legal and ethical face of genocide, it is useful to glance at the traditional role of the economic embargo as a coercive tool.

THE SANCTIONS OPTION

The use of sanctions/embargo/blockade[2] has been a common feature of conflict over the centuries, whether to apply coercion in circumstances of domestic confrontation (as in civil war) or as a weapon in wars between states (Table 4.1). The most celebrated early example of economic sanctions was the Megarian decree in ancient Greece, enacted by Pericles in 432 BC in response to the kidnapping of three Aspasian women. Thucydides mentions the enactment in *The Peloponnesian War*; while Aristophanes, in his comedy *The Acharnians*, judges the Megarian decree to have been a major cause of that war:

> Then Pericles the Olympian in his wrath
> thundered, lightened, threw Hellas into confusion,
> passed laws that were written like drinking songs
> [decreeing] the Megarians shall not be on our land, in our
> market, on the sea or on the continent . . .

The sanctions worked. The Megarians, denied the necessities of life, capitulated, and were spurned – an action that led to war:

> Then the Megarians, since they were starving little by little,
> begged the Laecedaemonians to have the decree
> arising from the three strumpets withdrawn.
> But we were unwilling, though they asked us many times.
> Then came the clash of the shields.[3]

The main purpose of sanctions, that of reducing an enemy to starvation, characterised countless military conflicts over the ages; as, for example,

TABLE 4.1   Selected pre-First World War examples of economic sanctions

Sender country	Target country	Active years	Background and resolution
Athens	Megara	c. 432 BC	Pericles issued decree limiting access to Megara's products – contributed to starting the Peloponnesian War
American colonies	Britain	1765	Colonies boycotted English goods – Britain repealed the Stamp Act in 1766
American colonies	Britain	1767–70	Boycott of English goods – Britain repealed Townshend Acts except on tea (tea tax led to Boston Tea Party of 1774)
Britain and France	France and Britain	1793–1815	Napoleonic Wars – economic warfare deemed inconclusive; France developed sugar beet as substitute product
United States	Britain	1812–14	US embargoed British goods in response to British economic pressure – revocation of the Acts failed to prevent war
Britain and France	Russia	1853–56	Danube blockaded – Russia defeated; Turkish partition was prevented
US North	Confederate States	1861–65	Civil War – blockade enhanced North's industrial superiority over the South; South lost
France	Germany	1870–71	Franco-Prussian War – blockade of German coast and occupied ports; Germany prevailed
France	China	1883–85	Indochina War – France declared rice contraband; China ceded to France control of the Annamese territory
United States	Spain	1898	Spanish-American War – naval blockade of Cuba and Philippines; Spain forced to cede the various territories
Britain	Dutch South Africa	1899–1902	Denial of contraband articles to the Boers – Boers eventually defeated; South Africa added to the British Empire
Russia	Japan	1904–05	Russo-Japanese War – blockade on rice, fuel, cotton, etc.; Russia defeated
Italy	Turkey	1911–12	Limited blockade – Italy acquired Libya from Ottoman Empire

Source: Hufbauer *et al.*, *Economic Sanctions Reconsidered: History and Current Policy*, Washington, D.C., 1990.

typified in the overcoming of fortresses through siege. Here it was essential – as with the US onslaught on modern Iraq – that people be denied the very essentials to survival; in particular, food and water. It was necessary, in furthering such an objective, to burn (or bomb) the crops, to destroy food stocks, to seek the contamination of the enemy's water supply. Thus Jim Bradbury, an authority on mediaeval European warfare, notes the importance of destroying the food crop before a siege and of denying the enemy access to water. When, in the twelfth century, the English rebel Baldwin de Redvers fought against King Steven his revolt was crushed when he twice ran out of water. Bradbury observes, of such mediaeval conflict: 'It was common to test the defenders as severely as possible in the early stages ... but if all the various forms of pressure proved unavailing, then *they might have to settle down to cutting off supplies and starving out the garrison*' (my italics).[4] (This is nicely analogous to Washington's onslaught on Iraq. Though the United States had the military power to prosecute the war to achieve the overthrow of the Iraqi regime, there were political constraints – the danger of significant American casualties, the fragility of the Coalition, etc. – that prevented such a course. Instead Washington was forced to rely on the embargo, 'cutting off supplies and starving out' the Iraqi people.)

Siege plans were plain enough in the context of mediaeval war. The besiegers might have to settle down 'to a prolonged blockade, interspersed with further attempts at storm'.[5] Again the nice analogy: throughout the US embargo on Iraq, Washington continued to launch frequent bombing strikes, that often produced civilian casualties, on one pretext or another (Iraqi radars were 'locking on' to US aircraft, Iraq was not complying with UN demands, there was an assassination attempt on George Bush, and so on). The maintenance of a siege was never regarded as precluding other military initiatives where possible.

The main siege tactics were straightforward: 'Once more the maxim "first destroy the land and then one's foe" applied' (Bradbury) – an approach adopted by the US military planners in targeting the Iraqi infrastructure. If a mediaeval fortification had an internal supply of water it was often possible for the attackers to contaminate it (just as through war and sanctions the United States took steps to deny the Iraqi population access to clean water). During the mediaeval siege at Alençon the attackers tunnelled underground and managed to rupture the pipes that supplied the castle with water (the equivalent of the modern US bombing of Iraqi water pumping plant), and so forced the defenders to surrender. At Tortona the Turkish corsair Barbarossa polluted the water supply by throwing putrid corpses of men and animals into the spring, so encouraging the spread of disease[6] (the equivalent of US bombing of sewage treatment plants to force the Iraqi civilian population to drink contaminated water).

The traditional siege deployed a mix of economic and military pressure as a means of coercing an enemy over time. With the growth of technology and the development of military technique, the scope of the siege approach expanded to the point that it could undermine the resistance of entire nations. If, like Iraq, a country had become massively reliant on foreign imports any interruption of such commerce could have devastating consequences for the civilian population. Where in mediaeval times a castle might be characteristically subjected to siege the modern age saw the possibility of imposing economic blockades on entire nations. However, where a single fortress might be effectively ringed by attackers, it proved much more difficult to subject a whole country to decisive siege. A nation may be able to organise a degree of economic self-sufficiency; it may be able to cajole friends and allies into providing assistance; it may be able to exploit the mercenary instincts of blockade runners. Clearly, if a blockade could be organised with virtually universal international support – as with the US-contrived blockade of Iraq – there would be a good chance of reducing the entire population to an impoverished state.

The Napoleonic Wars provided one of the first examples of economic blockade on a large scale, though the efforts made by the various belligerents in this context have been seen as less than decisive.[7] The warring countries were more or less self-sufficient in food and, though a measure of inconvenience was caused, the military capabilities of the parties were scarcely affected. At the same time it seemed obvious that if an enemy's supply routes could be blocked his war-making powers would be impeded. On 19 April 1861 President Abraham Lincoln introduced an economic blockade against Confederate ports, and within weeks the Union had bought or chartered scores of merchant ships, armed them, and sent them off on blockade duty. For a time Confederate privateers tried to break the blockade, but their efforts were short lived. On 3 February 1862 the Lincoln administration ruled that captured privateer crews would be treated as prisoners of war, and neutral nations, under Union pressure, were refusing to support Confederate trade. A few blockade runners achieved notoriety but the Confederate navy could not match Union prowess on the high seas or along the rivers of the South. In June 1861 the five-gun steam sloop CSS *Sumter* managed to evade the blockade at the mouth of the Mississippi, captured or burned 18 Union vessels over the next sixth months, and was finally trapped in January 1862 in the harbour at Gibraltar.

The Confederacy had 3500 miles of coastline with 10 major ports and some 180 inlets and bays accessible to smaller vessels. Three dozen blockade ships were patrolling this coastline by June 1861, with additional blockaders being commissioned or chartered every week. The difficulties in maintaining an effective blockade encouraged the Union to seize southern ports to act as bases from which the blockade vessels could operate. Still the blockade remained porous to a degree, and there was debate as to the extent of its success. Around 500 ships took part in the blockade, with an average of about 150 on patrol at any given time; over the full period of the war some 1500 blockade runners were either captured or destroyed.[8] One Union officer wrote to his mother of the burdens of blockade duty: she would know what it was like if she were to 'go to the roof on a hot summer day, talk to a half-dozen degenerates, descend to the basement, drink tepid water full of iron rust, climb to the roof again, and repeat the process until fagged out, then go to bed with everything shut tight'.[9] There was some compensation in the fact that the blockade sailors shared with the government the proceeds from every captured prize. Thus a notable success was achieved by the small gunboat *Aeolus*, which captured two blockade runners, winning $40,000 for the captain, $8000 to $20,000 for each officer, and $3000 for each seaman.[10]

Confederate envoys declared that Union efforts to block its trade constituted no more than a 'paper blockade', with the Confederate wartime president Jefferson Davis declaring the 'so-called blockade' a 'monstrous pretension'; in the same vein the historian Frank L. Owsley pronounced the blockade an 'absurdity', 'old Abe's . . . practical joke on the world'.[11] Many southerners saw a different picture. One, Mary Boykin Chesnut, noted on 16 July 1861 that the blockade was beginning to shut ammunition out, adding in March 1862 that it constituted 'a stockade which hems us in'. In July 1861 a southern trader observed in his diary that because of the blockade 'every article of consumption particularly in the way of groceries are [sic] getting very high'; and noted four months later that business was 'perfectly prostrated', with 'hardly any shoes to be had' and 'dry goods of every kind running out'. After the war a southern naval officer admitted that the blockade had 'shut the Confederacy out from the world, deprived it of supplies, weakened its military and naval strength'.[12] In fact the scale of the impact of the blockade on the Confederacy remains a matter of debate.

The technique of economic warfare developed further during the course of the First World War, by then a technique 'vastly different from anything that had been known before, with a new range of effectiveness'.[13] Both sides did what they could to impose an effective blockade, with German submarines taking a heavy toll of British merchant shipping and Britain imposing an official blockade on Germany in March 1915 as a declared response to the damaging submarine warfare. Then a bureaucratic administrative system had to be established to allow for the continuation of neutral commerce. The examination of neutral shipping at suitable 'control ports' had led to considerable delays; and so a system of 'navicerts', documents issued at source to certify neutral destination, was developed. Agreements with neutral governments and trade associations were negotiated to constrain the trade with Germany; blacklists were compiled of neutral countries with suspected enemy leanings; and a wide-ranging intelligence service was established. The technique of economic embargo, to be increasingly important in the decades ahead, had now evolved a new level of sophistication: 'This was a new kind of blockade, enforced at long range through control of contraband and by agreement with neutrals, and bearing little resemblance to the old-style direct naval blockade of the enemy coast.'[14]

An official British statement summarised some of the main features of the blockade:

1. German exports to overseas countries have been almost entirely stopped. Such exceptions as have been made are in cases where a refusal to allow the export of the goods would hurt the neutral concerned without inflicting any injury upon Germany.

2. All shipments to neutral countries adjacent to Germany are carefully scrutinised with a view to the detection of a concealed enemy destination. Wherever there is reasonable ground for suspecting such a destination the goods are placed in the prize court. Doubtful consignments are detained until satisfactory guarantees are produced.

3. Under agreements in force with bodies of representative merchants in several neutral countries adjacent to Germany, stringent guarantees are exacted from importers, and so far as possible all trade between the neutral country and Germany . . . is restricted.

4. By agreements with shipping lines and by a vigorous use of the power to refuse bunker coal, a large proportion of the neutral mercantile marine which carries on trade with Scandinavia and Holland has been induced to agree to conditions designed to prevent goods carried in these ships from reaching the enemy.

5. Every effort is being made to introduce a system of rationing which will ensure that the neutral countries concerned only import such quantities of the articles specified as are normally imported for their own consumption.

Thus a comprehensive system with international weight was set in place, a detailed framework set to evolve further in the years to come. In the early years of the First World War not all countries were happy to conform with the international requirements of the blockade. The United States, for example, objected to such elements as bunker control and blacklisting as manifest infringements of American sovereignty; but when Washington entered the war it agreed the various blockade practices and helped Britain to enforce them. By the end of the war Germany's export trade had been largely destroyed, with an effective block established on many of Germany's most vital imports (cotton, wool, rubber and others). Massive shortages of other products (such as fats, oils and dairy produce) had caused rocketing price inflation; and there was abundant evidence of massive discontent amongst various sections of the German population, with food riots in many of the towns. The blockade has been judged to have been 'undoubtedly a factor in Germany's eventual defeat'.[15]

The theory of economic warfare had been developing in parallel on several important fronts. The experience of young American officers in running the blockade on the confederacy (the Anaconda Plan of 1861–65) had led to contingency blockade plans for various possible confrontational situations. For example, early in the twentieth century Washington strategists were already developing *War Plan Orange* as a detailed scheme for the economic subjugation of Japan. Here it was believed that the 'final and complete commercial isolation' of Japan would guarantee its 'eventual impoverishment and exhaustion'; and that this was a war that the United States would be sure to win.[16] Already the explicit concept of *siege* was being developed for the modern world.[17] Many of the associated ideas were to be introduced in the 1930s as practical options, expanded through the Second World War, and used frequently thereafter, often in the service of Cold War strategy and most comprehensively in the siege of Iraq that began in August 1990.

After Japan invaded China in July 1937 the Washington strategists continued to consider how War Plan Orange might be used to contain the mounting crisis. The principal US response would be economic pressure, whereby Japan might be defeated in 'an economic war of exhaustion'. There were still uncertainties: did Washington want a

comprehensive victory over an expanding Japan or limited containment? By early 1940 the United States had imposed various economic
restrictions on Japan. Harold Stark, the US Chief of Naval Operations,
had already speculated on the possibility of a siege of 'several years'
(with War Plan Orange itself projecting a 'long and exhausting' struggle of two years, including a year of siege).[18] In the event President
Franklin D. Roosevelt had been careful not to impose a total embargo
on Japanese access to oil, knowing that this would serve as a massive
provocation. Harold L. Ickes, Roosevelt's Interior Secretary, commented
in July 1941 that Roosevelt 'was still unwilling to draw the noose
tight'; that he thought 'it might be better to slip the noose around
Japan's neck and give it a jerk now and then'.[19] A total embargo on
oil was avoided by blocking only high-octane gasoline exports and by
restricting the heavy oil exports to just below the 1940 level. But this
effort at a limited blockade was doomed to failure. Hardliners in both
Washington and Tokyo were quick to interpret the freeze as total, with
the *New York Times* dubbing the Roosevelt initiative 'the most drastic
blow short of war'. At the same time Washington pressured the Australian government not to allow Japan access to its abundant supplies
of iron ore – another provocative act. Japan's Imperial Navy, seeing
the new American policy as immensely hostile, one that threatened the
very survival of the Japanese fleet, urged military expansion to the
south to secure the oil resources in the East Indies. And the tentative
Roosevelt blockade was seen later as one of the contributing causes to
the bombing of Pearl Harbor on 7 December 1941.

   The economic warfare waged against Germany and Japan necessarily involved the characteristic mix of military and economic measures:
the concentrated bombing of industrial targets constituted an economic
onslaught, just as did the military efforts to interdict Germany's commerce. It is significant that the techniques introduced in the First World
War were now being developed and refined for the new international
conflict. Again compulsory navicerts were employed, this time supplemented by ship warrants issued to signal compliance with British regulations; and again blacklists were compiled. Essential raw materials
were purchased on a pre-emptive basis; neutrals were subjected to import
rationing; and diplomacy was exercised with care to avoid pushing
neutral states into the Axis camp. At the same time Germany, with
allies and substantial conquered territory, was able to resist what might
otherwise have been the decisive effects of the blockade. None the
less the economic embargo had significant successes, noted in Medlicott's
authoritative analysis:[20]

1. The drastic limitation of German imports;

2. The creation of a blockade neurosis impacting on German politics and military strategy;

3. The hampering of Axis armament efforts through raw material shortages;

4. The hampering of the Axis economy through strains on manpower and transportation;

5. The strengthening of neutral resistance to Axis pressure by economic aid and other measures.

Japan, coping with different circumstances from those of Germany, was similarly weakened by economic pressures that mounted through the war years. In particular, the crippling blockade, at its peak denying Japan access to raw materials, all but halted the nation's war industries.

The experience of blockade in various military conflicts (especially the American Civil War and two world wars) had confirmed the importance of economic pressure as an element in military conflict. In the post-Second World War years, mainly through the period of the Cold War, economic sanctions were used in dozens of cases, sometimes as a substitute for overt military action and sometimes in concert with military initiatives. Hufbauer *et al.* (1990) first list 11 selected case histories involving the use of economic sanctions (1948–1990), and then explore the use of sanctions for particular purposes (to change target-country politics, to destabilise governments, to disrupt military adventures, to impair military potential, etc.).[21] It is of interest for our purposes that the selected case studies all involve the imposition of sanctions by the United States (9 times acting alone, once with COCOM, and once with the United Nations). In the associated *Supplemental Case Histories* Hufbauer *et al.* provide detailed profiles of 108 case histories (55 where the United States acted alone, 16 with others).[22] Again the hegemony of Washington in its unrivalled power to punish and intimidate other states is manifest (see 'The US and Sanctions', below).

The collapse of the Soviet Union in the early 1990s served to enlarge Washington's freedom of political manoeuvre. Now the United States, newly freed from the constraint of a Soviet veto in the Security Council, could run UN affairs as it wished (though the US still declined to pay its financial dues); Washington could decide where and when to activate NATO; and it could decide where and when to activate economic sanctions against states that remained unsympathetic to American strategic aims. The United States remained far from omnipotent (various constraints remained), but in the 1990s Washington rejoiced in being universally regarded as 'the sole surviving superpower'. This circumstance was bound to influence the character of US-supported economic sanctions in the post-Cold War world.

THE LEAGUE AND THE UNITED NATIONS

The drafters of the League Covenant and the UN Charter, which in part grew out of it, were sensitive to the traditional role of economic sanctions in conflicts between nations. There was never a time when sanctions/embargo/blockade was not seen as a possible means of coercing enemy states (see Table 4.1). This does not mean that economic pressure was invariably decisive; if only because *all* the belligerents would try to use the sanctions weapon, and not all could prevail. The League Covenant, despite the League's limited membership and its Eurocentric focus, was one of the first 'universal' attempts to provide a framework equipped to guarantee international peace. Inevitably the formula gave a place to economic sanctions, what Woodrow Wilson had dubbed 'a terrible remedy'. Sanctions would be invoked precisely because, applied robustly and with international co-operation, they could achieve devastating results. After the First World War, one German observer noted: 'Of all implements of mass murder, [a fleet] is the most sophisticated. The striking force, the drive of will and the destructive skill of entire nations are concentrated in a couple of gigantic hulls. Millions of warriors can annihilate provinces, but hardly destroy a whole nation: a dozen grey dreadnoughts, besieging a country, invisible in the far distance, can spread hunger and misery over an entire continent.'[23] The theory and practice that would lay waste to Iraq in the 1990s was well known at the time of the First World War and before.

The League Covenant specifies its sanctions provisions in Article 16.* Here it is stated that if 'any Member of the League resort to war in disregard of its coventants . . . it shall . . . be deemed to have committed an act of war against all other Members of the League, which

---

* I have profiled the origins of the League of the Nations and the United Nations in *The United Nations: A Chronology of Conflict* (Macmillan, 1994).

hereby undertake immediately to subject it to the severance of all trade
or financial relations, the prohibition of all intercourse . . . and the
prevention of an [sic] financial, commercial or personal intercourse
between the nationals of the Covenant-breaking State and the nationals
of any other State . . .'. It is acknowledged that the imposition of sanctions may affect states other than those against whom the sanctions are
imposed, and so the Coventant stipulates mutual support: 'The Members of the League agree that they will mutually support one another
in the financial and economic measures . . . in order to minimise the
loss and inconvenience . . .'.

The ambiguities in the Covenant, similar to those that would later
plague the UN Charter, meant that member states were allowed an
unhelpful latitude. Members were left plenty of scope, within the Covenant wording, to decide whether to join a sanctions regime. The League
Council, the equivalent of the UN Security Council, had no powers to
coerce recalcitrant states into supporting an international trade embargo.
There were many aggressions ('resorts to war') during the history of
the League but, despite calls from aggrieved parties, sanctions were
only resorted to once, namely against Italy in 1935/6 following the
invasion of Abyssinia (today Ethiopia). An embargo was placed on
the export to Italy of arms, munitions and other war supplies; financial
dealings were restricted; and prohibitions were placed on imports from
Italy, with various exemptions (books and printed material, gold, sil-
ver, coin, goods under existing contracts, and goods of Italian origin
to which more than 25 per cent of value had been added by processing elsewhere). Also banned were the export to Italy of transport animals, rubber, bauxite, aluminium, iron ore, chromium, manganese,
titanium, nickel, tungsten, tin and vanadium; and a host of re-exports.
One observer, Frank Hardie, noted that 'In nine days the committee
had created, in outline, a new world of international sanctions'; by the
end of 1935 some fifty League members had reported that they were
applying sanctions. None the less the sanctions were partial and ineffective. The League decided not to impose an embargo on oil, coal,
iron, steel and other essential materials. On 9 May 1936 Benito Mus-
solini, satisfied that the war was over, announced the annexation of
Abyssinia; and a month later, on 10 June, the British chancellor of the
exchequer, Neville Chamberlain, declared that any idea that continued
sanctions would help Abyssinia was the 'very midsummer of madness', a position that was subsequently upheld by the new foreign secretary, Anthony Eden. On 15 July, despite South Africa and New Zealand
(alone) supporting continued sanctions, the League Sanctions Committee

convened to recommend the lifting of all the measures imposed under Article 16 of the Covenant.

The collapse of sanctions against Italy contributed to the demise of the League. The situation was plain. There was no consensus among League members for united action in the event of aggression; and the League Council had no powers to demand compliance. Efforts to reform the League in the 1936–39 period, in the face of Hitler's re-occupation of the Rhineland on 7 March 1936, were almost wholly negative, focusing on how the obligations on members might be reduced rather than how the League might become a more effective international body. Eleven members had left the League between 1936 and 1939, with the Soviet Union expelled in December 1939 following its attack on Finland. In April 1946, with the United Nations already in existence, the League was formally dissolved by unanimous vote.

Unlike the League Covenant, the UN Charter offers no guidelines for determining whether economic sanctions should be imposed on a particular state. The Charter leaves such judgement to the discretion of the Security Council. Thus Article 39 states:

The Security Council shall determine the existence of any threat to the peace, breach of the peace, or act of aggression and shall make recommendations, or decide what measures shall be taken . . . to maintain or restore international peace and security.

Such a provision confers immense power on the Council; in particular, in a United Nations with 185 members, on the five Permanent Members of the Council. Moreover, Article 39 is further bolstered by other provisions in Chapter VII of the Charter. Thus Article 41, the sanctions provision, states:

The Security Council may decide what measures not involving the use of armed force are to be employed to give effect to its decisions, and it may call upon the Members of the United Nations to apply such measures. These may include complete or partial interruption of economic relations and of rail, sea, air, postal, telegraphic, radio, and other means of communication, and the severance of diplomatic relations.

Subsequent Articles define provisions for the use of force, if the Security Council considers that Article 41 measures 'would be inadequate or have proved to be inadequate' (Article 42). What this means in reality is that the United States, today clearly dominant in the Council, decides in what circumstances UN sanctions and UN force are to be used. Today the Security Council, and thus the United Nations, is an unambiguous tool of American foreign policy (see 'The US and Sanctions' and 'Law and the Gulf', below).

As with the League sanctions provisions, the use of sanctions by the United Nations has been 'sparse'[24] – at least until the post-Cold War years (see below). The United Nations, over its first half-century, has imposed sanctions against the People's Republic of China and North Korea (in 1951), South Africa (1963), Portugal (1969), Rhodesia (1965), and Angola, the former Yugoslavia, Iraq, Libya* and Haiti (1990s). The various economic pressures have been applied for many different purposes and with varying degrees of success. In addition to UN-authorised sanctions, many individual states and alliances have imposed their own sanctions regimes to coerce other countries and/or alliances into assuming new political postures.

THE US AND SANCTIONS

Where the League of Nations and the United Nations had, over a combined three-quarters of a century, applied economic sanctions only sparsely, the United States imposed them frequently and robustly in support of foreign policy. The list shown in Table 4.2, compiled mainly from the two Hufbauer *et al.* volumes (notes 1 and 22), is not exhaustive but indicates the enthusiasm with which Washington has been prepared to exert economic pressure over the decades. Table 4.3 lists cases where the United States, acting with regional alliances and the United Nations, has been prepared to impose economic sanctions. In some of these cases, especially those of Iraq and Libya (see below), the semblance of an *international* initiative is misleading: Washington has never been averse to using blackmail, bribery and intimidation to secure international support for American strategic objectives. Thus the United States, acting alone or in concert with other countries, has imposed sanctions regimes in something approaching a hundred cases.

---

* There is now abundant and accumulating evidence of US manipulation of the UN Security Council: what is represented as the view of the 'international community' is often no more than Washington fiat. For example, on the sanctions issue, Libya is supported by the Organisation of the Islamic Conference (45 states), the Organisation of African Unity (35 states), the Arab League (22 states), and the Members of the Non-Aligned Movement (120 states).

TABLE 4.2　Countries targeted by US (acting alone) for sanctions

Country	Year imposed	Issue	Country	Year imposed	Issue
Japan	1917	Containment	Uruguay	1976	Human rights
Japan	1940	Withdrawal from	Taiwan	1976	Nuclear
		South-east Asia	Ethiopia	1976	Expropriation
Argentina	1944	Remove Peron	Paraguay	1977	Human rights
Netherlands	1948	Indonesian Federation	Guatemala	1977	Human rights
Israel	1956	Borders	Argentina	1977	Human rights
UK and			Nicaragua	1977	Somoza
France	1956	Suez	El Salvador	1977	Human rights
Laos	1956	Communism	Brazil	1977	Human rights
Dominican			Libya	1978	Gaddafi
Republic	1960	Trujillo	Brazil	1978	Nuclear
Cuba	1960	Castro	Argentina	1978	Nuclear
Ceylon	1961	Expropriation	India	1978	Nuclear
Brazil	1962	Goulart	USSR	1978	Dissidents
United Arab			Iran	1979	Hostages
Republic	1963	Yemen and Congo	Pakistan	1979	Nuclear
Indonesia	1963	Containment	Bolivia	1979	Human rights
South Vietnam	1963	Diem	USSR	1980	Afghanistan
Chile	1965	Copper price	Iraq	1980	Terrorism
India	1965	Agriculture	Nicaragua	1981	Communism
Arab League	1965	Anti-boycott	Poland	1981	Martial law
Peru	1968	French jets	Argentina	1982	Falklands
Peru	1968	Expropriation	USSR	1982	Poland
Chile	1970	Allende	USSR	1983	Korean Air
India and					Lines Flight 007
Pakistan	1971	Bangladesh	Zimbabwe	1983	UN voting record
Various			Iran	1984	Terrorism; war
countries	1972	Terrorism	South Africa	1985	Apartheid
Various			Syria	1986	Terrorism
countries	1973	Human rights	Angola	1986	Cuban troops
South Korea	1973	Human rights	Panama	1987	Noriega
Chile	1973	Human rights	Haiti	1987	Democracy
Turkey	1974	Cyprus	El Salvador	1987	Amnesty
USSR	1975	Emigration	Sudan	1989	Human rights
Eastern Europe	1975	Emigration	Iran	1992	Terrorism
Vietnam	1975	Communism			
South Africa	1975	Nuclear			
Kampuchea	1975	Post-war			

By contrast, the United States has been *subject to* sanctions impositions in fewer than half a dozen cases, involving mainly the former Soviet Union and the Arab League; in none of these cases were sanctions effective.

The extensive use by the United States of economic sanctions as a policy option has required the development of a wide range of presidential and other powers. For example, the various US laws authorising the President to impose sanctions can be divided into five categories: the imposition of limits on 1. US government programmes (such as foreign aid, landing rights, etc.); 2. exports from the United States; 3. imports; 4. private financial transactions; and 5. international financial

TABLE 4.3 Countries targeted by US (acting in concert) for sanctions

US and UK v. Mexico (1938–47): expropriation

Alliance Powers v. Germany and Japan (1939–45): Second World War

US and COCOM v. USSR and COMECON (1948–91): technology controls

US and CHINCOM v. China (1949–70): communism in China

US and United Nations v. North Korea (1950–): Korean War, etc.

US and UK v. Iran (1951–53): expropriation

US and South Vietnam v. North Vietnam (1954–75): Vietnam War, etc.

US, UK and France v. Egypt (1956): nationalisation of Suez Canal

Western Allies v. German Democratic Republic (1961–62): Berlin Wall

UN v. South Africa (1962–92): apartheid

UN and Organisation of African Unity (OAU) v. Portugal (1963–74): colonies

UN and UK v. Rhodesia (1965–79): black majority rule

US and UK v. Uganda (1972–79): Idi Amin

US and Canada v. countries pursuing nuclear option (1974)

US and Canada v. South Korea (1975–76): nuclear reprocessing

US and Netherlands v. Suriname (1982–): human rights

US and OECS v. Grenada (1983): democracy

US, Japan and West Germany v. Burma (1988–): human rights; elections

US and UK v. Somalia (1988–): human rights, civil war

US and UN v. Iraq (1990–): invasion of Kuwait

US and UN v. Libya (1992–): terrorism

US, UN and European Union (EU) v. former Yugoslavia (1992–6): civil war

US and UN v. Haiti (1993–94): democracy; human rights

institutions.[25] The presidential powers vary considerably between these categories: where the President has considerable discretion with exports and bilateral government programmes, he has much less power to curtail imports and international financial transactions. Congress, usually playing a secondary role once the relevant enabling laws are in place, may choose to limit its authorisation of foreign assistance requested by the President, but there are usually ways round such constraints. Specific laws, such as the Export Administration Amendments Act (1985), stipulate consultation and reporting requirements as

an intended brake on presidential initiative, but loopholes in the legislation generally allow a resourceful President to avoid significant
constraints.[26]

Many US government programmes can be used to apply economic
leverage in furtherance of foreign-policy objectives. Such programmes
include: bilateral foreign aid, low-interest credit facilities, loan guarantees, special insurance provisions, the granting of fishing rights, port
access, aircraft landing rights, the provision of advisories, and pass-
ports. The imposition of a sanctions regime may involve a number of
these programme facilities; and, for example, may be used to threaten
members of the UN Security Council in order to secure compliance
for US-drafted resolutions (see 'Law and the Gulf', below). Where the
United States has increased its aid to a country (as proverbial carrot),
any threat of a block to such vital assistance (stick) necessarily con-
centrates the collective government minds in dependent nations. At one
extreme, a country that has become reliant on food aid may be denied
it in the future unless it votes appropriately in the Security Council.

The Commodity Credit Corporation (CCC) in the US Department of
Agriculture helps to finance exports of agricultural products by arranging
export credit guarantees, insuring US exporters against defaults by foreign
banks (total CCC guarantees amount to billions of dollars every year).
The President is authorised to block any country's access to CCC guarantees, just as there is presidential discretion over the (P. L. 480) agricultural exports programmes. What this means in practice is that the
President can deny a country famine relief, or, having agreed such aid,
can threaten to withdraw it. For example, President Reagan invoked
these powers in 1981 when he froze Food for Peace aid to Nicaragua
and blocked a $9.6 million wheat sale to that country. In short, Wash-
ington characteristically uses starvation or the threat of it as a means
of securing its foreign policy objectives. The US policy of *food denial*
that was to afflict the Iraqi civilian population so grievously in the
1990s was one that had been used elsewhere, though never with such
comprehensive and dire consequences, in Washington's cynical pur-
suit of strategic goals.

The nominal limits on presidential powers over such international
financial institutions as the International Monetary Fund (IMF) and
the International Bank for Reconstruction and Development (World Bank)
give the impression of *international* rather than *American* financial
hegemony in such bodies. Again the impression is misleading. The
formal voting structures in the financial institutions do not grant Washington a dominant voice; instead it derives its overwhelming power

'from its alliances with other countries and from informal persuasion'.[27] Different national representatives can be encouraged by Washington to vote with the United States in the IMF and the World Bank, just as they can in the Security Council. It would be a grave error to assume that US powers in international bodies derive solely, or even mainly, from publicly-accessible statutes, protocols, regulations and rules of procedure. Real power means that rules can be ignored, 'corridor threats' can be made to effective purpose, and even the most unambiguous national legislation or international treaty can be treated with contempt. In such circumstances law is exploited as no more than a tool in cynical *realpolitik*: to be ignored when deemed unhelpful, to be righteously invoked whenever a 'pariah state' questions American virtue. In particular, for our purposes, the presidential powers plus those of Congress and various US government departments, allied to the many opportunities for the exercise of covert pressure on recalcitrant states, have evolved to enable the United States to exploit the economic sanctions option as a vital tool of foreign policy. In the post-Cold War world, with the demise of the Soviet veto in the UN Security Council, this US option took on a new power: for the first time there would be a real chance of applying truly *universal* sanctions against states that continued to irritate the Washington strategists.

After Iraq (see below), the regime of Libya's Colonel Muammar Gaddafi remained a principal source of irritation.* Here we do not need to rehearse the chronology of UN resolutions on Libya, from the Security Council's passing of Resolution 731 (20 January 1992) through the passing of Resolution 748 (31 March 1992) to the passing of Resolution 883 (11 November 1993). It is enough to note how Washington activated the Security Council against Libya, and how in particular it violated existing international law in the process. It deliberately ignored the requirements of the 1971 Montreal Convention, drafted specifically to address terrorist attacks on civilian aircraft, since the Convention protected Libya's right *not* to extradite the two Libyans charged by the United States with involvement in the Lockerbie bombing; and Washington proceeded to intimidate the members of the Security Council into agreeing the US-drafted sanctions resolution.

There was no legal requirement that Libya surrender its two nationals for trial in Scotland or the United States – simply because Libya had no extradition treaty with the UK or the US; and in its observance of

---

* I have explored this issue in *Libya: the Struggle for Survival* (Macmillan, 1993; reprinted 1996) and in *UN Malaise: Power, Problems and Realpolitik* (Macmillan, 1995).

the terms of the Montreal Convention Libya had acted in accord with the demands of international law. Thus Marc Weller, Research Fellow in International Law at St Catharine's College, Cambridge, noted that the claimant states (i.e. principally Washington) 'had to expend considerable political capital and goodwill in the Security Council, *bullying fellow members to obtain the necessary votes, and enraging many non-members of the Council who keenly observed this spectacle*' (my italics).[28] Weller judged that, in behaving in such a fashion, Washington and London 'may well have contributed to, or brought about, an abuse of rights by the Security Council'; and that it may now be necessary for the International Court of Justice at The Hague (the World Court) to seek a judicial review of Council decisions 'if the constitutional system of the UN Charter is to recover from the blow it has suffered in this episode'.[29]

The message was plain. With the Soviet Union no more, Washington felt free to bully the Security Council as never before. This had already been demonstrated in the case of Iraq (see below), but now it was clear that such tactics would be used whenever Washington thought appropriate. At the same time it is important to note the significant constraints on US attempts to bribe and intimidate. The European powers resisted the imposition of comprehensive sanctions on Libya (that would have included a ban on oil sales), China resisted the imposition of US-orchestrated UN sanctions on North Korea (over the nuclear weapons issue*), and Jordan has so far resisted US pressure to impose a full food/medicine blockade on the hapless Iraqi people. The United States has exploited the sanctions weapon to substantial effect, and continues to do so, but there remain some limits on the amount of punishment it can wreak through economic pressure on 'enemy' states.

In addition to imposing unilateral economic pressure on selected states, and orchestrating UN sanctions in support of American foreign policy, Washington also protects 'friendly' states that might otherwise invite UN economic pressure. Thus Israel, though repeatedly acting in violation of UN resolutions, never faces the real prospect of UN sanctions.[30] At the same time Washington could pressure the Security Council to implement sanctions against the former Yugoslavia, though this soon exposed the mounting tensions between the US and Europe on the issue. In January 1993, with Israel again in violation of a Security Council resolution (this time Resolution 799), UN Secretary-General

---

* I have covered this issue in *Korea: The Search for Sovereignty* (Macmillan, 1995, chapter 1).

Boutros Boutros-Ghali made the observation that the Council, 'by not pressing for Israeli compliance, does not attach equal importance to the implementation of all of its decisions'. An American diplomat in New York reportedly commented that the United States faced 'a tough decision. . . . There is pressure from Arab states, they're out there waiting.' They waited in vain: Israel ignored the specific demands of Resolution 799 and Washington supported the Israeli posture.

In early 1995 a US Senate committee urged that economic sanctions be imposed on Colombia to encourage action against the drug cartels; while at the same time the United States began framing intensified sanctions, including a ban on oil sales to US companies, against Iran. In April Washington moved to warn Russia that it would stop all nuclear co-operation unless Russia cancelled a $1 billion deal to build a nuclear power station for Iran. (This ignored the stipulation in the 1968 Non-Proliferation Treaty that the nuclear powers should help the non-nuclear states to develop nuclear power for peaceful purposes.) Now there were further suggestions that sanctions might be imposed on China unless it broke off talks with Iran for the supply of civilian nuclear technology. By May the Clinton administration had blocked US firms from trading with Iran (Clinton: 'I am convinced that instituting a trade embargo with Iran is the most effective way our nation can help curb Iran's drive to acquire devastating weapons and support for terrorist activities'). Washington's allies were reportedly thrown into 'confusion and doubt' by the unilateral US initiative.[31]

On 16 May 1995 the United States announced a record of almost $6 billion-worth of punitive sanctions against Japan, to become effective on 28 June unless Japan opened up its car market to American products. Japan immediately responded by making an appeal to the new World Trade Organisation (WTO), the trade court established under the GATT (General Agreement on Tariffs and Trade) provisions. At the same time it was reported that the US sanctions against Iran were 'a gift to extremists of Zionism and Islam'.[32] Some US factions were now also encouraging the imposition of sanctions on Nigeria, in addition to the arms ban (introduced in 1993), as a means of toppling the military regime. Susan Rice, President Clinton's special assistant for Africa, was quoted as saying that recent actions by General Sani Abacha's government 'do not give one hope for swift restoration of democracy and civilian rule'; and she hinted at the possibility of further sanctions that may include the freezing of Nigerian assets in the United States and a variety of other trade measures (the US is the largest buyer of Nigerian oil, which supplies about 90 per cent of Nigeria's foreign exchange and about 80 per cent of government revenue). On 22 June the United States declared that it might have to impose economic sanctions on China if it were found that Beijing had supplied missile components to Iran and Pakistan.

The Washington strategists were in no doubt that, in a world enmeshed in the constraints and opportunities of the global economy, trade and financial sanctions were an increasingly powerful foreign-policy weapon. Many possibly economic pressures could be exerted – from mere *threat* to *comprehensive universal sanctions*. Often threat alone has sufficed to achieve political compliance in weaker states, but at the other extreme it is obvious that the comprehensive and merciless imposition of economic sanctions can have genocidal consequences.

LAW AND THE GULF

Any attempt to understand the legal dimensions of the 1990/91 Gulf crisis must be set in the context of Washington's general attitude to treaty obligations, international law and the United Nations. The United States, through its reach and its power, was inevitably the principal player – in shaping the final stages of the Iran/Iraq War, in encouraging Kuwait to wage 'economic war' on Iraq, in giving Saddam Hussein the much-discussed 'green light', in cynically manipulating the United Nations for war, in running the military conflict, and in mercilessly administering a genocidal peace. In fact Washington played its part through these various phases with attention to no more than *realpolitik* concern for strategic advantage, indifferent to international law unless it could be cynically exploited. Noam Chomsky, the world-famous academic and dissident, has noted that the United States has always regarded diplomacy and international law 'as an annoying encumbrance, unless they can be used to advantage against an enemy'.[33] The contrived confrontation with Iraq has well illustrated the characteristic US posture. Before Saddam's illegal invasion of Kuwait on 2 August 1990 Washington was manifestly antipathetic to the United Nations; but then it was calculated that a UN mandate would be politically useful in underwriting a range of actions that were in reality unilateral American initiatives.

The US manipulation of law and the international community over Iraq is part of a pattern. It is useful to remember some significant US violations of the UN Charter, UN resolutions and Conventions, treaty obligations and international law (the list could easily be extended):

Korean War (1949–53): having artificially divided a sovereign nation by the simple expedient of drawing a line on a map, the United States acted initially without UN authorisation, lied to the Security Council about Russian involvement to secure the 'enabling' resolutions, and conducted a genocidal anti-civilian war in violation of the 1949 Geneva Protocol.

Vietnam War (1960–75): having ignored Paragraph 6 of the Final Declaration of the Geneva Accords (1954) (*'the military demarcation line is provisional and should not in any way be interpreted as constituting a political or territorial boundary'*), the United States waged a genocidal war, violated the UN Charter (Article 2(4)), violated the SEATO Treaty, and violated the US Constitution (waging war without Congressional approval).

Cuba (1960–): the United States, having supported military invasion and the use of terrorism against a sovereign UN member, in violation of the UN Charter, continues a trade blockade in violation of UN trade Conventions, the GATT protocols and national sovereignties. The continued occupation of the Guantánamo naval base, deriving from the coercive Platt Amendment (1903), violates the Vienna Convention on the Law of Treaties (Section 2(51/2)). On 2 November 1995 the UN General Assembly passed its fourth resolution (GA 50/10) condemning the illegal blockade by a vote of 117 to 3.

Grenada (1983): the US invasion violated national sovereignty, protected by Article 2(1) of the UN Charter, and violated Article 2(4) (*'All Members shall refrain . . . from the threat or use of force against the territorial integrity or political independence of any state . . .'*).

Nicaragua (1986): having orchestrated a terrorist campaign against a sovereign UN Member State, Washington refused to accept the ruling of the International Court of Justice (27 June 1986) that the United States was in violation of international law, that it should desist from its illegal actions, and that it should pay compensation. The US posture constituted a further violation of the UN Charter: *'Each Member . . . undertakes to comply with the decision of the International Court of Justice in any case to which it is a party'* (Article 94(1)).

Panama (1989): the US invasion violated the UN Charter (Article 2 (4)), the Charter of the Organisation of American States, the Rio Treaty (Interamerican Treaty of Reciprocal Assistance) of 1947, the

Declaration of Montevideo (1933), and the Panama Canal Treaties (1977–78).

Russian Federation (1991): in ensuring that the permanent Soviet seat on the UN Security Council was assumed by Russia, *without the necessary two-thirds majority vote in the General Assembly*, the United States violated Article 108 of the UN Charter.

Libya (1992): in refusing to observe its obligations under the 1971 Montreal Convention, drafted specifically to address terrorist acts against civilian aircraft, the United States was in violation of an international treaty enacted under the auspices of the International Civil Aviation Organisation (ICAO), a specialised UN agency, and properly lodged with the United Nations under Article 102.

North Korea (1991–93): in refusing to refer its nuclear dispute with North Korea to the International Court of Justice, the United States was in violation of Article 17 of the IAEA Statute (1956, amended 1973). In threatening war against North Korea, the United States was yet again in violation of Article 2(4) of the UN Charter.

Bosnia (1995): in supplying military aid to various factions, via Military Professional Resources Inc. (see *The Observer*, 5 November 1995), the US violated Security Council resolution 713 (25 September 1991). In April 1996 Washington admitted to violating 713 in allowing Iran to send arms to Bosnia.

Many countries violate treaty obligations and international law, characteristically viewing legal obligation as a variable quantity in a global politic shaped by cynical calculation of strategic advantage. But Washington's derelictions are uniquely significant, simply because of American economic sway and military unassailability. The corruptions of power are necessarily substantial in a *super*-power committed to upholding 'democracy' (i.e. US capitalist penetration for private profit) around the world. This was a highly significant factor in all Washington's efforts to shape the unfolding of the (1990–) Gulf crisis.

In order to secure the required Security Council authorisation (via Resolution 678) for the use of force, the long-settled US preference, and to establish a suitable international climate, Washington set about bribing and intimidating as many UN Members as seemed necessary. Thus:

- To avoid the possibility of a Chinese veto in the Security Council, Washington refrained from any criticism of the Tiananmen Square massacre, smoothed a substantial World Bank loan, and speedily arranged an initial World Bank payment of $114 million to Beijing. The Chinese scholar Liu Binyan observed that China had 'skilfully manipulated the Iraqi crisis to its advantage and rescued itself from being the pariah of the world'.

- The Soviet Union, particularly susceptible to bribery because of its parlous economic state, was promised $7 billion in aid from various (US-pressured) countries and substantial food shipments from the United States. Washington persuaded the Saudi foreign minister Saud al-Faysalwe to fly to Moscow with a $1 billion bribe, and once Resolution 678 had been passed a further $3 billion-worth of aid was donated by the Gulf states.

- Zaire was promised military aid and debt forgiveness.

- Ethiopia was offered an investment deal.

- A $7 billion loan to Egypt was written off, a presidential initiative that violated US law. At the same time Washington pressured other states, including Canada and Saudi Arabia, to 'forgive' or delay much of the rest of the Egyptian debt.

- Syria, though still on Washington's official list of terrorist states, was offered massive military assistance and the assurance that there would be no interference in its Lebanon operations. Syria's acquiescence earned the despotic regime – in many ways a Ba'athist mirror of Saddam's – $1 billion-worth of arms and aid.

- Saudi Arabia was promised $12 billion in arms sales.

- Turkey, particularly useful as a strategically placed NATO member, was given $8 billion-worth of military equipment, including tanks, ships, helicopters and fixed-wing aircraft (some of which were used to suppress the Turkish Kurds and to support later invasions into Iraq). Turkey was also offered $1 billion-worth of support for the building of the Sikorsky helicopter plant, an increased allocation of US textile exports, $1.5 billion-worth of low-cost loans from the IMF and the World Bank, and US sponsorship of Turkey's application for membership of the European Community (despite Turkey's appalling human-rights record).

- When Iran agreed to support the anti-Iraq blockade it was immediately rewarded with its first World Bank loan since the 1979 Islamic Revolution. Just before the ground attack on Iraq was launched the World Bank announced an unprecedented loan to the Islamic regime of $250 million dollars.

- Minutes after Yemen had registered its negative vote against Resolution 678, a senior American diplomat told the Yemeni ambassador: 'That was the most expensive "no" vote you ever cast.' Within days the US had blocked its $70 million aid programme to Yemen, one of the poorest countries in the world; the World Bank and the IMF moved to block further loans; and some 800,000 Yemeni workers were expelled from Saudi Arabia.

- Zimbabwe, initially hostile to Resolution 678, eventually voted in favour after being told that otherwise a projected IMF loan would be blocked.

- Ecuador was warned by Washington of the 'devastating economic consequences' that would follow a 'no' vote.

- Cuba, pressured by Secretary of State James Baker to support 678, refused to be bribed or intimidated.

The vote for Resolution 678 (29 November 1990), following Washington's best efforts, was 12 to 2 against (Yemen and Cuba) with one abstention (China). Now it seemed that the United States had unambiguously established its UN 'flag of convenience' for its long-projected war against Iraq; but there were still, for anyone who cared to notice, many procedural and legal uncertainties. These, however, would do nothing to deflect Washington from the course it had set.

One important consideration, ignored by the US war-planners, was that the 678 authorisation for 'all necessary means' [to evict Iraqi forces from Kuwait] was not unambiguously synonymous with authorisation for military force: if only because there could still be legitimate debate about what was *necessary*. The Soviet foreign minister Eduard Shevardnadze had made plain his doubts about including any reference to *force* in the resolution, though he clearly knew what Washington intended.[34] But now, with the agreed wording, who was to decide what was necessary? Every UN Member, acting independently? The Security Council? The General Assembly? The United States? The answer was plain. Washington was running the show. The United Nations had been excluded from further authorisation input, and any ambiguities in

Resolution 678 could be conveniently ignored by the military planners.

Another detail, given far too little attention, was the fact that China had abstained on the crucial vote – *which could reasonably be interpreted to mean that the vote had not been carried.* Article 27(3) of the UN Charter reads: 'Decisions of the Security Council . . . shall be made by an affirmative vote of nine members including the concurring votes of the permanent members . . .'. This suggests that a permanent-member abstention counts as a veto, an interpretation that is lent weight by the French text of Article 27(3): 'Les décisions du Conseil de Sécurité . . . sont prises par *un vote affirmatif* de neuf de ses membres dans lequel sont comprises les voix de *tous les membres permanent*' (my italics). That customary practice has *not* interpreted a permanent-member abstention as a veto does not detract from the clear wording of the Article (especially in French). This suggests that powerful states can interpret the UN Charter in a cavalier fashion, keen to invoke specific provisions when it suits but indifferent to Charter demands on other occasions. This indifference clearly characterised the US response to the Gulf crisis: not least in Washington's failure to work through the establishment of a Military Staff Committee (as specified in Article 47) for the military expulsion of Saddam's forces from Kuwait. In short, the 678 vote fell far short of granting Washington the legal right to attack Iraq whenever it chose.

Analysis of President George Bush's position during the events leading up to the Gulf War has also been taken to indicate various initiatives that violate the American Constitution.[35] Here it is pointed out that Bush made numerous threats against Iraq and, with no Constitutional authority, deployed 'enormous military force around Iraq in coalition with forces of other nations'. Moreover, the interception of ships carrying goods to Iraq, a manifest blockade exceeding the President's Constitutional powers, was an act of war. Such acts, without at that stage even a nominal Congressional approval, represented a violation of the US Constitution. In the same way the various alliances contracted by President Bush with Kuwait, Saudi Arabia and other governments, with the immediate aim of repelling the Iraqi invasion of Kuwait, had been made without the advice and consent of the Senate and in the absence of appropriate Presidential powers. Again the Senate is constitutionally required to agree such alliances and coalitions: the President has no legal power to make 'so-called "temporary alliances", or "coalitions", by calling them "Agreements" . . . with foreign Nations or foreign Powers'.[36] The President's authority as Commander-in-Chief of the American armed forces is subordinate to the authority of Congress to make war; it does not confer to the President any political authority to employ force abroad against a foreign nation. Even resolutions in the UN Security Council, bearing in mind the US United Nations Treaty, do not confer war-making powers on the President. It may be emphasised that Congress 'has no constitutional power to delegate to the President a discretionary power to contract war alliances by the medium of the UN Security Council . . . and to wage war by executing UN Security Council resolutions'. Here Webb argues that the very United Nations Treaty is unconstitutional since the Constitution grants neither the President nor the Congress the authority to provide armed forces to any Power other than the United States.[37]

The trade embargo on Iraq introduced by the President in early August 1990 has also been represented as unconstitutional on the ground that there are no constitutional powers conferred on the President whereby such sanctions could be imposed ('the Congress has no constitutional authority to delegate to the President the power to regulate commerce with foreign nations'). In fact, working through existing statutory provisions, the President has considerable powers to regulate trade (for example, to restrict exports), without needing to acquire additional powers.[38] Webb highlights also President Bush's decision to order units of the National Guard into federal service to augment the Gulf deployment. In fact the US government has no authority to order the National Guard (the State militia) out of the country, only the authority to employ such forces 'to execute the Laws of the Union, suppress Insurrections, and repel Invasions' (Article 1, Section 8 of the Constitution). Thus it is argued that President Bush's conduct of the confrontation with Iraq violated the US Constitution on many counts, quite apart from the various derelictions of international law that might be highlighted (see above and below).[39]

Hence, in arriving at the point when it was about to launch a military offensive against Iraq, Washington had threatened force (in violation of Article 2(4) of the UN Charter), had blockaded ships on the high seas (a recognised act of war in international law), had systematically bribed and intimidated UN Members (a form of 'jury tampering' that in the modern world passes for US diplomacy), had refused to make any realistic attempt to seek a pacific solution to the Gulf crisis (so violating Article 2(3) of the UN Charter), and had in addition violated the United States Constitution in various ways. The scene was now set for comprehensive violations of international law during the prosecution of a war and its aftermath.

It is now undisputed that the US forces in Iraq used various 'weapons of mass destruction' that stand condemned in successive UN resolutions and in the deliberations of the Commission for Conventional Armaments (12 August 1948). Thus GA Resolution 32/84 (12 December 1977), recalling earlier resolutions (3479 (XXX), 11 December 1975; 31/74, 10 December 1976):

1.   *Urges* States to refrain from developing new weapons of mass destruction based on new scientific principles;

2.   *Calls upon* States to apply scientific discovery for the benefit of mankind;

3.   *Reaffirms* the definition of weapons of mass destruction contained in the resolution of the Commission for Conventional Armaments of 12 August 1948, which defined weapons of mass destruction as atomic explosive weapons, radioactive material weapons, lethal chemical and biological weapons and any weapons developed in the future which might have characteristics comparable in destructive effect to those of the atomic bomb or other weapons mentioned above ...

A subsequent resolution (33/84, 13 December 1978) calls for Member States to ban 'weapons of mass destruction', as defined. Clearly a number of the devices used by the US forces in Iraq belong in this category. The depleted-uranium (DU) projectiles, made of radioactive materials, are prohibited; as are the fuel-air bombs (with 'destructive effect' comparable to that 'of the atomic bomb'). Fuel-air bombs, causing asphyxiation by burning the oxygen over several square kilometres, also stand condemned by the Geneva Protocol on 17 June 1925, by the 1st and 4th Geneva Conventions (1949), and by the 1st additional Protocol (1977) to the 1949 Geneva Convention. In the same spirit the 1922 Washington Conventions prohibit the use of asphyxiating gases and incendiary devices (later napalm), also condemned in the 1925 Protocol.

The Hague and Geneva Conventions include general prohibitions on the use of weapons that cause unnecessary harm to combatants; again ruling out the use of DU projectiles, fuel-air explosives, napalm, cluster bombs ('flesh shredders') and various other devices possibly used against Iraqi troops, such as the sting-ray blinding laser system, designed to destroy the optical systems on weapons but capable also of blinding human beings. Protocol 1 of the Geneva Convention urges protection of the natural environment against widespread and severe damage – so outlawing the deliberate bombing of nuclear power stations, chemical plants, oil refineries, etc., all of which were targeted by allied aircraft and missiles. The 1954 Hague Convention and Protocol 1 of the Geneva Convention both prohibit the targeting of historic monuments, works of art, cultural sites, spiritual centres, etc.; again all attacked by allied bombers. Other violations, individually condemned in one or more of the various Conventions (Hague, Washington, Geneva, UN), included:

- The bombing of 'dual use' (civilian/military) targets without prior warning;

- The bombing of materials essential for the survival of the civilian population;

- The bombing of dams and bridges;

- The bombing of schools, colleges, hospitals and laboratories;

- The bombing of civilian communications facilities;

- The bombing of retreating enemy forces;

- The bombing of soldiers no longer able to offer resistance;

- Deliberate neglect of the 'life preservation' principle (Protocol 1, 1949 Geneva Convention: 'It is prohibited to order that there shall be no survivors');

- Withholding information about prisoners of war from the International Red Cross;

- Denial of permission to International Red Cross representatives to visit prisoners of war to ascertain living conditions, health status, etc.;

- Denial of permission to International Red Cross representatives and other agencies to ascertain numbers and identities of dead, places of burial, etc.;

- Denial of rights of prisoners of war to correspondence, communication with legal or other representatives, contact with relatives, etc.;

- The establishment of undeclared detention centres for prisoners of war;

- Brutal treatment of prisoners of war.

Such violations (the list could be extended) indicate a comprehensive neglect of the evolved humanitarian provisions designed to establish rules of war and the protection of civilian populations trapped in battle zones. Illegal weapons, the targeting of civilians (even remote Bedouin tents in the desert) and the social infrastructure essential to civilian survival, massacres to no military purpose, the abuse of prisoners' rights, and the ultimate protracted genocide of a nation – all this indicates an unrestrained military colossus, striking unassailably from a distance, neglectful of the rights of combatants and civilians alike, indifferent to massive environmental and cultural damage, totally oblivious to the humanitarian corpus of international law.

Many observers, including eminent Americans, have addressed the question of US war crimes against Iraq. Thus Francis Boyle, Professor of International Law at the University of Illinois, served as an advisor to Congressman Henry Gonzales on the preparation of an impeachment resolution against President Bush. Professor Boyle also advised the Commission of Inquiry for the International War Crimes Tribunal, initiated by the former US Attorney-General Ramsey Clark. In February 1992, at a final judgement of the Tribunal, 22 judges from 18 nations met in New York to consider the charges against Bush and other American leaders: here it was concluded that President George Bush and others were guilty on 19 charges of crimes against peace, war crimes, and crimes against humanity.[40] Interviewed in 1991 by John M. Miller, Professor Boyle discussed some of the main issues that had developed out of the Gulf crisis.[41] Here it is stated that prewar computer modelling clearly indicated what would be the effects of extensive destruction of oil facilities in the region ('... it would be difficult to segregate responsibility between the Iraqis and the U.S. In law, you can have two perpetrators of the same crime'). In the event the US government, in knowingly causing considerable environmental damage, violated Geneva Protocol 1 of 1977, the Convention on the Prohibition of Military or Any Other Hostile Use of Environmental Modification Techniques (ENMOD, United Nations, 1977), and customary international law.

It was emphasised also that Washington's failure to sign the relevant Geneva Protocol did not absolve the United States from its legal responsibilities. At the Nuremberg Tribunal the Nazi war criminals argued that, since Germany was not a signatory to the Hague Regulations (1907) or the Kellogg–Briand Pact (1928), they could not be charged with war crimes: they were none the less convicted under the Hague Regulations.[42] In 1991 there were calls for Saddam Hussein to be tried for war crimes, a charge for which evidence could well be adduced. At the same time if an international court were to be set up at the United Nations all possible war criminals should be arraigned. (Professor Boyle: 'If they set the court up, we will bring to that court our case against Bush, Baker, Cheney, Quayle, Powell, Schwarzkopf, everyone else. Let them create the court. We will go in there with our evidence, and they will have to hear it'.)

The deliberate destruction of the civilian infrastructure by American forces also constituted a war crime, as defined in the Nuremberg Charter, the Nuremberg Judgement, and the Nuremberg Principles (Boyle also cites the Hague Regulations of 1907 and the Hague Rules of Aerial Warfare of 1923). In this connection, and for many other associated reasons, it is important to consider the additional Protocol 1 (already cited), appended (10 June 1977) to the Geneva Conventions of 1949 (see Appendix 9). Here it is emphasised (Article 35(1)) that 'the right of the Parties to the conflict to choose methods or means of warfare is not unlimited'; unnecessary suffering must be avoided, as must 'widespread, longterm and severe damage' to the environment. Indiscriminate attacks must be avoided, as must attacks on civilian targets, places of worship, and 'objects indispensable to the survival of the civilian population'.

It is clear that how the US-directed allied forces waged war in the Gulf (using indiscriminate weapons, causing severe damage to the natural environment, perpetrating massacres on helpless troops, bombing churches and mosques, deliberately targeting the civilian infrastructure, etc.) constituted a multifaceted violation of Protocol 1. We need to note that today (early 1996), five years after the war ended, *the gross violation continues – in what amounts to a protracted war of mass destruction*. We need to heed Article 54 of Protocol 1:

1. Starvation of civilians as a method of warfare is prohibited.

2. It is prohibited to attack, destroy, remove or render useless objects indispensable to the survival of the civilian population, such as foodstuffs, agricultural areas for the production of foodstuffs, crops, livestock, drinking water installation and supplies and irrigation works, for the specific purpose of denying them for their sustenance value to the civilian population or to the adverse Party, whatever the motive, whether in order to starve out civilians, to cause them to move away, or for any other motive.

We have seen, in this connection, that the US-led forces directly and indirectly targeted foodstuffs and water supplies (bombing food warehouses, food distribution facilities, refrigeration plant, electrical supply facilities, water pumping systems, water purification plant, water distribution systems, etc.); and that today, via the mechanism of the sanctions regime, Washington blocks food imports to Iraq, blocks the vaccines and drugs that are essential to animal husbandry, blocks the pesticides that are essential to productive agriculture, blocks the equipment and spare parts that are essential to water purification and distribution systems, etc. The *starvation of civilians* that is prohibited by Protocol 1 *as a method of warfare* is being deliberately perpetrated as one of several genocidal measures in a desolate peace.

THE FACE OF GENOCIDE

Genocides have run through all human history: *homo sapiens*, unique among species, has a keen propensity to exterminate its kind. At the same time human beings have made countless efforts to mitigate – by dint of regulation, law, international convention *inter alia* – the extremes of biological self-destruction. Thus on 11 December 1946 the General Assembly of the young United Nations, sensitive to the recent horrors of the Second World War, passed Resolution 96(I) to address 'The Crime of Genocide'. The resolution declares:

> Genocide is a denial of the right of existence of entire human groups, as homicide is the denial of the right to live of individual human beings; such denial of the right of existence shocks the conscience of mankind, results in great losses to humanity in the form of cultural and other contributions represented by these human groups, and is contrary to moral law and to the spirit and aims of the United Nations.

It notes that such 'crimes of genocide' have often occurred 'when racial, religious, political or other groups have been destroyed, entirely or in part'. The General Assembly therefore 'affirms that *genocide is a crime under international law ... and for the commission of which principals and accomplices – whether private individuals, public officials or statesmen, and whether the crime is committed on religious, racial, political or any other grounds – are punishable*' (my italics). Resolution GA 96(I) then invites Member States to enact the necessary legislation for the punishment of genocide, and recommends international co-operation to this end. The subsequent General Assembly Resolution 260A(III) (9 December 1948) approved and proposed for signature and ratification the Convention on the Prevention and Punishment of the Crime of Genocide (see Appendix 11).

The Convention, citing Resolution 96(I), states that genocide occurs with 'acts committed with intent to destroy, in whole or in part, a national, ethnical, racial or religious group, as such: (a) Killing members of the group; (b) Causing serious bodily or mental harm to members of the group; (c) Deliberately inflicting on the group conditions of life calculated to bring about its physical destruction in whole or in part; (d) Imposing measures intended to prevent births within the group; (e) Forcibly transferring children of the group to another group'. Article III of the Convention stipulates that five specific acts shall be punishable: genocide, conspiracy to commit genocide, direct and public incitement to commit genocide, the attempt to commit genocide, and complicity in genocide.

It is important to note also that punishable perpetrators of genocide may be 'constitutionally responsible rulers, public officials or private individuals' (Article IV); that persons charged with genocide 'shall be tried by a competent tribunal of the State in the territory of which the act was committed' or by an agreed international penal tribunal (Article VI); and that the Contracting Parties pledge themselves 'to grant extradition' (Article VII). Before speculating on the relevance of Resolution 96(I) and the genocide Convention to what the United States is perpetrating in Iraq, it is useful to recall the scale of genocide in the twentieth century.

Efforts to comprehend the nature of genocide have focused on its racial, religious and imperialistic aspects; on the sociological and psychological characteristics that make it possible; and on such considerations as the phases of what may be considered to be a typical genocidal process. Hervé Savon, as a member of the *Institut français de polémologie* (polemology = the study of war), grouped genocides into three classes: *substitution* (where one indigenous or ethnic group is supplanted by another), *devastation* (where a group is deliberately annihilated), and *elimination* (involving, for example, forced emigrations). Such arbitrary distinctions do at least indicate what is reflected in GA 96(I) and the Convention: namely that genocides can be of many different types. Hence simply that the US action on Iraq does not involve Holocaust-style extermination camps does not mean that it is any the less genocidal in intent or illegality. Nor does Germany's comprehensive slaughter in the 1940s mean that lesser exterminations both before and after do not qualify as genocides. Pre-twentieth-century genocides have included the extermination of the Samnites by Sulla after 91 BC, the annihilation of the Jews in Palestine under Hadrian, the Roman destruction of Carthage, the slaughter of the Cathars, the burning of witches, the killing of the Jews and Marranos in Spain, phases of the French Revolution (including *la terreur*, *les noyades* and Babeuf's *système de dépopulation*). Conquerors have traditionally sacked fortresses, towns and cities, slaughtering populations and stealing their possessions. In the twentieth century the scale of extermination, lubricated by new technologies and characteristic human enterprise, has surpassed all previous genocides combined.

Some 20,000 Armenian Christians were slaughtered by the Turks in Cilicia in 1909; followed by the mass extermination of more than one million Armenians in 1915/16 – an event that the US Congress voted (1990) by 51 to 48 to write out of history to protect the Turkish ally (Hitler, planning his 'final solution' to the Jewish Question, asked: 'Who remembers the Armenians now?'). Further slaughters took place in the Soviet Union (through forced collectivisation, purges and other events), throughout Europe with the Nazi holocaust, in India and Pakistan with the 'ethnic cleansing' that accompanied partition, in China (through class exterminations, the Cultural Revolution and other causes), in Rwanda and Burundi with reciprocal genocides of Tutsi and Hutu, and in many other countries that were less publicised. In the Liberia of the early 1990s more than 150,000 people were killed; in Zaire unknown thousands (half a million forced from their homes through 'ethnic cleansing'); in Sierra Leone one million people displaced, some 60,000 dead through war and famine in 1990 alone; in Angola 20,000 dead through the 8-month UNITA siege of Cuito, one such event among many; and the little-exposed US strategic policies in Africa – 'supporting bad men in the cause of anti-Communism and the cost has been counted in dead Africans'.[43]

In the twentieth century five countries – because of their size and the scale of their ambition – stand out in their genocidal accomplishments: the Soviet Union, Japan, Communist China, Nazi Germany and the United States of America. Italy committed genocide in the conquest of Libya; France slaughtered perhaps one million Algerians and hundreds of thousands more in Indo-China; Indonesian generals massacred 800,000 of their countrymen and 200,000 East Timorese; South Africa killed more than a million in Namibia, Angola and Mozambique, and so on and so forth – but only the five named countries can number their genocides in the many millions.

The United States, born through ethnic cleansing and genocide, developed its capacity for mass extermination through an unprecedented technology and a vigorous market imperialism. Most of Washington's genocidal prowess was developed during and after the Second World

War. The pre-war German bombing of Guernica, as an event in the Spanish Civil War, evoked much protest in the United States, not least from President Franklin D. Roosevelt. When the European war began in 1939 Roosevelt declared: 'The ruthless bombing from the air of civilians in unfortified centers of population during the course of the hostilities which have raged in various quarters of the earth during the past few years, which has resulted in the maiming and in the deaths of thousands of defenseless men, women and children has sickened the hearts of every civilized man and woman, and has profoundly shocked the conscience of humanity.'[44] In 1940 Roosevelt urged all parties to refrain from bombing civilians, at the same time recalling 'with pride that the United States has taken the lead in urging that this inhuman practice be prohibited'.[45] Before long, Washington had performed a remarkable U-turn: ' . . . the Royal Air Force and the US Army Air Force became the apostles of strategic bombing and proceeded to perfect the techniques of massive urban destruction with incendiary bombs. . .'.[46]

In fact General George C. Marshall, the chief of staff, had already ordered his aides to plan incendiary attacks that would 'burn up the wood and paper structures of the densely populated Japanese cities'. On the night of 9–10 March 1945 some 334 US aircraft destroyed sixteen square miles of Tokyo with incendiary bombs, killing 80–100,000 people and making one million homeless. Major-General Curtis LeMay observed with satisfaction that the Japanese men, women and children had been 'scorched and boiled and baked to death':[47] the heat was such that canals boiled, metal structures melted, and human beings burst spontaneously into flames. Through the course of the war some 64 Japanese cities, apart from Hiroshima and Nagasaki, were subjected to this type of attack. One estimate suggests that perhaps around 400,000 people were killed in this way.[48] This was a preparation for the genocides that the United States would commit against countries that were no threat to Washington.

From 1950 to 1973 the United States slaughtered, at a conservative estimate, around 10,000,000 Chinese, Koreans, Vietnamese, Laotians and Cambodians (the 'killing fields' of Cambodia did not begin with Pol Pot). One estimate suggests that two million North Korean civilians were killed in the Korean War, many of them in the firestorms in Pyongyang and other major cities, reminiscent of the incendiary attacks on Tokyo (the highest estimate for the Chinese dead is set at around three million). At the MacArthur Hearings Major-General Emmet O'Donnell, Commander of the Far East Air Force Bomber Command, testified: 'Almost the whole of the Korean peninsula is in an awfully tragic state. Everything is being destroyed. Nothing worth mentioning remains intact.' The sudden entry of the Chinese forces into North Korea, to deter MacArthur from crossing the Yalu River into China, provided the US bombers with new opportunities for mass slaughter: 'We had been free from our flying mission until the Chinese army came. For there had already been no target left in Korea' (*Records of the MacArthur Hearings*). Within little more than a decade Vietnam, Laos and Cambodia were being subjected to the same sort of treatment.

The Vietnamese Buddhist the Venerable Thich Thien Hao claimed that by mid-1963 the Vietnam War had caused: 160,000 dead, 700,000 tortured and maimed, 31,000 raped, 3000 disembowelled while alive, 4000 burned to death, 1000 temples destroyed, 46 villages attacked with poisonous chemicals, and so on.[49] The US bombing of Hanoi and Haiphong over Christmas 1972 produced some 30,000 children with permanent deafness; by which time the deaths and injuries had mounted into the millions. After the war, while the Americans anguished over (in one estimate) 2497 Missing-in-Action (MIA) US soldiers, Vietnamese families struggled to adjust to their own 300,000 MIAs. The dead in Vietnam numbered perhaps four million, with many millions more maimed, blinded, traumatised and deformed. Vietnam had been reduced to a land of graves, amputees, poisoned land, orphans and deformed babies. Perhaps the grand tally of Asian dead and mutilated, the victims of Western ideology, reached 20,000,000. But American anguish over the 'Vietnam Syndrome' had nothing to do with that.

It was not only the blood of Korea/Vietnam/Laos/Cambodia that indelibly coloured American hands. The United States was also a direct or indirect accomplice to the tortures, maimings and deaths in many other countries around the world. There is manifest US complicity in the Indonesian massacres, in the wars against the suffering people of Central America (Nicaragua, El Salvador,* Guatemala, Honduras: hundreds of thousands more dead through US arms, US training and advice, US proxies), in the African civil turmoils (the bloody struggles in Angola, Mozambique, Namibia and others), in the repressions perpetrated by US-sustained tyrants over the decades (Somoza, Pinochet, Marcos, Mobutu, Batista, Diem, Ky, Rhee, Duvalier, Suharto, Savimbi *inter alia*).

In such a context the genocidal onslaught on Iraq, part of a pattern

---

* As one example among many, about one thousand unarmed peasants, including 139 children, were massacred by US-trained troops in El Mozote in 1981. The US-trained army in Guatemala killed more than 150,000 peasants between 1966 and 1986.

spanning much of the twentieth century, is characteristic and familiar. We need to emphasise the criminal nature of this habitual behaviour; and to indicate, albeit briefly, the psychological mechanisms that enable otherwise decent people to become accomplices to genocide.

It should now be obvious that when American behaviour towards Iraq (through the protracted chronology of sanctions–war–sanctions) is set against Protocol 1 (1977) to the 1949 Geneva Convention, General Assembly Resolution 96(I) and the 1948 Genocide Convention, the United States is guilty of war crimes and genocide. The guilt, according to the terms of the Convention, extends to national leaders, public officials and private individuals. Reference has already been made to the US national leaders who might properly be arraigned before a war-crimes/genocide tribunal. Such individuals, subject on a daily basis to strategic pressures and personal ambition, have perhaps the greatest responsibility for crimes committed by nation states. But it is useful to look also at the officials who administer the mechanisms of genocide.

Any state system that exists to determine whether foreigners in some besieged country shall be allowed to eat requires an appropriate bureaucracy. To this end, suitable 'sanctions units' have been established to liaise with the United Nations Sanctions Committee. Procedures have been laid down and guidelines have been published; in particular, there is nice attention to record-keeping, tidy documentation, form-filling and the like. The UK Sanctions Unit, working under the auspices of the DTI Export Control Organisation, is happy to supply a well-printed document (two-colour, shiny paper) explaining how you, as a trader, are required to negotiate the thicket of sanctions legislation. The Bank of England offers similar documentation to advise on financial transactions. There is no reason to suppose that the individuals in such organisations are uniquely malicious or vindictive; when one speaks with them they give every indication of being normal human beings, committed to the task in hand and convinced that it is all worth while. In particular, they are keen to ensure that the bureaucracy works efficiently. As officials, perhaps unaware of Article IV of the Genocide Convention, they have no discernible views on the broader morality of what they are doing. It is clear that they are only obeying orders.

Any attempt to confront someone (official or other) with the fact of a prevailing genocide in which they may be implicated, albeit indirectly, immediately generates various defensive reactions. Ideology and propaganda have already prepared the ground. An initial response may be silence, while the water is tested. Why am I being challenged in such a way? Then the exculpations are presented. In the case of Iraq the demonisation of Saddam Hussein has accomplished everything. If the Iraqi people are suffering, it is Saddam's fault. If Iraqi infants are going blind through want of insulin, he should have thought of that. If Iraqi women are being forced to endure caesarian sections without anaesthetic, what a monster Saddam Hussein must be. Guilt transference – if I, my country, our allies, my ideology are full of rectitude, then who can be blamed for the manifest fact that Iraqi babies lie dying in their thousands in dirty hospital wards? The propaganda has done its filthy work. If I or my government are withholding medicine and food from sick and malnourished children then there must be a very good reason. What can it be? It is obviously the fault of the demon.

Attempts have been made to identify the psychological elements that combine to shape the mentalities of those involved in genocide. Thus Robert Jay Lifton, a professor of psychiatry and psychology at the City University of New York, and Eric Markusen, an associate professor of sociology at Carthage College (Kenosha, Wisconsin), have highlighted the 'psychological mechanisms that protect individual people from inwardly experiencing the harmful effects, immediate or potential, of their own actions on others'.[50] Such devices, 'all of which blunt feelings', include such elements as *'dissociation or splitting'* (where a part of the mind separates from the whole), *'psychic numbing'* (a reduced capacity or inclination to feel), *'brutalization'* (allowing sustained behaviour that causes harm to others), and *'doubling'* (akin to splitting, but where a second self emerges to allow the person some sanctuary from otherwise unsettling experiences).

All such mechanisms, along with guilt transference, are evident in public and private people that today support the continuation of the anti-Iraq sanctions regime. It must be right or we would not be doing it. If the Iraqis are dying and diseased, it isn't my fault, my government's fault, President Clinton's fault, the UN's fault. It's all Saddam's fault. If he won't say what happened to some biological material eight years ago then of course we should starve another one million Iraqis to death. In any case, I've enough to think about, you're too argumentative, and politicians are all the same. I don't really care, I've enough to think about. Yes, it's all very sad, but that's how things are.

EPILOGUE

It began, in large part, because of oil; it continues, in large part, because of oil. In the months leading up to Iraq's invasion of Kuwait it was known that Kuwait was flooding the oil market in violation of the agreed OPEC quotas. One consequence was a massive drop in oil prices which 'in turn, hurt Iraq, which was already short on funds'.[51] This caused Iraq's oil revenue to slump by $7 billion, and it was clear that Baghdad 'was facing economic suffocation'.[52] The substantial over-production of oil by Kuwait and the United Arab Emirates (UAR) in the spring of 1990 depressed the oil price well below the OPEC refer-ence (agreed in November 1989) of $18 a barrel. On 30 May Saddam Hussein, speaking at an Arab summit in Baghdad, declared: ' . . . for every US dollar drop in the price of a barrel of oil, the Iraqi loss amounted to $1 billion annually. . . . War is fought with soldiers and harm is done by explosions, killing and coup attempts, but it is also done by economic means sometimes. I say to those who do not mean to wage war on Iraq, that this is in fact a kind of war against Iraq.'[53] While Saddam was trying desperately to stabilise oil prices, Kuwait's oil minister, Ali Khalifa al-Sabah, was urging that the OPEC agree-ment be scrapped: 'Kuwait neither accepts nor is bound by its as-signed quota.' Those present at the Arab summit noted the indifference of Kuwait's Emir Jaber to the Iraqi problems, his reply evincing 'something close to contempt for the Iraqi position . . .'.[54] At the same time it was pointed out that Kuwait had been illegally extracting oil from the 'Iraqi Rumeila oilfield' (which extends into Kuwait), a practice that had so far cost Iraq $2.4 billion. On 17 July 1990 Saddam Hussein declared in a televised speech: 'At the behest of the US, certain Arab states had deliberately overproduced oil in defiance of the will of the OPEC majority. As a result . . . Iraq had been losing $14 billion a year.'[55] Washington's clear priority was being achieved: a flow of cheap oil.

After the invasion of Kuwait, over which it was easy to demonise Saddam, various US and international factions found further financial benefits to be gained. Now the sudden *rise* in oil prices meant that Britain, the Soviet Union and China were making enormous windfall profits, according to a UN report totalling $154 billion; and that Texas oilmen (including George Bush and James Baker) were seeing the value of their oil reserves increase by $140 billion.[56] Now the economies of many poorer countries were being devastated by the soaring oil prices.

Throughout the entire period of economic sanctions the world oil markets saw advantage in the absence of Iraqi oil. When, in August 1995, Rolf Ekeus, head of the special commission for disarming Iraq, suggested that the unprecedented level of Iraqi co-operation meant that sanctions should be lifted, there was immediate alarm on the markets.

If Iraq were to be allowed to sell its oil this could only add to the burgeoning problem of oversupply in the North Sea and elsewhere. Terry Dallas, finance director of the US oil company Arco, gave voice to the general dismay: 'We believe Iraq will severely depress markets for some time. We are very concerned about that scenario.'[57] In the same vein, Peter Bogin, at Cambridge Energy Research Associates in Paris, estimated that if Iraq was allowed back into the market, 'the price would fall by $2 a barrel'.[58] And another specialist, *The Independent's* diplomatic editor, Michael Sheridan, commented: 'there are commercial pressures in the world oil market to keep sanctions in place. Oil industry analysts believe Saudi Arabia and other producers want to keep Iraqi production off the market, because of weakening crude prices and the fact that Opec is in disarray over its collective marketing policy.'[59] Presumably, Washington would continue working to maintain sanctions – not because of any significant Iraqi derelictions but because the profits of global capitalism demanded it.

At one level the Iraqi invasion of Kuwait and its aftermath are about human rights and illegal aggression – matters that Washington has never addressed outside its cynical calculation of strategic advantage. At another, the one on which important political events are shaped, the situation in the Gulf region is about capitalist exploitation and Western economic imperialism. For such cultural icons the merciless sacrifice of Iraqi men, women and children will continue. The pain of distant peoples has never mattered if profits are to be made.

5 The New Holocaust

Lesley Stahl: 'We have heard that half a million children have died [as a result of sanctions against Iraq]. I mean, that is more children than died in Hiroshima ... is the price worth it?'

Madeleine Albright (then US Ambassador to the United Nations, now Secretary of State): '... we think the price is worth it'.

Interview, CBS '60 Minutes', 12 May 1996

PREAMBLE

There is an obvious sense in which the escalating catastrophe in Iraq is no secret. Details of civilian morbidity and mortality, the scale of sickness and malnutrition, the grim statistics of emaciated babies and dying children, the cruel fabric of a modern genocide – all this can be easily gleaned by comfortable observers in the West and elsewhere, if one knows where to look, if one has an interest, if one cares. After all, are we not constantly told that we live in properly Christian societies with due concern for human rights? No one would want to disguise or evade the truth about a dying nation – unless, that is, one in reality had direct or indirect responsibility for this slow extermination of a national people.

Information about the suffering of the Iraqi civilian population is available but never seriously advertised in the West: for example, after seven years of this cruel economic siege of Iraq we are never granted detailed television reports of the terrible consequences. Were it otherwise, indifferent publics may become agitated, questions may be asked, demands made for a change in the genocidal policies of the United States and the United Kingdom – possibilities that Washington and London, well satisfied with compliant media, can safely ignore.

We do well to remember – and to feel – what is being done in our name. We do well to acknowledge the character of a 1990s genocide, the comprehensive Western propaganda that sustains it, and the psychopathic malevolence of an unassailable superpower that remains blind and deaf to the demands of decency, compassion and international law.

214

SLOW EXTERMINATION

The impact of sanctions on Iraq has been well documented over the years. Thus Dieter Hannusch, Chief Emergency Support Officer of the UN World Food Programme, noted how sanctions-induced food short-ages were causing *irreparable damage to an entire generation of Iraqi children*: 'After 24 years in the field, mostly in Africa starting with Biafra, I didn't think anything could shock me, but this was com-parable to the worst scenarios I have ever seen.' Mona Hamman, the WFP Regional Manager, commented: 'There actually are more than 4 million people, a fifth of Iraq's population, at severe nutritional risk. That number includes 2.4 million children under five, about 600,000 pregnant/nursing women and destitute women heads of households as well as hundreds of thousands of elderly without anyone to help them . . . 70 per cent of the population has little or no access to food. . . . Nearly everyone seems to be emaciated. . . . We are at the point of no return. . . . The social fabric of the nation is disintegrating. People have exhausted their ability to cope.'[1]

The UN Food and Agriculture Organisation, reporting on the dete-riorating plight of Iraqi civilians in 1995, noted: 'More than one million Iraqis have died – 567,000 of them children – as a direct consequence of economic sanctions . . . as many as 12 per cent of the children sur-veyed in Baghdad are wasted, 28 per cent stunted and 29 per cent underweight.'[2] The International Red Cross was protesting at the 'dire effects' of sanctions on civilians, with reputable journalists such as Victoria Brittain reporting 'chronic hunger . . . with 20,000 new cases of child malnutrition every month'.[3] In March 1996 the UN World Health Organisation reported that the economic sanctions had caused a six-fold increase in the mortality rate of children under five with '*the vast majority of Iraqis*' surviving '*on a semi-starvation diet*'.

In this context it is not difficult to believe Iraqi claims that the sanc-tions have so far killed more than 2 million civilians, among them in excess of one million children. The United Nations Children's Fund (UNICEF) reported in October 1996 that 4500 children under five were dying every month as a result of sanctions-induced starvation and dis-ease. A more recent report, noting pre-sanctions mortality for the under fives at 540 a month, stated that the figure for May 1997 was around 5600 a month *and still rising*.[4] The same report, noting pre-sanctions adult deaths at 1800 a month, signalled the current figure at more than 8000. The West remains largely indifferent to this mounting genocide. A multinational group of doctors, public health experts, economists, lawyers and health surveyors visited Iraq in April–May 1996 and noted *'the astonishing lack of public debate over the UN's participation in this massive violation of human rights and particularly child rights'.*[5]

In January 1996 the Iraqi Permanent Mission at the UN Office at Geneva issued a *note verbale* to the 52nd session of the Commission on Human Rights to highlight the 'Impact of the economic embargo on the economic, social and cultural situation in Iraq'.[6] Here it is noted that the sanctions continue to affect 'all fields and aspects of daily life', with 'a direct impact on all' the human rights of the Iraqi people. The children continue to be the 'most severely affected by environmental and health conditions' (here reference is made to an earlier UNICEF study indicating soaring child mortality rates[7]). A growing number of births were requiring intensive care because of malnutrition among pregnant women. A further inevitable consequence of the drastically reduced access to adequate nutrition was a massive growth in the incidence of disease: anaemia, measles, mumps, cholera, typhoid, malaria, meningitis and others (reference to UNICEF report[8]). The deteriorating situation was compounded by the embargo on 'medical equipment, medicines and requisites for laboratory tests'. A cited FAO study confirmed that in mid-1993 the Iraqi government food supply system was able to meet only 45.7 per cent of individual nutritional needs; a subsequent FAO study (for the period 25 July to 1 September 1995) noted a worsening situation, with only 34 per cent of nutritional needs being met.

The collapse of health provision was being paralleled in the education sector:

> ... every year it has become increasingly difficult to meet the educational requirements. . . . The ongoing embargo has also had a profound psychological impact on most pupils and students, as well as their teachers. . . . The UN Sanctions Committee . . . refused to permit a Pakistani company to supply Iraq with a quantity of lead pencils to be used by pupils and students. . . . It has become difficult to supply school chairs . . . blackboards, pens, chalk and school copybooks.

The report notes also the large number of drop-outs at both the kindergarten and school levels because of malnutrition, disease and other factors. Inadequate access to food and medical attention was also causing a severe reduction in the numbers of teachers at all levels because of disease and premature death. The report comments that the 'destruction' of the people of Iraq 'is a form of genocide . . . punishable under international law regardless of whether it is committed in time of peace or war' (see *1990s Genocide*, below). Finally there is reference to the final sentence of Paragraph 2 of Article 1 in the International Covenant on Economic Social and Cultural Rights: '*In no case may a people be deprived of its own means of subsistence.*'

On 25 March 1996 the WHO released an Iraq health study (already cited) that was based on analysis of epidemiological data supplemented by various studies carried out by WHO, other UN agencies and non-governmental organisations.[9] The report confirmed the findings of earlier studies and emphasised that health conditions were continuing to decline at an alarming rate under the impact of sanctions. A 600 per cent increase in child mortality was reported, with drastic rises in the incidence of many vaccine-preventable diseases. Most Iraqis were forced to tolerate chronic shortages of both food and the cash to buy it. Maternal mortality had increased several-fold, and now there were epidemics of malaria, cholera, typhoid and other infectious diseases. The findings were unambiguous: '. . . the quality of health care in Iraq, due to the six-week 1991 war and the subsequent sanctions imposed on the country, has been literally put back at least 50 years. Diseases . . . once almost under control, have rebounded since 1991 to epidemic levels, with the health service as a helpless witness.'

It was now obvious to anyone who bothered to notice that a helpless people was being targeted for the sins of their leader; and that this was an odious policy. Sanctions were 'as much a violation of the rights of the Iraqi people as the brutal tactics used by Saddam . . .'.[10] In the same vein Roger Normand, policy director of the New York Centre for Economic and Social Justice, commented (in a joint Harvard University/London School of Economics report, May 1996) that the continuation of sanctions was 'tantamount to shooting down a plane full of innocent people because there are hijackers aboard'. The WHO report (March 1996) urged the international community to reconsider the implications of the sanctions regime. Similarly Abdullah Mutawi, a human rights lawyer who worked on the Harvard/LSE report (May 1996) noted the gross violation of human rights that the embargo represented:

Iraq is a clear example of the Security Council allowing human rights to be violated through the imposition of sanctions right across the board. We argue that limited military sanctions could be used without causing such hardship to the people.

TABLE 5.1   Malnutrition, children under five, monthly average

Year	kwashiorkor	marasmus	other malnutrition
1990	41	433	8,063
1991	1,066	8,015	78,990
1992	1,145	9,289	93,610
1993	1,261	11,612	102,971
1994	1,748	16,025	131,349
1995[a]	2,237	20,549	140,354

(a) January to July

Source: Government of Iraq, Vital and Health Statistics Department. Cited in Clark, 1996.

In these circumstances it was clear that the Security Council was ignoring its obligations under the UN Charter. The case against the US posture was – as it remains – overwhelming in logic, ethics and law.

The evidence of a genocidal onslaught on a national people had continued to accumulate through 1995 and 1996 – as shown by, for example, the rocketing scale of child deaths, the escalating incidence of food-deficiency diseases (see Table 5.1), or the manifest shortages of food requirements in all categories (see Table 5.2). An entire society was being knowingly and callously exterminated: all the studies and reports – from the UN agencies, non-governmental sources, research academics and journalists – were providing a broadly consensual view of what was happening in Iraq. For example, in August and September 1996 the charity Medical Aid for Iraq (MAI, see also Chapter 3) made its fourteenth tour of Iraq to supply beleaguered hospitals (on this occasion five in Baghdad and one in Kerbala).[11] The convoy again encountered a depressed and demoralised people, existing on semi-starvation rations: '*The monthly rations are enough to last approximately ten days and the World Health Organisation estimates that they provide 34 per cent of calorie needs.*' With static salaries, for those in work, some food prices had again increased.

The morale in the visited hospitals 'was even lower than in April . . . when MAI reported very poor conditions and very little hope'. There were more children suffering from malnutrition, with rickets 'a major problem' and diarrhoeal illnesses 'rife'. A large number of babies were being born with very low birth weights, and 'severely malnourished' children were common in all the hospitals visited by the MAI personnel.

There was in general further deterioration in the hospital conditions,

TABLE 5.2 Food shortages in Iraq, 1995–96

Commodity	Estimated Production[a] ('000 tons)	Total Requirement[b] ('000 tons)	Shortage or Import Requirement ('000 tons)	Shortage as % of Total Requirement
Wheat flour	989	3209	2220	69
Rice	221	994	773	78
Barley	892	1217	327	27
Maize	90	213	123[c]	58
Pulses[d]	50	120	70	58
Vegetable oil	100	298	198	66
Red Meat	94	227	133	58
Poultry Meat	20	227	207	90
Fish	5	62	57	92
Eggs (million)	150	1966	1816	92
Milk	n.a.	372	223[e]	93
Tea	none	62	62	100
Sugar	80	814	734	90
Baby Milk (for children under one year)	negligible	43	43	100

(a) Government and mission estimates. Conversion of wheat into flour is 80 per cent, reflecting the high rate of non-grain impurities in the 1995 wheat output; the recovery rate in the case of paddy into rice is 70 per cent.
(b) Calculated using standard per person annual requirement of each item in Iraq.
(c) If maize for feed for poultry and livestock is included, the quantity will be much larger.
(d) Include peas, green grain, lentil, broad beans, beans.
(e) Milk production in the country has declined sharply. It has been generously assumed that some 40 per cent of the requirement will be met through domestic production of fresh milk or that many poor people may not consume milk.

n.a. = not available.

Note: Total population 1995–96: 20.7 million.
Source: cited in Clark, 1996.

now in an even worse state than that reported in April (1996). Thus MAI reported on hospitals visited in September 1996:[12]

The general situation here was clearly worse than when MAI visited in April 1996. The hospital's cooling system had not worked...

high temperatures caused the deterioration of many medicines. . . . The medical situation here had visibly worsened. There were many more children with gastroenteritis and the hospital did not even have the basic intravenous fluids needed to treat them . . . many of the patients with gastroenteritis will die. . . . The cancer ward was full . . . the majority of the patients will die unless their parents can find the drugs . . . more than 500 disposable syringes for intravenous use were needed per day and only 20–25 were available. (*Saddam's Children's Teaching Hospital*)

The situation here was also worse. . . . Some aid had stopped after the United Nations announced the sale-of-oil agreement [see *Propaganda and 986* below] and the hospital had fewer supplies as a result. . . . Morale was at its lowest ebb ever. . . . Sheets were no longer available . . . they had been cut up and used by mothers to wrap their babies in as most cannot afford to buy baby clothes. . . . There were increasing incidents of children with respiratory problems not being able to be treated as the hospital had run out of supplies of oxygen. One child's family went to five hospitals . . . in an attempt to buy oxygen to treat their newborn child. None of the hospitals had any and the child died. (*Ibn Al Baldi Children's and Obstetric Hospital*)

We saw that the out-patient pharmacy was virtually empty of medicines and the Medical Director reported much worse conditions than in April 1996. He told the team of severe shortages in most of the drugs and equipment in high demand. . . . Most of the cancer patients were dying as a consequence of these shortages. (*Al-Mansour Children's Hospital*)

The conditions were bad, with filthy rooms and corridors . . . there were no sheets and none of the incubators were working. . . . There had been an increase in marasmus . . . and a steep increase in the levels of malnourishment. There were also cases of children suffering bloody diarrhoea, which results from drinking contaminated water, and many underweight babies. (*Kerbala Children's Hospital*)

There had been an increase in rickets. . . . As always there were many malnourished children. . . . Typhoid fever was also becoming increasingly problematic. There were a growing number of children who were relapsing after treatment for brucellosis. . . . Levels of candida were also increasing . . . there were no sheets; there have not been any for three years here. (*Khadamiva Children's Hospital*)

TABLE 5.3   Reduction in consumption of basic items

Item	1990	1996
Flour	14 kg	5 kg
Rice	3 kg	1.25 kg
Infant formula	4.430 kg	1.8 kg
Sugar	3.250 kg	500 g
Tea	270 g	100 g
Oils	1.330 kg	750 g
Detergent	540 g	250 g

The situation of these hospitals in Baghdad and Kerbala is plain enough: the United States works hard to deprive the Iraqi civilian population of food and medicine – so the sick and dying are constantly growing in numbers and the entire health system is forced, through sanctions, into terminal collapse. A 61-year-old Iraqi – his wife Haifa and his four children (Saddad, 6; Lina, 7; Fuad, 12; and Zina, 14) killed by the US bombing of the Amiriya shelter – notes that people 'live in a daze after six years of sanctions', not thinking any more, except 'about where to get food'. An Iraqi teacher wonders at American motives: 'We all understand that the Americans want to keep him [Saddam] in the kennel – but why are they starving us?'[13]

In September 1996 Nizar Hamdoon, the Iraqi ambassador to the United Nations, issued a document to the UN Secretary-General profiling the impact of the economic embargo on human rights in Iraq.[14] It notes that the block on Iraq selling its oil is a violation of Article 1, Paragraph 2 of the International Covenant on Economic, Social and Cultural Rights: '*All peoples may, for their own ends, freely dispose of their natural wealth and resources without prejudice to any obligations arising out of international economic cooperation, based upon the principle of mutual benefit, and international law. In no case may a people be deprived of its own means of subsistence.*' A consequence of preventing Iraq selling its oil to buy food and other essentials – a gross US violation of international law – has been a drastic impairment of the Iraqi rationing system. The pre-sanctions daily per capita calorie intake was 2306; in July 1996 this figure had been reduced to 1263 calories, a situation of semi-starvation for the average Iraqi civilian. Consumption of basic items had been massively reduced (as shown in Table 5.3, with the subsequent tables taken from the Iraqi submission to the United Nations[15]).

The inevitable corollary has been a rapid increase in deaths from

TABLE 5.4　Deaths resulting from the economic embargo

Under-5 age group		Over-5 age group	
Time period	Average monthly deaths	Time period	Average monthly deaths
1989	593	1989	1685
1990	742	1990	1963
1991	2289	1991	4872
1992	3911	1992	6377
1993	4107	1993	6522
1994	4409	1994	6731
1995	4651	1995	6913
January 1996	6165	January 1996	6664
February 1996	4210	February 1996	7179
March 1996	4234	March 1996	8089
April 1996	3266	April 1996	7491
May 1996	4127	May 1996	7955
June 1996	4434	June 1996	6460

TABLE 5.5　Infant deaths from various causes

Period	Condition					
	Diarrhoea		Pneumonia		Malnutrition	
	Deaths	Rate of increase	Deaths	Rate of increase	Deaths	Rate of increase
June 1989	156	–	108	–	123	–
June 1996	2057	1215.98%	775	617.59%	1958	1498.71%

various causes (already documented and see also Table 5.4). Where statistics have been compiled for particular causes of infant death massive increases in the mortality rate are demonstrated (see Table 5.5). The drastic escalation of baby and child death rates, as a direct consequence of the sanctions regime, are paralleled by increased mortality in other age groups (see Tables 5.6 and 5.7).

The Iraqi submission catalogues the multifaceted impact of the economic embargo on the entire civilian population. Reference is made to infant deaths, the acute shortage of food, the inevitable increase in the school drop-out rates (among both pupils and teachers), soaring delinquency rates, and the likelihood of total social collapse: *'The suffering of the Iraqi people has reached a point where it can no longer be*

TABLE 5.6   Over-50 mortality rates

| Period | Condition | | | | | |
| | Hypertension | | Diabetes | | Malignant neoplasia | |
	Deaths	Rate of increase	Deaths	Rate of increase	Deaths	Rate of increase
June 1989	128	–	70	–	236	–
June 1995	412	221.88%	274	291.43%	1133	380.1%

TABLE 5.7   Total deaths caused by the economic embargo

| Time period | Age group | | Total |
	Under-5	Over-5	
1990	5903	23 561	32 464
1991	27 473	58 469	85 942
1992	46 933	76 530	123 463
1993	49 762	78 261	128 023
1994	52 905	80 776	133 681
1995	55 823	82 961	138 784
January–June 1996	26 436	43 838	70 274
Total	268 235	444 396	712 631

ignored or overlooked because it now threatens to bring upon the society as a whole a horrendous disaster that may lead to its collapse.' In his 1995 report on the work of the United Nations, UN Secretary-General Boutros Boutros-Ghali acknowledged the desperate plight of the Iraqi people:

Health conditions have continued to deteriorate throughout the country because of shortages of essential drugs and medical supplies. The situation is further aggravated by the inadequate supply of potable water and poor sanitation facilities, as essential equipment and spare parts are lacking to rehabilitate the water, sewage and electricity supply systems . . . children are increasingly dying of ailments linked to malnutrition and lack of adequate medical care.

In the same vein, as noted, other UN agencies have acknowledged the appalling situation of the Iraqi civilian population. Thus the London-based UN Information Centre reported the '*deteriorating humanitarian*

*situation in a country [Iraq] where the majority of the population are
living below the poverty line and malnutrition is rampant with over 50
per cent of women and children receiving less than half their caloric
needs*'.[16] On 17 November 1996 an official of the UN World Food
Programme noted that the condition of some children in Iraqi hospitals in the sanctions-hit country was comparable to that of children in
Somalia. The WFP director in Iraq, Holdbrook Arthur said: 'If we are
not able to support this most vulnerable group . . . it would be a major
disaster. . . . It is pretty imminent.' The WFP food supplies in Iraq had
reportedly run out in October.[17] At the same time the heads of three
UN humanitarian agencies (UNICEF, WFP and DHA) made a joint
appeal for urgent contributions to the UN aid programme for Iraq.
They declared that the cumulative effects of war, economic sanctions,
hyperinflation, unemployment and a 30 per cent drop in crop production
in 1996 were starting to exact a terrible humanitarian toll.[18] Here the
cruel paradox was plain: while one UN element (the Security Council)
worked to crush a society and exterminate a people other UN agencies
struggled in impossible circumstances to bring humanitarian relief to
millions of suffering men, women, children and babies. And the paradox
persisted into 1997. While Washington continued to insist that the
sanctions regime would be maintained Dr Hiroshi Nakajima, Director-
General of the UN World Health Organisation (WHO) visited Iraqi
health facilities (in Najaf, Kerbala, Babil and Baghdad) and reported:
'*The consequences of this situation are causing a near breakdown of
the health care system, which is reeling under the pressure of being
deprived of medicine, other basic supplies and spare parts . . . its inability
to cope with, and provide services which the Iraqi people used to receive
is of grave concern.*' Malaria, typhoid and other diseases were now
threatening large areas of the country that had never been affected
before.[19]

The attitude of Washington in prosecuting its genocidal enterprise
has been amply demonstrated.* Aware that an American charity *Voices
in the Wilderness* was working to send medical relief and other humanitarian supplies to the Iraqi people, the US Department of the Treasury
(Washington D.C.) issued what it called a WARNING LETTER to
Kathy Kelly, organiser of the charity. The following is an extract from
the Treasury letter (2 January 1996):

* I am grateful to Felicity Arbuthnot, journalist and Iraq expert, for bringing to my
attention the courageous and humbling work of *Voices in the Wilderness: A Campaign to End the Sanctions Against Iraq*, and the response of the Department of the
Treasury, Washington, D.C.

The Regulations prohibit US persons from engaging in virtually all direct or indirect commercial, financial or trade transactions with Iraq, unless authorised by OFAC [Office of Foreign Assets Control].

This Office has learned that you and other members of Voices in the Wilderness recently announced your intention to collect medical relief supplies for the people of Iraq . . . and to personally transport the supplies to Iraq. . . .

OFAC has no record that your organization has requested a specific license to export medical supplies to Iraq and to travel to Iraq to supervise the delivery of such supplies.

Accordingly, you and members of Voices in the Wilderness are hereby warned to refrain from engaging in any unauthorised transactions related to the exportation of medical supplies and travel to Iraq. Criminal penalties for violating the Regulations range up to 12 years in prison and $1 million in fines. Civil penalties of up to $250,000 per violation may be imposed administratively by OFAC.

The letter is signed by David H. Harmon, the Acting Supervisor of the OFAC Enforcement Division. So it is that American charity workers, conveying anti-cancer medicines to dying children in Baghdad's Al-Mansour Children's Hospital, risked a 12-year incarceration and a $1 million fine on their return to the United States.

Kathy Kelly herself wrote (3 April 1997) of the heroism encountered in Iraq: 'doctors working round the clock for next to no income; hotel desk clerks who introduce us to the neediest families in their neighborhood; a widow managing somehow to care for eight children. . . . I saw a child fling a rock at a car whose passengers didn't respond to his begging plea, then the child sat down and slapped the cement in frustration. How I wish we could hold him, that little one, in his innocence and vulnerability, his defeat and frustration.' And she adds: 'the economic sanctions continue to kill quietly . . . we will try our best to break the silence . . . our motivation will be drawn from the goodness we encounter, across borders, among the many people who long to end the US/UN sanctions against Iraq'.

Chuck Quilty, who travelled to Iraq with three out of the five delegations of *Voices in the Wilderness*, recorded his impressions after the fifth visit (17–27 March 1997). He wept as he learnt more about the suffering of dying Iraqi children ('The young doctor is obviously touched . . . I show him news coverage we have received and how we are willing to risk jail to bring the truth to the American people about the suffering innocents of Iraq. . . . At the hospital I force myself to do my job, blow up balloons, pass out Tootsie Pops, and make the children laugh if only for a moment. . . . I race round to all the children, talk to the mothers. I am really trying to kill my own grief. . . . The children of Iraq will continue to die as long as these cruel sanctions remain in place.') Elsewhere Quilty urges the world community not 'to indifferently watch as thousands of innocent children die. . . . Please add your voice to those protesting this crime against humanity.'[20]

Another *Voices* peace activist, George Capaccio, wrote after the March visit to Iraq how it had been necessary to commit an act of civil disobedience – and so to risk imprisonment and fines. And he described what he had witnessed:

> . . . the mothers watching over their children day and night; the filthy uncovered mattresses; the aura of flies . . . the silent, sentry-like oxygen tanks that lacked the proper release valves and were thus useless . . .
>
> I could feel in my arms the child I had cradled in Basra . . . eight months old, Sahar was severely malnourished and wasted. Her mother watched me with tears in her eyes as I embraced her only daughter . . .
>
> . . . Shaima, a fourteen-year-old girl. . . . She looked up at me but was too weak to move, much less speak. Her mother and grandmother wept openly by her side and pleaded with me for medicine . . .
>
> . . . I brought them my clumsy greetings in Arabic, my ridiculous attempts at humor in the midst of profound suffering, my deep, undeniable need to nurture and heal, to mend what has been broken and defiled by an official policy whose dispassionate cruelty knows no bounds.
>
> One thing more I brought with me to Iraq: my own childlike nature and love of play and playfulness. Tucked among my more practical items were two hand puppets, with a mix-and-match wardrobe, and two acrylic glitter-filled wands . . .
>
> In the pediatric wards we visited, I tried, with varying degrees of success, to communicate with some of the children via my puppets. I soon realized, however, that I was no pied piper summoning forth the spirit of even the most withdrawn and afflicted child. Instead I felt more like a fool finding himself in a concentration camp barrack and behaving as though his antics might somehow transfigure the horror around him.
>
> I left one of my puppets with Haitham, a sixteen-year-old boy . . . severely depressed and dying from leukemia . . . he raised himself on his elbows and, after much effort, whispered his greetings to all

the children of the world and his hope for health and prosperity, and the end to sanctions. To twelve-year-old Ward . . . I gave the other puppet . . . she stood to have her picture taken that others might see and understand what is happening to the children of Iraq, and that her imminent death be not in vain.*

The American genocide of the Iraqi children is sustained by rhetoric and fuelled by a monstrous psychopathology. It is important to note the enabling role of *propaganda* in general and the propaganda significance of *Security Council Resolution 986* in particular.

PROPAGANDA AND 986

The unending economic onslaught on the helpless Iraqi people is facilitated by the systematic demonisation of Saddam Hussein. Because of Saddam, *anything* is legitimate; because of Saddam, Washington insists that 100,000 Iraqi children should be starved to death every year. The position has only to be stated for its indecent absurdity to be exposed. There is no crime that Saddam Hussein has committed against the Iraqi people that weighs in the balance against what the United States is today perpetrating against the helpless civilians of Iraq. And today it is not only Saddam's real or invented derelictions against his own people or the international community that justifies the American policy of slow extermination; it is what he *might* be doing, what might be *hidden, disguised, intended.* The sublime Catch-22 – if Saddam is shown to be in violation of Security Council resolutions then Washington will self-righteously continue to starve his people to death; and if *no* violation can be demonstrated then – *Saddam is not to be trusted* – Washington will continue to starve the Iraqi people to death.

The ploy is useful as a crude propaganda device to justify the endless sanctions regime. Thus the predictable allegations are publicised at regular intervals to justify the confirmation of the economic embargo every 60 days, as the UN resolutions require. Many examples of the genocidal Catch-22 can be cited. In March 1997 David Albright, a one-time member of the International Atomic Energy team that searched Iraq after the 1991 Gulf War for evidence of 'weapons of mass destruction' (a co-author of a text on nuclear materials), asserted: '*The*

* I am grateful to Kathy Kelly for encouraging me to publish these extracts.

nightmare of Iraq is that they will steal the material [plutonium, weapons-grade uranium] and we'll only know when they have the weapons'.[21] At the same time Iraq '*may be hiding* up to 16 modified Scud ballistic missiles and their chemical and biological warheads. . . . Mr Ekeus's team believes that between six and 16 missiles are *probably* being concealed . . .'.[22] Moreover, experts 'have warned that there is *still a danger* of Iraq rebuilding its biological capacity despite stringent controls. . . . All it has to do is to wait for the West to lose interest in the monitoring process'.[23] Nor should it be forgotten that the Iraqis are 'congenital liars' – unnamed source.[24] Rolf Ekeus, then the UN's chief weapons inspector, had the task of 'judging when, *if ever*, Iraq is finally free of weapons programmes. . . .'[25] And he thought that debris of missile engines '*may have been* stripped' of sophisticated Russian-built parts.[26] At the same time an (unnamed) American officer was asserting that he '*thought* Saddam could attempt to re-take Kuwait with a deft, surprise attack at night. . . .'[27] And a dump of chemical weapons '*may have been uncovered* in Iraq, according to an intelligence report . . .'.[28] Moreover, even if Saddam had *no* hidden weapons he '*could* start' building Scud missiles in a month.[29] Ekeus was happy to declare that little remained unknown about Baghdad's weapons potential – but '*what was unknown* could still cause devastating damage and casualties'.[30] (My italics throughout)

In such a fashion, *hypothesis* ('may be', 'probably', 'may have been', 'could') rather than undisputed *fact* is being used to underwrite the genocide of a people. Nonetheless, the international disquiet grew over the years, until the United States became virtually isolated in its insistence that helpless Iraqi civilians must continue to die (see *Superpower Isolation*, below). Another supplementary ploy was called for: Washington could no longer ignore with such callous cynicism the demands of humanity and reason. What the US strategists needed was a cloak for the continued genocide, a seeming amelioration that in fact had no real practical consequence. The Iraqis must be made to die at the same rate while the impression was created that American compassion now had a role. The device whereby this could be accomplished was Resolution 986, passed unanimously by the UN Security Council on 14 April 1995 (see Appendix 5)

The background to 986 has already been profiled (pp. 98–104), and subsequent events have amply justified the judgment made at that time: '*Resolution 986, like 706 and 712 before it, appeared to be no more than a cynical political ploy, a fresh public-relations diversion from on-going US efforts to tighten the embargo yet further*'. A self-serving chronology of the implementation of Resolution 986 (provided by the UN Department of Public Information for the UN Department of Humanitarian Affairs) is included here (see Figure 5.1), but it should be viewed with circumspection. The nominal purpose of 986 is to allow Iraq to sell limited quantities of oil to raise revenue for humanitarian purposes (the provision of foodstuffs and medicines). In fact four criticisms can be made of the implementation of 986 under the principal influence of the United States:

1. Resolution 986 is constantly misrepresented by Western politicians, officials, pundits and the media. It is repeatedly claimed (following 986, Clause 1) that $1 billion can be raised by the sale of petroleum and petroleum products every 90 days for the purchase of humanitarian supplies. In fact there are many calls on the realised revenues; not least the servicing of the Compensation Fund, the costs of the UN inspection agents, the costs of the Special Commission, and any other 'reasonable expenses' (see 986, Clause 8). This means that at best only a part of the realised revenues will be used for humanitarian purposes.

2. It is claimed that 986 is making and will make a significant contribution to the relief of suffering in Iraq. In fact even on official figures the revenues will yield no more than two-thirds of the $2 billion total every six months; that is, about $1.3 billion for the Iraqi population of around 20 million. This amounts to about $2 worth of humanitarian supplies in total for each Iraqi citizen per week, and this in a land where the entire health and food production/distribution systems are in a state of terminal collapse.

3. The propaganda claims that the contribution of 986 is/will be significant, however specious, rest on the assumption that implementation is carried out effectively in good faith. There is now abundant evidence that the United States has deliberately frustrated even the pathetically inadequate contribution that 986 has the potential to make.

4. There is also evidence that the existence of 986, with all the attendant propaganda, has discouraged existing aid agencies from continuing to work in Iraq – so to some extent and in some areas 986 has made many suffering Iraqis worse off than they were before.

230 *The Scourging of Iraq*

FIGURE 5.1   Chronology of implementation of Resolution 986

14 April 1995	Resolution 986 is unanimously adopted by the Security Council.
20 January 1996	Iraq and the UN commence discussion concerning the implementation of Resolution 986 (1995).
20 May 1996	Memorandum of Understanding is signed between the Government of Iraq and the United Nations Secretariat.
June 1996	A technical reconnaissance mission, comprising senior members of the UN Secretariat, and petroleum and customs experts, is dispatched to Iraq.
18 July 1996	The UN Secretary-General accepts the Distribution Plan submitted by the Government of Iraq for the purchase and distribution of humanitarian supplies.
9 August 1996	Four independent overseers are appointed by the Secretary-General to assist UN Headquarters with expertise in international oil trade.
20 August 1996	Gualtiero Fulcheri is appointed as the United Nations Humanitarian Coordinator in Iraq to succeed Mohammed Zejjari.
1 September 1996	The UN Secretary-General decides to delay the implementation of Resolution 986 (1995) due to security reasons in the northern Governorates.
22 October 1996	A technical team from Saybolt Nederland BV arrives in Iraq to test the reliability of the metering equipment near Zakho and Mina al-Bakr.
25 November 1996	The interim report of the Secretary-General on the implementation of Security Council Resolution 986 (1995) is released (S/1996/978).
27 November 1996	The Security Council Committee established by Resolution 661 (1990) concerning the situation between Iraq and Kuwait approves a pricing mechanism for the sale of Iraqi oil.
9 December 1996	A Mission is sent to Iraq by the Department of Humanitarian Affairs to assess the require-

ments of the UN Inter-Agency Programme, including logistical and support arrangements.

Report of the Secretary-General on the implementation of Security Council Resolution 986 (1995) (S/1996/1015).

15 December 1996	Loading of oil starts at Mina al-Bakr.
15 January 1997	The first proceeds from the sale of oil are deposited in the United Nations Iraq Account (Escrow Account), in the Banque Nationale de Paris.
23 January 1997	The first application for export of humanitarian supplies is approved by the Secretariat of the 661 Committee.
14 February 1997	The first letters of credit for the supply of humanitarian goods are issued.
28 February 1997	Staffan de Mistura is appointed as United Nations Humanitarian Coordinator in Iraq to succeed Gualtiero Fulcheri.
3 March 1997	Following are a number of important activities that had been completed by this date:

• The total sales allowed during the first 90 days, through the issuance of the final contract for 52.3 million barrels of oil, amounted to US\$ 1.07 billion.

• The four oil overseers reviewed a total of 38 contracts, 35 of which are approved.

• Two hundred twenty-two applications for the export of humanitarian supplies to Iraq are received by the Secretariat of the 661 Committee. Out of 37 applications submitted to the 661 Committee, 9 are approved.

• The 32 independent Inspection Agents (Lloyds Register) had been deployed, ready to confirm the arrival of authorised goods at the agreed entry points: 10 inspectors at Umm Qasr, 11 at Zakho on the Turkish border and 11 at Trebil on the Jordanian border.

• The United Nations Treasury had processed letters of credit for approximately US\$ 1 billion worth of petroleum and petroleum products. A total of US\$ 625,596,347.69 is paid into the Iraq Account.

FIGURE 5.1 *continued*

5 March 1997	UN Secretary-General Kofi Annan met the Foreign Minister of Iraq, Mohammed Said Al-Sahaf, who reaffirmed his Government's commitment to cooperate with the United Nations in implementing all provisions of Resolution 986 (1995) and the Memorandum of Understanding.
10 March 1997	Two hundred ninety applications are received by the Secretariat of the 661 Committee. Out of 37 applications submitted to the 661 Committee, 15 are approved. A total of US$ 633,621,080 is deposited in the Iraq Account.
	The 90-day report of the Secretary-General on the implementation of Security Council Resolution 986 (1995) is released (S/1997/206).
11 March 1997	The report of the Security Council Committee established by Resolution 661 (1990) is released (S/1997/213).
13 March 1997	The 90-day report is presented to Security Council members by Yasushi Akashi, Under-Secretary-General for Humanitarian Affairs.
17 March 1997	Three hundred twenty-four applications are received by the Secretariat of the 661 Committee. Out of 56 applications submitted to the 661 Committee, 34 are approved. A total of US$ 718,748,249 is paid in the Iraq Account.
20 March 1997	The first food supplies under Security Council Resolution 986 arrive in Iraq, a total of 125.2 tons of chickpeas and vegetable ghee through the Habur border crossing.
24 March 1997	Three hundred fifty-nine applications are received by the Secretariat of the 661 Committee. Out of 82 applications submitted to the 661 Committee, 57 are approved. A total of US$ 786,639,442 is deposited in the Iraq Account.
26 March 1997	The first substantial food supplies, 13,000 tons of Thai rice, arrive in Iraq through the Port of Umm Qasr.
31 March 1997	Three hundred ninety-one applications are received by the Secretariat of the 661 Committee. Out of 96 applications submitted to the 661 Committee, 62 are approved. A total of US$ 824,430,844 is deposited in the Iraq Account.

	66,402 tonnes of Australian and French wheat arrive in Iraq through the Port of Umm Qasr.
2 April 1997	Distribution of wheat flour begins.
3 April 1997	781.3 tonnes of toilet soap and detergent powder arrive in Iraq through the Trebil border crossing.
7 April 1997	Four hundred fourteen applications are received by the Secretariat of the 661 Committee; of 107 applications submitted to the 661 Committee, 77 are approved. A total of US$ 976,255,114 is deposited in the Iraq Account.

Source: UN Department of Information for UN DHA, April 1997.

Resolution 986 (passed unanimously on 14 April 1995) was influenced in no particular by Iraq. It was Iraq that was supposed to be the beneficiary but since Iraq was not a member of the Security Council it was allowed no comment. Drafted by American or US-proxy officials, 986 was aimed in part at feeding Iraqi oil money to Kuwait through the Compensation Fund to facilitate the payment of American contractors (not least the arms suppliers). Humanitarian pressure for the relief of Iraqi suffering was nicely exploited for the benefit of US companies.

The question then was whether Iraq could be induced to agree the terms of 986. Could it be expected to agree a measure that might indefinitely prolong the just lifting of sanctions *in toto*? Could it be expected to sacrifice a part of its principal asset for administration by a superpower dedicated to the overthrow of the Iraqi regime? Could it be expected to sacrifice its inherent sovereignty (as protected in Article 2(1) of the UN Charter) over important elements of its own industrial and social policy: in short to accept trusteeship status? Could Iraq be confident that 986 would be implemented in good faith? In conditions of mounting desperation Iraq eventually agreed to negotiate the implementation of 986.[31]

In January 1996 John English of the British Red Cross commented on returning from Iraq: 'The level of malnutrition is on a par with famine-ravaged countries like Sudan.' UN officials were estimating that four million of the Iraqi population (total population 20 million) faced starvation. It was inevitable, in these circumstances, that the Iraqi regime would be forced to clutch at any straw. Washington was quick to denounce Saddam's 'about-face' and the media repeated the falsehood that Iraq would now be able to spend $2 billion every six months to relieve the suffering of its people (see Point 1, above).

Even at this late stage the talks were protracted. Saddam was accused of making a propaganda effort and the international oil markets were nervous at the prospect of new Iraqi oil sales, however limited.[32] In April 1996 agreement on 986 was prevented when US and British negotiators 'insisted on 20 new conditions before the deal could be ratified' – a deliberately obstructive move that frustrated the other members of the Security Council (among them Italy, Germany, Russia and Egypt): 'The other member countries were very angry. The only people who are told what is going on are the Americans and the British. We have asked them for a copy of the draft agreement and a copy of the 20 conditions they have set, but we have not been given anything' (member of Sanctions Committee).[33] Such matters delayed the negotiations but eventually a nominal agreement was reached. On 20 May 1996 the UN Secretary-General submitted a Memorandum of Understanding (MOU) between the UN Secretariat and the Iraq government on the implementation of Resolution 986. Among the MOU 'General provisions' was the risible declaration (Paragraph 3) that 'Nothing in the present memorandum should be construed as infringing upon the sovereignty or territorial integrity of Iraq.' Later in the document were detailed the precise and many ways in which Iraqi sovereignty would be infringed for the effective implementation of 986.[34] Already there were signs that Iraqi oil would not be sold in the immediate future, and that therefore any minuscule amounts of humanitarian aid would be correspondingly delayed. A UN Legal Counsel briefing for *the information of the UN Secretariat ONLY* emphasised that it would be wrong 'to indicate any time-frame before oil would begin to flow. . . . Because of the nature of the oil market mechanism, he did not want to speculate on a specific timetable.'[35]

The United States and Britain were quick to point out that the agreement on the implementation of 986 said nothing about an early end to sanctions. The economic embargo would remain, with the British foreign secretary Malcolm Rifkind going so far as to declare that it would be hard to imagine sanctions being lifted while Saddam Hussein remained in power[36] – a comment with no support in any UN resolution. On 22 May 1996 the UN Legal Counsel briefed the Iraq Sanctions Committee on the various steps that would have to be taken: the adoption of procedures, the adoption of a bank by the Secretary-General to carry the required escrow account, and the submission of an aid distribution plan by Iraq for the Secretary-General's approval. Other matters included the appointment of oil experts for monitoring oil sales, the appointment of independent inspectors, and the creation of an observation mechanism for the distribution of aid. As it became clear that some limited amount of Iraqi oil would dribble onto the world market, oil prices dropped by $1 a barrel and oil shares were marked down.[37]

Now Washington was acting to delay the implementation of 986. For some time the United States scrutinised the Iraqi distribution plans and then declared them unacceptable. This meant that the plan might be delayed 'by several weeks or months'. In July the US spokesman at the United Nations, James Rubin, accused Iraq of trying 'to turn this humanitarian exception into a partial lifting of sanctions'; and the British government chose this time – when Iraq was denied all access to funds – to persuade 12 lenders (Midland, Barclays, National Westminster and nine others) to issue 25 writs claiming more than £400 million from Iraq. A spokesman from the government's Export Credit Guarantees Department (ECGD) commented: 'We are putting down a marker that legal action has started to recover the money and the banks have issued the writs on our behalf.'[38]

It was now clear that Washington was insisting on conditions for the implementation of 986 that went far beyond what most other Security Council members were prepared to accept. In August 1996 Washington was demanding many more monitors to oversee the oil exports and food imports than had been originally envisaged. Iraq was now being forced to accept a 'highly intrusive UN presence' with monitors 'allowed to roam anywhere in the country . . .'.[39] (So much for Paragraph 3 of the Memorandum of Understanding stating that Iraqi sovereignty would not be infringed.) Even now, following Iraq's acceptance of the inflated US/UK demands, there were still impediments to the implementation of 986 – to the dismay of the aid agencies and many other observers.

In September, after Iraqi forces moved into Erbil during the turmoil in the Kurdish region (see *Superpower Isolation*, below), the United States demanded reconsideration of the 986 plan, so delaying the entire implementation. Now the British Red Cross was warning of the 'catastrophic conditions' in Iraq as the United Nations was forced to wrangle over fresh American objections. John English (British Red Cross) commented: 'The suspension of the oil for food deal is only going to make things much worse.' With Iraqi civilians continuing to die at the rate of thousands a month there would be no relief to their suffering, even at the margins of the national catastrophe. Said Abdullah

Mutawi, of the New York Centre for Economic and Social Rights (which had carried out two health/nutrition surveys in Iraq) stated: 'Iraqi civilians will continue to die in the same numbers.'[40] By October the United Nations declared itself ready to approve the implementation plan 'in a matter of weeks': the United States, while exploiting Resolution 986 to maximum propaganda advantage, had managed to delay the implementation of its relatively trivial provisions for many months. On 24 October, France's President Jacques Chirac, speaking to the Jordanian parliament, urged the United Nations to allow Iraq to sell its oil to buy food and medicine: 'France is alarmed at the humanitarian situation in Iraq, and calls solemnly on the international community to apply at long last Resolution 986.'

Throughout this period Iraq, while now welcoming the crumbs nominally offered by 986, continued to emphasise that this was a totally inadequate approach to the suffering of the Iraqi people. Thus Nizar Hamdoon, the Iraqi Ambassador to the United Nations, quoted the UN Secretary-General (before specifically addressing 986):

> Sanctions, as is generally recognised, are a blunt instrument. They raise the ethical question of whether suffering inflicted on vulnerable groups in the target country is a legitimate means of exerting pressure on political leaders whose behaviour is unlikely to be affected by the plight of their subjects.[41]

He then commented that the implementation of 986 '*does not in reality meet the minimum needs of the population*'; and that moreover the agreement was reached '*six months after negotiations on the matter began, the same period of time as that established for the agreement to remain in effect*' – a delay caused by the '*constant interference*' of the United States and its policy '*of procrastination and deliberate and unwarranted delay motivated by political intentions and plans to inflict more harm on the life of the Iraqi people*'.[42] It is difficult to avoid Hamdoon's charge that the United States 'is intentionally endeavouring to annihilate the Iraqi people'.[43] (See 1990s Genocide, below.)

With the procrastination and delay seemingly at an end, the oil began to flow. Washington, having milked 986 for propaganda advantage, now seemed reluctant to allow it any humanitarian affect, though forced to respond to international complaints about the cruelty of economic sanctions: 'By so grudgingly acquiescing in it [implementation of 986], the US in effect concedes what others have long proclaimed: prolonged sanctions do not punish President Saddam, only his people. . . . The

US has floundered about without any discernible plan for the future of Iraq. As long as that is so, sanctions will come under the increasing assault of moral imperatives . . .'[44] On 10 December 1996 limited quantities of Iraqi oil began to flow, for the first time since Saddam's invasion of Kuwait in August 1990. But now there were fresh doubts about how efficiently any newly purchased foodstuffs and medical supplies would be distributed. The United States was now withdrawing aid-linked personnel from the region, with inevitable consequences for the distribution of purchased humanitarian supplies. In September 2130 aid workers had been evacuated, with a further 4500 aid personnel withdrawn from the Kurdish areas in December. The Clinton administration was now declaring that in future aid would have to be distributed by the UN agencies. Bronwen Lewis, of Save the Children Fund, commented: 'I don't know how, without reliable NGO [non-governmental organisation] partners, the aid will be distributed. We've been trying to get an answer from the United Nations on just how they expect to implement the oil-for-food deal without large numbers of NGOs on the ground.' And even with adequate distribution facilities in place the new arrangements were set to offer little to the suffering Iraqi people. Set against the scale of the civilian deprivation only minuscule amounts of aid would be distributed and there was no provision for rebuilding the economy. A diplomat in the Gulf declared: *'There is still a long way to go before the Iraqi people really have anything to celebrate.'*

In early 1997 the United Nations began receiving funds from the Iraqi oil sales. Now it was predicted that Iraq would experience significant economic growth from its massive level of depression. According to the Economist Intelligence Unit (*World Outlook 1997*, London) there would be rapid GDP growth but no sustained rehabilitation of the national economy: 'For as long as overall sanctions remain in force, the dinar will continue to depreciate against the dollar and the price of foods and other essentials outside the rationing system will continue to rise.' As expected, observers were estimating that it would still be weeks or longer before the Iraqi civilian population saw any benefits from the 986 implementation. By March 1997, while Iraq had agreed 222 contracts for the provision of humanitarian supplies, only nine had been approved by the United Nations. Thus, in one judgment, with Security Council members still able to veto any purchase, the supply of food and medicine to Iraq – even under the terms of 986 – remained subject to a harsh sanctions regime.[45] On 10 March 1997 the UN Secretary-General, under his obligation of Paragraph 11 of Resolution 986, reported to the Security Council on the progress of the implementation plan. This report, made 90 days after the nominal commencement of the implementation, demonstrates what little emphasis had been given to the provision of humanitarian aid to the Iraqi population.[46]

It is important to note the Secretary-General's Observations under Section VII of the Report. He notes that the 'full ramifications' of the arrangements, 'specifically *the time lag* between the initial flow of oil and the actual delivery of foodstuffs, are *only now* becoming clear'. In consequence there had been 'a direct impact on the implementation of the Inter-Agency Humanitarian Programme' (Paragraph 23). In particular, '*I have had strong concerns about the pace at which the provisions of resolution 986 (1995) are being implemented*'; it was important '*to look for innovative and flexible approaches to overcome the constraints that the Programme has encountered*' (Paragraph 24).

Nor had adequate resources been allocated to the 986 implementation: 'The amount actually available for operational and administrative expenses has been *very limited*. . . . Several agencies have used their own funds to meet these costs' (Paragraph 25). *No* humanitarian goods had so far been delivered and '*it appears unlikely that all the humanitarian goods in the distribution plan will be delivered and distributed* within the initial 180 days established by the resolution'. The UN agencies in the three northern governorates had also 'raised *concerns* about the *constraints* caused by the limited time-frame of the resolution for the proper implementation of their activities'. The Security Council '*may wish to consider the implications*' (Paragraph 27). (My italics throughout)

In short, a US-dominated Security Council able to accomplish with great success millions of Iraqi casualties in the 1991 Gulf War and millions more by a years-long economic siege was seemingly incapable of organising the speedy and efficient provision of humanitarian supplies to a starving population. *Washington, highly motivated in the management of genocide, had no interest in aiding the starving and diseased Iraqi people.*

By the end of March 1997, two years after the passing of Resolution 986 in the Security Council, some humanitarian supplies had begun arriving in Iraq (see Figure 5.1): chickpeas and vegetable ghee, Thai rice, Australian and French wheat, iodized salt from Jordan. But Iraq continued to proclaim the inadequacy of 986, even if all its terms were to be scrupulously observed. In a further communication addressed to the Secretary General, Iraqi Minister for Foreign Affairs Mohammed Said Al-Sahaf cited the concern of the UN Subcommission on Prevention of Discrimination and Protection of Minorities (session 48, decision 1996/107, adopted without a vote) at the 'reliable information according to which children will continue to die after the agreement [between Iraq and the UN on 986 implementation], since it does not correspond to the minimum needs, in particular for food and medicines, of the civilian population'.[47] Resolution 986, declared Said Al-Sahaf, 'is a temporary and feeble measure, and it should not be characterised as otherwise'. But even the paltry provisions agreed in 986 could be relied upon.

In April the United States was again blocking the shipment of humanitarian supplies to Iraq – this time to signal disapproval of Iraqi helicopter flights over the US-imposed 'no-fly zone' in southern Iraq to ferry pilgrims to Mecca in Saudi Arabia. On 24 April seven humanitarian contracts were blocked by the Sanctions Committee: including rice from Vietnam, beans from Sudan, and plastic bags, cooking oil, detergent, sugar and soap from Jordan. Of 217 contracts received by the Committee, 95 were on hold, pending or blocked.[48] Kofi Annan, the UN Secretary-General, agreed that the matter needed to be addressed. In a further letter (25 April 1997) addressed to the Secretary-General, Mohammed Said Al-Sahaf declared that the United States had blocked 21 contracts for the supply of medical equipment on a priority list submitted by the World Health Organisation. This unilateral US action (21 April) was followed (22–23 April 1997) by US blocks on 19 further contracts from the WHO priority list. Thus over a period of three days Washington had blocked 40 contracts for essential medical supplies required for humanitarian purposes:

- Two contracts for medical supplies from Italy;
- Two contracts for medical equipment from France;
- Twenty-four contracts for medical equipment from Jordan;
- Twelve contracts for medical supplies from the United Kingdom.

In addition, the United States had blocked seven contracts for the purchase of foodstuffs and other supplies: one contract for rice from Vietnam, and six contracts for sugar, cooking oil, cleaning materials and soap from Jordan.[49] Said Al-Sahaf pointed out that despite earlier top-level meetings with UN staff with a view to improving the procedures none of the practical suggestions had been acted upon: 'On the contrary, recently the United States of America has increased the number of the holds and blocks it has put on contracts, including those on the [medical] priority list itself.'[50]

Resolution 986, already plainly inadequate, was being deliberately frustrated by the United States. Washington had been shamed by an increasingly disgusted world community into making some gesture of humanitarian concern towards the starving and diseased Iraqi population. But having grudgingly acceded to 986, Washington worked hard both to exploit it as a propaganda public-relations tool and to thwart its letter and spirit. The dying Iraqi people would be allowed no relief: the genocide would continue.

1990s GENOCIDE

The precept that it is wrong to kill large numbers of innocent people – including babies, children, the sick and the old – by the deliberate infliction of disease and starvation has a certain ethical weight. Yet we cannot assume that everyone is sensitive to it: powerful political leaders, buttressed by pliant and largely ignorant and uncomprehending populations, have frequently demonstrated their capacity to act without moral constraint. Before indicating the character and status of the United States genocide against the helpless Iraqi people, we should note the full body of existing law and ethical prescription that leaves current US policy exposed as both formally criminal and morally derelict.

Attention has already been drawn (see Appendix 9) to the Protocol 1 Addition to the Geneva Conventions, 1977. It is useful to emphasise some key elements in the first two paragraphs of Article 54:

1. Starvation of civilians as a method of warfare is prohibited.

2. It is prohibited to attack, destroy, remove or render useless objects indispensable to the survival of the civilian population, such as foodstuffs, agricultural areas . . . crops, livestock, drinking water installations and supplies and irrigation works, for the specific purpose of denying them their sustenance value to the civilian population . . .

Such prescriptions, framed to limit the effects of war on innocent civilians, may be judged to be particularly relevant to genocidal action targeting civilians in peace time. Yet Washington is today blocking Iraqi access to food (even delaying or blocking the small quantities allowed under 986), to pesticides and animal vaccines (for crop and livestock management), to water purification chemicals, to spare parts for the repair of irrigation works and so on. Washington's violation of the Geneva Conventions is a compound dereliction.

FIGURE 5.2   UN declarations prohibiting food embargoes

'Everyone has the right to a standard of living adequate for the health and well being of himself and his family, including food, clothing, housing and medical care and necessary social services, and the right to security in the event of unemployment, sickness, disability, widowhood, old age, or other lack of livelihood in circumstances beyond his control.' **Universal Declaration of Human Rights,** *1948*

'The enjoyment of the highest standard of health is one of the fundamental rights of every human being without distinction of race, religion, political belief, economic, or social condition.' **Constitution of World Health Organisation, 1946**

'Calls upon the developed countries to refrain from exercising political coercion through the application of economic instruments with the purpose of inducing changes in the economic or social systems, as well as in the domestic or foreign policies, of other countries;
   Reaffirms that developed countries should refrain from threatening or applying trade and financial restrictions, blockades, embargoes, and other economic sanctions, incompatible with the provisions of the Charter of the United Nations . . .' **UN General Assembly Resolution 44/215 (22 December 1989). Economic measures as a means of political and economic coercion against developing countries.**

'We recognise that access to nutritionally adequate and safe food is a right of each individual. We affirm . . . that food must not be used as a tool for political pressure.' **International Conference on Nutrition, World Declaration on Nutrition, United Nations FAO/WHO 1992**

'Food should not be used as an instrument for political and economic pressure. We reaffirm . . . the necessity of refraining from unilateral measures, not in accordance with the international law and the Charter of the United Nations and that endanger food security.' **Rome Declaration on World Food Security adopted by the World Food Summit, 13 November 1996**

It is useful to record also that many UN-linked organisations are sensitive to how *denial of food* can be used illicitly by powerful states to punish civilian populations and to coerce national governments. We should note various sample prescriptions from UN-linked sources (see Figure 5.2).

The framing of the UN genocide decision, Resolution 96(I), by the General Assembly on 11 December 1946; the subsequent General Assembly Resolution 260A (III) (9 December 1948); and the resulting

Convention on the Prevention and Punishment of the Crime of Genocide – all have been cited (see pp. 205–6 and Appendix 11). It is useful to quote Article II of the Genocide Convention (12 January 1951):

> In the present Convention, genocide means any of the following acts committed with intent to destroy, in whole or in part, a national, ethnical, racial or religious group, as such:
> (a) Killing members of the group;
> (b) Causing serious bodily or mental harm to members of the group;
> (c) Deliberately inflicting on the group conditions of life calculated to bring about its physical destruction in whole or in part;
> (d) Imposing measures intended to prevent births within the group;
> (e) Forcibly transferring children of the group to another group.

Consider this clear definition of genocide in relation to the known effects of the US policy of extermination in Iraq, as documented in Chapter 3 and *Slow Extermination*, above. Consider the scale of sanctions-induced deaths throughout the Iraqi civilian population; the soaring levels of trauma, depressive illness and hypertension casualties; the 600,000 pregnant/nursing women and destitute widows starving to death (United Nations WFP, 26 September 1995); the soaring levels of miscarriages, low birth-weights and infant deaths. Was ever an ongoing genocide so unambiguously acknowledged by the world community, and so cynically and dispassionately tolerated?

Consider also important affirmations that the United States itself has made:

- It *Condemns* [via its signing of Security Council Resolution 787 of 16 November 1992 on Bosnia and Herzegovina] *all violations of international humanitarian law, including . . . the deliberate impeding of the delivery of food and medical supplies to the civilian population . . .'* (Paragraph 7);

- It defines 'international terrorism' as '*acts dangerous to human life . . . that appear intended to coerce a civilian population or to influence the policy of a government by intimidation or coercion'* (Title 18, 2331, US Legal Code).

Hence Washington stands condemned – not only by the copious evidence of a years-long, US-orchestrated genocide but also by legal documents to which the United States offers unqualified support. When US policy on Iraq is set against UN Resolution 787 (16 November 1992) and the definition of international terrorism in the US Legal Code, the United States is demonstrably guilty of international criminal behaviour. In response to such considerations, Ramsey Clark, a former US Attorney General has issued a *'Criminal Complaint Against the United States of America ... for Causing the Deaths of More Than 1,500,000 People Including 750,000 Children Under Five ... By Genocidal Sanctions'* (see Appendix 10). The US genocide in Iraq faces a clear – if impotent – challenge in law.[51]

SUPERPOWER ISOLATION

The United States has repeatedly implied that the economic embargo on Iraq the 986 trivia apart will be maintained *in perpetuity*: the Washington strategists are conscious that such a stranglehold, on one of the most energy-rich regions of the world, may be too useful to relinquish. Thus in March 1997 Secretary of State Madeleine Albright evoked the 'future threat' hypothesis (see *Propaganda and 986*, above) to justify the continuing hard line on sanctions. Speaking at a symposium on Iraq at Georgetown University, she declared: 'We do not agree with those nations who argue that if Iraq complies with its obligations concerning weapons of mass destruction, sanctions should be lifted ...'.[52] Dialogue might be possible with a successor regime, but even then there would be no predictable end to the economic embargo.

In this context Iraq's neighbours felt free to perpetrate the very crime for which Iraq itself was being so mercilessly punished – namely, the illegal invasion of sovereign territory. Thus there were frequent military invasions of Iraq by Iran and Turkey, but Washington declined to respond to such clear violations of the UN Charter and international law. Thus in July 1996 some 2000 Iranian troops invaded Iraq at various points and converged on the historic town of Koisinjak, 50 miles inside Iraqi territory. Now, according to one pro-Western Iraqi politician, the 'idiotic result of US policies toward Saddam' was that the mullahs could 'do as they please'.[53] In the same vein more than 50,000 Turkish troops invaded northern Iraq on 14 May 1997 – yet one more of many Turkish aggressions since the end of the 1991 Gulf War – with the aim of rooting out Kurdish separatists. Iraqi Kurds, noting the 'huge' scale of the invasion, claimed that the military aggresion had been approved by Washington.[54] American tolerance of such illegal incursions should be set against its response of Iraqi attempts to move military forces *within its own internationally-recognised sovereign territory.*

On 3 September 1996, following alleged Iraqi involvement in the on-going conflict between the Patriotic Union of Kurdistan (PUK) and the Kurdistan Democratic Party (KDP) in northern Iraq, the United States launched missile strikes against various targets south of Baghdad. Some 27 cruise missiles – costing $1.2 million each – were fired from B-52 bombers and warships in the Gulf to accomplish what President Clinton called 'limited but clear' objectives: 'To make Saddam pay a price for the latest act of brutality, reducing his ability to threaten his neighbors and America's interests.' At the same time Washington unilaterally extended the 'no-fly' zone in southern Iraq – *and declared that the UN plan under the terms of 986 to allow Iraq to sell oil to buy food could not proceed.* A fresh means had been found to block the paltry food shipments to the millions of starving Iraqi civilians. British premier John Major, predictably supine, declared his full support for the American action and judged that others would offer support.

In fact the initial US action, clear aggression with no legal justification, was condemned throughout the world – which did not prevent the launch of a further 17 cruise missiles from warships and a submarine in the Gulf the following day. Russia declared that the American missile attacks were designed to boost Clinton's chances in the November presidential elections; and the strikes were criticised also by Iran, Syria, Egypt, Jordan and Turkey. An Egyptian foreign ministry spokesman went so far as to comment: 'Egypt underlines the importance of principles and goals of the UN Charter, which guarantees Iraq's sovereignty, integrity and non-interference in its internal affairs.'[55] The 22-country Arab League issued a statement noting that the American action had no international legitimacy. Britain, Israel and Kuwait maintained their support for Washington; and events had a predictable impact on the oil market. The blocking of 986 implementation meant that now between 650,000 and 750,000 barrels would be kept off the world's oil markets. Oil prices climbed, shares rose, and Irene Himona, an oil analyst with Societe Generale Strauss Turnbull, expressed the general industry view: *'It's all very helpful for oil prices, and with winter coming and low stocks, the price strength will remain.'*[56] The Kurdish turmoil in northern Iraq had drastically impeded the 986 implementation in that region, with the US missile strikes effectively blocking the implementation elsewhere. The United States had succeeded in wrecking the Gulf alliance[57] – but military hardware had been usefully field-tested, Clinton had gained a pre-election boost, 986 had been sabotaged, and the Iraqi people would continue to starve.

The UN Secretary-General had now put 986 implementation on hold because of concerns for the security of UN officials working in northern Iraq. At the same time Washington was indicating that the Memorandum of Understanding, tortuously negotiated over months, might have to be renegotiated in the light of the new developments inside Iraq. The United States would have no difficulty in maintaining the economic embargo, due for formal extension, and it was now obvious that any 986 amelioration would be blocked. In the Security Council Sergei Lavrov, the Russian ambassador, denounced the United States for its 'disproportionate' response to Saddam's incursion into northern Iraq, and made it clear that Russia would veto a US-proxy (British) resolution condemning Baghdad and supporting the US missile attacks: 'We believe that the response to these events by the United States was disproportionate and we don't think that it is acceptable.' Lavrov declared also that the Secretary-General *'should continue to implement Resolution 986'*.[58] Now Russia, France and China – three of the five Permanent Members of the Security Council – were expressing disapproval of the American aggression. On 4 September 1996 a commentary on state-run Tehran radio evinced Iranian anxieties about the US military initiative: 'By continuing its attacks against Iraq, America is pursuing objectives far beyond stopping the Iraqi military operations in the city of Erbil ... Clinton not only takes personal advantage of developments in Iraq, he also paves the way for the advancement of the long-term strategy for maintaining a permanent presence in the Persian Gulf region.'

The Russian Federation had blocked the anti-Iraq resolution in the Security Council; France was refusing to patrol the extended US-defined 'no-fly' zone in southern Iraq; and the 1991 coalition of anti-Saddam states had been finally ruptured. The Russian foreign minister Yevgeny Primakov denounced the American action as 'very dangerous' and one that could lead to 'anarchy' on the world scene; and even Syria, obsessively anti-Saddam, claimed that the US strikes had violated the laws against 'interference in the internal affairs of other countries'. Washington was now able to rely on the unequivocal support of only Britain among the major powers, with even some British officials expressing disquiet about US threats of 'disproportionate' strikes against Baghdad. (Nor was the American case helped by a missile fired from a US Air Force F-16 in error.[59])

The American political posture was now visibly crumbling. In late

November 1996 Washington offered to evacuate thousands of US-sponsored personnel, many of them CIA-backed, from northern Iraq; on 20 December the Iraqi News Agency reported that an unspecified number of members of a sabotage and espionage ring working for the CIA had been arrested. A week later, France announced that having refused to police the US's unilaterally expanded southern 'no-fly' zone, it would soon be withdrawing its aircraft from operations over the northern 'no-fly' zone – further proof, were it needed, that France was seeking to distance itself from US policy. The British Foreign Office 'noted the French position', with the Clinton administration reportedly annoyed at France's decision to pull out.[60] Such developments, and internal tensions, were also eroding the Iraqi National Congress, the main umbrella organisation of anti-Saddam political parties. In March 1997 the London-based INC was reportedly near to collapse, wracked by leadership disputes, conflict between the two main Kurdish parties, and disagreements over strategy.[61] And at the same time, witnessed by a bemused UN High Commissioner for Refugees (UNHCR), Kurdish refugees from Turkish oppression were seeking sanctuary with Saddam Hussein. Said one refugee, Ahmet Vurgun: *'We are not saying Saddam is totally respectful of human rights, but he is the one who is supporting us. Saddam is better than the UN and he is much better than Turkey.'*[62] Even Kuwait now appeared willing to soften its hard-line anti-Saddam line, declaring that the emirate would not oppose Saddam's presence at an Arab summit called in April 1997 to discuss the stalled Middle East peace process.

Such obvious signs of fragmentation in the anti-Saddam coalition were inducing the Iraqi regime to respond with growing confidence. The hope was growing that Resolution 986 – despite its inadequate provision and the frequent implementation delays contrived by Washington – might represent a useful breach in the sanctions wall. Now Baghdad felt bold enough to mount a symbolic challenge to the embargo. On 9 April an Iraqi aeroplane carrying 104 Haj pilgrims crossed the Iraqi frontier to be given safe escort by two Saudi Arabian fighters. Despite the Saudi obligation to receive pilgrims bound for Mecca and Medina, Washington UN envoy Bill Richardson denounced the 'outright violation of sanctions' and urged the Security Council to condemn the flight.

It now seemed plain that, despite US political pressure, there was mounting international opposition to the indefinite prolongation of the sanctions regime. In December 1996 Jordan had agreed to supply Baghdad with $35 million worth of goods (including vegetable oil, detergents, soap and fertiliser), in addition to the negotiation of an earlier $200 million trade protocol. Throughout 1997 the pressure mounted for an end to the genocidal sanctions regime. In March – following an earlier (16 March 1995) condemnation of sanctions – the Pope moved to recognise Libya, despite intense private lobbying by Washington, and so signalled the clear Vatican disapproval of American sanctions policy. On 5 May the Chinese foreign minister, Qian Qichen, declared in Beijing that China wanted to see an end to the sanctions against Iraq as soon as possible. At the same time, speaking to Iraqi deputy prime minister Tariq Aziz, President Jiang Zemin expressed his sympathy for the Iraqi people in their suffering under sanctions. Throughout 1997 the international view became increasingly plain. The vast majority of UN members – including three Permanent Members of the Security Council – were now implacably opposed to the continued starvation of the Iraqi people. The motives were often mixed: commercial interest, as well as humanitarian concern, clearly played a part. But one fact was obvious. In continuing to perpetrate its 1990s genocide against the Iraqi people the United States was forced to acknowledge ever diminishing support from the international community.

EPILOGUE

The United States has succeeded in converting Iraq into a land of the dead and the dying. Here is the mediaeval city under siege, a house of horrors, a vast and swelling grave. An entire generation of children is being exterminated: as I write in July 1997, after seven years of the cruelest economic embargo, tens of thousands of infants, blind for want of insulin, black-hollowed eyes, stick limbs, damaged brains, in coma or feverish agony – emaciated all – wait for their early death. (I know Western observers who have been plunged into depression and nervous breakdown at what they have witnessed of the US torture of Iraqi children.) Many of the children die far from the urban hospitals. How can hungry parents convey their dying babies to medical centres far away? And what point is there – with the hospitals denuded of drugs and disinfectants, of bandages and sheets even, where dying infants lie on plastic or blood-stained mattresses and have their wounds wrapped in dirty cardboard?

It should not be thought that the American policy on Iraq is an isolated and mysterious aberration, an inexplicable departure from the norms of decency and justice. The genocidal US approach to the Iraq

Question is manifestly typical of a wider American strategy. It has nothing to do with expelling Saddam from Kuwait: that was accomplished long ago. It has nothing to do with Saddam's abuse of human rights: Washington has no interest in human rights beyond the cynical calculation of strategic advantage. It has nothing to do with locating 'weapons of mass destruction': even Rolf Ekeus has admitted that there is little left in that category to uncover. The US aims are simple and transparent – to maintain a military and commercial grip on an oil-rich region; to develop a multifaceted strategy that will continue to deter any effective challenge to American hegemony, not only in the Gulf region but elsewhere.

In March 1997 the American Association for World Health published documents (an Executive Summary and Report) on the impact of US sanctions on health and nutrition in Cuba.[63] The *Summary of Findings* begins with the words:

> After a year-long investigation, the American Association for World Health has determined that the US embargo of Cuba has dramatically harmed the health and nutrition of large numbers of ordinary Cuban citizens ... it is our expert medical opinion that the US embargo has caused a significant rise in suffering – and even deaths – in Cuba.

The US embargo has contributed to 'serious nutritional deficits, particularly among pregnant women ... an increase in low birth-weight babies ... food shortages linked to a devastating outbreak of neuropathy numbering in the tens of thousands ... serious cutbacks in supplies of safe drinking water ... rising incidence of morbidity and mortality rates from water-borne diseases'. The embargo has brought 'untold hardship' to sick patients; with, for example, 35 children being treated with chemotherapy in a cancer ward denied nausea-relieving drugs, and so vomiting an average of 28-to-30 times a day; and a heart-attack patient denied access to an implantable defibrillator (the firm CPI was willing to make the sale but the US government denied a licence) – the man died two months later.

A report, on release of the AAWH documents, was carried under the heading: '*Children die in agony as US trade ban stifles Cuba*'.[64] This is what the United States stands for in the modern world. This is the policy that is being so comprehensively and so mercilessly imposed on the Iraqi people; and which – were the Washington strategists allowed – would be applied to many other identifiable countries around the world. The United States is orchestrating a new Holocaust in Iraq; and is working to accomplish a similar genocide in Cuba ('Such a stringent embargo, if applied to most other countries in the developing world, would have had catastrophic effects on the public health system. Cuba's healthcare system, however, is uniformly considered the preeminent model in the Third World' – AAWH[65]). The American policy of bringing catastrophe to national populations through starvation and disease – that is, through biological warfare – is nicely portable from one country to another.

The policy of the United States in this regard is a manifest genocide under the terms of the Convention (see Appendix 11 and also 1990s Genocide, above). The policy deliberately targets 'national' groups, 'killing' their members, 'causing serious bodily or mental harm', 'deliberately inflicting . . . conditions of life calculated to bring about its physical destruction in whole or in part' and 'imposing measures intended to prevent births within the group' (Genocide Convention, Article II). The Convention indicates also (Article III) the acts that shall be punishable and the persons (Article IV) that shall be punished. Genocide, as defined, is punishable; but so also are 'conspiracy', 'incitement', 'attempt' and 'complicity'. Therefore Washington stands condemned not only for its *accomplished* genocide in Iraq but also for its *attempted* genocide in Cuba.

It is easy to identify the culpable individuals – the 'constitutionally responsible rulers, public officials or private individuals'. The principal names have already been published by Ramsey Clark, former US Attorney General (see Appendix 10). It remains to be seen whether the successors to Boutros Boutros-Ghali, John Major *inter alia* (namely, Kofi Annan, Tony Blair *inter alia*) will earn exemption from Clark's 'Criminal Complaint' (Annan at least has called for an end to the US embargo on Cuba[66]).

I remember private discussions and public debates about the perpetration and nature of past genocides; in particular, about the Holocaust. How could such things have been allowed to happen? How could responsible states have fallen under such leaderships? Did literate and educated publics really know nothing of what was happening? How are we to avoid such human catastrophes, such moral and legal derelictions in high places, in the future?

Today, in contemplation of such matters, we do not need to make imaginative leaps into the past. We do not need to consider only past genocides. With the example of what is being perpetrated in 1990s Iraq we are all contemporaries of genocide. In particular, with the current players on the scene, we need contemplate only the psychologies, ethics and politics of President Bill Clinton, Secretary of State Madeleine Albright *inter alia* and the unfeeling indifference of comfortable populations in Western states.

Appendix 1

Security Council Resolutions 660 and 661

UNITED NATIONS SECURITY COUNCIL RESOLUTION 660
2 August 1990

The Security Council,

Alarmed by the invasion of Kuwait on 2 August 1990 by the military forces of Iraq,

Determining that there exists a breach of international peace and security as regards the Iraqi invasion of Kuwait.

Acting under Articles 39 and 40 of the Charter of the United Nations,

1. Condemns the Iraqi invasion of Kuwait;

2. Demands that Iraq withdraw immediately and unconditionally all its forces to the positions in which they were located on 1 August 1990;

3. Calls upon Iraq and Kuwait to begin immediately intensive negotiations for the resolution of their differences and supports all efforts in this regard, and especially those of the League of Arab States;

4. Decides to meet again as necessary to consider further steps to ensure compliance with the present resolution.

Adopted by 14 votes to none, with one abstention (Yemen)

UNITED NATIONS SECURITY COUNCIL RESOLUTION 661
6 August 1990

The Security Council,

Reaffirming its resolution 660 (1990) of 2 August 1990,

Deeply concerned that the resolution has not been implemented and that the invasion by Iraq of Kuwait continues with further loss of human life and material destruction,

Determined to bring the invasion and occupation of Kuwait by Iraq to an end and to restore the sovereignty, independence and territorial integrity of Kuwait,

251

Noting that the legitimate Government of Kuwait has expressed its readiness to comply with resolution 660 (1990),

Mindful of its responsibilities under the Charter of the United Nations for the maintenance of international peace and security,

Affirming the inherent right of individual or collective self-defence, in response to the armed attack by Iraq against Kuwait, in accordance with Article 51 of the Charter,

Acting under Chapter VII of the Charter of the United Nations,

1. Determines that Iraq so far has failed to comply with paragraph 2 of resolution 660 (1990) and has usurped the authority of the legitimate Government of Kuwait;

2. Decides, as a consequence, to take the following measures to secure compliance of Iraq with paragraph 2 of resolution 660 (1990) and to restore the authority of the legitimate Government of Kuwait;

3. Decides that all States shall prevent:

   (a) The import into their territories of all commodities and products originating in Iraq or Kuwait exported therefrom after the date of the present resolution;

   (b) Any activities by their nationals or in their territories which would promote or are calculated to promote the export or transshipment of any commodities or products from Iraq or Kuwait; and any dealings by their nationals or their flag vessels or in their territories in any commodities or products originating in Iraq or Kuwait and exported therefrom after the date of the present resolution, including in particular any transfer of funds to Iraq or Kuwait for the purposes of such activities or dealings;

   (c) The sale or supply by their nationals or from their territories or using their flag vessels of any commodities or products, including weapons or any other military equipment, whether or not originating in their territories but not including supplies intended strictly for medical purposes, and, in humanitarian circumstances, foodstuffs, to any person or body in Iraq or Kuwait or to any person or body for the purposes of any business carried on in or operated from Iraq or Kuwait, and any activities by their nationals or in their territories which promote or are calculated to promote such sale or supply of such commodities or products;

4. Decides that all States shall not make available to the Government of Iraq or to any commercial, industrial or public utility undertaking in Iraq or Kuwait, any funds or any other financial or economic resources and shall prevent their nationals and any persons within their territories from removing from their territories or otherwise making available to that Government or to any such undertaking any such funds or resources and from remitting any other funds to persons or bodies within Iraq or Kuwait,

except payments exclusively for strictly medical or humanitarian purposes and, in humanitarian circumstances, foodstuffs;

5. Calls upon all States, including States non-members of the United Nations, to act strictly in accordance with the provisions of the present resolution notwithstanding any contract entered into or licence granted before the date of the present resolution;

6. Decides to establish, in accordance with rule 28 of the provisional rules of procedure of the Security Council, a Committee of the Security Council consisting of all the members of the Council, to undertake the following tasks and to report on its work to the Council with its observations and recommendations:

(a) To examine the reports on the progress of the implementation of the present resolution which will be submitted to the Secretary-General;

(b) To seek from all States further information regarding the action taken by them concerning the effective implementation of the provisions laid down in the present resolution;

7. Calls upon all States to co-operate fully with the Committee in the fulfilment of its task, including supplying such information as may be sought by the Committee in pursuance of the present resolution;

8. Requests the Secretary-General to provide all necessary assistance to the Committee and to make the necessary arrangements in the Secretariat for the purpose;

9. Decides that, notwithstanding paragraphs 4 through 8 above, nothing in the present resolution shall prohibit assistance to the legitimate Government of Kuwait, and calls upon all States.

(a) To take appropriate measures to protect assets of the legitimate Government of Kuwait and its agencies;

(b) Not to recognize any regime set up by the occupying Power;

10. Requests the Secretary-General to report to the Council on the progress of the implementation of the present resolution, the first report to be submitted within thirty days;

11. Decides to keep this item on its agenda and to continue its efforts to put an early end to the invasion by Iraq.

Adopted by 13 votes to none,
with two abstentions (Cuba and Yemen)

Appendix 2

EEC Declaration concerning the Iraqi invasion of Kuwait; and Council Regulation (EEC) No. 2340/90

DECLARATION, ROME, 4 AUGUST 1990

The European Economic Community and its Member states affirm their unre-served condemnation of the brutal Iraqi invasion of Kuwait and demand an immediate unconditional retreat of the Iraqi armed forces from the Kuwaiti territory, as already expressed in their declaration of August 2.

Iraq's motives justifying its military invasion of Kuwait are deemed unjusti-fied and unacceptable by the members of the economic community which will refrain from any action which could be considered as an implicit recognition of the government imposed by the invaders in Kuwait.

To protect the interests of the legitimate government in Kuwait, the members decided to take steps in order to protect all assets belonging directly or indi-rectly to Kuwait.

The European Economic Community and its Member states confirm their backing of resolution 660 of the United Nations Security Council and request that Iraq respect the provisions of this resolution. If the Iraqi authorities do not respect these provisions, the European Economic Community and its Member states shall apply a resolution of the Security Council introducing obligatory global sanctions.

The following decisions were reached with immediate effect:

• an embargo on petrol imports from Iraq and Kuwait.

• appropriate measures in order to freeze Iraqi assets in Member states of the European Economic Community.

• an embargo on the sale of arms and other military equipment to Iraq.

• the suspension of all military cooperation with Iraq.

• the suspension of technical and scientific cooperation with Iraq.

• the suspension and application of the general preference system in Iraq.

The European Economic Community and its Member states reiterate their firm conviction that any dispute between countries should be resolved pacifically and that they are prepared to participate wholeheartedly in assisting to reduce the tension in the region.

They are in close contact with the governments of several Arab countries and follow attentively all discussions within the Arab League and the Cooperation Council of the Gulf. They hope that Arab initiatives will contribute to the reestablishment of international order and of the legitimate Kuwaiti government. The European Economic Community and its Member states are prepared to strongly back those initiatives as well as all efforts to resolve the problem by negotiating the disputes between the concerned countries.

The European Economic Community and its Member states are attentively following the situation of their fellow countrymen resident in Iraq and in Kuwait. They are closely coordinating in order to assure their security.

COUNCIL REGULATION (EEC) No. 2340/90
of 8 August 1990
preventing trade by the Community as regards Iraq and Kuwait

THE COUNCIL OF THE EUROPEAN COMMUNITIES,

Whereas the serious situation resulting from the invasion of Kuwait by Iraq, which was the subject of United Nations Security Council Resolution 660 (1990) of 2 August 1990, has led to a declaration by the Community and its Member States, adopted on 4 August 1990 in the framework of political cooperation, condemning outright the invasion of Kuwait by Iraq and demanding an immediate and unconditional withdrawal of Iraqi forces from the territory of Kuwait, as well as to the Decision that economic measures will be taken against Iraq;

Whereas, faced with Iraq's refusal to conform to Resolution 660, the Security Council adopted Resolution 661 (1990) of 6 August 1990 establishing an embargo on trade with Iraq and Kuwait,

Whereas, in these conditions, the Community's trade as regards Iraq and Kuwait must be prevented;

Whereas the Community and its Member States have agreed to have recourse to a Community instrument in order to ensure uniform implementation, throughout the Community, of the measures concerning trade with Iraq and Kuwait decided upon by the United Nations Security Council;

Whereas it is appropriate to avoid a situation in which this Regulation affects exports from these countries conducted before 7 August 1990 as well as the supply of products intended strictly for medical purposes, and, where humanitarian reasons so warrant, of foodstuffs;

Having regard to the Treaty establishing the European Economic Community, and in particular Article 113 thereof,

Having regard to the proposal from the Commission,

HAS ADOPTED THIS REGULATION:

Article 1

As from 7 August 1990, the following shall be prohibited:

1. the introduction into the territory of the Community of all commodities or products originating in, or coming from, Iraq or Kuwait;

2. the export to the said countries of all commodities or products originating in, or coming from, the Community.

Article 2

As from the date referred to in Article 1, the following shall be prohibited in the territory of the Community or by means of aircraft and vessels flying the flag of a Member State, and when carried out by any Council national:

1. all activities or commercial transactions, including all operations connected with transactions which have already been concluded or partially carried out, the object or effect of which is to promote the export of any commodity or product originating in, or coming from, Iraq or Kuwait;

2. the sale or supply of any commodity or product, wherever it originates or comes from:

   – to any natural or legal person in Iraq or Kuwait,
   – to any other natural or legal person for the purposes of any commercial activity carried out in or from the territory of Iraq or Kuwait;

3. any activity the object or effect of which is to promote such sales or supplies.

Article 3

1. Article 1(2) and Article 2(2) shall not apply to the products listed in the Annex.

2. Article 1(1) and Article 2(1) shall not prevent the introduction into the territory of the Community of the commodities or products referred to in Article 1(1) which originate in, or come from, Iraq or Kuwait and are exported before 7 August 1990.

Article 4

This Regulation shall enter into force on the day of its publication in the *Official Journal of the European Communities*.

This Regulation shall be binding in its entirety and directly applicable in all Member States.

Done at Brussels, 8 August 1990.

For the Council
The President
G. DE MICHELIS

ANNEX

LIST OF PRODUCTS REFERRED TO IN ARTICLE 3 (1)

A. Medical products

ex chapter 29

All the products which are international nonproprietary names (INN) or modified international nonproprietary names (INNM) of the World Health Organization

2937 Hormones, natural or reproduced by synthesis; derivatives thereof, used primarily as hormones; other steroids used primarily as hormones

2941 Antibiotics

3001 Glands and other organs for organotherapeutic uses, dried, whether or not powdered; extracts of glands or other organs or of their secretions for organotherapeutic uses; hepatin and its salts; other human or animal substances prepared for therapeutic or prophylactic uses, not elsewhere specified or included

3002 Human blood; animal blood prepared for therapeutic, prophylactic or diagnostic uses; antisera and other blood fractions; vaccines, toxins, cultures of micro-organisms (excluding yeasts) and similar products

3003 Medicaments (excluding goods of heading Nos 3002, 3005 or 3006) consisting of two or more constituents which have been mixed together for therapeutic or prophylactic uses, not put up in measured doses or in forms or packings for retail sale

3004 Medicaments (excluding goods of heading Nos 3002, 3005 or 3006) consisting of mixed or unmixed products for therapeutic or prophylactic uses, put up in measured doses or in forms or packings for retail sale.

3005 Wadding gauze, bandages and similar articles (for example, dressings, adhesive plasters, poultices), impregnated or coated with pharmaceutical substances or put up in forms or packings for retail sale for medical, surgical, dental or veterinary purposes

3006 Pharmaceutical goods specified in note 3 to this chapter

B. Foodstuffs

Any foodstuff intended for humanitarian purposes as part of emergency aid operations.

Appendix 2

Corrigendum to Council Regulation (EEC) No. 2340/90 of 8 August 1990 preventing trade by the Community as regards Iraq and Kuwait

(Official Journal of the European Communities No. L 213 of 9 August 1990)

On page 1 in Article 2, introductory part:

for: '... Member State, and when carried out by any Community national:',

read: '... Member State, or when carried out by any Community national:'.

Appendix 3

Security Council Resolution 687

RESOLUTION 687 (1991)
of 3 April 1991

The Security Council,

Recalling its resolutions 660 (1990), 661 (1990), 662 (1990), 664 (1990), 665 (1990), 666 (1990), 667 (1990), 669 (1990), 670 (1990), 674 (1990), 677 (1990), 678 (1990) and 686 (1990),

Welcoming the restoration to Kuwait of its sovereignty, independence and territorial integrity and the return of its legitimate government,

Affirming the commitment of all Member States to the sovereignty, territorial integrity and political independence of Kuwait and Iraq, and noting the intention expressed by the Member States co-operating with Kuwait under paragraph 2 of resolution 678 (1990) to bring their military presence in Iraq to an end as soon as possible consistent with paragraph 8 of resolution 686 (1991),

Reaffirming the need to be assured of Iraq's peaceful intentions in light of its unlawful invasion and occupation of Kuwait,

Taking note of the letter sent by the Foreign Minister of Iraq on 27 February 1991 (S/22275) and those sent pursuant to resolution 686 (1990) (S/22273, S/22276, S/22320, S/22321, and S/22330),

Noting that Iraq and Kuwait, as independent sovereign States, signed at Baghdad on 4 October 1963 'Agreed Minutes Regarding the Restoration of Friendly Relations, Recognition and Related Matters', thereby recognizing formally the boundary between Iraq and Kuwait and the allocation of islands, which were registered with the United Nations in accordance with Article 102 of the Charter and in which Iraq recognized the independence and complete sovereignty of the State of Kuwait within its borders as specified and accepted in the letter of the Prime Minister of Iraq dated 21 July 1932, and as accepted by the Ruler of Kuwait in his letter dated 10 August 1932,

Conscious of the need for demarcation of the said boundary,

Conscious also of the statements by Iraq threatening to use weapons in violation of its obligations under the Geneva Protocol for the prohibition of the Use in War of Asphyxiating, Poisonous or Other Gases, and of Bacteriological Methods of Warfare, signed at Geneva on 17 June 1925, and of its prior use of chemical weapons and affirming that grave consequences would follow any further use by Iraq of such weapons,

Recalling that Iraq has subscribed to the Declaration adopted by all States participating in the Conference of States Parties to the 1925 Geneva Protocol and Other Interested States, held at Paris from 7 to 11 January 1989, establishing the objective of universal elimination of chemical and biological weapons,

Recalling further that Iraq has signed the Convention on the Prohibition of the Development, Production and Stockpiling of Bacteriological (Biological) and Toxin Weapons and on Their Destruction, of 10 April 1972,

Noting the importance of Iraq ratifying this Convention,

Noting moreover the importance of all States adhering to this Convention and encouraging its forthcoming Review Conference to reinforce the authority, efficiency and universal scope of the Convention,

Stressing the importance of an early conclusion by the Conference on Disarmament of its work on a Convention on the Universal Prohibition of Chemical Weapons and of universal adherence thereto,

Aware of the use by Iraq of ballistic missiles in unprovoked attacks and therefore of the need to take specific measures in regard to such missiles located in Iraq,

Concerned by the reports in the hands of Member States that Iraq has attempted to acquire materials for a nuclear-weapons programme contrary to its obligations under the treaty on the Non-Proliferation of Nuclear Weapons of 1 July 1968,

Recalling the objective of the establishment of a nuclear-weapons-free zone in the region of the Middle East,

Conscious of the threat which all weapons of mass destruction pose to peace and security in the area and of the need to work towards the establishment in the Middle East of a zone free of such weapons,

Conscious also of the objective of achieving balanced and comprehensive control of armaments in the region,

Conscious further of the importance of achieving the objectives noted above using all available means, including a dialogue among the states of the region,

Noting that resolution 686 (1991) marked the lifting of the measures imposed by resolution 661 (1990) in so far as they applied to Kuwait,

Noting that despite the progress being made in fulfilling the obligations of resolution 686 (1991), many Kuwaiti and third country nationals are still not accounted for and property remains unreturned,

Recalling the International Convention against the taking of hostages, opened for signature at New York on 18 December 1979, which categorizes all acts of taking hostages as manifestations of international terrorism,

Deploring threats made by Iraq during the recent conflict to make use of terrorism against targets outside Iraq and the taking of hostages by Iraq,

Taking note with grave concern of the reports of the Secretary-General of 20 March 1991 (S/22366) and 28 March 1991 (S/22409), and conscious of the necessity to meet urgently the humanitarian needs in Kuwait and Iraq,

Bearing in mind its objective of restoring international peace and security in the area as set out in recent Council resolutions,

Conscious of the need to take the following measures acting under Chapter VII of the Charter,

1. Affirms all thirteen resolutions noted above, except as expressly changed below to achieve the goals of this resolution, including a formal cease-fire;

A

2. Demands that Iraq and Kuwait respect the inviolability of the international boundary and the allocation of islands set out in the 'Agreed Minutes Between the State of Kuwait and the Republic of Iraq Regarding the Restoration of Friendly Relations, Recognition and Related Matters', signed by them in the exercise of their sovereignty at Baghdad on 4 October 1963 and registered with the United Nations and published by the United Nations in document 7063, United Nations Treaty Series, 1964;

3. Calls on the Secretary-General to lend his assistance to make arrangements with Iraq and Kuwait to demarcate the boundary between Iraq and Kuwait, drawing on appropriate material including the map transmitted by Security Council document S/22412 and to report back to the Security Council within one month;

4. Decides to guarantee the inviolability of the above-mentioned international boundary and to take as appropriate all necessary measures to that end in accordance with the Charter;

B

5. Requests the Secretary-General, after consulting with Iraq and Kuwait, to submit within three days to the Security Council for its approval a plan for the immediate deployment of a United Nations observer unit to monitor the Khor Abdullah and a demilitarized zone, 10 kilometres into Iraq and 5 kilometres into Kuwait from the boundary referred to in the 'Agreed Minutes Between the State of Kuwait and the Republic of Iraq Regarding the Restoration of Friendly Relations, Recognition and Related Matters' of 4 October 1963; to deter violations of the boundary through its presence in and surveillance of the demilitarized zone; to observe any hostile or potentially hostile action mounted from the territory of one State to the other; and for the Secretary-General to report regularly to the Council on the operations of the unit, and immediately if there are any serious violations of the zone or potential threats to peace;

6. Notes that as soon as the Secretary-General notifies the Council of the completion of the deployment of the United Nations observer unit, the

conditions will be established for the Member States co-operating with Kuwait in accordance with resolution 678 (1990) to bring their military presence in Iraq to an end consistent with resolution 686 (1991);

C

7. Invites Iraq to reaffirm unconditionally its obligations under the Geneva Protocol for the Prohibition of the Use in War of Asphyxiating, Poisonous or Other Gases, and of Bacteriological Methods of Warfare, signed at Geneva on 17 June 1925, and to ratify the Convention on the Prohibition of the Development, Production, and Stockpiling of Bacteriological (Biological) and Toxin Weapons and on Their Destruction, of 10 April 1972;

8. Decides that Iraq shall unconditionally accept the destruction, removal, or rendering harmless, under international supervision, of:

   (a) all chemical and biological weapons and all stocks of agents and all related subsystems and components and all research, development, support and manufacturing facilities;

   (b) all ballistic missiles with a range greater than 150 kilometres and related major parts, and repair and production facilities;

9. Decides for the implementation of paragraph 8 above, the following:

   (a) Iraq shall submit to the Secretary-General, within fifteen days of the adoption of this resolution, a declaration of the locations, amounts and types of all items specified in paragraph 8 and agree to urgent, on-site inspection as specified below;

   (b) the Secretary-General, in consultation with the appropriate Governments and, where appropriate, with the Director-General of the World Health Organization (WHO), within 45 days of the passage of this resolution, shall develop, and submit to the Council for approval, a plan calling for the completion of the following acts within 45 days of such approval:

      (i)   the forming of a Special Commission, which shall carry out immediate on-site inspection of Iraq's biological, chemical and missile capabilities, based on Iraq's declarations and the designation of any additional locations by the Special Commission itself;

      (ii) the yielding by Iraq of possession to the Special Commission for destruction, removal or rendering harmless, taking into account the requirements of public safety, of all items specified under paragraph 8 (a) above including items at the additional locations designated by the Special Commission under paragraph 9 (b) (i) above and the destruction by Iraq, under supervision of the Special Commission, of all its missile capabilities including launchers as specified under paragraph 8 (b) above;

      (iii) the provision by the Special Commission of the assistance and co-operation to the Director-General of the International Atomic Energy Agency (IAEA) required in paragraphs 12 and 13 below;

10. Decides that Iraq shall unconditionally undertake not to use, develop, construct or acquire any of the items specified in paragraphs 8 and 9

above and requests the Secretary-General, in consultation with the Special Commission, to develop a plan for the future ongoing monitoring and verification of Iraq's compliance with this paragraph, to be submitted to the Council for approval within 120 days of the passage of this resolution;

11. Invites Iraq to reaffirm unconditionally its obligations under the treaty on the Non-Proliferation of Nuclear Weapons, of 1 July 1968;

12. Decides that Iraq shall unconditionally agree not to acquire or develop nuclear weapons or nuclear-weapons-usable material or any subsystems or components or any research, development, support or manufacturing facilities related to the above; to submit to the Secretary-General and the Director-General of the International Atomic Energy Agency (IAEA) within 15 days of the adoption of this resolution a declaration of the locations, amounts and types of all items specified above; to place all of its nuclear-weapons-usable material under the exclusive control, for custody and removal, of the IAEA, with the assistance and co-operation of the Special Commission as provided for in the plan of the Secretary-General discussed in paragraph 9 (*b*) above; to accept in accordance with the arrangements provided for in paragraph 13 below, urgent on-site inspection and the destruction, removal and rendering harmless as appropriate of all items specified above; and to accept the plan as discussed in paragraph 13 below for the future ongoing monitoring and verification of its compliance with these undertakings;

13. Requests the Director-General of the International Atomic Energy Agency (IAEA) through the Secretary-General, with the assistance and co-operation of the Special Commission as provided for in the plan of the Secretary-General in paragraph 9 (*b*) above, to carry out immediate on-site inspection of Iraq's nuclear capabilities based on Iraq's declarations and the designation of any additional locations by the Special Commission; to develop a plan for submission to the Security Council within 45 days calling for the destruction, removal, or rendering harmless as appropriate of all items listed in paragraph 12 above; to carry out the plan within 45 days following approval by the Security Council; and to develop a plan, taking into account the rights and obligations of Iraq under the Treaty on the Non-Proliferation of Nuclear Weapons, of 1 July 1968, for the future ongoing monitoring and verification of Iraq's compliance with paragraph 12 above, including an inventory of all nuclear material in Iraq subject to the Agency's verification and inspections to confirm that IAEA safeguards cover all relevant nuclear activities in Iraq, to be submitted to the Council for approval within 120 days of the passage of this resolution;

14. Takes note that the actions to be taken by Iraq in paragraphs 8, 9, 10, 11, 12 and 13 of this resolution represent steps towards the goal of establishing in the Middle East a zone free from weapons of mass destruction and all missiles for their delivery and the objective of a global ban on chemical weapons;

D

15. Requests the Secretary-General to report to the Security Council on the steps taken to facilitate the return of all Kuwaiti property seized by Iraq, including a list of any property which Kuwait claims has not been returned or which has not been returned intact;

E

16. Reaffirms that Iraq, without prejudice to the debts and obligation of Iraq arising prior to 2 August 1990, which will be addressed through the normal mechanisms, is liable under international law for any direct loss, damage, including environmental damage and the depletion of natural resources, or injury to foreign Governments, nationals and corporations, as a result of Iraq's unlawful invasion and occupation of Kuwait;

17. Decides that all Iraqi statements made since 2 August 1990, repudiating its foreign debt are null and void, and demands that Iraq scrupulously adhere to all of its obligations concerning servicing and repayment of its foreign debt;

18. Decides to create a Fund to pay compensation for claims that fall within paragraph 16 above and to establish a Commission that will administer the Fund;

19. Directs the Secretary-General to develop and present to the Council for decision, no later than 30 days following the adoption of this resolution, recommendations for the Fund to meet the requirement for the payment of claims established in accordance with paragraph 18 above and for a programme to implement the decisions in paragraphs 16, 17, and 18 above, including: administration of the Fund; mechanisms for determining the appropriate level for Iraq's contribution to the Fund based on a percentage of the value of the exports of petroleum and petroleum products from Iraq not to exceed a figure to be suggested to the Council by the Secretary-General, taking into account the requirement of the people of Iraq, Iraq's payment capacity as assessed in conjunction with the international financial institutions taking into consideration external debt service, and the needs of the Iraqi economy; arrangements for ensuring that payments are made to the Fund; the process by which funds will be allocated and claims paid; appropriate procedures for evaluating losses, listing claims and verifying their validity and resolving disputed claims in respect of Iraq's liability as specified in paragraph 16 above; and the composition of the Commission designated above;

F

20. Decides, effective immediately, that the prohibitions against the sale or supply to Iraq of commodities or products, other than medicine and health supplies, and prohibitions against financial transactions related thereto, contained in resolution 661 (1990) shall not apply to foodstuffs notified to the Committee established by resolution 661 (1990) or, with the ap-

proval of that Committee, under the simplified and accelerated 'no-objection' procedure, to materials and supplies for essential civilian needs as identified in the report of the Secretary-General dated 20 March 1991 (S/22366), and in any further findings of humanitarian need by the Committee.

21. Decides that the Council shall review the provisions of paragraph 20 above every sixty days in light of the policies and practices of the Government of Iraq, including the implementation of all relevant resolutions of the Security Council, for the purposes of determining whether to reduce or lift the prohibitions referred to therein;

22. Decides that upon the approval by the Council of the programme called for in paragraph 19 above and upon Council agreement that Iraq has completed all actions contemplated in paragraphs 8, 9, 10, 11, 12, and 13 above, the prohibitions against the import of commodities and products originating in Iraq and the prohibitions against financial transactions related thereto contained in resolution 661 (1990) shall have no further force or effect;

23. Decides that, pending action by the Council under paragraph 22 above, the Committee established by resolution 661 (1990) shall be empowered to approve, when required to assure adequate financial resources on the part of Iraq to carry out the activities under paragraph 20 above, exceptions to the prohibition against the import of commodities and products originating in Iraq;

24. Decides that, in accordance with resolution 661 (1990) and subsequent related resolutions and until a further decision is taken by the Council, all States shall continue to prevent the sale or supply, or promotion or facilitation of such sale or supply, to Iraq by their nationals, or from their territories or using their flag vessels or aircraft, of:

   (a) arms and related material of all types, specifically including conventional military equipment, including for paramilitary forces, and spare parts and components and their means of production, for such equipment;

   (b) items specified and defined in paragraph 8 and paragraph 12 above not otherwise covered above;

   (c) technology under licensing or other transfer arrangements used in production, utilization or stockpiling of items specified in subparagraphs (a) and (b) above;

   (d) personnel or materials for training or technical support services relating to the design, development, manufacture, use, maintenance or support of items specified in subparagraphs (a) and (b) above;

25. Calls upon all States and international organizations to act strictly in accordance with paragraph 24 above, notwithstanding the existence of any contracts, agreements, licences, or any other arrangements;

26. Requests the Secretary-General, in consultation with appropriate Governments, to develop within sixty days, for approval of the Council, guidelines

to facilitate full international implementation of paragraphs 24 and 25 above and paragraph 27 below, and to make them available to all States and to establish a procedure for updating these guidelines periodically;

27. Calls upon all States to maintain such national controls and procedures and to take such other actions consistent with the guidelines to be established by the Security Council under paragraph 26 above as may be necessary to ensure compliance with the terms of paragraph 24 above, and calls upon international organizations to take all appropriate steps to assist in ensuring such full compliance;

28. Agrees to review its decisions in paragraphs 22, 23, 24, and 25 above, except for the items specified and defined in paragraphs 8 and 12 above, on a regular basis and in any case 120 days following passage of this resolution, taking into account Iraq's compliance with this resolution and general progress towards the control of armaments in the region;

29. Decides that all States, including Iraq, shall take the necessary measures to ensure that no claim shall lie at the instance of the Government of Iraq, or of any person or body in Iraq, or of any person claiming through or for the benefit of any such person or body, in connection with any contract or other transaction where its performance was affected by reason of the measures taken by the Security Council in resolution 661 (1990) and related resolutions;

G

30. Decides that, in furtherance of its commitment to facilitate the repatriation of all Kuwaiti and third country nationals, Iraq shall extend all necessary co-operation to the International Committee of the Red Cross, providing lists of such persons, facilitating the access of the International Committee of the Red Cross to all such persons wherever located or detained and facilitating the search by the International Committee of the Red Cross for those Kuwaiti and third country nationals still unaccounted for;

31. Invites the International Committee of the Red Cross to keep the Secretary-General apprised as appropriate of all activities undertaken in connection with facilitating the repatriation or return of all Kuwaiti and third country nationals or their remains present in Iraq on or after 2 August 1990;

H

32. Requires Iraq to inform the Council that it will not commit or support any act of international terrorism or allow any organization directed towards commission of such acts to operate within its territory and to condemn unequivocally and renounce all acts, methods, and practices of terrorism;

I

33. Declares that, upon official notification by Iraq to the Secretary-General and to the Security Council of its acceptance of the provisions above, a

formal cease-fire is effective between Iraq and Kuwait and the Member States co-operating with Kuwait in accordance with resolution 678 (1990);

34. Decides to remain seized of the matter and to take such further steps as may be required for the implementation of this resolution and to secure peace and security in the area.

Adopted by 12 votes to one (Cuba), with two abstentions (Ecuador and Yemen)

Appendix 4

Security Council Resolutions 707 and 715

RESOLUTION 707 (1991)
of 15 August 1991

The Security Council,

Recalling its resolution 687 (1991) of 3 April 1991 and its other resolutions on this matter,

Recalling also the letter of 11 April 1991 from the President of the Security Council to the Permanent Representative of Iraq to the United Nations, in which he noted that on the basis of Iraq's written agreement to implement fully resolution 687 (1991), the preconditions for a cease-fire established in paragraph 33 of that resolution had been met,

Taking note with grave concern of the letters dated 26 and 28 June and 4 July 1991 from the Secretary-General to the President of the Security Council, conveying information received from the Executive Chairman of the Special Commission and from the high-level mission to Iraq which establishes Iraq's failure to comply with its obligations under resolution 687 (1991),

Recalling further the statement issued by the President of the Security Council on 28 June 1991 requesting that a high-level mission consisting of the Executive Chairman of the Special Commission, the Director General of the International Atomic Energy Agency and the Under-Secretary-General for Disarmament Affairs be dispatched to meet with officials at the highest levels of the Government of Iraq at the earliest opportunity to obtain written assurance that Iraq will fully and immediately cooperate in the inspection of the locations identified by the Special Commission and present for immediate inspection any of those items that may have been transported from those locations,

Having taken note with dismay of the report of the high-level mission to the Secretary-General on the results of its meetings with the highest levels of the Iraqi Government,

Gravely concerned by the information provided to the Council by the International Atomic Energy Agency on 15 and 25 July 1991 regarding the actions of the Government of Iraq in flagrant violation of resolution 687 (1991),

Gravely concerned also by the letter of 7 July 1991 from the Minister for Foreign Affairs of Iraq addressed to the Secretary-General and subsequent statements and findings that Iraq's notifications of 18 and 28 April were incomplete and that certain related activities had been concealed, facts both of which constitute material breaches of its obligations under resolution 687 (1991),

Noting, having been informed by the letters dated 26 and 28 June and 4 July 1991 from the Secretary-General, that Iraq has not fully complied with all of its undertakings relating to the privileges, immunities and facilities to be accorded to the Special Commission and the Agency inspection teams mandated under resolution 687 (1991),

Affirming that in order for the Special Commission to carry out its mandate under paragraphs 9 (*b*) (i–iii) of resolution 687 (1991) to inspect Iraq's chemical and biological weapons and ballistic missile capabilities and to take possession of the elements referred to in that resolution for destruction, removal or rendering harmless, full disclosure on the part of Iraq as required in paragraph 9 (*a*) of resolution 687 (1991) is essential,

Affirming also that in order for the International Atomic Energy Agency, with the assistance and cooperation of the Special Commission, to determine what nuclear-weapon-usable material or any subsystems or components or any research, development, support or manufacturing facilities related to them need, in accordance with paragraph 13 of resolution 687 (1991), to be destroyed, removed or rendered harmless, Iraq is required to make a declaration of all its nuclear programmes, including any which it claims are for purposes not related to nuclear-weapon-usable material.

Affirming further that the aforementioned failures of Iraq to act in strict conformity with its obligations under resolution 687 (1991) constitute a material breach of its acceptance of the relevant provisions of that resolution which established a cease-fire and provided the conditions essential to the restoration of peace and security in the region,

Affirming moreover, that Iraq's failure to comply with the safeguards agreement it concluded with the International Atomic Energy Agency pursuant to the Treaty on the Non-Proliferation of Nuclear Weapons of 1 July 1968, as established by the Board of Governors of the Agency in its resolution of 18 July 1991, constitutes a breach of its international obligations,

Determined to ensure full compliance with resolution 687 (1991), and in particular its section C,

Acting under Chapter VII of the Charter of the United Nations,

1. *Condemns* Iraq's serious violation of a number of its obligations under section C of resolution 687 (1991) and of its undertakings to cooperate with the Special Commission and the International Atomic Energy Agency, which constitutes a material breach of the relevant provisions of that resolution which established a cease-fire and provided the conditions essential to the restoration of peace and security in the region;

2. *Also condemns* non-compliance by the Government of Iraq with its obligations under its safeguards agreement with the International Atomic Energy Agency, as established by the Board of Governors of the Agency in its resolution of 18 July 1991, which constitutes a violation of its commitments as a party to the Treaty on the Non-Proliferation of Nuclear Weapons of 1 July 1968;

3. *Demands* that Iraq:

(*a*) Provide without further delay full, final and complete disclosure, as required by resolution 687 (1991), of all aspects of its programmes to develop weapons of mass destruction and ballistic missiles with a range greater than one hundred and fifty kilometres and of all holdings of such weapons, their components and production facilities and locations, as well as all other nuclear programmes, including any which it claims are for purposes not related to nuclear-weapon-usable material;

(*b*) Allow the Special Commission, the International Atomic Energy Agency and their inspection teams immediate, unconditional and unrestricted access to any and all areas, facilities, equipment, records and means of transportation which they wish to inspect;

(*c*) Cease immediately any attempt to conceal, move or destroy any material or equipment relating to its nuclear, chemical or biological weapons or ballistic missile programmes, or material or equipment relating to its other nuclear activities, without notification to and prior consent of the Special Commission;

(*d*) Make available immediately to the Special Commission, the Agency and their inspection teams any items to which they were previously denied access;

(*e*) Allow the Special Commission, the Agency and their inspection teams to conduct both fixed-wing and helicopter flights throughout Iraq for all relevant purposes, including inspection, surveillance, aerial surveys, transportation and logistics, without interference of any kind and upon such terms and conditions as may be determined by the Special Commission, and to make full use of their own aircraft and such airfields in Iraq as they may determine are most appropriate for the work of the Commission;

(*f*) Halt all nuclear activities of any kind, except for use of isotopes for medical, agricultural or industrial purposes, until the Council determines that Iraq is in full compliance with the present resolution and with paragraphs 12 and 13 of resolution 687 (1991) and the Agency determines that Iraq is in full compliance with its safeguards agreement with the Agency;

(*g*) Ensure the complete enjoyment, in accordance with its previous undertakings, of the privileges, immunities and facilities accorded to the representatives of the Special Commission and the Agency and guarantee their complete safety and freedom of movement;

(*h*) Immediately provide or facilitate the provision of any transportation and medical or logistical support requested by the Special Commission, the Agency and their inspection teams;

(*i*) Respond fully, completely and promptly to any questions or requests from the Special Commission, the Agency and their inspection teams;

4. *Determines* that Iraq retains no ownership interest in items to be destroyed, removed or rendered harmless pursuant to paragraph 12 of resolution 687 (1991);

5. *Requires* the Government of Iraq forthwith to comply fully and without delay with all its international obligations, including those set out in the present resolution, in resolution 687 (1991), in the Treaty on the Non-Proliferation of Nuclear Weapons and in its safeguards agreement with the International Atomic Energy Agency;

6. *Decides* to remain seized of this matter.

Adopted unanimously at the 3004th meeting

Decision

At its 3008th meeting, on 19 September 1991, the Council invited the representative of Iraq to participate, without vote, in the discussion of the item entitled 'The situation between Iraq and Kuwait: report of the Secretary-General pursuant to paragraph 5 of Security Council resolution 706 (1991) (S/23006 and Corr. 2)'.

RESOLUTION 715 (1991)
of 11 October 1991

The Security Council,

Recalling its resolutions 687 (1991) of 3 April 1991 and 707 (1991) of 15 August 1991 and its other resolutions on this matter,

Recalling in particular that under resolution 687 (1991) the Secretary-General and the Director General of the International Atomic Energy Agency were requested to develop plans for future ongoing monitoring and verification and to submit them to the Security Council for approval,

Taking note of the report and note of the Secretary-General, transmitting the plans submitted by the Secretary-General and the Director General of the Agency,

Acting under Chapter VII of the Charter of the United Nations,

1. *Approves,* in accordance with the provisions of resolutions 687 (1991), 707 (1991) and the present resolution, the plans submitted by the Secretary-General and the Director General of the International Atomic Energy Agency;.

2. *Decides* that the Special Commission shall carry out the plan submitted by the Secretary-General, as well as continuing to discharge its other responsibilities under resolutions 687 (1991), 699 (1991) of 17 June 1991 and 707 (1991) and performing such other functions as are conferred upon it under the present resolution;

3. *Requests* the Director General of the Agency to carry out, with the assistance and cooperation of the Special Commission, the plan submitted by him and to continue to discharge his other responsibilities under resolutions 687 (1991), 699 (1991) and 707 (1991);

4. *Decides* that the Special Commission, in the exercise of its responsibilities as a subsidiary organ of the Security Council, shall:

(*a*) Continue to have the responsibility for designating additional locations for inspection and overflights;

(*b*) Continue to render assistance and cooperation to the Director General of the Agency by providing him, by mutual agreement, with the necessary special expertise and logistical, informational and other operational support for the carrying out of the plan submitted by him;

(*c*) Perform such other functions, in cooperation in the nuclear field with the Director General of the Agency, as may be necessary to coordinate activities under the plans approved by the present resolution, including making use of commonly available services and information to the fullest extent possible, in order to achieve maximum efficiency and optimum use of resources;

5. *Demands* that Iraq meet unconditionally all its obligations under the plans approved by the present resolution and cooperate fully with the Special Commission and the Director General of the Agency in carrying out the plans;

6. *Decides* to encourage the maximum assistance, in cash and in kind, from all Member States to support the Special Commission and the Director General of the Agency in carrying out their activities under the plans approved by the present resolution, without prejudice to Iraq's liability for the full costs of such activities;

7. *Requests* the Security Council Committee established under resolution 661 (1990) concerning the situation between Iraq and Kuwait, the Special Commission and the Director General of the Agency to develop in cooperation a mechanism for monitoring any future sales or supplies by other countries to Iraq of items relevant to the implementation of section C of resolution 687 (1991) and other relevant resolutions, including the present resolution and the plans approved hereunder;

8. *Requests* the Secretary-General and the Director General of the Agency to submit to the Security Council reports on the implementation of the plans approved by the present resolution, when requested by the Security Council and in any event at least every six months after the adoption of this resolution;

9. *Decides* to remain seized of the matter.

Adopted unanimously at the 3012th meeting

Decision

After the consultations held on 20 December 1991, the President of the Security Council made the following statement to the media on behalf of the members of the Council:

> The members of the Security Council held informal consultations on 6 December 1991 pursuant to paragraph 28 of resolution 687 (1991) of 3 April 1991, paragraph 6 of resolution 700 (1991) of 17 June 1991 and paragraph 21 of resolution 687 (1991). After hearing all the opinions expressed in the course of the consultations, the President of the Council concluded that there was no agreement that the necessary conditions existed for a modification of the regimes established in paragraphs 22 to 25, as referred to in paragraph 28 of resolution 687 (1991), in paragraph 6 of resolution 700 (1991), and in paragraph 20, as referred to in paragraph 21 of resolution 687 (1991).
>
> However, with a view to alleviating the humanitarian conditions for the civilian population in Iraq and in order to facilitate the utilisation of paragraph 20 of resolution 687 (1991), the Security Council Committee established under resolution 661 (1990) concerning the situation between Iraq and Kuwait is requested to study immediately those materials and supplies for essential civilian and humanitarian needs as identified in the Ahtisaari report with the purpose of drawing up a list of items which may, with the Council's approval, be transferred from the 'no-objection' procedure to a simple notification procedure. Members of the Council may submit proposals of items for this purpose.
>
> With regard to imports of items subject to prior approval under the 'no-objection' procedure by the Committee (i.e. items other than food and medicine), any member of the Committee putting forward an objection to such an import will offer a specific explanation at a meeting of the Committee.
>
> The members of the Council are aware of reports received concerning the approximately 2,000 Kuwaitis believed to be still detained in Iraq, access by the International Committee of the Red Cross to all detainees and places of detention, the return of Kuwaiti property, and particularly the return of Kuwaiti military equipment and their bearing upon the present state of Iraqi compliance with resolution 687 (1991).
>
> In light of the above, the Council will request the Secretary-General to prepare a factual report on Iraq's compliance with all the obligations placed upon it by resolution 687 (1991) and subsequent relevant resolutions. This report will be made available to the Council in good time before it undertakes its next review under paragraph 21 of resolution 687 (1991).
>
> In the course of consultations it was noted that resolutions 706 (1991) of 15 August 1991 and 712 (1991) of 19 September 1991 gave to Iraq the possibility for oil sales to finance the purchase of foodstuffs, medicines and materials and supplies for essential civilian needs for the purpose of providing humanitarian relief. However, this possibility has not yet been used.

Appendix 5

Security Council Resolutions 706, 712 and 986

RESOLUTION 706 (1991)
of 15 August 1991

The Security Council,

Recalling its previous relevant resolutions and in particular resolutions 661 (1990) of 6 August 1990, 686 (1991) of 2 March 1991, 687 (1991) of 3 April 1991, 688 (1991) of 5 April 1991, 692 (1991) of 20 May 1991, 699 (1991) of 17 June 1991 and 705 (1991) of 15 August 1991,

Taking note of the report dated 15 July 1991 of the inter-agency mission headed by the Executive Delegate of the Secretary-General for the United Nations Inter-Agency Humanitarian Programme for Iraq, Kuwait and the Iraq/ Turkey and Iraq/Iran border areas,

Concerned by the serious nutritional and health situation of the Iraqi civilian population as described in the report and by the risk of a further deterioration of this situation,

Concerned also that the repatriation or return of all Kuwaitis and third-State nationals or their remains present in Iraq on or after 2 August 1990, pursuant to paragraph 2 (*c*) of resolution 686 (1991) and paragraphs 30 and 31 of resolution 687 (1991), has not yet been fully carried out,

Taking note of the conclusions of the above-mentioned report, and in particular of the proposal for oil sales by Iraq to finance the purchase of food-stuffs, medicines and materials and supplies for essential civilian needs for the purpose of providing humanitarian relief,

Taking note also of the letters dated 14 April, 31 May, 6 June, 9 July and 22 July 1991 from the Minister for Foreign Affairs of Iraq and the Permanent Representative of Iraq to the United Nations to the Chairman of the Security Council Committee established by resolution 661 (1990) concerning the situation between Iraq and Kuwait, in regard to the export by Iraq of petroleum and petroleum products,

Convinced of the need to ensure equitable distribution of humanitarian relief assistance to all segments of the Iraqi civilian population through effective monitoring and transparency of the process,

Recalling and reaffirming in this regard its resolution 688 (1991), and in particular the importance which the Council attaches to Iraq's allowing unhindered access by international humanitarian organisations to all those in need of assistance in all parts of Iraq and making available all necessary facilities

274

for their operation, and in this connection stressing the continuing importance of the Memorandum of Understanding between the United Nations and the Government of Iraq signed on 18 April 1991,

Recalling that, pursuant to resolutions 687 (1991), 692 (1991) and 699 (1991), Iraq is required to pay the full costs of the Special Commission and the International Atomic Energy Agency in carrying out the tasks authorised by section C of resolution 687 (1991), and that the Secretary-General, in the report of 15 July 1991 that he submitted to the Council pursuant to paragraph 4 of resolution 699 (1991), expressed the view that the most obvious way of obtaining financial resources from Iraq to meet those costs would be to authorise the sale of some Iraqi petroleum and petroleum products; recalling also that Iraq is required to pay its contributions to the United Nations Compensation Fund and half the costs of the Iraq–Kuwait Boundary Demarcation Commission; and recalling further that, in its resolutions 686 (1991) and 687 (1991), the Council demanded that Iraq return in the shortest possible time all Kuwaiti property seized by it and requested the Secretary-General to take steps to facilitate this demand,

Acting under Chapter VII of the Charter of the United Nations,

1. *Authorizes* all States, subject to the decision to be taken by the Security Council pursuant to paragraph 5 and notwithstanding the provisions of paragraphs 3 (*a*), 3 (*b*) and 4 of resolution 661 (1990), to permit, for the purposes specified in the present resolution, the import, during a period of six months from the date of adoption of the resolution pursuant to paragraph 5, of a quantity of petroleum and petroleum products originating in Iraq sufficient to produce a sum to be determined by the Council following receipt of the report of the Secretary-General requested in paragraph 5, a sum, however, not to exceed 1.6 billion United States dollars, subject to the following conditions:

(*a*) Approval of each purchase of Iraqi petroleum and petroleum products by the Security Council Committee established by resolution 661 (1990) concerning the situation between Iraq and Kuwait, following notification to the Committee by the State concerned;

(*b*) Direct payment of the full amount of each purchase of Iraqi petroleum and petroleum products by the purchaser in the State concerned into an escrow account to be established by the United Nations and administered by the Secretary-General exclusively to meet the purposes of this resolution;

(*c*) Approval by the Council, following the report of the Secretary-General requested in paragraph 5, of a scheme for the purchase of foodstuffs, medicines and materials and supplies for essential civilian needs as referred to in paragraph 20 of resolution 687 (1991), in particular health related materials, all of which to be labelled to the extent possible as being supplied under this scheme, and for all feasible and appropriate United Nations monitoring and supervision for the purpose of assuring their equitable distribution to meet humanitarian needs in all regions of Iraq and to all categories of the Iraqi civilian population, as well as all feasible and appropriate management relevant to this purpose, such a United Nations role to be available if desired for humanitarian assistance from other sources;

(*d*) The total sum of purchases authorized in the present paragraph is to be released by successive decisions of the Committee in three equal portions after the Council has taken the decision provided for in paragraph 5 on the implementation of the present resolution; notwithstanding any other provision of the present paragraph, the Council may review the maximum total sum of purchases on the basis of an ongoing assessment of the needs and requirements;

2. *Decides* that a part of the sum in the account administered by the Secretary-General shall be made available to him to finance the purchase of foodstuffs, medicines and materials and supplies for essential civilian needs, as referred to in paragraph 20 of resolution 687 (1991), and to cover the cost to the United Nations of its activities under the present resolution and of other necessary humanitarian activities in Iraq;

3. *Decides also* that a part of the sum deposited in the account administered by the Secretary-General shall be used by him for appropriate payments to the United Nations Compensation Fund and to cover the full costs of carrying out the tasks authorized by section C of resolution 687 (1991), the full costs incurred by the United Nations in facilitating the return of all Kuwaiti property seized by Iraq, and half the costs of the Iraq–Kuwait Boundary Demarcation Commission;

4. *Decides further* that the percentage of the value of exports of petroleum and petroleum products from Iraq authorized under the present resolution to be paid to the Compensation Fund, as called for in paragraph 19 of resolution 687 (1991) and as defined in paragraph 6 of resolution 692 (1991), shall be the same as the percentage decided by the Council in paragraph 2 of resolution 705 (1991) for payments to the Fund, until such time as the Governing Council of the Fund decides otherwise;

5. *Requests* the Secretary-General to submit to the Council, within twenty days of the date of adoption of the present resolution, a report suggesting decisions to be taken on measures to implement paragraphs 1 (*a*), (*b*) and (*c*), on estimates of the humanitarian requirements of Iraq set out in paragraph 2 and on the amount of Iraq's financial obligations set out in paragraph 3 up to the end of the period of the authorization in paragraph 1, as well as on the method for taking the necessary legal measures to ensure that the purposes of the present resolution are carried out and the method for taking account of the costs of transportation of Iraqi petroleum and petroleum products;

6. *Also requests* the Secretary-General, in consultation with the International Committee of the Red Cross, to submit to the Council within twenty days of the date of adoption of the present resolution a report on activities undertaken in accordance with paragraph 31 of resolution 687 (1991) in connection with facilitating the repatriation or return of all Kuwaiti and third-State nationals or their remains present in Iraq on or after 2 August 1990;

7. *Calls upon* the Government of Iraq to provide to the Secretary-General and appropriate international organisations on the first day of the month

immediately following the adoption of the present resolution and on the first day of each month thereafter until further notice, a detailed statement of the gold and foreign currency reserves it holds, whether in Iraq or elsewhere;

8. *Calls upon* all States to cooperate fully in the implementation of the present resolution;

9. *Decides* to remain seized of the matter.

RESOLUTION 712 (1991)
of 19 September 1991

The Security Council,

Recalling its previous relevant resolutions, and in particular resolutions 661 (1990) of 6 August 1990, 686 (1991) of 2 March 1991, 687 (1991) of 3 April 1991, 688 (1991) of 5 April 1991, 692 (1991) of 20 May 1991, 699 (1991) of 17 June 1991, and 705 (1991) and 706 (1991) of 15 August 1991,

Expressing its appreciation for the report submitted by the Secretary-General on 4 September 1991 pursuant to paragraph 5 of resolution 706 (1991),

Reaffirming its concern about the nutritional and health situation of the Iraqi civilian population and the risk of a further deterioration of this situation, and underlining the need in this context for fully up-to-date assessments of the situation in all parts of Iraq as a basis for the equitable distribution of humanitarian relief to all segments of the Iraqi civilian population,

Recalling that the activities to be carried out by or on behalf of the Secretary-General to meet the purposes referred to in resolution 706 (1991) and the present resolution enjoy the privileges and immunities of the United Nations,

Acting under Chapter VII of the Charter of the United Nations,

1. *Confirms* the figure mentioned in paragraph 1 of resolution 706 (1991) as the sum authorized for the purpose of that paragraph, and reaffirms its intention to review this sum on the basis of its ongoing assessment of the needs and requirements, in accordance with paragraph 1 (*d*) of that resolution;

2. *Invites* the Security Council Committee established by resolution 661 (1990) concerning the situation between Iraq and Kuwait to authorize immediately, pursuant to paragraph 1 (*d*) of resolution 706 (1991), the release by the Secretary-General from the escrow account of the first one-third portion of the sum referred to in paragraph 1 above, such release to take place as required subject to the availability of funds in the account and, in the case of payments to finance the purchase of foodstuffs, medicines and materials and supplies for essential civilian needs that have been notified or approved in accordance with existing procedures, subject to compliance with the procedures laid down in the report of the Secretary-General as approved in paragraph 3 below;

3. *Approves* the recommendations contained in paragraphs 57(*d*) and 58 of the Secretary-General's report;

4. *Encourages* the Secretary-General and the Committee to cooperate, in close consultation with the Government of Iraq, on a continuing basis to ensure the most effective implementation of the scheme approved in the present resolution;

5. *Decides* that petroleum and petroleum products subject to resolution 706 (1991) shall, while under Iraqi title, be immune from legal proceedings and not be subject to any form of attachment, garnishment or execution, and that all States shall take any steps that may be necessary under their respective domestic legal systems to assure this protection and to ensure that the proceeds of sale are not diverted from the purposes laid down in resolution 706 (1991);

6. *Reaffirms* that the escrow account to be established by the United Nations and administered by the Secretary-General to meet the purposes of resolution 706 (1991) and the present resolution, like the United Nations Compensation Fund established by resolution 692 (1991), enjoys the privileges and immunities of the United Nations;

7. *Reaffirms also* that the inspectors and other experts on mission for the United Nations, appointed for the purpose of the present resolution, enjoy privileges and immunities in accordance with the Convention on the Privileges and Immunities of the United Nations, and demands that Iraq allow them full freedom of movement and all necessary facilities;

8. *Confirms* that funds contributed from other sources may, if desired, in accordance with paragraph 1 (*c*) of resolution 706 (1991), be deposited into the escrow account as a sub-account and be immediately available to meet Iraq's humanitarian needs as referred to in paragraph 20 of resolution 687 (1991) without any of the obligatory deductions and administrative costs specified in paragraphs 2 and 3 of resolution 706 (1991);

9. *Urges* that any provision to Iraq of foodstuffs, medicines or other items of a humanitarian character, in addition to those purchased with the funds referred to in paragraph 1 above, be undertaken through arrangements that assure their equitable distribution to meet humanitarian needs;

10. *Requests* the Secretary-General to take the actions necessary to implement the above decisions, and authorizes him to enter into any arrangements or agreements necessary to accomplish this;

11. *Calls upon* States to cooperate fully in the implementation of resolution 706 (1991) and the present resolution, in particular with respect to any measures regarding the import of petroleum and petroleum products and the export of foodstuffs, medicines and materials and supplies for essential civilian needs as referred to in paragraph 20 of resolution 687 (1991), and also with respect to the privileges and immunities of the United Nations and its personnel

implementing the present resolution, and to ensure that there are no diversions from the purposes laid down in these resolutions;

12. *Decides* to remain seized of the matter.

RESOLUTION 986 (1995)
of 14 April 1995

The Security Council,

Recalling its previous relevant resolutions,

Concerned by the serious nutritional and health situation of the Iraqi population, and by the risk of a further deterioration in this situation,

Convinced of the need as a temporary measure to provide for the humanitarian needs of the Iraqi people until the fulfilment by Iraq of the relevant Security Council resolutions, including notably resolution 687 (1991) of 3 April 1991, allows the Council to take further action with regard to the prohibitions referred to in resolution 661 (1990) of 6 August 1990, in accordance with the provisions of those resolutions,

Convinced also of the need for equitable distribution of humanitarian relief to all segments of the Iraqi population throughout the country,

Reaffirming the commitment of all Member States to the sovereignty and territorial integrity of Iraq,

Acting under Chapter VII of the Charter of the United Nations,

1. *Authorizes* States, notwithstanding the provisions of paragraphs 3 (*a*), 3 (*b*) and 4 of resolution 661 (1990) and subsequent relevant resolutions, to permit the import of petroleum and petroleum products originating in Iraq, including financial and other essential transactions directly relating thereto, sufficient to produce a sum not exceeding a total of one billion United States dollars every 90 days for the purposes set out in this resolution and subject to the following conditions:

(*a*) Approval by the Committee established by resolution 661 (1990), in order to ensure the transparency of each transaction and its conformity with the other provisions of this resolution, after submission of an application by the State concerned, endorsed by the Government of Iraq, for each proposed purchase of Iraqi petroleum and petroleum products, including details of the purchase price at fair market value, the export route, the opening of a letter of credit payable to the escrow account to be established by the Secretary-General for the purposes of this resolution, and of any other directly related financial or other essential transaction;

(*b*) Payment of the full amount of each purchase of Iraqi petroleum and petroleum products directly by the purchaser in the State concerned into the escrow account to be established by the Secretary-General for the purposes of this resolution;

2. *Authorizes* Turkey, notwithstanding the provisions of paragraphs 3 (*a*), 3 (*b*) and 4 of resolution 661 (1990) and the provisions of paragraph 1 above, to permit the import of petroleum and petroleum products originating in Iraq sufficient, after the deduction of the percentage referred to in paragraph 8 (*c*) below for the Compensation Fund, to meet the pipeline tariff charges, verified as reasonable by the independent inspection agents referred to in paragraph 6 below, for the transport of Iraqi petroleum and petroleum products through the Kirkuk–Yumurtalik pipeline in Turkey authorized by paragraph 1 above;

3. *Decides* that paragraphs 1 and 2 of this resolution shall come into force at 00.01 Eastern Standard Time on the day after the President of the Council has informed the members of the Council that he has received the report from the Secretary-General requested in paragraph 13 below, and shall remain in force for an initial period of 180 days unless the Council takes other relevant action with regard to the provisions of resolution 661 (1990);

4. *Further decides* to conduct a thorough review of all aspects of the implementation of this resolution 90 days after the entry into force of paragraph 1 above and again prior to the end of the initial 180 day period, on receipt of the reports referred to in paragraphs 11 and 12 below, and *expresses its intention*, prior to the end of the 180 day period, to consider favourably renewal of the provisions of this resolution, provided that the reports referred to in paragraphs 11 and 12 below indicate that those provisions are being satisfactorily implemented;

5. *Further decides* that the remaining paragraphs of this resolution shall come into force forthwith;

6. *Directs* the Committee established by resolution 661 (1990) to monitor the sale of petroleum and petroleum products to be exported by Iraq via the Kirkuk–Yumurtalik pipeline from Iraq to Turkey and from the Mina al-Bakr oil terminal, with the assistance of independent inspection agents appointed by the Secretary-General, who will keep the Committee informed of the amount of petroleum and petroleum products exported from Iraq after the date of entry into force of paragraph 1 of this resolution, and will verify that the purchase price of the petroleum and petroleum products is reasonable in the light of prevailing market conditions, and that, for the purposes of the arrangements set out in this resolution, the larger share of the petroleum and petroleum products is shipped via the Kirkuk–Yumurtalik pipeline and the remainder is exported from the Mina al-Bakr oil terminal;

7. *Requests* the Secretary-General to establish an escrow account for the purposes of this resolution, to appoint independent and certified public accountants to audit it, and to keep the Government of Iraq fully informed;

8. *Decides* that the funds in the escrow account shall be used to meet the humanitarian needs of the Iraqi population and for the following other purposes, and *requests* the Secretary-General to use the funds deposited in the escrow account:

(*a*) To finance the export to Iraq, in accordance with the procedures of the Committee established by resolution 661 (1990), of medicine, health supplies, foodstuffs, and materials and supplies for essential civilian needs, as referred to in paragraph 20 of resolution 687 (1991) provided that:

(i) Each export of goods is at the request of the Government of Iraq;
(ii) Iraq effectively guarantees their equitable distribution, on the basis of a plan submitted to and approved by the Secretary-General, including a description of the goods to be purchased;
(iii) The Secretary-General receives authenticated confirmation that the exported goods concerned have arrived in Iraq;

(*b*) To complement, in view of the exceptional circumstances prevailing in the three Governorates mentioned below, the distribution by the Government of Iraq of goods imported under this resolution, in order to ensure an equitable distribution of humanitarian relief to all segments of the Iraqi population throughout the country, by providing between 130 million and 150 million United States dollars every 90 days to the United Nations Inter-Agency Humanitarian Programme operating within the sovereign territory of Iraq in the three northern Governorates of Dihouk, Arbil and Suleimaniych, except that if less than one billion United States dollars worth of petroleum or petroleum products is sold during any 90 day period, the Secretary-General may provide a proportionately smaller amount for this purpose;

(*c*) To transfer to the Compensation Fund the same percentage of the funds deposited in the escrow account as that decided by the Council in paragraph 2 of resolution 705 (1991) of 15 August 1991;

(*d*) To meet the costs to the United Nations of the independent inspection agents and the certified public accountants and the activities associated with implementation of this resolution;

(*e*) To meet the current operating costs of the Special Commission, pending subsequent payment in full of the costs of carrying out the tasks authorized by section C of resolution 687 (1991);

(*f*) To meet any reasonable expenses, other than expenses payable in Iraq, which are determined by the Committee established by resolution 661 (1990) to be directly related to the export by Iraq of petroleum and petroleum products permitted under paragraph 1 above or to the export to Iraq, and activities directly necessary therefor, of the parts and equipment permitted under paragraph 9 below;

(*g*) To make available up to 10 million United States dollars every 90 days from the funds deposited in the escrow account for the payments envisaged under paragraph 6 of resolution 778 (1992) of 2 October 1992;

9. *Authorizes* States to permit, notwithstanding the provisions of paragraph 3 (*c*) of resolution 661 (1990):

(*a*) The export to Iraq of the parts and equipment which are essential for the safe operation of the Kirkuk–Yumurtalik pipeline system in Iraq, subject to the prior approval by the Committee established by resolution 661 (1990) of each export contract;

(*b*) Activities directly necessary for the exports authorized under subparagraph (*a*) above, including financial transactions related thereto;

10. *Decides* that, since the costs of the exports and activities authorized under paragraph 9 above are precluded by paragraph 4 of resolution 661 (1990) and by paragraph 11 of resolution 778 (1991) from being met from funds frozen in accordance with those provisions, the cost of such exports and activities may, until funds begin to be paid into the escrow account established for the purposes of this resolution, and following approval in each case by the Committee established by resolution 661 (1990), exceptionally be financed by letters of credit, drawn against future oil sales the proceeds of which are to be deposited in the escrow account;

11. *Requests* the Secretary-General to report to the Council 90 days after the date of entry into force of paragraph 1 above, and again prior to the end of the initial 180 day period, on the basis of observation by United Nations personnel in Iraq, and on the basis of consultations with the Government of Iraq, on whether Iraq has ensured the equitable distribution of medicine, health supplies, foodstuffs, and materials and supplies for essential civilian needs, financed in accordance with paragraph 8 (*a*) above, including in his reports any observations he may have on the adequacy of the revenues to meet Iraq's humanitarian needs, and on Iraq's capacity to export sufficient quantities of petroleum and petroleum products to produce the sum referred to in paragraph 1 above;

12. *Requests* the Committee established by resolution 661 (1990), in close coordination with the Secretary-General, to develop expedited procedures as necessary to implement the arrangements in paragraphs 1, 2, 6, 8, 9 and 10 of this resolution and to report to the Council 90 days after the date of entry into force of paragraph 1 above and again prior to the end of the initial 180 day period on the implementation of those arrangements;

13. *Requests* the Secretary-General to take the actions necessary to ensure the effective implementation of this resolution, authorizes him to enter into any necessary arrangements or agreements, and *requests* him to report to the Council when he has done so;

14. *Decides* that petroleum and petroleum products subject to this resolution shall while under Iraqi title be immune from legal proceedings and not be subject to any form of attachment, garnishment or execution, and that all States shall take any steps that may be necessary under their respective domestic legal systems to assure this protection, and to ensure that the proceeds of the sale are not diverted from the purposes laid down in this resolution;

15. *Affirms* that the escrow account established for the purposes of this resolution enjoys the privileges and immunities of the United Nations;

16. *Affirms* that all persons appointed by the Secretary-General for the purpose of implementing this resolution enjoy privileges and immunities as experts on mission for the United Nations in accordance with the Convention on the Privileges and Immunities of the United Nations, and *requires* the Government of Iraq to allow them full freedom of movement and all necessary facilities for the discharge of their duties in the implementation of this resolution;

17. *Affirms* that nothing in this resolution affects Iraq's duty scrupulously to adhere to all of its obligations concerning servicing and repayment of its foreign debt, in accordance with the appropriate international mechanisms;

18. *Also affirms* that nothing in this resolution should be construed as infringing the sovereignty or territorial integrity of Iraq;

19. *Decides* to remain seized of the matter.

Appendix 6

Rights of the Child, Note Verbale
(16 January 1995) from Iraq to UN Centre
for Human Rights, Geneva

THE IMPACT OF THE EMBARGO ON IRAQI CHILDREN IN THE LIGHT OF THE CONVENTION ON THE RIGHTS OF THE CHILD

I. THE RIGHTS OF THE CHILD IN INTERNATIONAL INSTRUMENTS

1. International concern for the rights of the child was first manifested in the days of the League of Nations, which adopted the Geneva Declaration on 26 September 1924. That Declaration contained seven principles, which focused on the protection, assistance, development, nutrition and upbringing of children, as well as their preservation from disasters and their enjoyment of social security.

2. On 10 December 1948, the General Assembly of the United Nations adopted the Universal Declaration of Human Rights, article 25, paragraph 2, of which stipulated that: 'Motherhood and childhood are entitled to special care and assistance. All children, whether born in or out of wedlock, shall enjoy the same social protection.'

3. On 20 November 1959, the General Assembly of the United Nations proclaimed a Declaration of the Rights of the Child, which comprised a preamble and 10 principles. These principles specified, for the first time, the most important human rights that children should enjoy, such as the right to physical, mental, moral and social development, the right to enjoy the benefits of social security, the right to treatment for the physically, mentally or socially handicapped, the right to parental care, the right to education, the right to protection against all forms of neglect, cruelty and exploitation and the right to protection from all practices which might foster racial, religious or any other form of discrimination. Since its proclamation, this Declaration has virtually become a guideline for private and public endeavours to further the interests of children.

4. The two International Covenants (the International Covenant on Economic, Social and Cultural Rights and the International Covenant on Civil and Political Rights), which were adopted on 16 December 1966, incorporated some of the fundamental rights of the child, such as: the right to protection from economic and social exploitation, the right to enjoy the highest standard of health and the right to enjoy the protection and care of their family and society as long as they are minors.

5. In view of the importance of children for the present and future of the world, there was a need to endow the rights of the child with the force of a legal instrument. Accordingly, in 1978, Poland submitted a draft convention on the rights of the child to the Commission on Human Rights, following which a working group was established, under the chairmanship of Professor Adam Lupatka, the delegate of Poland, to elaborate the draft convention. The group held a series of meetings from 1979 to 1989. The Convention on the Rights of the Child was adopted by the General Assembly of the United Nations on 20 November 1989 and entered into force on 2 September 1990 when it became part of international law.

6. The main principles embodied in the Convention can be summarized as follows:

(*a*) Every child has the inherent right to life and the States Parties shall ensure to the maximum extent possible the survival and development of the child.

(*b*) States shall ensure that every child enjoys his or her full rights without being subjected to any form of discrimination or segregation.

(*c*) Parents have the primary responsibility for the upbringing of the child and States shall render them the requisite assistance and shall ensure the development of institutions for the care of children.

(*d*) States shall ensure that the child is protected from physical or mental injury and neglect.

(*e*) Disabled children are entitled to receive special treatment, education and care.

(*f*) A child has a right to the highest attainable standard of health.

(*g*) States shall ensure that all children enjoy health care, with emphasis on preventive measures, health education and a diminution of infant mortality.

(*h*) Primary education must be compulsory and free of charge.

(*i*) Children must be granted time to rest and engage in recreational activities and must be given equal opportunities to engage in cultural activities.

(*j*) States shall protect children from economic exploitation and from any work that is likely to interfere with a child's education or to be harmful to the child's health.

(*k*) No child under 15 years of age shall be involved in military operations and children who are victims of armed conflict should be afforded special protection.

More than 160 States, including Iraq, have so far acceded to the Convention.

Appendix 6

II. IMPACT OF THE EMBARGO ON IRAQI CHILDREN

7. A compulsory and comprehensive embargo was imposed on Iraq under the terms of Security Council resolution 661 of 8 August 1990. Although medicines and foodstuffs were exempted, in practice this exemption was to no avail since Iraq was denied any opportunity to obtain financial resources following the ban on the export of its petroleum and the freezing of its assets abroad. In addition, Iraq was prevented from importing medical, laboratory and pharmaceutical requisites and various medicines that it had contracted to purchase and the price of which it had paid in hard currency before 2 August 1990.

8. The shortage of food and medicine had a greater impact on children due to their vulnerability and their physical and mental immaturity. The effects of their present sufferings will extend into the future, thereby paralysing and destroying society, particularly if we bear in mind the fact that, according to the latest UNICEF statistical report, the number of Iraqi children in the 0–15 age group amounted to about 8.9 million in 1992.

9. Since the embargo was imposed, the mortality rate from certain diseases among children under 15 years of age has increased in comparison with the pre-embargo rate.

For example, we find that the number of deaths from diarrhoea increased from 96 in November 1989 to 1,270 in November 1994. In the case of pneumonia, the number of deaths increased from 110 in November 1989 to 1,551 in November 1994. The number of deaths from malnutrition increased from 52 in November 1989 to 1,741 in November 1994.

10. The number of deaths in the under-five age group from various causes attributable to the embargo were as shown in the table.

Year	Number of deaths	Year	Number of deaths
1989	7,110	1992	46,933
1990	8,903	1993	49,762
1991	27,473	1994 (Jan.–Sept.)	38,844

11. All this is happening to the children of Iraq even though article 6, paragraph 1, of the Convention on the Rights of the Child stipulates that 'States Parties recognize that every child has the inherent right to life', while article 24, paragraph 2, places the States Parties under an obligation to take appropriate measures to diminish infant and child mortality. In paragraph 20 of the World Declaration on the Survival, Protection and Development of Children, the world leaders attending the World Summit for Children held at New York on 30 September 1990 undertook to work for a solid effort of national and international action to enhance children's health, to promote pre-natal care and to lower infant and child mortality in all countries.

12. Since the beginning of the embargo, the proportion of children born with a birth weight of less than 2.5 kg has risen sharply from around 4.5 per cent in 1990 to 21.5 per cent in 1994. This means that many of those Iraqi children will be afflicted with deformities or disabilities due to the shortage of basic foodstuffs for expectant mothers, who are therefore exposed to the dangers of anaemia and diseases associated with malnutrition, which stunt the natural growth of their unborn or newborn children.

13. The monthly average number of children under five years of age suffering from vitanition rose from 41 in 1990 to 1,797 in 1994 and the average number of cases of emaciation due to malnutrition increased from 433 in 1990 to 16,006 in 1994. The disease kwashiorkor (protein deficiency) had been unknown in Iraq for many years, but 1,744 cases of this disease are now reported every month.

14. The infliction of such suffering on Iraqi children is totally incompatible with the provisions of the Convention on the Rights of the Child, article 6, paragraph 2, of which stipulates that 'States Parties shall ensure to the maximum extent possible the survival and development of the child.' Article 24, paragraph 2, further stipulates that 'States Parties shall take appropriate measures: . . . (c) To combat disease and malnutrition, including within the framework of primary health care; (d) To ensure appropriate pre-natal and post-natal health care for mothers.'

15. The effects of the embargo are not confined to the physical aspect. A field survey undertaken by two members of the teaching staff at the Mustansiriya University and supervised by the Iraqi Child Support Association clearly showed that the psychological, social and educational consequences of the embargo were just as severe as its physical consequences. The survey, which took a whole year to complete and ended in March 1993, was based on a sample of 2,000 male and female children from 50 schools dispersed throughout the city of Baghdad. Its findings were as follows:

(a) There was an increased feeling of fear and anxiety due to the child's exposure to frustration and repression. Children's anxiety is usually expressed through tears and insomnia and, according to Fisher's formula (probable average), the incidence of this condition amounted to 22.2 before the embargo and increased to 49.4 after the embargo.

(b) There was an increased desire to acquire and possess things due to the fact that the children's basic needs were not satisfied. The incidence of this amounted to 20.9 before the embargo and increased to 48.8 after the embargo. This state of affairs led to the emergence of the phenomenon of theft among children, particularly in regard to money, academic requisites and food.

(c) There was an increase in excitability and irritability, the incidence of which amounted to 21.7 before the embargo and 47.4 after the embargo.

(d) There was an increase in lying among children, the incidence of which amounted to 24 before the embargo and 51.9 after the embargo.

(e) There was an increase in aggressive behaviour in some children, the incidence of which amounted to 22.5 before the embargo and increased to 43.9 after the embargo due to frustration, deprivation of desired items and hunger.

(f) There was an increase in the incidence of insularity and social introversion, which amounted to 21.6 before the embargo and increased to 40.6 after the embargo.

(g) The incidence of the phenomenon of falling asleep during studies increased from 18 before the embargo to 33.7 after the embargo due to the fact that children were deprived of proteins and vitamins, particularly vitamin B and iodine.

(h) The incidence of loss of self-confidence increased from 22.3 before the embargo to 40.1 after the embargo due to fear and the disturbed family environment.

(i) The degree of difficulty that children experienced in concentrating and paying attention increased from 25.3 before the embargo to 50.9 after the embargo. The degree of difficulty in assimilating and understanding increased from 25.2 before the embargo to 50.7 after the embargo. The degree of difficulty in remembering increased from 25.7 before the embargo to 49.7 after the embargo.

(j) Some adverse educational phenomena increased. For example, the incidence of failure to do homework increased from 24 before the embargo to 50.7 after the embargo; the incidence of failure to assume responsibility increased from 23 before the embargo to 45.8 after the embargo and the incidence of truancy from school increased from 19.3 before the embargo to 37.2 thereafter.

(k) The incidence of ill-treatment of children by their families increased from 21.6 before the embargo to 42.5 after the embargo due to the problems that families were experiencing and which usually lead to juvenile delinquency and a feeling of deprivation and mental anxiety.

The above-mentioned results are totally incompatible with the provisions of article 39 of the Convention on the Rights of the Child, which stipulates that 'States Parties shall take all appropriate measures to promote physical and psychological recovery and social reintegration of a child victim of cruel, inhuman or degrading treatment or punishment or armed conflicts. Such recovery and reintegration shall take place in an environment which fosters the health, self-respect and dignity of the child.'

16. The consequences of the embargo have not been confined to aspects of the physical and mental health of Iraq's children; they also extend to education, since the embargo has prompted large numbers of students to abandon their studies in order to work in the private sector and help their parents or guardians to meet their living expenses. Families are also faced with the need to buy clothing for their children, to meet the cost of transport from home to school and vice-versa and to pay high prices for stationery.

All this has helped to increase the phenomenon of drop-outs, the number of whom amounted to 73,381 primary school children during the academic year 1993/94. The number of drop-outs from secondary education during the same year amounted to 56,816 male and female students. There was also a decline in the primary school enrolment rate among children in the compulsory-education age group. The number of pupils enrolled for primary education during the present academic year 1994/95 amounted to 3,392,560 as compared with a planned enrolment of 3,745,532, i.e. a deficit of 352,972 children who should be attending school.

17. The embargo has had an extremely serious impact on the school environment. Out of a total of 11,000 school buildings, 8,613 are in need of renovation and are suffering from maintenance and sanitation problems due to the aerial bombardment by the Coalition States during the aggression against Iraq when those buildings that were not destroyed in the bombardment were destroyed by gangs of thugs. As a result, the remaining schools are overcrowded with students, who spend the shortest possible time there. The hygienic environment in the schools has deteriorated, thereby exposing students to the risk of infectious diseases, and the situation has been aggravated by the lack of disinfectants, detergents and medicines due to the embargo.

18. The impact of the embargo on the drop-out rate from primary and secondary schools, as well as the deplorable condition of those schools, are clearly shown by the above-mentioned statistics. This situation is incompatible with the provisions of article 28, paragraph 1, of the Convention on the Rights of the Child, which stipulates that 'States Parties recognize the right of the child to education.' Subparagraph (*a*) places the States Parties under an obligation to 'make primary education compulsory and available free to all', while subparagraph (*e*) obliges the States Parties to 'take measures to encourage regular attendance at schools and the reduction of drop-out rates'.
The need for students to drop out from school in order to seek employment is totally incompatible with article 32 of the Convention on the Rights of the Child, which stipulates that 'States Parties recognize the right of the child to be protected from economic exploitation and from performing any work that is likely to be hazardous or to interfere with the child's education.'

19. From the above, it is evident that the bodies, minds and mentalities of Iraqi children are constantly being sapped by the embargo, which is depriving them of the fundamental requirements needed to safeguard their lives. There are no basic vaccines, no balanced nutrition and no preventive or curative medication. This runs totally counter to the universal ethical principle to the effect that premature death or disability at a time when means to prevent them are available should be regarded, like colonialism and racism, as abhorrent to the human conscience.

20. The failure of States to take positive measures to lift or alleviate the embargo that has been imposed on the people of Iraq means that there is negative international cooperation to maintain it. This is incompatible with the Charter of the United Nations and the purposes and principle for which

that Organization was established. Article 1, paragraph 3, of the Charter stipulates that one of the purposes of the United Nations is to achieve international cooperation in solving international problems of an economic, social, cultural or humanitarian character, and in promoting and encouraging respect for human rights and for fundamental freedoms for all. That negative attitude is also incompatible with the Convention on the Rights of the Child, article 24, paragraph 4, of which stipulates that 'States Parties undertake to promote and encourage international cooperation with a view to achieving progressively the full realization of the right recognized in the present article (concerning enjoyment of the highest attainable standard of health). In this regard, particular account shall be taken of the needs of developing countries.'

21. The people of Iraq, and particularly their children, are faced with destruction by a weapon that is just as horrendous as any weapon of mass destruction, namely the economic embargo weapon to which one million persons, half of whom were children, have fallen victim during the last four years.

This destruction is a form of genocide of the people of Iraq: it is an international crime punishable under international law, regardless of whether it is committed in time of war or peace.

Article 2 of the Convention on the Prevention and Punishment of the Crime of Genocide defines acts of genocide as: killing members of the (ethnic or religious) group; causing serious bodily or mental harm to members of the group; or deliberately inflicting on the group conditions of life calculated to bring about its physical destruction in whole or in part.

22. These acts are undoubtedly being committed deliberately through the imposition and maintenance of the economic embargo which can no longer be justified now that the reasons that led to its imposition no longer apply.

Appendix 7

The Impact of the Blockade on Iraq, Note Verbale (16 January 1995) from Iraq to UN Centre for Human Rights, Geneva – Extract

The health care available in many parts of the world is significantly inferior to that available in North America and Western Europe. Many conditions go undiagnosed and untreated in these parts. The two primary reasons for these diminished health care conditions are capital constraint and lack of educational awareness. But here in Iraq it is not the awareness but the 'Educational Blockade', which has been imposed on Iraq. Medical equipment needs services, training and spare parts.

The impact of the sanctions on the health care is very serious and grave:

1. The capital constraint with reduced budget.

2. Partial utilization of the already squeezed budget of health care, because of the blockade on the import which has led to serious shortage in drugs and other life saving measures and medical equipment. Even a number of shipments of medicines ordered and paid for prior to August 1990 has not been delivered.

3. Reduction in the number of hospital beds available per capita of population in addition to reduced bed occupancy to 25–30%.

4. Lower nutritional status of the community which has led to increased morbidity and mortality.

5. Insecure local environment with its increased effect and added strains on the community plus lack of vaccines and irregular immunization programmes which has led to appalling increase in the morbidity and mortality from infectious diseases.

6. Delayed or Misdiagnoses

(*a*) Because of delayed attendance for consultations due to lack or very high cost of transportation.

(*b*) Lack of facilities for laboratory investigations to do minimum tests available for daily routine manual methods, let alone the absence of advanced methods which are not performed in the country. Those who can afford have to travel abroad to do these investigations.

(c) Lack of X-ray films, developers and dyes with breakdown of X-ray machines and other equipment due to lack of spare parts and inadequate maintenance.

(d) Lack of endoscopes with lack of newer endoscopic procedures and other non-invasive methods.

(e) Lack of new ultrasound and echocardiography equipment.

(f) Lack and breakdown of cardiac cath. Laboratories with the long waiting list of patients.

(g) C.A.T. Scan: no C.A.T. Scan available in the town.

(h) Magnetic Resonance Imaging is a dream.

So for diagnosis we are back to the era where we have to use our clinical sense and experience deprived of the new technology in medicine with frequent delayed or misdiagnosis.

7. The Treatment

The dilemma of the doctor and the patient starts when we have labeled the disease with a name i.e. the diagnosis, waiting hopefully for the treatment to relieve the patient's suffering or to cure his disease, with drugs adequate in quantity and quality, but in vain. Then we have to be satisfied with the nearest alternative and the minimum possible dose. Here the health care system rightly has introduced drug rationing.

8. 'Drug Ration'

Drug rationing is to secure the supply of drugs to those with chronic diseases, i.e. drugs for cardio vascular system (C.V.S.), indocrine disease, peptic ulcer, bronchial asthma, etc., with a cheap subsidised price, a very noble good policy which ensures the treatment to be continued, in spite of a few defects:

(1) The process of organizing the chronic diseases certificate is rather tedious for some patients, there is a gap between immediate diagnosis and immediate requirement of the patient 'which might be urgent', and the supply of the drug through the certificate.

(2) The treatment has to be changed according to the alternative drugs available.

(3) The dose has to be reduced by the centre because of the reduced storage, and sometimes has to be cut altogether.

9. Drugs in Private Pharmacies

The Ministry of Health is the only body responsible for drug importation and distribution. Because of the low amount of imported drugs or insufficient amount manufactured, the supply of the drugs to the private pharmacies (other than the items included in the chronic illness certificate) is not enough and there is the problem with those patients, obtaining the drug in lower quantities with rather higher prices. So you can imagine how this lack of drugs leads to increased suffering with increased morbidity and mortality rates.

10. Embargo and its Effect on Educational and Medical Experience

(1) Lack of medical journals, papers, periodicals, literature and recently published books.

(2) Lack of attendance to the medical conferences abroad:

   (a) No hard currency.
   (b) No visa issued.

(3) Lack of visiting expertise to the country, who used to come for teaching, consultation, to do surgical procedures and attend local medical conferences.

(4) No scholarships for postgraduate studies, refresher and training courses.

The health aspects of Iraqi children are severely affected by the embargo. The impact has included the nutritional, preventive, diagnostic, therapeutic, and psychological aspects of children.

Children with malignancy are among those who have suffered the most from the embargo. To demonstrate this effect, we will take the acute lymphocytic leukemia as an example because it is the most common malignancy in children and it is the first neoplasm in which the cure was achieved with the longest survival rate.

Basically in this study we will compare between the outcome of those children before and after embargo; the year of aggression (1991) will not be included because of the problems in transportation, the relocations of some families, etc.

The parameters studied are: the number of the new patients, the relapsing rate (recurrence of the disease) in terms of systemic and extramedullary (outside the bone marrow), and the mortality rate. The children studies are those who attend Saddam teaching hospital for children.

The study revealed a progressive increase in the number of the new patients after the embargo through the successive years (Table 1).

TABLE 1

Year	1990	1992	1993	1994 (first 6 months)
No. of new cases	10	47	75	47
percentage increase		470%	750%	940%

For the systemic relapse, a similar result was obtained in terms of increase in the rate of relapse (as we see from Table 2).

TABLE 2

Year	1990	1992	1993	1994 (first 6 months)
No. of relapses	19	58	75	45
percentage increase		300%	400%	470%

The extramedullary relapse (outside the bone marrow) revealed a similar result with a continuous increase in the number of patients who relapsed over the years during embargo (Table 3).

TABLE 3

Year	1990	1992	1993	1994 (first 6 months)
No. of relapses	5	19	27	19
Pecentage increase	100%	380%	540%	760%

The mortality rate also increased (as we see from Table 4).

TABLE 4

Year	1990	1992	1993	1994 (first 6 months)
No. of deaths	20	33	35	20
percentage increase	100%	160%	175%	200%

The results obtained in this study regarding the outcome of children with acute leukemia are highly significant in comparison between the embargo years and the year before in all parameters, which indicates a continuous deterioration in the health of our children as a result of unjustified embargo.

The aggressive war on Iraq in 1991 brought about massive destruction in many elements of the country's physical and service infrastructure. The most immediate consequence was the environment: there are reported outbreaks of cholera and of other infectious diseases, these communicable diseases which Iraq succeeded to eradicate are now widespread. According to the World Health Organization, Harvard Study Team and Unicef, the rate of mortality is 6–8 times greater than before the outset of the war. These may include but are in no way limited to: Typhoid, Paratyphoid, Dysentery, Hepatitis and Poliomyelitis.

Medical Supplies

1. It has frequently been announced by the United Nations that foodstuffs and medicines are exempted from the Sanction Resolutions. Yet, the following examples bear abundant evidence that medicine embargo is still in effect if not on the increase and that it is targeted mostly against the people of Iraq.

(a) We attach herewith a copy of the telex sent by the British B. Wellcome Drug Company. It is self-explanatory. It was received from Britain; a country which claims it promotes and advocates human rights. The telex informed us of the British Government's disapproval for the export of Angised tablets to Iraq. These tablets are normally used for the treatment of angina pectoris. They are very important as they are life-sustaining drugs, without which a patient has no or little opportunity for survival. Iraq has already paid US$150,000 for the supply of 150,000 bottles of the drug. The quantity asked for accounts for only 20 per cent of Iraq's annual needs. Yet, the British Government did not allow the export of the drug. It said it contained glycerin trinitrate and there was likelihood that Iraq might use this substance making bombs!! Everyone with special medical knowledge knows that this substance is made in the form of tablets and that it contains less than a milligram of it, and if Iraq, for the sake of argument, has ordered hundreds of tons of the substance, a quantity that takes several years for the company to produce, then it wouldn't be possible for Iraq to develop even one bomb.

(b) The second case in point is the letter addressed by the Ministry of Health to the Atomic Energy Agency in Vienna for the supply of radio-active isotopes for the treatment of cancerous diseases. The Agency told us that it had used its influence to obtain the isotopes from the manufacturing company but nothing happened in effect. If this kind of dealing is of any indication, it reveals a blatant desire to maintain the sanctions imposed on Iraq and to further increase the rate of deaths among the patients. The supply of the isotopes has been suspended since August 1990 in spite of the fact that Iraq has already paid their costs.

(c) International inspection teams have destroyed all the available quantities of ammonium nitrate, a substance used locally for the production of nitrous oxide in large cylinders. This anesthetic agent proved to be highly effective for the cases of difficult deliveries that need cesarean section operations. When manufactured locally it is more economical than the ones imported from abroad as they come in large cylinders and are sent by air. It followed that a severe and acute shortage of this preparation had been reported in ante-natal hospitals with the consequent deaths of pregnant women or of the foetuses in the wombs. The Unicef representative in Baghdad was formally invited to be actually present to see these cases. Full with amazement he sent a telex to his organization's headquarters asking for a prompt shipment of the cylinders that contain the substance. The process has proved to be both lengthy and complicated. The required cylinders had to be sent from Copenhagen to Amman by air and from Amman to Baghdad by land. It seems they haven't realized how much time and effort it will take to respond to such a matter of great urgency. It is clearly contrary to the medical code of ethics.

2. There are many other examples in support of our claim. It goes without saying that with the lack of life-sustaining drugs no quality medical care can be provided properly. It is the allied countries which try, from time to time, to obstruct the delivery of medical supplies on which the patients' continued existence depends. They adopted a far more uncompromising attitude when they turned down a proposal to unfreeze Iraq's assets held in foreign banks for the purchase of medicines and health supplies. Every time they asked to do so they gave and indeed are still giving numerous excuses for being more of a hindrance than a help. They began to ask such amusingly foolish questions as: What is the quantity required? What is your annual need? How much of the medicines asked for have you already dispensed? What is the rate of morbidity? Are the documents duly signed? Has our representative in Baghdad ratified them? All these questions and many others have one underlying purpose; to delay any shipment of medicines to Iraq.

3. Between January and August 1990 Iraq paid more than 56 million dollars in cash to different companies in Germany, Britain, Japan, USA, and Italy for the supply of medicines. However, a large number of the contracts negotiated and signed with these companies had not been executed. This happened in spite of our repeated confirmations and of the talks held with the companies' representatives in Geneva in 1992 under the supervision of the International Committee of the Red Cross. The delegates indicated that Iraq's goods had been withheld for the time being and that they all desire to deal with Iraq but they had instructions from their respective governments not to send the goods to Iraq!

4. The prevalence of malnutrition among the infants, lactating mothers and pregnant women together with the acute shortage of baby formula have diminished the children's resistance to diseases. This condition of not getting enough food or enough of the right kind of food has had a profoundly adverse impact on the health of pregnant women and lactating mothers. Hence, there has been a sudden and striking incidence of low birth weight babies (less than 2.5 kg) or of feeding difficulties. If we take these two factors combined they would eventually lead to further complications or even death.

5. Proceeding from the above, the number of deaths between August 1990 and March 1994, as a result of the international sanctions and of other reasons; direct and indirect, has totalled 431,093 of which 153,448 were for children under five years of age and 277,645 for the age group five and above. Besides, the functioning of the medical system in general has been severely and tremendously affected.

There are three factors influencing the treatment of patients: medical personnel, equipments and medical supplies for diagnosis, and thirdly drugs. This is a fact nobody can deny. Therefore, any disturbance or lack in one of these three elements will have negative reflexes on the social, economical, mental and physical aspects of the patient.

Drugs like antibiotics play a significant role in both the curative and preventive processes of treatment because they are prescribed and used in many diseases and surgical operations.

The impact of the sanctions affected health services all over the country due to the shortage of drugs and medical supplies. The reduction of drug supplies as well as the infected environment, malnutrition, unclean water supply, all these factors helped many diseases to spread out and make the situation even worse.

The figures and data mentioned in this paper are supplied by official sources concerning the amount of drug supplies to both sectors (Government and private).

OBJECTIVES

1. To demonstrate the effects of drug shortage due to the sanctions on health services.
2. To demonstrate the effects of continuous sanctions on the prevalence of diseases.

3. To give a comparison between the rate per person of drugs used for communicable and chronic diseases before and after the sanctions.

MATERIALS AND METHODS

The scope of work was to investigate in three main issues in order to find the relationship between these elements 'population, disease, and drugs'. To reach the objectives:

1. Select the total number of patients attacked in each of eight communicable diseases (measles, pneumonia, cholera, typhoid, amoebiasis, meningitis, Baghdad boil and Malta fever) and calculate the need of antibiotics per person.

2. Select the total number of patients attacked in each of three main chronic diseases (diabetes, cardiovascular, and hypertension) to compare the share for each patient of the drugs distributed for these particular diseases before and after the embargo.

3. To find the rate of increase in selected communicable and chronic diseases compared with the increased rate of population.

4. 1989 was considered as standard year.

RESULTS

1. There was a sharp decline in antibiotics supply per individual during the sanctions years 1990–93, compared with the year 1989, e.g. rate of decrease in no. of capsules was 33% for 1990 and jumped to 48% for 1993. Also for parenterals the percentage of decrease was 60% in 1993. The reduction of liquid forms of antibiotics reached to 67% for 1992.

2. There was a huge increase in the prevalence of communicable diseases, e.g. measles 100% increase for 1991 and raised to 203% for 1992. The no. of patients in the case of pneumonia reached 234% for 1991, also typhoid cases showed 850% increase in 1991 and 1060% for 1993.

3. The data collected for chronic diseases indicate drastic prevalence in no. of cases with drastic shortages and no availability of drugs used for their treatment during the sanction, e.g. in the case of diabetic patients the rate of medication decreased to 34% in 1991 and 25% in 1993.

4. Cardio-vascular diseases: the percent in reduction of drugs related to these diseases was 29% in 1991; for hypertension the decrease was estimated at 40% in 1991.

The document shown assesses the nature and magnitude of the health problem which the nation is facing with the continuation of the sanctions: reduction in drug supplies, increase of diseases will definitely influence the planning and development of the health services in Iraq. So the issue of treating patients in the right way and right doses with right diagnosis will be obscured and as a result, patients will always be the victims of the sanctions.

Although importation of drugs and medical supplies is not prohibited according to UN Security Council resolutions we found big difficulties in importing drugs because of great unjustified policies applied by drug supply companies and through political pressure of their governments which added a new factor to our bad situation for maintaining our needs of drugs and poor medical supplies in order to serve our patients in health centers to the minimum requirements.

Consumption of drugs increased after 1990 because of the population increase, polluted environment, polluted water, bad health care and malnutrition. All were reflected in a drastic increase in communicable and chronic diseases.

To justify the case with all the information and facts mentioned in this paper, we easily conclude that there is a dilemma in Iraq and a complete negligence of human rights. The existing condition due to the sanctions will deteriorate our national health system and lead us to fearful and worried speculations on health services and nutritional problems for the whole nation.

The embargo needs vital movement today from all nations and organizations to rescue a nation with a population of 20 millions from the greatest crime of the twentieth century, which certainly leaves millions of Iraqi children and elderly people affected by the sanctions with no proper nutrition, medicine or baby milk.

It is the responsibility of all nations and human rights organizations and individuals to start moving to play a bigger role in utilizing all measures, efforts, pressures and potentials to help in lifting this inhuman sanction.

At the end, I hope we have succeeded in our demonstration that the scopes of the sanctions really have a wide effect on our health services which directly influences the curative and health care and consequently on the prevalence of diseases and suffering of sick people, which should be condemned by all people who believe in and serve the cause of human rights and justice.

Appendix 8

Malaysian Conference Resolution (May 1994) against Economic Sanctions on Iraq

1. This International Conference against Economic Sanctions on Iraq, organized by Malaysian non-governmental organizations represented in the Organizing Committee of the Conference, meeting on 26 and 27 May 1994 in this city of Kuala Lumpur, Malaysia:

(*a*) *Noting* that it has been almost four years now since the United Nations Security Council imposed the severest economic sanctions ever witnessed in history on Iraq;

(*b*) *Noting* that Iraq has fully cooperated with various United Nations agencies, missions and teams, as openly admitted and fully acknowledged in particular by Mr Ekéus of the Special United Nations Commission;

(*c*) *Noting* that in spite of Iraq's compliance with all relevant Security Council resolutions, despite their harsh nature, the Security Council, under the influence of the United States of America and its ally the United Kingdom of Great Britain and Northern Ireland, has chosen to maintain economic sanctions against Iraq through the concoction of new demands unrelated to the texts of the relevant resolutions;

(*d*) *Noting* that these murderous sanctions against Iraq already claimed at least 400,000 lives, many of them children and women, while hundreds of thousands of others suffer from malnutrition, disease and hunger brought about by inadequate medical facilities and rapidly deteriorating health conditions;

(*e*) *Noting* that the sanctions regime is depriving Iraq of scientific, medical and educational and cultural materials;

(*f*) *Noting* also that the real motives behind the continued imposition of these cruel, inhuman sanctions against Iraq are to destroy and to render impotent the economic, scientific and technological capability and potential of an Arab nation which until the Gulf war was industrially more advanced than most other Arab States; to control the immense oil wealth of Iraq and the Gulf region; to interfere in Iraq's internal affairs; and to reinforce a power structure in the region which favours the United States, the West and Israel but is inimical to the independence, integrity and sovereignty of the Arab people; and

(*g*) *Noting* also that the economic sanctions imposed on Iraq have also negative impacts on other countries of the world, particularly those which have economic and trade dealings with Iraq, and that the lifting of the sanctions will improve their economic prospects and prosperity;

2. Now therefore solemnly:

(*a*) *Declares* that these sanctions are not only inhuman and unjust but also have been rendered illegal due to 1 (*b*) and (*c*) above;

(*b*) *Salutes* the brave people of Iraq for their indomitable courage, steadfastness and perseverance they have displayed in the face of great adversity, pain and suffering in the last 44 months since sanctions were imposed upon their country;

(*c*) *Calls upon* the Governments of the world to pressure the United Nations Security Council to lift immediately the sanctions against Iraq;

(*d*) *Calls upon* the Governments of the world, desirous of defending their own independence and sovereignty, to break the sanctions imposed upon Iraq by re-establishing trade and other economic ties with Iraq;

(*e*) *Calls upon* the Governments of the world to provide, as a matter of utmost urgency, extensive humanitarian assistance to the suffering people of Iraq. To this purpose, Iraqi frozen assets should be immediately released to allow for purchases of medicine, food and other basic necessities of life;

(*f*) *Calls upon* the Arab League, the Organization of the Islamic Conference (OIC), the Movement of Non-Aligned Countries, and other regional and international organizations to come to the defence of the people of Iraq in their hour of need, to resist United States and British dominance of the global system and to initiate concrete plans and programmes aimed at creating a just world;

(*g*) *Calls upon* citizens, groups and non-governmental organizations throughout the world to launch a massive global campaign to free the people of Iraq from the dominance and hegemony of super-powers so that men, women and children everywhere will be able to live in accordance with the noble values and principles embodied in their great moral and spiritual traditions now and in the future;

(*h*) *Calls upon* progressive governmental and non-governmental third world leaders and leaders of progressive groups in North America, Europe and Japan to initiate discussions and dialogues to work out a common general plan, policy and strategy to free mankind from super-power domination and/or comprehensive and overall cooperation to build a just new world; and

(*i*) *Instructs* the Organizing Committee of the Conference to establish an international working group to carry out the decisions of the Conference as well as to continue the work of this Conference.

ANNEX II

INTERNATIONAL CONFERENCE AGAINST ECONOMIC SANCTIONS ON IRAQ THE MALAYSIAN DECLARATION

Immediately following the end of the cold war, a new situation manifested itself in the form of an Anglo-American dominated 'new world order'. It was intended to give an absolute and unchallengeable lead to these imperialistic forces for world domination by coercive forces and through blatant interference in internal affairs of independent and sovereign nations. The result, however, has been a world characterized by chaos and disorder, a sad prelude to the coming of the twenty-first century.

One of the major manifestations of how this new world order worked was the massive bombing and genocidal war of aggression launched by the United States of America and the United Kingdom of Great Britain and Northern Ireland (with the active compliance of over 33 allies) against a small country, Iraq. It was a major aim of the war, as clearly stated by its instigators, to bomb Iraq back to what was described as 'the pre-industrial era'. The purpose was nothing less than total United States hegemony in the strategic and oil-rich Middle East region.

It was nothing less than the continuation of the policies of several past United States administrations that has led to the present impasse in this strategic region of the world. The United States and its allies partially realized their goals when they inflicted such huge human and material damage on Iraq.

At present, even when Iraq has complied with all the relevant Security Council resolutions, and in particular resolution 687 (1991), the iniquitous economic sanctions imposed on Iraq in 1990 have still not been lifted. They are maintained, and indeed intensified even until this moment, despite the compliance and the mounting sufferings of the Iraqi people.

We call upon the United States and its allies to withdraw all sanctions against the Iraqi people. A decent and humanitarian attitude towards the suffering of the people of Iraq would mandate the Clinton Administration to withdraw the United Nations sanctions immediately. We call for a day of action in different countries demanding the embargo be lifted at the 17 July Security Council meeting.

Even in other parts of the world the people have suffered from the so-called new world order. The United States also manipulated the General Agreement on Tariffs and Trade (GATT)/World Trade Organization (WTO) to serve its sole interests. The third world countries in particular have been made to suffer as a result of the schemings of the World Bank and the International Monetary Fund (IMF) through their high interest rates and loan conditions.

To face such abhorrent behaviour by the United States forces of domination, even though it was by an elite and oligarchic group there, the peace-loving and progressive forces need to unify their ranks and achieve unity of action. The oppressed in today's world are on the increase: injustices are reaching alarming scales. For instance, the implications of the iniquitous economic sanctions imposed on Iraq not only affect Iraq but extend to numerous countries of the world.

The South–South dialogue should be made to work effectively in a world dominated by the North. An objective and productive kind of South–North dialogue, however, must be based upon justice, equality and fair dealings. We should in no way permit the pillage of the wealth of nations; neither should interference in countries' internal affairs be allowed by greedy and power-thirsty countries.

The only way to survival and prosperity of all nations of the world is through building bridges and international coalitions amongst cultures having a universal outlook respecting man and all mankind; dialogues, seminars and conferences should be quickly convened bringing together cultural leaders and philosophers sharing the basic outlook of serving man for whose sake the universe was created, so that a powerful international movement united over socio-economic principles may emerge to bring about the establishment of a 'new just world order' instituted on the moral and spiritual values embodied in all great universal traditions.

Appendix 9

Protocol 1, Addition to the Geneva Conventions, 1977 – Extract

PART IV: CIVILIAN POPULATION

Section I: General Protection Against Effects of Hostilities

Chapter I: Basic Rule and Field of Application

Article 48: Basic Rule

In order to ensure respect for and protection of the civilian population and civilian objects, the Parties to the conflict shall at all times distinguish between the civilian population and combatants and between civilian objects and military objectives and accordingly shall direct their operations only against military objectives.

Article 49: Definition of Attacks and Scope of Application

1. 'Attacks' means acts of violence against the adversary, whether in offense or in defense.

2. The provisions of this Protocol with respect to attacks apply to all attacks in whatever territory conducted, including the national territory belonging to a Party to the conflict but under the control of an adverse Party.

3. The provisions of this Section apply to any land, air or sea warfare which may affect the civilian population, individual civilians or civilian objects on land. They further apply to all attacks from the sea or from the air against objectives on land but do not otherwise affect the rules of international law applicable in armed conflict at sea or in the air.

4. The provisions of this Section are additional to the rules concerning humanitarian protection contained in the Fourth Convention, particularly in Part II thereof, and in other international agreements binding upon the High Contracting Parties, as well as to other rules of international law relating to the protection of civilians and civilian objects on land, at sea or in the air against the effects of hostilities.

Chapter II: Civilians and Civilian Population

Article 50: Definition of Civilians and Civilian Population

1. A civilian is any person who does not belong to one of the categories of persons referred to in Article 4 A (1), (I), (3) and (6) of the Third Convention and in Article 43 of this Protocol. In case of doubt whether a person is a civilian, that person shall be considered to be a civilian.

2. The civilian population comprises all persons who are civilians.

3. The presence within the civilian population of individuals who do not come within the definition of civilians does not deprive the population of its civilian character.

Article 51: Protection of the Civilian Population

1. The civilian population and individual civilians shall enjoy general protection against dangers arising from military operations. To give effect to this protection, the following rules, which are additional to other applicable rules of international law, shall be observed in all circumstances.

2. The civilian population as such, as well as individual civilians, shall not be the object of attack. Acts or threats of violence the primary purpose of which is to spread terror among the civilian population are prohibited.

3. Civilians shall enjoy the protection afforded by this Section, unless and for such time as they take a direct part in hostilities.

4. Indiscriminate attacks are prohibited. Indiscriminate attacks are:

   (*a*) those which are not directed at a specific military objective;

   (*b*) those which employ a method or means of combat which cannot be directed at a specific military objective; or

   (*c*) those which employ a method or means of combat the effects of which cannot be limited as required by this Protocol; and consequently, in each such case, are of a nature to strike military objectives and civilians or civilian objects without distinction.

5. Among others, the following types of attacks are to be considered as indiscriminate:

   (*a*) an attack by bombardment by any methods or means which treats as a single military objective a number of clearly separated and distinct military objectives located in a city, town, village or other area containing a similar concentration of civilians or civilian objects; and

   (*b*) an attack which may be expected to cause incidental loss of civilian life, injury to civilians, damage to civilian objects, or a combination thereof, which would be excessive in relation to the concrete and direct military advantage anticipated.

6. Attacks against the civilian population or civilians by way of reprisals are prohibited.

7. The presence or movements of the civilian population or individual civilians shall not be used to render certain points or areas immune from military operations, in particular in attempts to shield military objectives from attacks or to shield, favor or impede military operations. The Parties to the conflict shall not direct the movement of the civilian population or individual civilians in order to attempt to shield military objectives from attacks or to shield military operations.

8. Any violation of these prohibitions shall not release the Parties to the conflict from their legal obligations with respect to the civilian population and civilians, including the obligation to take the precautionary measures provided for in Article 57.

Chapter III: Civilian Objects

Article 52: General Protection of Civilian Objects

1. Civilian objects shall not be the object of attack or of reprisals. Civilian objects are all objects which are not military objectives as defined in paragraph 2.

2. Attacks shall be limited strictly to military objectives. In so far as objects are concerned, military objectives are limited to those objects which by their nature, location, purpose or use make an effective contribution to military action and whose total or partial destruction, capture or neutralization, in the circumstances ruling at the time, offers a definite military advantage.

3. In case of doubt whether an object which is normally dedicated to civilian purposes, such as a place of worship, a house or other dwelling or a school, is being used to make an effective contribution to military action, it shall be presumed not to be so used.

Article 53: Protection of Cultural Objects and of Places of Worship

Without prejudice to the provisions of the Hague Convention for the Protection of Cultural Property in the Event of Armed Conflict of 14 May 1954, and of other relevant international instruments, it is prohibited:

  (*a*) to commit any acts of hostility directed against the historic monuments, works of art or places of worship which constitute the cultural or spiritual heritage of peoples;

  (*b*) to use such objects in support of the military effort;

  (*c*) to make such objects the object of reprisals.

Article 54: Protection of Objects Indispensable to the Survival of the Civilian Population

1. Starvation of civilians as a method of warfare is prohibited.

2. It is prohibited to attack, destroy, remove or render useless objects indispensable to the survival of the civilian population, such as foodstuffs, agricultural areas for the production of foodstuffs, crops, livestock, drinking water installations and supplies and irrigation works, for the specific purpose of denying them for their sustenance value to the civilian population or to the adverse Party, whatever the motive, whether in order to starve out civilians, to cause them to move away, or for any other motive.

3. The prohibitions in paragraph 2 shall not apply to such of the objects covered by it as are used by an adverse Party:

(a) as sustenance solely for the members of its armed forces; or

(b) if not as sustenance, then in direct support of military action, provided, however, that in no event shall actions against these objects be taken which may be expected to leave the civilian population with such inadequate food or water as to cause its starvation or force its movement.

4. These objects shall not be made the object of reprisals.

5. In recognition of the vital requirements of any Party to the conflict in the defense of its national territory against invasion, derogation from the prohibitions contained in paragraph 2 may be made by a Party to the conflict within such territory under its own control where required by imperative military necessity.

Article 55: Protection of the Natural Environment

1. Care shall be taken in warfare to protect the natural environment against widespread, long-term and severe damage. This protection includes a prohibition of the use of methods or means of warfare which are intended or may be expected to cause such damage to the natural environment and thereby to prejudice the health or survival of the population.

2. Attacks against the natural environment by way of reprisals are prohibited.

Article 56: Protection of Works and Installations Containing Dangerous Forces

1. Works or installations containing dangerous forces, namely dams, dikes and nuclear electrical generating stations, shall not be made the object of attack, even where these objects are military objectives, if such attack may cause the release of dangerous forces and consequent severe losses among the civilian population. Other military objectives located at or in the vicinity of

these works or installations shall not be made the object of attack if such attack may cause the release of dangerous forces from the works or installations and consequent severe losses among the civilian population.

2. The special protection against attack provided by paragraph 1 shall cease:

  (*a*) for a dam or a dike only if it is used for other than its normal function and in regular, significant and direct support of military operations and if such attack is the only feasible way to terminate such support;

  (*b*) for a nuclear electrical generating station only if it provides electric power in regular, significant and direct support of military operations and if such attack is the only feasible way to terminate such support;

  (*c*) for other military objectives located at or in the vicinity of these works or installations only if they are used in regular, significant and direct support of military operations and if such attack is the only feasible way to terminate such support.

3. In all cases, the civilian population and individual civilians shall remain entitled to all the protection accorded them by international law, including the protection of the precautionary measures provided for in Article 57. If the protection ceases and any of the works, installations or military objectives mentioned in paragraph 1 is attacked, all practical precautions shall be taken to avoid the release of the dangerous forces.

4. It is prohibited to make any of the works, installations or military objectives mentioned in paragraph 1 the object of reprisals.

5. The Parties to the conflict shall endeavor to avoid locating any military objectives in the vicinity of the works or installations mentioned in paragraph 1. Nevertheless, installations erected for the sole purpose of defending the protected works or installations from attack are permissible and shall not themselves be made the object of attack, provided that they are not used in hostilities except for defensive actions necessary to respond to attacks against the protected works or installations and that their armament is limited to weapons capable only of repelling hostile action against the protected works or installations.

6. The High Contracting Parties and the Parties to the conflict are urged to conclude further agreements among themselves to provide additional protection for objects containing dangerous forces.

7. In order to facilitate the identification of the objects protected by this Article, the Parties to the conflict may mark them with a special sign consisting of a group of three bright orange circles placed on the same axis, as specified in Article 16 of Annex I to this Protocol. The absence of such marking in no way relieves any Party to the conflict of its obligations under this Article.

Chapter IV: Precautionary Measures

Article 57: Precautions in Attack

1. In the conduct of military operations, constant care shall be taken to spare the civilian population, civilians and civilian objects.

2. With respect to attacks, the following precautions shall be taken:

   (*a*) those who plan or decide upon an attack shall:

      (i) do everything feasible to verify that the objectives to be attacked are neither civilians nor civilian objects and are not subject to special protection but are military objectives within the meaning of paragraph 2 of Article 52 and that it is not prohibited by the provisions of this Protocol to attack them;

      (ii) take all feasible precautions in the choice of means and methods of attack with a view to avoiding, and in any event to minimizing, incidental loss of civilian life, injury to civilians and damage to civilian objects;

      (iii) refrain from deciding to launch any attack which may be expected to cause incidental loss of civilian life, injury to civilians, damage to civilian objects, or a combination thereof, which would be excessive in relation to the concrete and direct military advantage anticipated;

   (*b*) an attack shall be canceled or suspended if it becomes apparent that the objective is not a military one or is subject to special protection or that the attack may be expected to cause incidental loss of civilian life, injury to civilians, damage to civilian objects, or a combination thereof, which would be excessive in relation to the concrete and direct military advantage anticipated;

   (*c*) effective advance warning shall be given of attacks which may affect the civilian population, unless circumstances do not permit.

3. When a choice is possible between several military objectives for obtaining a similar military advantage, the objective to be selected shall be that the attack on which may be expected to cause the least danger to civilian lives and to civilian objects.

4. In the conduct of military operations at sea or in the air, each Party to the conflict shall, in conformity with its rights and duties under the rules of international law applicable in armed conflict, take all reasonable precautions to avoid losses of civilian lives and damage to civilian objects.

5. No provision of this article may be construed as authorizing any attacks against the civilian population, civilians or civilian objects.

Appendix 10

Criminal Complaint Against the United States by Ramsey Clark (14 November 1996), former Attorney General of the United States

CRIMINAL COMPLAINT AGAINST THE UNITED STATES OF AMERICA AND OTHERS FOR CRIMES AGAINST THE PEOPLE OF IRAQ FOR CAUSING THE DEATHS OF MORE THAN 1,500,000 PEOPLE INCLUDING 750,000 CHILDREN UNDER FIVE AND INJURY TO THE ENTIRE POPULATION BY GENOCIDAL SANCTIONS

This Supplemental Complaint* charges: the United States of America, President Bill Clinton, Secretary of State Warren Christopher, Secretary of Defence William Perry, US Ambassador to the United Nations Madeleine Albright, State Department Spokesman Nicholas Burns, the United Kingdom Prime Minister John Major; aided and abetted by United Nations Secretary General Boutros Boutros-Ghali, Rolf Ekeus, Chairman of UN Special Commission on Iraq, and each Member Nation of the Security Council and its UN Ambassador from 1991 to date that failed to act affirmatively to relieve death and suffering caused by United Nations sanctions against the People of Iraq; and others to be named; with genocide, crimes against humanity, the use of a weapon of mass destruction and other crimes specified herein.

The criminal acts charged include the deliberate and intentional imposition, maintenance and enforcement of an economic blockade and sanctions against the people of Iraq from 6 August 1990 to this date will full knowledge constantly communicated that the blockade and sanctions were depriving the people of Iraq of essentials to support and protect human life. These essentials include medicines and medical supplies, safe drinking water, adequate food, insecticides, fertilisers, equipment and parts required for agriculture, food processing, storage and distribution, hospital and medical clinic procedures; a multitude of common items such as light bulbs and fluorescent tubes; equipment and parts for the generation and distribution of electricity, telephone and other communications, public transportation and other essential human services. Also denied the people of Iraq is knowledge of the existence of, and procedures and equipment to provide protection from, depleted uranium and dangerous chemical pollution released in the environment of Iraq by defendants. The United States has further subjected Iraq to random missile assaults which have killed civilians.

* These charges are supplemental to the 19 charges issued by Ramsey Clark early in 1991 relating to the causes, conduct and consequences of the war against Iraq, which were considered and endorsed by the International War Crimes Tribunal called by him.

310

The direct consequence of such acts and others is direct physical injury to the majority of the population in Iraq, serious permanent injury to a substantial minority of the population and death to more than 1,500,000 people including 750,000 children under five years of age.

The formal criminal charges are:

1. The United States and its officials aided and abetted by others engaged in a continuing pattern of conduct from 6 August 1990 until this date to impose, maintain and enforce extreme economic sanctions and a strict military blockade on the people of Iraq for the purpose of injuring the entire population, killing its weakest members, infants, children, the elderly and the chronically ill, by depriving them of medicines, drinking water, food, and other essentials in order to maintain a large US military presence in the region and dominion and control over its people and resources including oil.

2. The United States, its President Bill Clinton and other officials, the United Kingdom and its Prime Minister John Major and other officials have committed a crime against humanity as defined in the Nuremberg Charter against the population of Iraq and engaged in a continuing and massive attack on the entire civilian population in violation of Articles 48, 51, 52, 54 and 55 of Protocol I Additional to the Geneva Convention 1977.

3. The United States, its President Bill Clinton and other officials, the United Kingdom and its Prime Minister John Major and other officials have committed genocide as defined in the Convention against Genocide against the population of Iraq including genocide by starvation and sickness through use of sanctions as a weapon of mass destruction and violation of Article 54, Protection of Objects Indispensable to the Civilian Population, of Protocol I Additional to the Geneva Convention 1977.

4. The United States, its President Bill Clinton and other officials, the United Kingdom and its Prime Minister John Major and other officials have committed and engaged in a continuing course of conduct to prevent any interference with the long term criminal imposition of sanctions against the people of Iraq in order to support continuing US presence and domination of the region.

5. The United States, its President Bill Clinton and other officials, the United Kingdom and its Prime Minister John Major and other officials with US Ambassador Madeleine Albright as a principal agent have obstructed justice and corrupted United Nations functions, most prominently the Security Council, by political, economic and other coercions using systematic threats, manipulations and misinformation to silence protest and prevent votes or other acts to end sanctions against Iraq despite reports over a period of five years by every major UN agency concerned including UNICEF, UN World Food Program, UN Food and Agriculture Organisation, which describe the deaths, injuries and suffering directly caused by the sanctions.

6. The United States, its President Bill Clinton and other officials have engaged in a continuing concealment and cover-up of the criminal assaults during January through March 1991 on nuclear reactors, chemical, fertiliser, insecticide plants, oil refineries, oil storage tanks, ammunition depots and bunkers in violation of humanitarian law including Article 56, *Protecting Works and Installations Containing Dangerous Forces*, exposing the civilian population of Iraq, and military personnel of Iraq, the United States and other countries to radiation and dangerous chemical pollution which continues for the population of Iraq causing deaths, sickness and permanent injuries including chemical and radiation poisoning, cancer, leukaemia, tumours and diseased body organs.

7. The United States and its officers have concealed and failed to help protect the population of Iraq from the cover-up of the use by US forces of illegal weapons of a wide variety including rockets and missiles containing depleted uranium which have saturated soil, ground water and other elements in Iraq and are a constant presence affecting large areas still undefined with deadly radiation causing death, illness and injury which will continue to harm the population with unforeseeable effects for thousands of years.

8. The United States and its officials have endeavoured to extort money tribute from Iraq and institutionalise forced payments of money on a permanent basis by demanding more than one half the value of all oil sales taken from Iraq be paid as it directs as the price for reducing the sanctions to permit limited oil sales insufficient to feed the people and care for the sick. This is the functional and moral equivalent of holding a gun to the head of the children of Iraq and demanding of Iraq, pay half your income or we will shoot your children.

9. The United States has violated and condoned violations of human rights, civil liberties and the US Bill of Rights in the United States, in Kuwait, Saudi Arabia and elsewhere to achieve its purpose of complete domination of the region.

10. President Clinton, Ambassador Albright, Nicholas Burns and Rolf Ekeus have systematically manipulated, controlled, directed, misinformed, concealed from and restricted press and media coverage about conditions in Iraq, compliance with UN requirements, and the suffering of the people of Iraq to maintain overwhelming and consistent media support for genocide. This has been done in the face of their proclaiming that the deaths of more than half a million children is 'worth it' to control the region, that Saddam Hussein is responsible for all injury and could prevent this genocide by not putting 'his yacht on the Euphrates this winter', or by shutting down his 'palace for the winter and using that money to buy food and medicine' and by insisting that the sanctions will be maintained until a government acceptable to the US is installed in Iraq.

Appendix 11

Convention on the Prevention and Punishment of the Crime of Genocide

APPROVED AND PROPOSED FOR SIGNATURE AND RATIFICATION
OR ACCESSION BY GENERAL ASSEMBLY RESOLUTION 260 A(III)
OF 9 DECEMBER 1948

ENTRY INTO FORCE: 12 January 1951, in accordance with
Article XIII

The Contracting Parties,

Having considered the declaration made by the General Assembly of the United
Nations in its resolution 96(I) dated 11 December 1946 that genocide is a
crime under international law, contrary to the spirit and aims of the United
Nations and condemned by the civilized world,

Recognizing that at all periods of history genocide has inflicted great losses
on humanity, and

Being convinced that, in order to liberate mankind from such an odious scourge,
international co-operation is required,

Hereby agree as hereinafter provided:

Article I
The Contracting Parties confirm that genocide, whether committed in time of
peace or in time of war, is a crime under international law which they undertake to prevent and to punish.

Article II
In the present Convention, genocide means any of the following acts committed with intent to destroy, in whole or in part, a national, ethnical, racial or
religious group, as such:

(*a*) Killing members of the group;

(*b*) Causing serious bodily or mental harm to members of the group;

(*c*) Deliberately inflicting on the group conditions of life calculated to bring
about its physical destruction in whole or in part;

(*d*) Imposing measures intended to prevent births within the group;

(*e*) Forcibly transferring children of the group to another group.

Article III
The following acts shall be punishable:

(a) Genocide;

(b) Conspiracy to commit genocide;

(c) Direct and public incitement to commit genocide;

(d) Attempt to commit genocide;

(e) Complicity in genocide.

Article IV
Persons committing genocide or any of the other acts enumerated in Article III shall be punished, whether they are constitutionally responsible rulers, public officials or private individuals.

Article V
The Contracting Parties undertake to enact, in accordance with their respective Constitutions, the necessary legislation to give effect to the provisions of the present Convention, and, in particular, to provide effective penalties for persons guilty of genocide or any of the other acts enumerated in Article III.

Article VI
Persons charged with genocide or any of the other acts enumerated in Article III shall be tried by a competent tribunal of the State in the territory of which the act was committed, or by such international penal tribunal as may have jurisdiction with respect to those Contracting Parties which shall have accepted its jurisdiction.

Article VII
Genocide and the other acts enumerated in Article III shall not be considered as political crimes for the purpose of extradition.

The Contracting Parties pledge themselves in such cases to grant extradition in accordance with their laws and treaties in force.

Article VIII
Any Contracting Party may call upon the competent organs of the United Nations to take such action under the Charter of the United Nations as they consider appropriate for the prevention and suppression of acts of genocide or any of the other acts enumerated in Article III.

Article IX
Disputes between the Contracting Parties relating to the interpretation, application or fulfilment of the present Convention, including those relating to the responsibility of a State for genocide or for any of the other acts enumerated in Article III, shall be submitted to the International Court of Justice at the request of any of the parties to the dispute.

Article X
The present Convention, of which the Chinese, English, French, Russian and Spanish texts are equally authentic, shall bear the date of 9 December 1948.

Article XI
The present Convention shall be open until 31 December 1949 for signature on behalf of any Member of the United Nations and of any non-member State to which an invitation to sign has been addressed by the General Assembly.

The present Convention shall be ratified, and the instruments of ratification shall be deposited with the Secretary-General of the United Nations.

After 1 January 1950, the present Convention may be acceded to on behalf of any Member of the United Nations and of any non-member State which has received an invitation as aforesaid.

Instruments of accession shall be deposited with the Secretary-General of the United Nations.

Article XII
Any Contracting Party may at any time, by notification addressed to the Secretary-General of the United Nations, extend the application of the present Convention to all or any of the territories for the conduct of whose foreign relations that Contracting Party is responsible.

Article XIII
On the day when the first twenty instruments of ratification or accession have been deposited, the Secretary-General shall draw up a *procès-verbal* and transmit a copy thereof to each Member of the United Nations and to each of the non-member States contemplated in Article XI.

The present Convention shall come into force on the ninetieth day following the date of deposit of the twentieth instrument of ratification or accession.

Any ratification or accession effected, subsequent to the latter date shall become effective on the ninetieth day following the deposit of the instrument of ratification or accession.

Article XIV
The present Convention shall remain in effect for a period of ten years as from the date of its coming into force.

It shall thereafter remain in force for successive periods of five years for such Contracting Parties as have not denounced it at least six months before the expiration of the current period.

Denunciation shall be effected by a written notification addressed to the Secretary-General of the United Nations.

Article XV
If, as a result of denunciations, the number of Parties to the present Convention should become less than sixteen, the Convention shall cease to be in force as from the date on which the last of these denunciations shall become effective.

Article XVI
A request for the revision of the present Convention may be made at any time by any Contracting Party by means of a notification in writing addressed to the Secretary-General.

The General Assembly shall decide upon the steps, if any, to be taken in respect of such request.

Article XVII
The Secretary-General of the United Nations shall notify all Members of the United Nations and the non-member States contemplated in Article XI of the following:

(*a*) Signatures, ratifications and accessions received in accordance with Article XI;

(*b*) Notifications received in accordance with Article XII;

(*c*) The date upon which the present Convention comes into force in accordance with Article XIII;

(*d*) Denunciations received in accordance with Article XIV;

(*e*) The abrogation of the Convention in accordance with Article XV;

(*f*) Notifications received in accordance with Article XVI.

Article XVIII
The original of the present Convention shall be deposited in the archives of the United Nations.

A certified copy of the Convention shall be transmitted to each Member of the United Nations and to each of the non-member States contemplated in Article XI.

Article XIX
The present Convention shall be registered by the Secretary-General of the United Nations on the date of its coming into force.

Appendix 12

Verdict of the International Court for Crimes Against Humanity Committed by the UN Security Council on Iraq (October 1996)

The members of the International Court on Crimes Against Humanity Committed by the UN Security Council on Iraq, having today examined the accusation formulated by Ramsey Clark (former Attorney General of the United States of America and President of the *International Action Center*) against the United Nations (UN) Security Council and its permanent members, have met to deliberate on the evidence brought forward in the public hearing, namely:

The testimonies and documents presented by Peter L. Pellet (UN FAO Team Manager, University of Massachusetts, US), Khaldun Lutfi (President of the *Iraqi Red Crescent*), Siegwart-Horst Günther (President of the *International Yellow Cross, Austria*), Margret Fakhouri (Pediatrician, Germany and Jordan) regarding the state of public health among the Iraqi people and, specifically, the incidence of health problems among children, as well as the effects of non-conventional weapons used during the war;

The testimonies and documents presented by Sarah Zaidi (Member of UN FAO team, Science Director of the *Centre for Economic and Social Rights*, US and Pakistan), Tha'era, Mohamed (Doctor, Vice-President of the *General Federation of Iraqi Women*), María Durán (Lawyer, *Themis Association of Women Lawyers*, Spain), on socio-economic indicators of the embargo and its effects on women;

The testimonies and documents presented by Joaquín Córdoba Zoilo (teacher of Ancient History at A.U.M., Spain) on the consequences of the sanctions on the historical and cultural patrimony of humankind in Iraq;

The testimonies and documents presented by Saad Hamid (Jurist, *Centre for Economic and Social Rights*, Jordan), Patrick Brunot (Lawyer, Paris Appeal Court, Professor in International Law, *Paris High International Studies School*, France), Terrance Duffy (Lecturer in International Law, Director of the *International Direct Democracy Research Association*, Northern Ireland), Akram Witri (Lecturer in International Law, University of Baghdad) on the regime of sanctions against Iraq and International Law.

The accused failed to appear. The UN Security Council sent its apologies via the UN Office in Madrid and alleged its reiterated concern for the civil society affected by the embargo and the humanitarian situation in Iraq, which

317

was reflected in its 1991 Resolutions nos. 776 and 712. Resolution 712 drew attention to the deteriorating levels of nutrition and health among the Iraqi population. The UN also stated that the Directors of UNICEF and the World Food Programme, and the Under-Secretary for Humanitarian Affairs have launched an appeal to collect urgent financial contributions to the humanitarian aid programme for Iraq. These statements were submitted in a fax from the UN Office in Madrid, dated 31 October 1996.

EVIDENCE

Point ONE   From 6 August 1990 to date, the UN Security Council, under the hegemony of the United States, has adopted a form of conduct oriented towards imposing, maintaining and applying extreme economic sanctions and a strict embargo on the people of Iraq in order to harm the entire population, killing its weaker members (children of all ages, the elderly, chronically ill and pregnant and nursing women), and depriving them of medicine, drinking water, food and other essential elements.

Point TWO   The accused have obstructed Justice and corrupted the operation of the UN by all kinds of coercion, systematically using threats, manipulation and disinformation to silence protests and prevent the sanctions against Iraq from being lifted, despite the reports issued over the last five years by the main UN agencies and various humanitarian and pacifist organisations, which have repeatedly denounced the high death rate and suffering of the Iraqi people.

Point THREE   The accused have perpetrated criminal attacks against fertiliser and insecticide chemical factories, warehouses of agricultural and food products, oil storage tanks, and so on, exposing the Iraqi population to chemical contamination and radiation, and causing death, disease and permanent injuries.

Point FOUR   The accused have hidden the existence and use of a wide range of illegal weapons, including rockets and missiles containing impoverished uranium, which have contaminated the soil and groundwaters with seriously hazardous, sometimes lethal radiation that will affect the population for thousands of years.

Point FIVE   The accused have coercively enforced illegal levies and payments and have institutionalised disproportionate economic reparations that ignore the unjust damages inflicted on Iraq, which mean that more than half the value of all the oil sales made from Iraq must be used to pay the sanctions, giving rise to hunger, malnutrition and lack of elementary resources to care for the needs of the most vulnerable sectors of the population.

Point SIX   The accused, under a sectarian policy of hiding and disguising the facts, have manipulated, controlled and given misleading information on the failure to meet the UN's own requirements and on the suffering of the

Iraqi people, in order to propitiate the support or the ignorance of international public opinion regarding what is really being done.

Point SEVEN   All the above has had an especially brutal effect on the most vulnerable, most unprotected sectors of the Iraqi people: its children, women and the elderly. Several reports from international UN agencies and humanitarian and pacifist organisations have drawn attention to the deaths of over a million and a half people, of whom 750,000 were children below the age of five. These figures do not take into account the high rate of death at childbirth and the thousands of children born with congenital malformations. The situation of women has been set back drastically by brutal attacks on women's dignity and their physical and moral integrity.

Point EIGHT   The accused have, by default, passiveness or complicity, propitiated the destruction and plundering of much of the historical, artistic, monumental and documentary wealth of the Iraqi nation, which belongs to Humankind as a whole.

LEGAL FUNDAMENTALS

Point ONE   This Court considers itself to be supported by the legal and ethical legitimacy accorded to it by the reprobation of broad sectors of worldwide public opinion and the brutality of the UN Security Council against the Iraqi people. The Court deems that no power is authorised to act without Law or against the Law, taking advantage of the terrible, inexistent faculty to commit crimes with impunity. The UN Security Council has perpetrated atrocious crimes against the very principles of peace, freedom and justice that, it is called upon to defend, violating fundamental UN declarations and resolutions and the moral and legal Code that constitutes the ethical minimum for international co-existence.

Point TWO   The facts presented constitute evidence of the *crime of genocide*, described and typified under the UN Convention of 9 December 1948. These facts have entailed, and continue to entail, the destruction of the Iraqi people, through the following acts:

- *First*: killing members of that population.

- *Second*: seriously injuring the physical and mental integrity of the Iraqi people.

- *Third*: intentionally and consciously subjecting the Iraqi people to conditions of existence that lead to its destruction.

   The Court considers that this crime of genocide may constitute a specific kind of *institutional terrorism* perpetrated by the United Nations Security Council.

Point THREE   The member States of the UN Security Council that have given support to the acts described are responsible, as *authors*, for the material execution, induction or cooperation needed in the above mentioned crimes, and the crimes against humanity therein incorporated.

Those who, by *abetment or complicity*, have decisively collaborated in committing or abetting such crimes, are also responsible.

Point FOUR   The facts declared proven violate, among others, the following rules of *international law* approved by the United Nations itself:

A – The UNIVERSAL DECLARATION OF HUMAN RIGHTS, 10 December 1948;
B – The INTERNATIONAL COVENANT ON CIVIL AND POLITICAL RIGHTS, 19 December 1966;
C – The CONVENTION ON THE ELIMINATION OF ALL FORMS OF DISCRIMINATION AGAINST WOMEN, 18 December 1979;
D – The CHILD RIGHTS CONVENTION, 20 November 1989.
E – The first additional Protocol to the 1977 GENEVA CONVENTION.

Given the above, this International Court *condemns* the accused, the United Nations Security Council and, especially, the Government of the United States of America, as responsible for the crime described herein.

It also *demands*:

1. – immediate lifting of the sanctions imposed on the Iraqi people.

2. – immediate withdrawal of all military forces and armaments accumulated since the war to exterminate Iraq.

3. – compensation for the Iraqi people for all the damage caused.

In Madrid, Spain, 17 November 1996

MEMBERS OF THE COURT

Algeria:
Ahmed Ben Bella (First President of Algeria, Vice-President of Bertrand Russell Court).
Louisa Hannoun (General Secretary of PTA).

Austria:
Hans Koechler (President of *International Progress Organization*, IPO).

Egypt:
Saber Mohamed Mahmoud Ammar (member of Permanent Boureau of *Arab Lawyer Union*)

Italia:
Domenico Gallo (former Senator, Judge in Rome Court, AEJDDH)

Jordan:
Tujan Feisal (MP)
Husain Mujali (President of the Lawyer's College)

Morocco:
Mohamed Al-Basry (member of USPP)

Palestine:
Haider Abdel Shafi (Doctor, President of *Palestinian Red Crescent*, Palestinian Legislative Board)
Raji Sourani (Lawyer, Director of *Palestinian Center for Human Rights*)

Spanish State:
Najib Abu-Warda (Teacher of Foreign Relations in Madrid Complutense University, member of *Jerusalem Spanish-Palestinian Association*).
Juan María Bandrés (Lawyer, President of *Spanish Center for Refugees Help*, CEAR).
Aurora Bilbao (Doctor, Professor in Basque Country University, President of IPPNW).
Marcelino Camacho (Sindicalist, former President of the Trade Union CCOO).
Pablo Castellano MP, Spokesman of United Left in the Justice Commission of Spanish Congress).
Francisco Doñate (Medicine Professor in Basque Country University).
Francisco Frutos (MP United Left and Federal Coordinator of the Communist Party, PCE).
Juan Francisco Martín Seco (Economist).
Pedro Martínez Montávez (Professor, M.A.U.).
Joaquín Navarro (Judge).
Carmen Pujol (Jurist, President of *Themis Association of Women Lawyers*).
Nicolás Redondo (Sindicalist, former General Secretary of the Trade Union UGT).
Francisco Rodríguez (MP Galician Nationalist Bloc (BNG) in the Spanish Congress).
Juan José Romeo Laguna (Judge at Sevilla County High Court and member of *Judges for Democracy*).
Javier Sádaba (Professor, M.A.U.).
Eloy Terrón (former President of *UNESCO Friends Club*, CAUM).
Endika Zulueta (Lawyer, *Lawyer's Free Union*).

Turkey:
Turkkaya Ataöv (Professor of Foreign Relations in Ankara University).

Appendix 13

Sanctions Details in UN Documents (Extracts) – March 1997 to October 1997

The course of sanctions on Iraq is abundantly described in documents prepared by the United Nations (and by UN-related bodies) and by documents submitted to various UN authorities. The following brief extracts (giving reference, date and source) convey the flavour of the on-going holocaust:

S/1997/250, 22 March 1997, Iraqi Minister for Foreign Affairs

3. While all the relevant international covenants, conventions and instruments, and pre-eminently the Charter of the United Nations, 'reaffirm faith in fundamental human rights [and] in the dignity . . . of the human person', the measures being taken against the people of Iraq and the policies and practices that seek to starve it and deprive it of its most elementary and basic humanitarian needs rob these covenants of all humanitarian substance.

In his report entitled *Supplement to an Agenda for Peace*, the Secretary-General of the United Nations states as follows:

> Sanctions, as is generally recognised, are a blunt instrument. They raise the ethical question of whether suffering inflicted on vulnerable groups in the target country is a legitimate means of exerting pressure on political leaders . . .

4. It was the experience forced on the people of Iraq by the imposition of sanctions that prompted the careful assessment made by the Secretary-General in his position paper, which he has reaffirmed on numerous occasions in his reports to the General Assembly on the work of the Organization. In paragraph 821 of the most recent such report (A/51/1) he states that the humanitarian assistance provided to Iraq:

> . . . remained significantly below the requirements resulting from the difficulties faced by children, women, elderly people and an increasing number of indigent families in Iraq. Several United Nations agencies operating in the field reported a continued deterioration of health and nutritional conditions, with an estimated four million people, the majority of them children under five, being in danger of severe physical and mental damage as a result of malnutrition.

5. This alarming number of four million Iraqi children under the age of five whose lives are in jeopardy was confirmed in the joint appeal launched by the Department of Humanitarian Affairs of the United Nations Secretariat,

UNICEF and the World Food Programme on 26 October 1996, which stressed that there was a need to meet the urgent basic needs of the Iraqi people given that rates of malnutrition were rising among children and women in particular and that water contamination and the deteriorating level of health services had contributed to rising mortality rates owing to transmissible and contagious diseases.

In a statement made at Geneva on 4 October 1996, the representative of UNICEF in Baghdad said that 4,500 Iraqi children under five were dying every month from the consequences of malnutrition and treatable diseases.

6. The March 1996 World Health Organization report, entitled *The health conditions of the population in Iraq since the Gulf crisis* (WHO/EHA/96.1) concludes that:

> The vast majority of the country's population has been on a semi-starvation diet for years. This tragic situation has tremendous implications on the health status of the population and on their quality of life, not only for the present generation, but for the future generation as well.

CERD/C/SR.1203, 25 April 1997, note appending contributions to the 1203rd meeting of the Committee on the Elimination of Racial Discrimination (14 March 1997)

8. Both UNICEF (E/ICEF/1994/PL.2) and WHO (WHO/EHA/96.4) had described the catastrophic consequences of the health situation for children, more than 600,000 of whom had died in Iraq between 1990 and August 1995.

9. . . . A slow genocide, more dramatic than a swift genocide, was clearly under way. (Mr al-Azawi, Iraq).

11. . . . Since 1993, the situation had worsened for most of the population, especially children, the number of whom admitted to hospital had increased 50 times since 1990. Infant mortality among children under five had increased sixfold . . . (Mr Wolfrum, Country Rapporteur).

S/1997/402, 25 May 1997, Iraqi Minister for Foreign Affairs
The representative of the United States of America in the Security Council Committee established by Resolution 661 (1990) has placed on hold the contracts for the supply of pharmaceuticals numbered 252, 253, 391, 428, 429 and 553 and has done so on the pretext that they would include free merchandise or free medical samples. The use of this pretext only confirms, once again, that the United States of America is pursuing a policy, which has become evident to one and all, of impeding the smooth implementation of the Memorandum of Understanding and blocking the contracts of sale submitted by various foreign companies to the secretariat of the 661 Committee in order to ensure the provision of basic supplies to Iraq.

The inclusion of free merchandise and medical samples in contracts for medicines is a standard commercial practice in all countries of the world. Pharmaceutical companies distribute them to physicians in order to introduce their products and to provide information on a particular medication and on its ingredients and uses as well as other details of a scientific nature that are useful in the treatment of patients. There is no doctor's office in the world, not even in the United States, that is without medical samples of this kind, and the doctor usually gives them to his patients free of charge.

In his summary presentation to the Security Council on 22 May 1997, Mr Yasushi Akashi, Under-Secretary-General for Humanitarian Affairs, referred to the disgraceful state of the hospitals he visited, without prior arrangement, in Baghdad and Mosul during his visit to Iraq from 3 to 9 May 1997.

Mr Nakajima, Director-General of WHO, in a statement issued after his visit to Iraq, also said that the country's health system was on the verge of collapse. These facts have not been enough to persuade the representative of the United States of America to desist from using irresponsible methods to prevent thousands of sick children, older persons and women from obtaining the medicines they need. . . .

S/1997/419, 2 June 1997, UN Secretary-General

49. Any assessment of the adequacy of Resolution 986 (1995) medical supplies in meeting the health needs of the population is hampered by the slow and partial arrival of medicines and medical supplies . . . the continuous degradation of the health sector has been exacerbated by this situation. According to information provided by the Ministry of Health, no more than four per cent of the medicines needed in Iraq were available during the past five months . . .

50. Although the non-arrival to date of supplies for the water, sanitation, agricultural, education and electricity sectors makes it impossible to comment from observation on the adequacy of these inputs, United Nations agencies stress that the allocations in the distribution plan are not, in their assessment, sufficient to meet the basic needs . . .

51. Recently, United Nations agencies have highlighted urgent needs that are not covered in the present distribution plan . . .

53. . . . I am troubled by the persistent lags and other difficulties . . . which have resulted in major delays in the provision of several items, in particular medicine and pharmaceutical supplies, of which there is demonstrably a critical and sometimes desperate shortage . . .

S/1997/452, 11 June 1997, Iraqi Minister for Foreign Affairs

. . . The representative of the United States has also placed on hold a significant number of contracts for medical supplies, more than 40 of them. . . . The [US] representative . . . also placed on hold the medical contracts numbered 252, 253, 391, 428, 429 and 553 on the grounds that they included free merchandise or free medical samples . . .

S/1997/548, 14 July 1997, Iraqi Minister for Foreign Affairs

. . . I wish to draw your attention to the information which appeared in the *Washington Post* of 26 June 1997, as well as to that given in a television programme broadcast the same day on the American ABC network, which confirmed that the United States Government continues to pursue towards Iraq an official policy based on intervention in the internal affairs of my country, and to take measures and engage in concrete and deliberate action designed to threaten the national security of Iraq and place it in danger. . . . The Washington Post article states that Warren Marik of the CIA . . . persuaded . . . Ahmed Chalabi and the members of the so-called Iraqi National Congress to work for the CIA and recruited various groups of agents and mercenaries to organise an armed attack against the institutions of the Iraqi State. He organised an attempted *coup d'état* against the regime. Warren Marik has acknowledged that considerable sums of money, at least $100 million, were swallowed up by these efforts, just as he has acknowledged the role played by the United States Senate Intelligence Committee in mounting a secret action against the legitimate authorities of Iraq and preparing a programme of aggression against Iraq

Warren Marik says *inter alia* that the former President of the United States, George Bush, ordered the CIA to organise sabotage operations in order to topple the regime in power in Iraq. Mention should also be made of the establishment by the CIA of radio and relay stations to broadcast hostile propaganda to Jeddah, Kuwait, Cairo and Amman in which Iraqi officers, among others, were urged to desert and abandon the Iraqi armed forces. The author of the article states also that the United States Senate Intelligence Committee authorised the CIA to set up a secret, semi-permanent American group in the north of Iraq to train rebels, outlaws and bands of brigands and mercenaries and to supply them with *matériel* to conduct sabotage, assassination and plundering operations.

Warren Marik also revealed the existence of a plan aimed at launching an armed attack on 4 March 1995 against garrisons of the Iraqi army at Mosul and Kirkuk. The attack was to be led by rebels, saboteurs, brigands and outlaws. The article also states that the CIA agent asked the CIA lackey Ahmed Chalabi to use his contacts with the ayatollahs in power in Iran to convey to them the message that 'Washington would look with favor on Iran moving troops along its border to distract Saddam as the offensive began. . . .'

S/1997/606, 4 August 1997, UN Secretary-General (acknowledging receipt of Iraqi distribution plan) (extracts from plan)

5. The condition of clean water supply and sanitation services remains critical all over Iraq . . . the rehabilitation of this sector requires over $500 million . . . the Plan allocates only $44.17 million . . .

6. Full rehabilitation of electric power generation, transmission and distribution, requires approximately $675 million of which $49.17 million was provided under the previous Distribution Plan. The current Plan allocates a further $55.3 million . . .

10. The humanitarian requirements for the whole population of Iraq are enormous due to the cumulative deterioration of living and environmental conditions . . .

S/1997/663, 25 August 1997, Iraqi Charge D'Affaires to United Nations
. . . when the Vietnamese ship Kwang Myong, laden with 4000 tons of

detergent imported from Vietnam under the terms of the memorandum of understanding between Iraq and the United Nations, was in sight of Iraqi territorial
waters on its way to Iraq, the United States navy subjected it to a search. The
crew was interrogated over a period of three days and nights before being
ordered either to turn back and abandon its journey to Iraq, or throw into the
sea some electrical equipment (a refrigerator, a television, a video and a piano),
which was the property of the ship's crew. Pursuant to that order, the crew
and the United States forces threw the electrical equipment into the sea . . .

S/1997/664, 21 August 1997, Iraqi Minister for Foreign Affairs

. . . The Turkish forces in question carried out 19 military operations against
Iraqi territory between 20 June . . . and 12 August 1997. . . . Turkey is persisting in its attacks. . . . (A three page listing of the details of 31 Turkish violations of Iraqi territory between 4 June 1997 and 12 August 1997 is appended.)

S/1997/672, 28 August 1997, Chairman of UN Security Council Committee

Humanitarian flights

32. The Committee could not approve a request . . . for . . . authorisation of
one or more weekly flights . . . in order to carry United Nations personnel and
for humanitarian reasons, that is, to transport the sick and elderly to and from
Baghdad . . . and to transport medical, pharmaceutical and food supplies . . .

S/1997/696, 8 September 1997, Iraqi Charge D'Affairs to United Nations

. . . on 6 August 1997 United States naval forces . . . intercepted the Cam-
bodian freighter . . . inside Iraqi territorial waters. The vessel was loaded with
packaged laundry detergent being imported by Iraq under the terms of the
memorandum of understanding. . . . It was searched by these forces in a coercive manner, and part of the cargo was removed to the gangways, cabins and
deck. A large part of the cargo was lost as a result of this handling and through
exposure to moisture and sea water . . .

S/1997/717, 16 September 1997, Iraqi Minister for Foreign Affairs

. . . In paragraph 56 of his recent report (S/1997/685), the Secretary-General . . .
states that uncertainties in the arrival of food and other items have caused
great difficulties. . . . In paragraph 19 . . . the Secretary-General points out that
in the water and sanitation, electricity, education and agricultural sectors no
supplies have yet arrived. Although more than 100 days have elapsed . . . the
secretariat of the Security Council Committee . . . still has around 60 contracts that it has yet to process . . . More than 70 contracts are still on hold at
the request of . . . the United States and the United Kingdom, and these countries have blocked a further 21 contracts . . .

CONCLUSION

At the time of publication of the second edition of the present book the sanctions regime against Iraq will have been in place for approaching eight years. Over that period the civilian deaths caused by US-induced starvation and disease (that is, by *biological warfare*) have continued to mount. We may estimate that almost 2,000,000 people, the majority babies and children, have been killed in this fashion. With a tenth of the population slaughtered, the remainder have been reduced to malnutrition, sickness, trauma and despair. The present book has made plain the violations of ethics and law that this obscene American policy represents. This is the cruel reality behind all Washington's talk of morality, human rights, terrorism and war crimes.

In the seven years up to August 1997 the biological warfare waged by the United States against the people of Iraq had killed 1,211,285 babies and children. (The statistic, compiled by the Iraqi Ministry of Health, is accepted as accurate by UNICEF and other UN agencies). Today (early 1998) tens of thousands more dead and dying are being reported every month.

Notes

Notes to Chapter 1: The Legacy of War

1. Quoted by Dr Fadia Faqir, 'Tales of war: Arab women in the eye of the storm', in Victoria Brittain (ed.), *The Gulf Between Us: The Gulf War and Beyond* (London: Virago Press, 1991) pp. 85–6; Faqir points out that some Vietnamese witnesses to the horrors of the Vietnam War suffered a psychologically induced blindness.
2. H. V. F. Winstone and Zahra Freeth, *Kuwait: Prospect and Reality* (London: George Allen and Unwin, 1972) p. 111.
3. *Transcript of House Subcommittee Hearing on US–Iraqi Relations*, in James Ridgeway (ed. and Introduction), *The March to War* (New York: Four Walls Eight Windows, 1991) pp. 47–9.
4. Ridgeway, ibid., p. 30.
5. I have considered in detail the events leading up to the 1991 Gulf War – including Iraq's grievances, the US 'green light', Western support for Saddam, and US manipulation of the United Nations – in Geoff Simons, *Iraq: From Sumer to Saddam* (London: Macmillan, 1994).
6. When Saddam Hussein commented to UN Secretary-General Javier Perez de Cuellar that the UN resolutions were in reality *American* resolutions, 'not what the Security Council wants', Perez de Cuellar said: 'I agree with you' (*The Independent*, London, 12 December 1991).
7. *US and Its Allies' Crimes and Violations of Human Rights in Iraq. A Report on Part I: Crimes of the Military Aggression Against Iraq, Part II: The Blockade and Its Violations*, prepared by a panel of international law experts in Iraq, The International Symposium, Baghdad, 5–8 February 1994, p. 13.
8. *Incendiary Weapons*, a SITPRO (Stockholm International Peace Research Institute) monograph (Stockholm: Almqvist & Wiksell, 1975) pp. 153–4.
9. Colonel Richard White, US pilot, quoted in *The Independent*, London, 6 February 1991.
10. *US and Its Allies' Crimes and Violations of Human Rights in Iraq, op. cit.*, p. 14.
11. *The Washington Post*, 16 and 17 February 1991; Robert Lifton, 'The US fantasy of kicking ass', *The Guardian*, London, 20 June 1991.
12. Reuter pool report, 'Apache pilots in ground attack shooting gallery', *The Independent*, London, 25 February 1991.
13. Paul Rogers, 'Myth of a clean war buried in the sand', *The Guardian*, London, 19 September 1991.
14. See, for example, John R. MacArthur, *Second Front, Censorship and Propaganda in the Gulf War* (New York: Hill and Wang, 1992) pp. 146–98.
15. Dilip Hiro, *Desert Shield to Desert Storm: The Second Gulf War* (London: Paladin, 1992) p. 389.
16. *Newsweek*, 11 March 1991, quoted in Philip M. Taylor, *War and the Media:*

Propaganda and Persuasion in the Gulf War (Manchester: Manchester University Press, 1992) p. 251.

17. Quoted by Taylor, ibid., p. 253.
18. Ibid.
19. Michael Kelly, 'Carnage on a forgotten road', *The Guardian*, London, 11 April 1991.
20. Ibid.
21. *Los Angeles Times*, 10 March 1991; Kelly, 'Carnage on a forgotten road', *op. cit.*
22. Kelly, ibid.
23. BBC2 Television 'Late Show', 8 June 1991.
24. *The Washington Post*, 28 February 1991.
25. *Wall Street Journal*, 2 March 1991.
26. Patrick Sloyan, 'Iraqi troops buried alive say American officers', *The Guardian*, London, 13 September 1991.
27. Quoted in MacArthur, *Second Front, op. cit.*, p. 105.
28. Barton Gellman, 'Allied air war struck broadly in Iraq: officials acknowledge strategy went beyond purely military targets', *The Washington Post*, 23 June 1991.
29. Ibid.
30. Amy Kasslow, 'Shifting fortunes in the Arab world', *The Christian Science Monitor*, 26 June 1991, p. 7.
31. *War Crimes: A Report on United States War Crimes Against Iraq*, Reports to the Commission of Inquiry for the International War Crimes Tribunal and the Tribunal's Final Judgement (Washington, D.C.: Maisonneuve Press, 1992) p. 15.
32. Ibid.
33. *US and Its Allies' Crimes and Violations of Human Rights in Iraq, op. cit.*, pp. 9–11.
34. John Vidal, 'Poisoned sand and seas', in Victoria Brittain (ed.), *The Gulf Between Us, op. cit.*, p. 137.
35. Ibid., p. 141; a draft Pentagon report leaked to *The New York Times* suggested in 1992 that the damage to the Iraqi infrastructure was heavier than intended because US Air Force commanders failed to pass on targeting restrictions to bomber pilots (Mark Tran, 'US destruction of Iraq's power plants a "mistake"', *The Guardian*, London, 24 February 1992).
36. Bob Woodward, *The Commanders* (New York: Simon and Schuster, 1991) p. 291.
37. Andre Petersen, 'Archaeological sites a forgotten casualty of war', letter, *The Guardian*, London, 4 February 1991.
38. Patrick Cockburn, 'Iraq's ancient treasures are the hidden casualties of war', *The Independent*, London, 15 July 1991.
39. Muayad S. Damirji, editorial, *Akkad*, Department of Antiquities and Heritage, Baghdad, Number 2 (December 1994).
40. *Chicago Herald Tribune*, 15 January 1993.
41. Isabel Boucher ('The haemorrhage of looted art continues', *The Art Newspaper*, Number 47, April 1995) describes the commercial flood of archaeological artefacts from Iraq, caused by the Gulf War. The British School of Archaeology in Iraq has published a 153-page document (*Lost*

Heritage: Antiquities Stolen from Iraq's Regional Museums) listing the thousands of archaeological artefacts – amulets, arrowheads, beads, bottles, bowls, bracelets, cups, figurines, goblets, jars, necklaces, rings, seals, statues, tumblers, vases, etc. – looted from Iraq following the war.

42. Christopher Bellamy, 'Arithmetic of death in wake of Gulf conflict', *The Guardian*, London, 1 March 1991.
43. Simon Jones, 'US demographer sacked for exposing Iraqi civilian deaths', *The Independent*, London, 23 April 1992.
44. Robert Lifton, 'Last refuge of a hi-tech nation', *The Guardian*, London, 12 March 1991.
45. Lee Hockstadter, 'Health crisis looms in Baghdad', *The Guardian*, London, 5 March 1991.
46. *Public Health in Iraq after the Gulf War*, Harvard Study Team Report, May 1991.
47. Richard Norton-Taylor, 'Gulf war allies had nuclear option, claims officer', *The Guardian*, London, 28 September 1991.
48. Mohamed Heikal, *Illusions of Triumph: An Arab View of the Gulf War* (London: HarperCollins, 1992) p. 289.
49. Nick Cohen, 'Radioactive waste left in Gulf by allies', *The Independent on Sunday*, London, 10 November 1991.
50. Ibid.
51. Nick Cohen and Tom Wilkie, 'Gulf teams not told of risk from uranium', *The Independent on Sunday*, London, 10 November 1991.
52. Greg Philo and Greg McLaughlin, 'The first casualties of war', *New Statesman and Society*, London, 29 January 1993.
53. Ibid.
54. Felicity Arbuthnot, 'Allies' shells leave deadly radiation', *Scotland on Sunday*, 18 March 1993.
55. David Albright, 'The desert glows – with propaganda', *The Bulletin of the Atomic Scientists*, May 1993, pp. 11–12, 46.
56. Fact Sheet 2, Stichting LAKA, Ketelhuisplein 43, 1054 RD Amsterdam, Netherlands.
57. *The International Scientific Symposium on Post War Environmental Problems in Iraq*, editors: Layth F. Al-Kassab, Ph.D., Sami R. Al-Araji, Ph.D., Walid G. Al-Tawil, Ph.D., Muna Al-Jubori, Ph.D., Adil A. Al-Khafaji, Ph.D., and Khidher A. Putrus, M.Sc., Iraqi Society for Environmental Protection and Improvement (ISEPI), Baghdad, 10–12 December 1994.
58. Ibid., pp. 16–18.
59. From ibid., pp. 28–9. Table compiled by Dr Arsien Abdul-Karim Hana, B.Sc., Ph.D. (Birmingham University, UK).
60. *The Impact of War on Iraq*, Report to the Secretary-General on humanitarian needs in Iraq in the immediate post-crisis environment by a mission to the area led by Mr Martti Ahtisaari, Under-Secretary-General for Administration and Management, United Nations, New York, 20 March 1991.
61. Ibid.
62. Ibid.
63. Ibid.
64. Peter Jenkins, 'War continues by other means', *The Independent*, London, 24 April 1991.

65. Louise Cainkar, 'Desert sin: a post-war journey through Iraq', in Phillis Bennis and Michel Moushabeck (eds), *Beyond the Storm: A Gulf Crisis Reader* (London: Canongate, 1992) pp. 335–55.
66. Patrick E. Tyler, 'Bush links ending of trading ban to Hussein exit', *The New York Times*, 21 May 1991.
67. Cainkar, 'Desert sin', *op. cit.*, p. 340.

Notes to Chapter 2: The Chronology of Sanctions

1. *Woodrow Wilson's Case for the League of Nations*, compiled with his approval by Hamilton Foley (Princeton: Princeton University Press, 1932) pp. 67, 71, 72.
2. Evans Clark (ed.), *Boycotts and Peace*, a Report by the Committee of Economic Sanctions (New York and London: Harper and Brothers, 1923) p. 21.
3. Danforth Newcomb, 'Old tools for a new job: US sanctions against Iraq', in Barry R. Campbell and Danforth Newcomb (eds), *The Impact of the Freeze of Kuwaiti and Iraqi Assets* (London: Graham and Trotman, and International Bar Association, 1990) p. 27.
4. Charles Richards, 'Jordan is "breaking embargo" say Iraqi officials', *The Independent*, London, 13 August 1990.
5. Ibid.
6. Colin Hughes, 'US insists Iraq cordon is not an act of war', *The Independent*, London, 14 August 1990.
7. David Pallister, 'Coarser bread a sign of things to come as Iraqis prepare for sanctions to bite', *The Guardian*, London, 25 September 1990.
8. Bob Woodward, *The Commanders* (New York: Simon and Schuster, 1991) p. 229.
9. Leonard Doyle, 'Iraq "will still face sanctions after crisis"', *The Independent*, London, 18 January 1991.
10. Martin Walker and Hella Pick, 'British and American aims include finishing Saddam', *The Guardian*, London, 23 January 1991.
11. *Middle East Economic Survey*, 29 March 1993; Martin Walker, 'US to stand firm on Iraqi sanctions', *The Guardian*, London, 30 March 1993.
12. 'Iraq and the UN', Gulf Information Project, Newsbriefing Number 17 (15 June 1993).
13. Ibid.
14. Ibid.
15. *Middle East Economic Survey*, 24 May 1993.
16. *The New York Times*, 29 April 1994.
17. Ian Black, 'Pressure grows for end to UN sanctions against Iraq', *The Guardian*, London, 29 September 1994.
18. Ibid.
19. Kenneth R. Timmerman, 'Saddam heads for final victory in the Gulf war', *The Sunday Times*, London, 2 October 1994.
20. Ibid.
21. Robert Fisk, 'Let's not cry for Kuwait', *The Independent*, London, 24 October 1994.
22. Ibid.

23. David Hirst and Ian Black, 'Iraq recognises Kuwait', *The Guardian*, London, 11 November 1994.

24. Jonathan Freedland and Ian Black, 'US and Britain claim virtual no-go zone in southern Iraq', *The Guardian*, London, 27 October 1994.

25. 'Iraq challenges Security Council', *Gulf Newsletter*, Gulf Information Project, London, Number 11 (November/December 1994).

26. Suzanne Lowry, 'France acts to bring Iraq out of isolation', *The Daily Telegraph*, London, 7 January 1995; Marie Colvin, 'France breaks rank on Iraq', *The Sunday Times*, London, 8 January 1995.

27. Patrick Cockburn, 'Iraq uses poison on political opponents', *The Independent*, London, 1 February 1995; Ian Black, 'UK treats poisoned Iraqi', *The Guardian*, London, 1 February 1995.

28. Ibid.

29. ITAR–TASS news agency (World Service), Moscow, 31 January 1995.

30. Ian Black, 'Losing out in the battle for Iraq', *The Guardian*, London, 4 February 1995.

31. Ibid.

32. Patrick Cockburn, 'Saddam is left weaker after crushing revolt', *The Independent*, London, 16 June 1995; Marie Colvin, 'Saddam shaken as his most loyal clan revolts', *The Sunday Times*, London, 18 June 1995.

33. Karen Dabrowska, 'Saddam gloats as foes fight each other', *The Guardian*, London, 1 July 1995.

34. David Hirst, 'Saddam's top henchmen flee to Jordan', *The Guardian*, London, 11 August 1995; Maryann Bird, 'Family vows to topple Saddam', *The Independent on Sunday*, London, 13 August 1995; David Hirst, 'West probes top Saddam defectors', *The Guardian*, London, 12 August 1995.

35. See, for example, Kenneth R. Timmerman, *The Death Lobby: How the West Armed Iraq* (London: Fourth Estate, 1992); 'Terror Arsenal the West ignored', *The Independent*, London, 12 September 1990; and the findings of the Scott enquiry, London, 1996.

36. See, for example, Seymour M. Hersh, *The Samson Option: Israel, America and the Bomb* (London: Faber and Faber, 1991); and William E. Burrows and Robert Windrem, *Critical Mass* (New York: Simon and Schuster, 1994).

37. Dr H. M. Al-Shaibani, 'Destruction of 14 Tammuz reactor during the war against Iraq', *The International Scientific Symposium on Post-War Environmental Problems in Iraq*, Iraqi Society for Environmental Protection and Improvement (ISEPI), Baghdad, 10–12 December 1994, p. 19.

38. NPT review conference, Document NPT/Conf. IV/MC. iii/L1, Add. 2, p. 4, September 1990.

39. On 2 June 1991 the UN Secretary-General issued a report ('pursuant to paragraph 26 of Security Council Resolution 687') including, amongst other items, details of guidelines to facilitate implementation of key parts of the resolution; in particular, those parts governing the prohibition of Iraqi weapons development. The report declared that 'further action may be necessary to ensure the implementation of the arms and related sanctions against Iraq'.

40. Leonard Doyle, 'Experts are certain Iraq has bomb technology', *The Independent*, London, 16 July 1991.

41. Ibid.

42. Leonard Doyle and Tom Wilkie, 'UN denies Iraq was close to making bomb', *The Independent*, London, 5 October 1991.
43. Frank Barnaby, 'Iraqi nuclear frisson', *The Guardian*, London, 1 November 1991.
44. *The Independent*, London, 29 February 1992.
45. *The Independent on Sunday*, London, 1 March 1992.
46. *The Sunday Times*, London, 1 March 1992.
47. *The Guardian*, London, 12 March 1992.
48. Harvey Morris and Tom Wilkie, 'Iraq's bomb project back to square two', *The Independent*, London, 21 March 1992.
49. Leonard Doyle, 'UN may resort to force over Iraqi weapons', *The Independent*, London, 21 July 1992.
50. Ibid.
51. *The Guardian*, London, 25 July 1992.
52. *The Independent*, London, 25 July 1992.
53. *The Observer*, London, 26 July 1992.
54. *The Independent on Sunday*, London, 26 July 1992.
55. Seth Faison, 'Tracker of Iraqi arms: Rolf Ekeus', *The New York Times*, 28 July 1992.
56. George F. Seib, 'US gets ready for military conflict with Iraq over weapons inspections', *The Wall Street Journal*, 17 August 1992.
57. *The Guardian*, London, 17 August 1992.
58. *The Independent on Sunday*, London, 23 August 1992.
59. Ian Katz, 'Mission improbable', *The Guardian*, London, 18 February 1993.
60. *The New York Times*, editorial, 28 June 1993.
61. David Usborne, 'Allies in new Saddam alert', *The Independent*, London, 1 July 1993.
62. *MidEast Mirror*, 13 July 1993, p. 18.
63. *Report of the Secretary-General on the Status of the Implementation of the Plan for the Ongoing Monitoring and Verification of Iraq's Compliance with Relevant Parts of Section C of Security Council Resolution 687 (1991)*, S/1994/489, United Nations, New York, 22 April 1994.
64. Thomas Sancton, 'No longer fenced in', *Time*, 22 May 1994, p. 31.
65. Ibid.
66. *Report of the Secretary-General on the Status of the Implementation of the Special Commission's Plan for the Ongoing Monitoring and Verification of Iraq's Compliance with Relevant Parts of Section C of Security Council Resolution 687 (1991)*, S/1994/1138, United Nations, New York, 7 October 1994.
67. For example, S/1994/1422, United Nations, New York, 15 December 1994.
68. Robin Wright, 'UN recovers Iraqi germ warfare plan', *The Guardian*, London, 1 March 1995.
69. James Bone, 'Iraq admits to germ warfare', *The Times*, London, 24 August 1995.
70. *Report by the Secretary-General pursuant to Paragraph 5 of Security Council Resolution 706 (1991)*, S/23006, United Nations, New York, 4 September 1991.
71. Evelyn Leopold, 'UN set to let Iraq sell oil worth $2bn', *The Independent*, London, 14 April 1995.

Notes to Chapter 3: Targeting the Powerless

1. Sabah Jawad and Kamil Mahdi, 'Responsibility and the Gulf', letter, *The Guardian*, London, 14 November 1991.
2. *The Impact of War on Iraq*, Report to the Secretary-General on humanitarian needs in Iraq in the immediate post-crisis environment by a mission to the area led by Mr Martti Ahtisaari, Under-Secretary-General for Administration and Management, United Nations, New York, 20 March 1991.
3. *Iraq Situation Report for SCF (UK)*, The Save the Children Fund, London, March 1991.
4. Ibid.
5. Ibid.
6. Ibid.
7. Ed Vulliamy, 'Doctors find Iraq is slowly dying', *The Guardian*, London, 16 April 1991.
8. John Pienaar and Leonard Doyle, 'UK maintains tough line on sanctions against Iraq', *The Independent*, London, 11 May 1991.
9. Diane Weathers, 'Life under sanctions', *WFP Journal*, World Food Programme, Rome, Number 18 (June 1991) p. 24.
10. Ibid.
11. 'Relief programmes in Iraq', CFA:35/SCP:10/5, World Food Programme (WFP), Rome, 20 April 1993.
12. Dr Eric Hoskins, *Children, War and Sanctions*, Report on the effects of sanctions on Iraqi women and children, commissioned by UNICEF and subsequently shelved as politically inconvenient, April 1993 (see Annika Savill, 'UN back-pedals on Baghdad sanctions report', *The Independent*, London, 24 June 1993).
13. *FAO/WFP Crop and Food Supply Assessment Mission to Iraq*, Special Alert Number 237, Food and Agriculture Organisation (FAO) and World Food Programme (WFP), Rome (July 1993).
14. Ibid., p. 1.
15. Ibid.
16. *Iraq, EIU Country Report, 2nd Quarter 1994*, Economist Intelligence Unit, London, 1994.
17. Ibid.
18. Ross B. Mirkarimi, 'The environmental and human health impacts of the Gulf region with special reference to Iraq', The Arms Control Research Centre, San Francisco, now Arc Ecology, May 1992.
19. Ibid.
20. Ibid.
21. Willem C. Smit and Jean Pierre Revel, *Report of the Assessment Mission to Iraq, 11 January 1994–11 February 1994*, International Federation of Red Cross and Red Crescent Societies, Amman, February 1994.
22. *Impact of Oppressive Sanctions on Health, Nutrition and Environment in Iraq*, Ministry of Culture and Information, Baghdad, June 1994, p. 6.
23. Kais Al-Kaisy, 'The sanctions that bring death', letter, *The Guardian*, London, 5 July 1994.
24. 'Sanctions against Iraq', World Chronicle (recorded 20 May 1992), Information Products Division, Department of Public Information, United

Nations, New York; Guest: Ambassador Peter Hohenfellner, Chairman of Committee on Sanctions against Iraq; journalists: Bruno Franseschi, Raghida Dergham, Ian Williams; moderator: Michael Littlejohns.
25. Ibid.
26. Ibid.
27. Ibid.
28. S/25761, 12 May 1993; S/26204, 2 August 1993, United Nations, New York.
29. Felicity Arbuthnot, 'Sanctions stop decent burial', *Al-Muhajir Newspaper*, London, 1 November 1993.
30. Seumas Milne, 'Sanctions snare medical journal', *The Guardian*, London, 9 May 1994.
31. See the comments by Iraqi UN ambassador Abd al-Amir Al-Anbari, in S/24338, United Nations, New York, 22 July 1992, pp. 8–10, 12–14; and, for example, the Bank of England Notice for Iraq, *Emergency Laws (Re-Enactments and Repeals) Act 1964*, 7 August 1990.
32. Margit Fakhoury, 'A German doctor tells how Iraq's children are being killed', *Committee to Save the Children in Iraq*, funded by the Schiller Institute, Washington D.C., 1991, pp. 14–18.
33. Felicity Arbuthnot, 'Children condemned to a lingering death', *Asian Times*, 16 March 1993.
34. Miriam Ryle, 'Child victims of the sanctions syndrome', letter, *The Guardian*, London, 15 July 1994.
35. Yves Bonnet (French deputy), 'Sanctions that should shame the UN', *The Guardian*, London, 8 August 1995, reprinted from *Le Monde*.
36. Fakhoury, 'A German doctor tells how Iraq's children are being killed', *op. cit.*, p. 15.
37. Ibid.
38. Ibid., pp. 16–17.
39. All these figures are taken from Iraqi sources.
40. See Magne Raundalen, 'The long-term impact of the Gulf war on the children of Iraq', Centre for Crisis Psychology, Bergen, Norway, 1991; Atle Dyregrov and Magne Raundalen, 'The impact of the Gulf war on the children of Iraq', Centre for Crisis Psychology, paper delivered at the International Society for Traumatic Stress Studies World Conference, 'Trauma and Tragedy', Amsterdam, 21–6 June 1992; Atle Dyregrov, 'Traumatized kids, traumatized rescuers', *Emergency Medical Services*, Volume 21, Number 6 (June 1992) pp. 21–4.
41. Felicity Arbuthnot, interviewed by Gillian Harris, 'Journalist claims sanctions killing children in Iraq', *The Scotsman*, Edinburgh, Scotland, 29 June 1992.
42. Alberto Ascherio, Robert Chase, Tim Coté, Godelieave Dehaes, Eric Hoskins, Jilali Laaouej, Megan Passey, Saleh Zaidi, 'Effect of the Gulf war on infant and child mortality in Iraq', *The New England Journal of Medicine*, Volume 327, Number 13 (24 September 1992).
43. Ibid.
44. Ibid.
45. S/25653, United Nations, New York, 22 April 1993.
46. Hoskins, *Children, War and Sanctions*, *op. cit.*

47. Ibid.
48. S/25653, *op. cit.* Another estimate suggests that 4000 schools were damaged or completely destroyed (see UN Department of Humanitarian Affairs, UN Inter-Agency Humanitarian Programme in Iraq, *Report*, May 1993).
49. *Impact of Oppressive Sanctions, op. cit.*, p. 8.
50. Miriam Ryle, 'Child victims of the sanctions syndrome', *op. cit.*
51. Siegwart Gunther, 'Iraq: children mortality dramatically increased', *The International Scientific Symposium, op. cit.*, pp. 94–8.
52. 'Rights of the Child', Note verbale dated 16 January 1995 from the Permanent Mission of the Republic of Iraq to the United Nations Office at Geneva addressed to the Centre for Human Rights (Economic and Social Council, United Nations), enclosing a study, 'The impact of the embargo on Iraqi children in the light of the Convention on the Rights of the Child', E/CN.4/1995/135, 7 February 1995.
53. Bonnet, 'Sanctions that should shame the UN', *op. cit.*
54. Ibid.
55. Ibid.
56. Bela Bhatia, Mary Kawar and Miriam Shahin, *Unheard Voices: Iraqi Women on War and Sanctions*, International Study Team, Change, International Reports: 'Women and Society', London, 1992.
57. Ibid., pp. 39–40.
58. Ibid., p. 44.
59. *Report to the Secretary-General on Humanitarian Needs in Iraq*, mission led by Sadruddin Aga Khan, Executive Delegate of the Secretary-General for a United Nations Inter-Agency Humanitarian Programme for Iraq, Kuwait and the Iraq/Turkey and Iraq/Iran border aeas, Geneva, 1991.
60. Bela Bhatia, *et al.*, *Unheard Voices, op. cit.*, p. 44.
61. Ibid., pp. 44–5.
62. Ibid., p. 46.
63. Ibid., p. 52.
64. UN Department of Humanitarian Affairs, UN Inter-Agency Humanitarian Programme in Iraq Co-operation Programme, 1 April 1993 to 31 March 1994, *Report*, May 1993, p. 11.
65. Andrée Michel, 'Women and war', paper given at the international forum, 'Human Rights and Women', organised by the General Federation of Iraqi Women, Baghdad, 20–22 April 1994.
66. John Pilger, *Distant Voices* (London: Vintage, 1992) p. 142.
67. E. E. Reynolds, *The League Experiment* (London: Thomas Nelson and Sons, 1939) p. 102.
68. Hoskins, *Children, War and Sanctions, op. cit.*, p. 19.
69. United Nations Children's Fund (UNICEF), *Children and Women in Iraq: A Situation Analysis*, March 1993.
70. 'Sanctions hit poor Iraqis but Saddam's rule stays secure', *The Guardian*, London, 1 August 1991.
71. Leonard Doyle, 'Iraq facing famine if UN sanctions stay', *The Independent*, London, 3 September 1991.
72. John Osgood Field and Robert M. Russell, *Nutrition Mission to Iraq*, Final Report to UNICEF by Tufts University, 14 August 1991.
73. Ibid.

74. Helga Graham, 'Starving Iraqis riot as food crisis deepens', *The Observer*, London, 3 November 1991.
75. Alfred Picardi, Ross Mirkarimi and Mahmoud Al Khoshman, 'Waterborne diseases and agricultural consequences', International Study Team – ARC Arms Control Research Centre, in Saul Bloom, John M. Miller, James Warner and Philippa Winkler (eds), *Hidden Casualties: Environmental Health and Political Consequences of the Persian Gulf War* (San Francisco, ARC/Arms Control Research Centre; London: Earthscan Publications, 1994) pp. 156–7.
76. Cited in ibid., pp. 160.
77. Cited in ibid., p. 161.
78. H. A. Ali, 'The postwar impact on the speciation in Iraq', *The International Scientific Symposium, op. cit.*, pp. 44–5.
79. Ibrahim J. Al-Jboory, 'Effects of military operations, pollution and sanctions on agricultural pests in Iraq', in *The International Scientific Symposium, op. cit.*, pp. 46–8.
80. Emad Al-Hafiath and D. Hussein Al-Saadi, 'The ecological effects of war and sanctions on the status of agricultural pests in Iraq', in *The International Scientific Symposium, op. cit.*, pp. 53–5.
81. Rahd Abdul-Kareem, 'The effects of sanctions on animal resources in Iraq', in *The International Scientific Symposium, op. cit.*, pp. 56–9.
82. *Situation of Human Rights in Iraq*, note by UN Secretary-General following report by Max van der Stoel, Special Rapporteur of the Commission on Human Rights, dealing with food and health situation in Iraq, A/46/647, 13 November 1991.
83. 'Food supply situation and crop outlook in Iraq', in *Food Outlook*, Food and Agriculture Organisation (FAO), Rome, July 1993, pp. 22–6 (see also note 88).
84. Ibid.
85. Ibid.
86. John Osgood Field, 'From food security to food insecurity: the case of Iraq, 1990–1991', *GeoJournal*, 30.2 (1993) pp. 185–94.
87. Ibid., p. 189.
88. *FAO/WFP Crop and Food Supply Assessment Mission to Iraq, op. cit.* (see also note 83).
89. Ibid., p. 6.
90. Ibid., p. 2.
91. *Report of the Nutritional Status Assessment Mission to Iraq (November 1993)*, Project TCP/IRQ/23T6(E), Food and Agriculture Organisation (FAO), Rome, December 1993.
92. Ibid., p. 2.
93. Ibid., pp. 2–3.
94. Ibid., p. 20.
95. Smit and Revel, *Report of the Assessment Mission to Iraq, op. cit.*, p. 4.
96. Ibid., p. 5.
97. 'Iraq', *News Summary (12 April–12 May 1995)*, United Nations Information Centre, London, 16 May 1995.
98. 'Iraq (14 June)', *Foodcrops and Shortages*, Food and Agriculture Organisation, Rome, Number 3 (May/June 1995) p. 28.

99. 'Iraq (11 July)', *Foodcrops and Shortages*, Food and Agriculture Organisation, Rome, Number 4 (July 1995) p. 25.
100. Eric Hoskins, 'The truth behind economic sanctions: a report on the embargo of food and medicines to Iraq', in Ramsey Clark *et al.*, *War Crimes: A Report on United States War Crimes Against Iraq*, (Washington D.C.: Maisonneuve Press, 1992) p. 165.
101. Ibid., p. 166.
102. Ibid.
103. *Iraq Situation Report for SCF (UK)*, The Save the Children Fund, London, March 1991, pp. 2–3.
104. Ibid., p. 5.
105. Ibid., p. 6.
106. Louise Cainkar, 'Desert sin: a post-war journey through Iraq', in Phyllis Bennis and Michel Moushabeck (eds), *Beyond the Storm: A Gulf Crisis Reader*, (Edinburgh: Canongate, 1992) p. 346.
107. Ibid., p. 346.
108. Report by Middle East Action Network (MEAN) team, following visits to children's hospitals in Baghdad, 24 April 1991.
109. Marnie Johnson, report by Medical Aid for Iraq (MAI), London, following medical supplies delivery, September 1991.
110. Ibid.
111. Diane Weathers, 'Life under sanctions', *WFP Journal*, World Food Programme, Rome, June 1991, p. 27.
112. Ibid.
113. Noriko Sato, Omar Obeid and Tierry Brun, 'Malnutrition in southern Iraq', letter, *The Lancet*, London, Volume 338 (9 November 1991) p. 1202.
114. *Situation of Human Rights in Iraq, op. cit.*, p. 4.
115. *The Sanctions Committee – working procedures and economic and humanitarian impact of the sanctions on Iraq*, submission to UN Secretary-General from Ministry of Foreign Affairs of the Republic of Iraq, S/24338, 22 July 1992.
116. Ibid., p. 17.
117. *Health Status in Iraq*, report from Medicine for Peace (MFP), New York, February 1993; team led by Dr Michael Viola, Oncology Division, Stony Brook University, New York.
118. Ibid., p. 4.
119. Hoskins (April 1993), *Children, War and Sanctions, op. cit.*, citing Beth Osborne Daponte, 'Iraqi casualties from the Persian Gulf War and its aftermath', unpublished manuscript, 1992.
120. Report by Medical Aid for Iraq (MAI), London, following medical supplies delivery, January/February 1993.
121. Ibid.
122. Letter dated 18 May 1993 from the Permanent Mission of the Republic of Iraq to the United Nations Office at Geneva addressed to the Assistant Secretary-General for Human Rights, E/CN.4/Sub.2/1993/36, 2 July 1993.
123. Ibid.
124. Report by Medical Aid for Iraq (MAI), London, following medical supplies delivery (September/October 1993), January 1994.
125. Ibid.

126. Ibid.
127. Iraq Factsheet Number 1, *Focus*, British Red Cross, London, February 1994.
128. Ibid., report by John English, British Red Cross Desk Officer.
129. Smit and Revel, *Report of the Assessment Mission to Iraq, op. cit.*
130. Ibid., p. 8.
131. Report by Medical Aid for Iraq (MAI), London, following medical supplies delivery (3–22 April 1994), May 1994.
132. Ibid., p. 9.
133. Harvey Marcovitch, 'Saddam's atrocity – or ours?', *The Times*, London, 31 May 1994.
134. Ibid.
135. *Impact of Oppressive Sanctions, op. cit.*, p. 9.
136. Report by Medical Aid for Iraq (MAI), London, following medical supplies delivery (October 1994), December 1994.
137. Ibid., pp. 2–3.
138. *The International Scientific Symposium, op. cit.*
139. Ibid., pp. 91–106.
140. Note verbale dated 16 January 1995 from the Permanent Mission of Iraq to the United Nations Office at Geneva addressed to the Centre for Human Rights, enclosing study entitled 'The impact of the blockade on Iraq', E/CN.4/1995/137, 21 February 1995.
141. 'A life in the day of Dr Tariq Abbas Hady', *The Sunday Times*, colour supplement, London, 12 March 1995, p. 58.
142. Report by Medical Aid for Iraq (MAI), London, following medical supplies delivery (7–29 April 1995), May 1995.
143. Felicity Arbuthnot, 'Zoo animals share the suffering', *Irish Times*, 15 January 1995.
144. Warren A. J. Hamerman, International Progress Organisation, presentation (denouncing sanctions against Iraq) to UN Organisation Subcommission on Prevention of Discrimination and Protection of Minorities, 43rd Session, 13 August 1991.
145. Edward Pearce, 'Death and indecency in a time of cholera', *The Guardian*, London, 25 October 1991.
146. Charles Richards, 'Iraq plagued by wave of violent crime', *The Independent*, London, 1 February 1993; Marie Colvin, 'Iraq's lost legions become the thieves of Baghdad', *The Sunday Times*, London, 31 January 1993.
147. Patrick Cockburn, 'The face of Saddam's new terror', *The Independent*, London, 13 January 1995; 'Savage justice', *Time*, 6 February 1995.
148. Letter dated 22 June 1994 from the Chargé d'Affaires A.I. of the Permanent Mission of Iraq to the United Nations Addressed to the Secretary-General, S/1994/771, 28 June 1994, appending: the Resolution of the International Conference against Economic Sanctions on Iraq, held at Kuala Lumpur, Malaysia, on 26–7 May 1994; and the Malaysian Declaration.

Notes to Chapter 4: The Face of Genocide

1. Gary Clyde Hufbauer, Jeffrey J. Schott and Kimberly Ann Elliott, *Economic Sanctions Reconsidered: History and Current Policy* (Washington, D.C.: Institute for International Economics, 1990) p. 114.

2. The individual terms admit of different definitions and interpretations (see, for example, M. S. Daoudi and M. S. Dajani, *Economic Sanctions: Ideals and Experience* (London: Routledge and Kegan Paul, 1983) pp. 2–9) However, because of the comprehensive nature of the anti-Iraq sanctions regime, I have tended to use the terms as functional synonyms. We should remember that Washington preferred to talk, in the early days of sanctions, of *interdiction* rather than *blockade* to avoid charges that it was guilty of acts of war.

3. Quoted in Charles Fornara, 'Plutarch and the Megarian decree', *24 Yale Classical Studies*, 1975, pp. 213–28.

4. Jim Bradbury, *The Medieval Siege* (Woodbridge, Suffolk: UK, The Boydell Press, 1992) p. 81.

5. Ibid., p. 82.

6. Ibid., p. 84.

7. D. T. Jack, *Studies in Economic Warfare* (London: King, 1940) pp. 1–42.

8. James M. McPherson, *Battle Cry of Freedom: The American Civil War* (London: Penguin, 1988) p. 378.

9. Richard S. West Jr, *Mr Lincoln's Navy* (New York, 1957) p. 60, cited in ibid.

10. McPherson, *Battle Cry of Freedom, op. cit.*, p. 378.

11. Citations in ibid., p. 381.

12. Citations in ibid.

13. W. N. Medlicott, *The Economic Blockade* (London: HMSO and Longmans Green, Volume 1, 1952) p. 9.

14. Margaret P. Doxey, *Economic Sanctions and International Enforcement* (London: Macmillan for The Royal Institute of Economic Affairs, 1980) p. 12.

15. Ibid.

16. Edward S. Miller, *War Plan Orange: The US Strategy to Defeat Japan, 1897–1945* (Annapolis, Maryland: United States Naval Institute, 1991) p. 28.

17. Ibid., chapter 14.

18. Ibid., p. 365.

19. John Costello, *The Pacific War* (London: Pan Books, 1981) p. 99.

20. Medlicott, *The Economic Blockade, op. cit.*; plus Volume 2, 1959.

21. Hufbauer *et al.*, *Economic Sanctions Reconsidered, op. cit.*

22. Gary Clyde Hufbauer, Jeffrey J. Schott and Kimberly Ann Elliott, *Economic Sanctions Reconsidered: Supplemental Case Histories* (Washington D.C.: Institute for International Economics, 1990).

23. Wilhelm Dibelius, *England* (London: Jonathan Cape, 1930) p. 103.

24. Margaret P. Doxey, *International Sanctions in Contemporary Perspective* (London: Macmillan, 1987) p. 32.

25. Barry E. Carter, *International Economic Sanctions* (New York: Cambridge University Press, 1988) p. 32.

26. Ibid., p. 35.

27. Ibid., p. 159.

28. Marc Weller, 'The Lockerbie case: a premature end to the "New World Order"?', *African Journal of International and Comparative Law*, Number 4 (1992) pp. 1–15.

29. Ibid., p. 15.
30. Simon Tisdall and John Hooper, 'US plays down illegal Israeli missile sales', *The Guardian*, London, 28 October 1991; Rupert Cornwell, 'Bush turns blind eye to Israeli arms deals', *The Independent*, London, 28 October 1991.
31. Michael Sheridan, 'US allies alarmed at trade ban on Iran', *The Independent*, London, 2 May 1995.
32. David Hirst, 'US sanctions against Iran are a gift to extremists of Zionism and Islam', *The Guardian*, London, 19 May 1995.
33. Noam Chomsky, *Deterring Democracy* (London: Verso, 1991) p. 3.
34. Bob Woodward, *The Commanders* (New York: Simon and Schuster, 1991) p. 34.
35. See, for example, the paper by Richard E. Webb, 'Analysis of the Constitution with respect to the authority to make war and alliances, and the employment of force against Iraq by Presidential act', Bavaria, Germany, 15 January 1991.
36. Ibid., p. 2.
37. Ibid., p. 3.
38. Carter, *International Economic Sanctions*, *op. cit.*, chapter 4.
39. Webb, 'Analysis of the Constitution', *op. cit.*, presents a detailed analysis of the US Constitution (pp. 4–11) to provide 'essential proof' of the Constitutional violations (listed pp. 1–3).
40. Ramsey Clark, *The Fire this Time* (New York: Thunder Mouth's Press, 1992).
41. Saul Bloom, John M. Miller, James Warner and Philippa Winkler (eds), *Hidden Casualties: The Environmental, Health and Political Consequences of the Persian Gulf War* (San Francisco: ARC/Arms Control Research Center; London: Earthscan, 1994) pp. 298–302.
42. Ibid., p. 300.
43. Richard Dowden, 'Not as nice as he looked', *The Independent*, London, 16 October 1992.
44. *The Public Papers and Addresses of Franklin D. Roosevelt, 1939, Volume: War – and Neutrality* (New York: Macmillan, 1941) pp. 454, 511–12, 587–9.
45. Robert Batchelder, *The Irreversible Decision, 1939–1950* (New York: Houghton Mifflin, 1961) pp. 172–3.
46. John Dower, *War Without Mercy: Race and Power in the Pacific War* (London: Faber and Faber, 1986) p. 40.
47. Quoted in ibid., pp. 40–41.
48. Ibid., with citations.
49. Bertrand Russell, *War Crimes in Vietnam* (London: George Allen and Unwin, 1967) p. 59; see also *US War Crimes in Vietnam* (Hanoi: Juridical Science Institute, 1968); *The Winter Soldier Investigation: An Inquiry into American War Crimes*, by Vietnam Veterans Against the War (Beacon Press, US, 1972); Martha Hess, *Then the Americans Came: Voices from Vietnam* (New York: Four Walls Eight Windows, 1993).
50. Robert Jay Lifton and Eric Markusen, *The Genocidal Mentality: Nazi Holocaust and Nuclear Threat* (London: Macmillan, 1991) p. 13.
51. Bishara A. Bahbah, 'The Crisis in the Gulf – Why Iraq invaded Kuwait',

in Phyllis Bennis and Michel Moushabeck (eds), *Beyond the Storm* (London: Canongate, 1992) p. 52.

52. Mohamed Heikal, *Illusions of Triumph* (London: HarperCollins, 1992) p. 137.

53. Baghdad Radio, 18 June 1990, cited by Dilip Hiro, *Desert Shield to Desert Storm* (London: Paladin, 1992) pp. 83–4.

54. Pierre Salinger and Eric Laurent, *Secret Dossier: The Hidden Agenda Behind the Gulf War* (London: Penguin, 1991) p. 33.

55. Hiro, *Desert Shield to Desert Storm, op. cit.*, p. 89.

56. Leonard Doyle, 'Gulf threat "is earning billions for Britain"', *The Independent*, London, 22 October 1990; Michael Kinsley, 'Where the Gulf crisis is a barrel of laughs', *The Guardian*, London, 5 November 1990; Irwin Stelzer, 'Gulf war allies collude to raise the price of oil', *The Sunday Times*, London, 17 March 1991.

57. David Bowen, 'Iraq sparks fears of oil price crash', *The Independent on Sunday*, London, 27 August 1995.

58. Ibid.

59. Michael Sheridan, 'Future of Iraq rests on germ war checks', *The Independent*, London, 30 September 1995.

Notes to Chapter 5: The New Holocaust

1. UN World Food Programme (WFP), *News Update*, 26 September 1995.

2. UN Food and Agriculture Organisation (FAO), December 1995.

3. Victoria Brittain, *The Independent*, London, 4 December 1995.

4. Umeed Mubarak, Iraqi Health Minister, *Reuters*, 12 May 1997.

5. Center for Economic and Social Rights (CESR, formerly known as the Harvard Study Team), visit to Iraq, April–May 1996.

6. Note verbale (29 January 1996) from the Permanent Mission of the Republic of Iraq to the United Nations Office at Geneva addressed to the Centre for Human Rights: '*Impact of the economic embargo on the economic, social and cultural situation in Iraq*'; published by UN Economic and Social Council, E/CN.4/1996/140, 21 March 1996.

7. United Nations Children's Fund (UNICEF), E/ICEF/1994/P/L.23, April 1994.

8. United Nations Children's Fund (UNICEF), '*The Status of women and children in Iraq*', September 1995.

9. UN World Health Organisation (WHO), report on health situation in Iraq, 25 March 1996.

10. *Index on Censorship*, 3, 1996, p. 9.

11. Report of the Delivery of Medical Supplies to Hospitals in Iraq, 29 August to 17 September 1996 (Fourteenth Convoy), Medical Aid for Iraq, London.

12. *Ibid.*

13. Maggie O'Kane, 'Bomb his palace – we understand that – but why are they starving us?', *The Guardian*, London, 17 September 1996.

14. Paper submitted by Government of Iraq on the impact of the economic embargo on human rights in Iraq, 29 September 1996, from Iraqi UN ambassador to UN Secretary-General, A/C.3/51/6, 1 October 1996.

15. *Ibid.*

16. *News Summary*, 20 September to 20 October 1996, United Nations Information Centre, London.

17. 'Iraq "on verge of food disaster"', *The Guardian*, London, 18 November 1996.
18. *News Summary*, 21 October to 22 November 1996, United Nations Information Centre, London.
19. 'Iraqi health system close to collapse says WHO Director-General', *Press Release*, WHO/16, 27 February 1997.
20. Chuck Quilty, 'Children of the Sanctions', *The Nonviolent Activist*, March–April 1997.
21. David Fairhall, 'Iraq "could steal" nuclear surplus', *The Guardian*, London, 17 March 1997.
22. Christopher Bellamy, 'Scuds may be hidden in Iraq says UN', *The Independent*, London, 23 March 1997.
23. Jon Leyne, 'UN destroys Iraqi germ war plant', *The Observer*, London, 9 June 1996.
24. *Ibid.*
25. David Usborne, 'UN clash with Iraq "worst since Gulf war"', *The Independent*, London, 20 June 1996.
26. 'Iraq gives up missile parts', *The Daily Telegraph*, London, 24 February 1997.
27. Hugh Davies, 'Saddam wife held in power struggle', *The Daily Telegraph*, London, 30 January 1997.
28. Ed Vulliamy, 'UN may have found weapon dump in Iraq', *The Guardian*, London, 28 February 1997.
29. 'Saddam's deadly sting', *The Sunday Times*, London, 19 January 1997.
30. Peter Beaumont, 'US has N-bomb bunker-buster', *The Observer*, London, 13 April 1997.
31. See, as two examples among dozens, Ian Black, 'Iraq close to agreeing UN "oil deal"', *The Guardian*, London, 18 January 1996; Michael Sheridan, 'Stricken Iraq set to sell oil on UN terms', *The Independent*, London, 19 January 1996.
32. John Waples, 'Oil market braces for Iraqi sales', *The Sunday Times*, London, 21 April 1996.
33. Maggie O'Kane, 'The Wake of War', *The Guardian*, London, 18 May 1996.
34. Letter (20 May 1996) from Secretary-General to the President of the Security Council, S/1996/356, Annex 1: Memorandum of Understanding between the Secretariat of the United Nations and the Government of Iraq on the implementation of Security Council Resolution 986 (1995).
35. Press briefing by UN Legal Counsel on 'Oil-for-Food' Agreement, 20 May 1996.
36. Ian Black and Mark Tran, 'Iraq accepts UN oil for food deal', *The Guardian*, London, 21 May 1996.
37. Magnus Grimond, 'Oil sector falls as Iraq strikes UN deal', *The Independent*, London, 21 May 1996.
38. Rufus Olins, 'Britain sues Iraq over its £400 m debt', *The Sunday Times*, London, 7 July 1996.
39. Mark Tran, 'US agrees "oil for food" plan to aid Iraq', *The Guardian*, London, 8 August 1996.

40. Maggie O'Kane, 'Burden falls on the sick and the hungry', *The Guardian*, London, 5 September 1996.
41. Secretary-General, *Supplement to An Agenda for Peace*, United Nations, A/50/60-S/1995/1.
42. Paper submitted by Government of Iraq on the impact of the economic embargo on human rights in Iraq, 29 September 1996, *op. cit.*
43. *Ibid.*
44. David Hirst, 'UN "oil for food" deal greases Saddam's wheels and palms', *The Guardian*, London, 30 November 1996.
45. Riad El-Tahir, *Friendship Across Frontiers*, London, 7 March 1997.
46. Report of the Secretary-General pursuant of Paragraph 11 of Resolution 986 (1995), United Nations, S/1997/206, 10 March 1997.
47. Letter (24 March 1997) from the Permanent Representative of Iraq to the United Nations addressed to the Secretary-General, S/1997/250, 25 March 1997; letter (22 March 1997) from the Minister for Foreign Affairs of Iraq addressed to the Secretary-General.
48. 'Iraq complains to UN chief on food deliveries', *Reuter*, 25 April 1997.
49. Letter (25 April 1997) from the Permanent Representative of Iraq to the United Nations addressed to the Secretary-General, S/1997/338, 28 April 1997, letter (25 April 1997) from the Minister for Foreign Affairs of Iraq addressed to the Secretary-General.
50. *Ibid.*
51. Ramsey Clark's 'Criminal Complaint . . .' was published in *Journal of Independence Studies*, Number 1, March 1997, Institute for Independence Studies, London.
52. Mary Dejevsky, 'US committed to hard line against Saddam's Iraq', *The Independent*, London, 27 March 1997.
53. David Hirst, 'Iran raid strengthens grip on northern Iraq', *The Guardian*, London, 30 July 1996.
54. Amberin Zaman, 'Iraq angry at Turkey's attack on Kurd rebels', *The Daily Telegraph*, London, 15 May 1997.
55. Derek Brown, 'Attack upsets friends and foes alike', *The Guardian*, London, 4 September 1996.
56. Magnus Grimond, 'UN action against Iraq sends oil price surging', *The Independent*, London, 3 September 1996.
57. In the international tally, the following countries disapproved of the US strikes: France, Spain, Russia, China, Egypt, Turkey, Jordan, Syria and Iran. The following approved: Britain, Germany, Japan, Canada, Israel and Kuwait. Saudi Arabia remained non-commital.
58. Phil Reeves and Mary Dejevsky, 'Russia leads attack on US action', *The Independent*, London, 4 September 1996.
59. 'US jet missile fired in error', *The Daily Telegraph*, London, 9 November 1996.
60. Mary Dejevsky, Christopher Bellamy and Rupert Cornwell, 'France quits watch over northern Iraq', *The Independent*, London, 28 December 1996.
61. Kathy Evans, 'Anti-Saddam alliance set to break-up', *The Guardian*, London, 10 March 1997.
62. Chris Nuttall, 'Saddam offers sanctuary', *The Guardian*, London, 2 April 1997.

63. Executive Summary and Report, 'Denial of Food and Medicine', *The Impact of the US Embargo on Health and Nutrition in Cuba*, American Association for World Health (AAWH), US Committee for the World Health Organisation (WHO) and the Pan American Health Organisation (PAHO), Washington D.C., March 1997.

64. Victoria Brittain, 'Children die in agony as US trade ban stifles Cuba', *The Guardian*, London, 7 March 1997.

65. Executive Summary and Report, AAWH, *op. cit.*

66. 'Annan wants Cuban embargo to end', *The Guardian*, London, 30 April 1997.

Bibliography

Akehurst, Michael, *A Modern Introduction to International Law* (London: HarperCollins, 6th edition, 1987).

Atkinson, Rick, *Crusade: The Untold Story of the Gulf War* (London: HarperCollins, 1994).

Bailey, Martin, *Oilgate: The Sanctions Scandal* (London: Coronet, 1979).

Bloom, Saul; Miller, John M.; Warner, James; and Winkler, Philippa (eds), *Hidden Casualties: The Environmental, Health and Political Consequences of the Persian Gulf War* (San Francisco, Calif.: ARC/Arms Control Research Center; London: Earthscan, 1994).

Boyd, Andrew, *Fifteen Men on a Powder Keg: A History of the UN Security Council* (London: Methuen, 1971).

Bresheeth, Haim and Yuval-Davis, Nira (eds), *The Gulf War and the New World Order* (London: Zed Books, 1991).

Brierly, J. L., *The Law of Nations: An Introduction to the International Law of Peace* (London: Oxford University Press, 6th edition, 1963).

Campbell, Barry R. and Newcomb, Danforth (eds), *The Impact of the Freeze of Kuwaiti and Iraqi Assets* (London: Graham & Trotman and International Bar Association, 1990).

Carter, Barry E., *International Economic Sanctions* (New York: Cambridge University Press, 1988).

Chomsky, Noam, *Deterring Democracy* (London: Verso, 1991).

Clark, Ramsey, *The Children are Dying* (New York: World View Forum, 1996).

Clark, Ramsey, *The Fire this Time* (New York: Thunder Mouth's Press, 1992).

Clark, Ramsey and Others, *War Crimes: A Report on United States War Crimes against Iraq* (Washington D.C.: Maisonneuve Press, 1992).

Claude, Inis L. Jr, *Swords into Plowshares: The Problems and Progress of International Organization* (London: University of London Press, 1965).

Cookson, John and Nottingham, Judith, *A Survey of Chemical and Biological Warfare* (New York: Monthly Review Press, 1969).

Daoudi, M. S. and Dajani, M. S., *Economic Sanctions: Ideals and Experience* (London: Routledge and Kegan Paul, 1983).

Dower, John, *War without Mercy: Race and Power in the Pacific War* (London: Faber and Faber, 1986).

Doxey, Margaret P., *Economic Sanctions and International Enforcement* (London: Macmillan for The Royal Institute of Economic Affairs, 1980).

——, *International Sanctions in Contemporary Perspective* (London: Macmillan, 1987).

Fehrenbach, T. R., *This Kind of Peace* (London: Leslie Frewin, 1967).

George, Alexander (ed.), *Western State Terrorism* (Cambridge: Polity Press, 1991).

Glaser, Kurt and Possony, Stefan T., *Victims of Politics: The State of Human Rights* (New York: Columbia University Press, 1979).

Green, L. C., *The Contemporary Law of Armed Conflict* (Manchester, UK: Manchester University Press, 1993).

Hayes, J. P., *Economic Effects of Sanctions on South Africa* (London: Trade Policy Research Centre, 1987).

Hazelton, Fran (ed.), *Iraq Since the Gulf War: Prospects for Democracy* (London: Zed Books, 1994).

Hess, Martha, *Then the Americans Came: Voices from Vietnam* (New York: Four Walls Eight Windows, 1993).

Hiro, Dilip, *Desert Shield to Desert Storm: The Second Gulf War* (London: Paladin, 1992).

Hufbauer, Gary Clyde; Schott, Jeffrey J. and Elliott, Kimberly Ann, *Economic Sanctions Reconsidered: History and Current Policy* (Washington D.C.: Institute for International Economics, 1990).

——, *Economic Sanctions Reconsidered: Supplemental Case Histories* (Washington D.C.: Institute for International Economics, 1990).

Leyton-Brown, David (ed.), *The Utility of International Economic Sanctions* (London: Croom Helm, 1987).

Lifton, Robert Jay and Markusen, Eric, *The Genocidal Mentality: Nazi Holocaust and Nuclear Threat* (London: Macmillan, 1990).

MacArthur, John R., *Second Front: Censorship and Propaganda in the Gulf War* (New York: Hill and Wang, 1992).

McPherson, James M., *Battle Cry of Freedom: The American Civil War* (London: Penguin, 1990).

Miller, Edward S., *War Plan Orange: The US Strategy to Defeat Japan, 1897–1945* (Annapolis, Maryland, US: Naval Institute Press, 1991).

Northedge, F. S., *The League of Nations: Its Life and Times 1920–1946* (Leicester, UK: Leicester University Press, 1986).

Patil, Anjali V., *The UN Veto in World Affairs: A Complete Record and Case Histories of the Security Council's Veto, 1946–1990* (London: Mansell, 1992).

Political Symbol or Political Tool? Making Sanctions Work, Report of the 24th United Nations Issues Conference, sponsored by The Stanley Foundation, convened at Arden House, Harriman, New York, 19–21 February 1993.

Russell, Bertrand, *War Crimes in Vietnam* (London: George Allen and Unwin, 1967).

Salinger, Pierre and Laurent, Eric, *Secret Dossier: The Hidden Agenda Behind the Gulf War* (London: Penguin, 1991).

Segal, Ronald, *Sanctions Against South Africa* (London: Penguin, 1964).

Sifry, Micah L. and Cerf, Christopher (eds), *The Gulf War Reader: History, Documents, Opinions* (New York: Random House, 1991).

Simons, Geoff, *Iraq: From Sumer to Saddam* (London: Macmillan, 1994).

——, *The United Nations: A Chronology of Conflict* (London: Macmillan, 1994).

——, *UN Malaise: Power, Problems and Realpolitik* (London: Macmillan, 1995).

Taylor, Philip M., *War and the Media: Propaganda and Persuasion in the Gulf War* (Manchester, UK: Manchester University Press, 1992).

The Winter Soldier Investigation: An Inquiry into American War Crimes, by the Vietnam Veterans Against the War (Beacon Press, US, 1972).

Timmerman, Kenneth R., *The Death Lobby: How the West Armed Iraq* (London: Fourth Estate, 1992).

Weeks, John and Gunson, Phil, *Panama: Made in the USA* (London: Latin American Bureau, 1991).

Wight, Martin, *Power Politics* (London: Penguin, 2nd edition, 1986).

Woodward, Bob, *The Commanders* (New York: Simon and Schuster, 1991).

Index